BASIC VLSI DESIGN
Systems and Circuits

SECOND EDITION

PRENTICE HALL
SILICON SYSTEMS ENGINEERING SERIES
Editor: Kamran Eshraghian

HASKARD & MAY   *Analog VLSI Design: nMOS and CMOS*
PUCKNELL & ESHRAGHIAN *Basic VLSI Design: Systems and Circuits*

BASIC VLSI DESIGN
Systems and Circuits
SECOND EDITION

Douglas A. Pucknell
Kamran Eshraghian
Department of Electrical and Electronic Engineering The University of Adelaide and Directors of Integrated Silicon Design Pty Ltd Adelaide, South Australia.

PRENTICE HALL

New York   London   Toronto   Sydney   Tokyo

© 1988 by Prentice-Hall of Australia Pty Ltd

Prentice-Hall, Inc., *Englewood Cliffs, New Jersey*
Prentice-Hall of Australia Pty Ltd, *Sydney*
Prentice-Hall Canada, Inc., *Toronto*
Prentice-Hall Hispanoamericana, S.A., *Mexico*
Prentice-Hall of India Private Ltd, *New Delhi*
Prentice-Hall International, Inc., *London*
Prentice-Hall of Japan, Inc., *Tokyo*
Prentice-Hall of Southeast Asia Pty Ltd, *Singapore*
Editora Prentice-Hall do Brasil Ltda, *Rio de Janeiro*

Typeset by Abb-typesetting Pty Ltd,
Collingwood, Victoria

Printed and bound in Australia by
Brown Prior Anderson Pty Ltd, Burwood, Victoria

Cover design by Philip Eldridge

1 2 3 4 5 91 90 89 88 87

ISBN 0 7248 0105 7

National Library of Australia
Cataloguing-in-Publication Data

Pucknell, Douglas A. (Douglas Albert), 1927–
  Basic VLSI design.

  2nd ed.
  Bibliography.
  Includes index.
  ISBN 0 7248 0106 5.
  ISBN 0 7248 0105 7 (pbk.)

  1. Integrated circuits — Very large scale integration —
  Design and construction. I. Eshraghian, Kamran,
  1945–   . II. Title.

621.395

 PRENTICE HALL

A division of Simon & Schuster

To Ella, Douglas and Christopher
and
Deidre, Michelle and Kylie

Contents

List of color plates

Between pages 236 and 237

Acknowledgments

Most text books based on course work which has been conducted over a period of time must inevitably constitute a team effort. In this respect *Basic VLSI Design* is no exception and the authors have benefited greatly from discussions, criticism, constructive suggestions, and direct assistance in one form or another from many colleagues, postgraduate research workers, post-experience and undergraduate students. We have been most fortunate in being associated with very creative and talented groups and individuals and it is impossible to mention all those who have contributed. However, we will do our best to cover at least a representative cross-section of those who have assisted directly with our work.

First of all, we must acknowledge the contributions of Marcus Paltridge, Professor Jonathon Rosenberg and Professor Kishor Trivedi. They have each supplied useful and much appreciated material and their contributions will be found in Chapters 4, 12 and 11 respectively.

Our VLSI program has benefited significantly from support provided through Gary Kennedy, by Orbit Semiconductor, Inc. of Sunnyvale California. Orbit 2 micron design rules have been reproduced in this text. We are also indebited to B. McClusky and V. Svoboda of Amalgamated Wireless (Australasia) Ltd (AWA) for their cooperation in supplying AWA design rules which we also reproduced.

Research and teaching activity in the University was greatly enhanced by a joint research program with the Microelectronics Center of North Carolina (MCNC), North Carolina. The venture owed much to the foresight of Professor Peter Calingaert of MCNC, and his collaborative role has been ably continued by Jonathon Rosenberg (who also contributed material for this text).

We also owe much to the University of Adelaide and, in particular, to the Department of Electrical and Electronic Engineering. At a time of financial stringency the university has, nevertheless, directed resources into the microelectronics area. It says much for the resourcefulness of Department Chairman, Don Griffin, and Deputy Chairman, Tony Parker, that this has been so, and we are grateful for their help and for the tolerance and support of all our departmental colleagues. Peter Cole and Michael Liebelt, who both played essential roles, deserve a special mention.

No teaching developments could ever take place without interaction with those who wish to learn, the students. We have been most fortunate in having a steady flow of high-quality students in both the undergraduate and post-experience areas. We are particularly grateful to those who have used expertise gained from our courses to produce and test designs in silicon.

In the teaching arena, we must acknowledge the initiatives taken by Dr Craig Mudge in organising the first 'teach the teachers' course in Australia and for providing, through the CSIRO, the chip fabrication resources of the AUSMPC concept. We have, over the years, also benefited greatly from our association with Integrated Silicon Design Pty Ltd of Adelaide who have organised regular VLSI courses in this and other parts of the world. In particular we must mention the support we have received from Laird Varzaly, Alf Grasso and Greg Zyner.

Our overseas teaching ventures have also been greatly assisted by our association with the Applied Research Corporation (ARC) of Singapore and, most recently, from our association with the Microelectronics Center of the Middlesex Polytechnic in London.

In forward-looking areas, such as VLSI design, research and teaching are closely allied and this desirable situation has resulted in most significant contributions to the teaching program from postgraduate students and young engineers. Yet again, we have been blessed with some very talented, imaginative, and energetic co-workers among whom Alex Dickinson, Peter Evans, Paul Franzon, Peter Heath, Michael Pope, and Roman Woloszczuk stand out for their exceptional efforts.

To turn now to the actual production of this text, we must thank the secretarial staff of the Electrical and Electronic Engineering Department of the University of Adelaide. We thank Mrs Mary Parry for making available the facilities used to produce this substantial manuscript and we are also indebted to Mrs Jillian Sandison and Mrs Margaret Drake.

We also owe much to the editorial and production staff of Prentice-Hall in Sydney, in particular we must mention Ted Gannan, Richard Dahl and Ian MacArthur. They have maintained the highest standards in producing this text.

Finally, we acknowledge with gratitude the patience and understanding of our respective wives, Ella and Deidre, without whose tolerance and support this text would never have been completed without any reasonable time scale.

Preface

Seldom, if ever, have there been such dramatic changes in any field of engineering as have taken place in electronics in the past 25 years. The early 1960s saw the start of the integrated circuit concept and developments have taken place at a revolutionary rate since then. Already there have been four clearly distinguishable generations of integrated circuits, ranging from the SSI (Small Scale Integration) of the early 1960s through MSI (Medium Scale Integration) which evolved in the late 1960s, followed, in the next decade, by very important developments attendant upon the application of LSI (Large Scale Integration) and now, VLSI (Very Large Scale Integration) which has become the technology of the 1980s.

VLSI chips which are readily available 'off the shelf' or may be custom designed are the 'components' with which the engineer (and others) may now create systems. VLSI chips have complexities equivalent to circuits containing, say, fifty thousand or more transistors and, in consequence, the systems which may be readily contemplated and realized are limited only by the imagination of the designer. The technology is available to extend creativity to the limit.

The ability to design VLSI circuits is an increasingly important, if not essential, attribute of the professional engineer and computer scientist. Indeed, the applications of VLSI promise to be widespread and the need to design will extend beyond the boundaries of electronic engineering into a wide range of disciplines. Thus, there exists a widespread need for education in VLSI in an easily assimilated but yet comprehensive form.

The microscopic dimensions of VLSI systems make possible the design of fast circuits and VLSI is finding ready application in areas requiring high speed processing. Although silicon MOS based circuitry will meet most requirements in such systems, there are ultimate limitations associated with the velocity of electrons (and holes) in silicon which make MOS circuitry unsuitable for some of the very fast systems which are now being contemplated. Thus other techniques are being actively investigated including the use of materials other than silicon for the production of integrated circuits. One promising technology is the production of very fast circuits in Gallium Arsenide.

VLSI systems in silicon utilise both nMOS and CMOS technology and it is advantageous to understand and to be able to design in either as the need arises. This added learning load is no real burden since they are closely interrelated and design is based on common concepts. It is further possible to carry these concepts into the design of Gallium Arsenide circuits.

A structured course in digital MOS (nMOS and CMOS) VLSI design and an introduction to the design of Gallium Arsenide circuits is contained in this book.

The essential material is provided for undergraduate courses for electrical/ electronic engineers or computer scientists, for post-experience courses, or for reading by practising professionals. In this latter context it is also suitable reading for those needing to acquire a background in the subject. In view of the wide range of backgrounds of potential readers, this text has been written in a direct and concise manner which does not presuppose a deep knowledge of electronic engineering or semiconductor physics. It is in the digital systems area that VLSI will have its widest immediate application and this book, therefore, concentrates on digital rather than analog circuits and systems.

Thanks to some very enlightened yet down to earth work on VLSI design methodology by Mead and Conway[1] and others, it is now possible to learn the essential elements of integrated circuit design very readily. For a relatively modest investment of time, it is possible to acquire a level of expertise enabling the design of circuits of VLSI complexity. This gives the designer a new and significant degree of freedom and an ability to create and utilize special purpose processors where appropriate.

This text is the result of more than five years' experience in teaching VLSI systems design to engineering undergraduates, practising engineers, and computer scientists. The text is closely aligned with material taught in the Department of Electrical and Electronic Engineering of the University of Adelaide, and many of the design examples used have been tried out and verified in silicon.

The essential material may be lectured and supporting tutorials catered for by devoting, for example, a minimum of three hours per week throughout a nine-week term or two hours per week for one semester. However, if practical laboratory exercises are to be given, using CAD tools, then at least a further twelve hours will be required. A rough guide to the allocation of hours is as follows:

Lectures   16 hours
Tutorial work   10 hours
Laboratory exercises   12 hours

It should be noted that the lecture and tutorial material can also be presented as a four-day full-time course.

Essential matters for MOS digital circuit design are covered in Chapters 1 to 10, including an illustrative system design exercise over Chapters 8 to 10. There are three further design projects in Chapter 13. Lambda-based design rules (Mead and Conway style) are given and used in all exercises except for the CMOS project work in Chapter 13. Here, micron-based rules are used and two fabricator's micron-based rule sets are included in this text; one set from an Australian fabrication house, AWA Ltd, and the second set from Orbit Semiconductor Inc. of California U.S.A. The latter rule set covers a 'state-of-the-art' 2-micron double-metal CMOS process.

Chapter 11 serves a dual purpose in the text. First, it is intended to review aspects of system design brought out in the preceding chapters from a more practical point of view and with a greater depth of insight. Second, the authors have gathered together, and in some cases elaborated upon, design procedures and

---

[1] Mead and Conway, *Introduction to VLSI Systems*, Addison-Wesley, 1980.

ground rules established earlier in the text. It is hoped that this will provide a useful reference area and save much searching through the text.

It is essential that at least ten hours of tutorial work (a minimum of two hours per tutorial) be completed at the points indicated in the text. Tutorials are most effective if supervised, but the tutorial work included in the text can be tackled by referring to material in this text alone.

CAD tools will be needed for laboratory work and a discussion of particular CAD tools is presented in Chapter 12. This also provides the basis around which lectures or further reading in these areas can be constructed. The relevant material from Chapter 12 is usually presented during the early part of the twelve hours allowed here for laboratory exercises. However, in a particular undergraduate course for electrical and electronic engineering students, this aspect and a further treatment of basic MOS fabrication processes were allocated a further nine hours of lectures in total.

Depending on the availability of computer-aided tools and the computing facilities available, it is highly beneficial for each student to spend some ten to twelve hours at a computer terminal (preferably in two-hour rather than one-hour sessions) completing exercises and project work in the design of MOS VLSI circuits.

Chapter 14 introduces Gallium Arsenide technology and establishes stick diagram and layer encoding notation. Basic logic circuit arrangements are examined.

The black and white figures used in the text present mask layout detail in the form in which it may appear on a monochrome graphics terminal. The color outline layouts (between pages 236 and 237) have been presented as they would appear when output to a multipen plotter. Both these forms of presentation are generated by readily available software and commonly available terminals. A black and white encoding of stick diagrams and mask layouts has been used through the text so that, for example, instructors may produce further material in the same format for reproduction in quantity. This representation copies easily and does not lose the layer information as occurs when copying color stick diagrams in monochrome form (color copying being generally ruled out on price and availability).

For those who have based coursework on the first edition of this text, all essential material from the first edition is included here and appears in the same order and mostly in the same chapters as before so that existing courses should not be adversely affected.

In conclusion, the authors have set out to present a balanced and structured course in the design of circuits, subsystems and systems in MOS technology without treating nMOS and CMOS as separate topics. The introduction to Gallium Arsenide is presented using a compatible design methodology. The material presented is mostly based on coursework taught over a number of years and is therefore "tried and trusted" and we have set out to present this text in a form which is readily used and easily assimilated.

Douglas Pucknell and Kamran Eshraghian
Adelaide, June 1987.

1 A review of microelectronics and an introduction to MOS technology

1.1   Introduction to integrated circuit technology

There is no doubt that our daily lives are significantly affected by electronic engineering technology. This is true on the domestic scene, in our professional disciplines, in the workplace, and in leisure activities. Indeed, even at school, tomorrow's adults are exposed to and are coming to terms with quite sophisticated electronic devices and systems. There is no doubt that revolutionary changes have taken place in a relatively short time and it is also certain that even more dramatic advances will be made in the next decade.

Electronics as we know it today is characterized by reliability, low power dissipation, extremely low weight and volume, and low cost, coupled with an ability to cope easily with a high degree of sophistication and complexity. Electronics, and in particular the integrated circuit, has made possible the design of powerful and flexible processors which provide highly intelligent and adaptable devices for the user. Integrated circuit memories have provided the essential elements to complement these processors and, together with a wide range of logic and analog integrated circuitry, they have provided the system designer with components of considerable capability and extensive application. Furthermore, the revolutionary advances in technology have not yet by any means run their full course and the potential for future developments is exciting to say the least.

Up until the 1950s electronic active device technology was dominated by the vacuum tube and, although a measure of miniaturization and circuit integration did take place, the technology did not lend itself to miniaturization as we have come to accept it today. Thus the vast majority of present-day electronics is the result of the invention of the transistor in 1947 and the subsequent invention of the integrated circuit at the start of the 1960s.

1.2   The integrated circuit (IC) era

Such is the potential of the integrated circuit that there have already been four generations of integrated circuits, and the number of transistors commercially integrated on a single chip has risen from 2 to more than 500,000 in just over two decades. This rapid rate of growth was observed and predicted by Gordon Moore, now of Intel, and is conveniently graphed as Moore's First Law in Figure 1–1. The course of microelectronics evolution can also be represented in the concise form of Table 1–1.

At the beginning of the semiconductor era, manufacturers concentrated on germanium devices, but the emphasis soon shifted to silicon and it was on silicon substrates that the integrated circuit (IC) was developed. Integrated circuit development has also taken place in two main streams, bipolar and MOS technologies. At the outset, bipolar technology seemed to provide the most promising approach to fast logic arrays, but MOS technology held the promise of higher levels of integration and the latest MOS circuits are capable of high-speed operation.

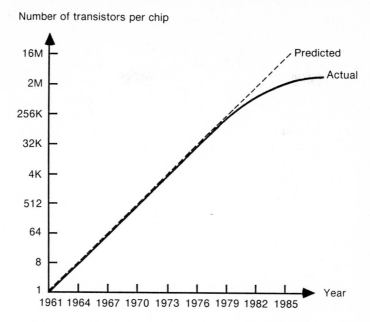

Number of transistors per chip

Note: K signifies a multiplier of 1024 and M signifies a multiplier of $1024^2 = 1,048,576$.

Figure 1–1   Moore's first law: Transistors integrated on a single chip (commercial products)

1.3   Metal-oxide-semiconductor (MOS) technology and VLSI

Within the field of MOS technology the possible streams are based on pMOS, nMOS, and CMOS devices, each of which has properties which make it attractive in one way or another. pMOS offers ease of manufacture, nMOS offers faster devices, and CMOS offers very high regularity and often achieves much lower power dissipation than other MOS circuits.

However, this text will concentrate on nMOS and CMOS which are currently the leading integrated circuit technologies, although aspects of future trends will be discussed in the final chapter. There, gallium arsenide-based technology is introduced which is destined to become the fast front end of VLSI systems of the 1990s.

A number of the examples used to illustrate the design processes and methodology will be presented in nMOS form. The reasons for this are:

1.   nMOS design methodology and the design rules are easily learned and provide an excellent introduction to structured design for VLSI.
2.   nMOS technology and design processes provide an excellent background for other technologies. In particular, familiarity with nMOS allows for a relatively easy transition to CMOS design.

Table 1–1   Microelectronics evolution

Year	1947	1950	1961	1966	1971	1980	1985	1990
Technology	*Invention of the transistor*	*Discrete components*	*SSI*	*MSI*	*LSI*	*VLSI*	*ULSI**	*GSI†*
Approximate number of transistors per chip in commercial products	1	1	10	100–1000	1000–20,000	20,000–500,000	>500,000	>10,000,000
Typical products	—	Junction transistor and diode	Planar devices Logic gates Flip-flops	Counters Multiplexers Adders	8 bit micro-processors ROM RAM	16 and 32 bit micro-processors Sophisticated peripherals	Special processors Real time image processing	?

* Ultra large-scale integration
† Giant-scale integration

Note. The boundary lines between technologies in the table are *not* artificially created. Crossing each boundary requires new design methodology, simulation approaches, and new methods for determining and routing communications and for handling complexity.

3. Both CMOS and nMOS technologies are likely to be current for some time, as there are areas of application where one or the other is more suitable. Both are well suited to VLSI systems requirements.

VLSI technology, then, is not only providing the user with a new and more complex range of 'off the shelf' circuits, but MOS VLSI design processes are such that system designers can readily design their own special circuits of considerable complexity. This provides a new degree of freedom for designers and it is probable that some very significant advances will result. Couple this with the fact that integration density is increasing rapidly, as advances in technology shrink the feature size for circuits integrated in silicon. Typical manufacturers' commercial IC products have shown this trend quite clearly as shown in Figure 1–2 and, simultaneously, the effectiveness of the circuits produced has increased with scaling down. A common measure of effectiveness is the speed power product of the basic logic gate circuit of the technology (for nMOS, the *Nor* gate, with *Nand* and *Nor* gates for CMOS). Speed power product is measured in picojoules (pJ) and is the product of the gate switching delay in nanoseconds and the gate power dissipation in milliwatts. Typical figures are given in Figure 1–3.

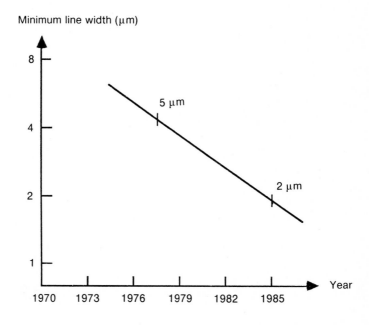

Figure 1–2 Approximate minimum line width of commercial products versus year

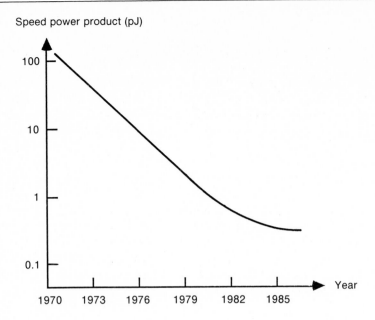

Speed power product (pJ)

Figure 1-3   Speed power product per gate versus year

1.4   Basic MOS transistors

Having now established some background, let us turn our attention to basic MOS processes and devices. In particular, let us examine the basic nMOS enhancement and depletion mode transistors as shown in Figures 1–4 (a) and (b).

nMOS devices are formed in a p-type substrate of moderate doping level. The source and drain regions are formed by diffusing n-type impurities through suitable masks into these areas to give the desired n-impurity concentration and give rise to depletion regions which extend mainly in the more lightly doped p-region as shown. Thus, source and drain are isolated from one another by two diodes. Connections to the source and drain are made by a deposited metal layer. In order to make a useful device there must be the capability for establishing and controlling a current between source and drain, and this is commonly achieved in one of two ways, giving rise to the enhancement mode and depletion mode transistors.

Consider the enhancement mode device first, shown in Figure 1–4(a). A polysilicon gate is deposited on a layer of insulation over the region between source and drain. Figure 1–4(a) shows a basic enhancement mode device in which the channel is not established and the device is in a nonconducting condition, $V_D = V_S = V_{gs} = 0$. If this gate is connected to a suitable positive voltage with respect to the source, then the electric field established between the gate and the substrate

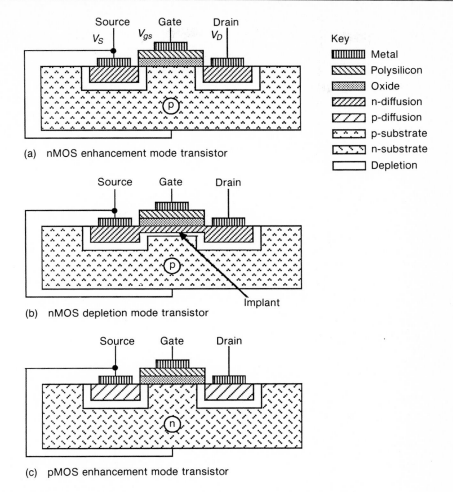

Key

▥▥▥ Metal
▨▨▨ Polysilicon
▦▦▦ Oxide
▨▨▨ n-diffusion
▨▨▨ p-diffusion
▨▨▨ p-substrate
▨▨▨ n-substrate
☐ Depletion

(a) nMOS enhancement mode transistor

(b) nMOS depletion mode transistor

(c) pMOS enhancement mode transistor

Figure 1–4 MOS transistors (V_D=0 V. Source and gate to 0 V.)

gives rise to a charge inversion region in the substrate under the gate insulation and a conducting path or channel is formed between source and drain.

The channel may also be established so that it is present under the condition V_{gs}=0 by implanting suitable impurities in the region between source and drain during manufacture and prior to depositing the insulation and the gate. This arrangement is shown in Figure 1–4(b). Under these circumstances, source and drain are connected by a conducting channel but the channel may now be closed by applying a suitable negative voltage to the gate.

In both cases, variations of the gate voltage allow control of any current flow between source and drain.

Figure 1–4(c) shows the basic pMOS transistor structure for an enhancement mode device. In this case the substrate is of n-type material and the source and drain diffusions are consequently p-type. In the figure the conditions shown are those for an unbiased device; however, the application of a *negative* voltage of suitable magnitude ($>|V_t|$) between gate and source will give rise to the formation of a channel (p-type) between the source and drain and current may then flow if the drain is made negative with respect to the source. In this case the current is carried by holes as opposed to electrons (as is the case for nMOS devices). In consequence, pMOS transistors are inherently slower than nMOS, since hole mobility μ_p is less by a factor of 2.5 approximately than electron mobility μ_n. However, bearing these differences in mind, the discussions of nMOS transistors which follow relate equally well to pMOS transistors.

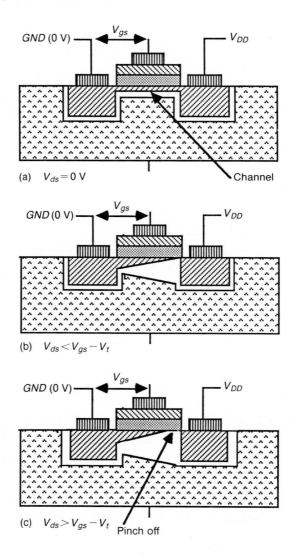

(a) $V_{ds} = 0$ V   Channel

(b) $V_{ds} < V_{gs} - V_t$

(c) $V_{ds} > V_{gs} - V_t$ Pinch off

Figure 1–5   Enhancement mode transistor for particular values of V_{ds} ($V_{gs} > V_t$)

1.5 Enhancement mode transistor action

To gain some understanding of this mechanism, let us further consider the enhancement mode device, as in Figure 1–5, under three sets of conditions. It must first be recognized that in order to establish the channel in the first place a minimum voltage level of *threshold voltage* V_t must be established between gate and source (and of course between gate and substrate as a result). Figure 1–5(a) then indicates the conditions prevailing with the channel established but no current flowing between source and drain ($V_{ds} = 0$). Now consider the conditions prevailing when current flows in the channel by applying a voltage V_{ds} between drain and source. There must of course be a corresponding IR drop $= V_{ds}$ along the channel. This results in the voltage between gate and channel varying with distance along the channel with the voltage between gate and channel being a maximum of V_{gs} at the source end. Since the effective gate voltage is $V_g = V_{gs} - V_t$ (no current flows when $V_{gs} < V_t$) there will be voltage available to invert the channel at the drain end so long as $V_{gs} - V_t \geq V_{ds}$. The limiting condition comes when $V_{ds} = V_{gs} - V_t$. For all voltages $V_{ds} \leq V_{gs} - V_t$, the device is in the nonsaturated region of operation which is the condition shown in Figure 1–5(b).

Consider now what happens when V_{ds} is increased to a level greater than $V_{gs} - V_t$. In this case, an IR drop $= V_{gs} - V_t$ takes place over less than the whole length of the channel so that over part of the channel, near the drain, there is no electric field available to give rise to an inversion layer to create the channel. The channel is, therefore, 'pinched off' as indicated in Figure 1–5(c). Diffusion current completes the path from source to drain in this case, causing the channel to exhibit a high resistance and behave as a constant current source. This region, known as *saturation*, is characterized by almost constant current for increase of V_{ds} above $V_{ds} = V_{gs} - V_t$. In all cases, the channel will cease to exist and no current will flow when $V_{gs} < V_t$. Typically, for enhancement mode devices, $V_t = 1$ volt for $V_{DD} = 5$ V or, in general terms, $V_t = 0.2\ V_{DD}$.

1.6 Depletion mode transistor action

For depletion mode devices the channel is established, due to the implant, even when $V_{gs} = 0$, and to cause the channel to cease to exist a negative voltage V_{td} must be applied between gate and source.

V_{td} is typically $< -0.8\ V_{DD}$, depending on the implant and substrate bias, but, threshold voltage differences apart, the action is similar to that of the enhancement mode transistor.

Commonly used symbols for nMOS and pMOS transistors are set out in Figure 1–6.

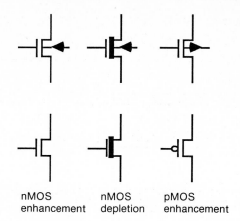

nMOS   nMOS   pMOS
enhancement   depletion   enhancement

Figure 1-6   Transistor circuit symbols

1.7   nMOS fabrication

A brief introduction to the polysilicon gate self-aligning nMOS process will be given now so that the reader may appreciate those aspects of design determined by the process. This is most easily achieved by considering the production of a single enhancement mode transistor in and on a silicon substrate. The process is illustrated in Figure 1-7 and outlined as follows:

1. Processing is carried out on a thin wafer cut from a single crystal of silicon of high purity into which the required p-impurities are introduced as the crystal is grown. Such wafers are typically 75 to 100 mm in diameter and 0.4 mm thick and are doped with, say, boron to impurity concentrations of $10^{15}/cm^3$ to $10^{16}/cm^3$ giving resistivity in the approximate range 25 ohm cm to 2 ohm cm.

2. A layer of silicon dioxide (SiO_2), typically 1 μm thick, is grown all over the surface of the wafer to protect the surface, act as a barrier to dopants during processing, and provide a generally insulating substrate on to which other layers may be deposited and patterned.

3. The surface is now covered with a photoresist which is deposited onto the wafer and spun to achieve an even distribution of the required thickness.

4. The photoresist layer is then exposed to ultraviolet light through a mask which defines those regions into which diffusion is to take place together with transistor channels. Assume, for example, that those areas exposed to ultraviolet radiation are polymerized (hardened) but that the areas required for diffusion are shielded by the mask and remain unaffected.

5. These areas are subsequently readily etched away together with the underlying silicon dioxide so that the wafer surface is exposed in those areas defined by the mask.

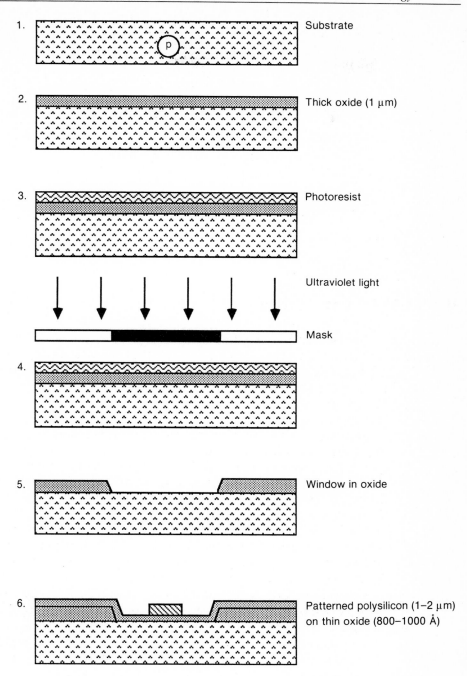

1.   Substrate

2.   Thick oxide (1 μm)

3.   Photoresist

      Ultraviolet light

      Mask

4.

5.   Window in oxide

6.   Patterned polysilicon (1–2 μm)
      on thin oxide (800–1000 Å)

Figure 1–7   nMOS fabrication process

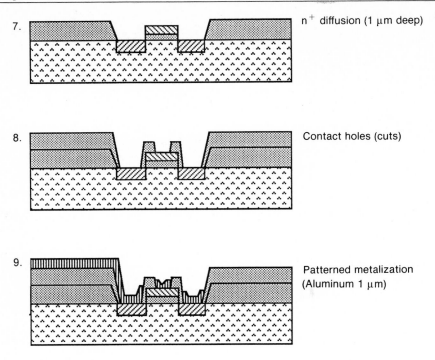

Figure 1-7   continued

6. The remaining photoresist is removed and a thin layer of SiO_2 (0.1 µm typical) is grown over the entire chip surface and then polysilicon is deposited on top of this to form the gate structure. The polysilicon layer consists of heavily doped polysilicon deposited by chemical vapour deposition (CVD). In the fabrication of fine pattern devices, precise control of thickness, impurity concentration, and resistivity is necessary.

7   Further photoresist coating and masking allows the polysilicon to be patterned (as shown in Step 6) and then the thin oxide is removed to expose areas into which n-type impurities are to be diffused to form the source and drain as shown. Diffusion is achieved by heating the wafer to a high temperature and passing a gas containing the desired n-type impurity (for example, phosphorus) over the surface as indicated in Figure 1-8. It will be noted that the polysilicon and underlying SiO_2 act as a mask during diffusion — the process is self-aligning.

8. Thick oxide (SiO_2) is grown over all again and is then masked with photoresist and etched to expose selected areas of the polysilicon gate and the drain and source areas where connections are to be made.

9. The whole chip then has metal (aluminum) deposited over its surface to a thickness typically in excess of 1 µm. This metal layer is then masked and etched to form the required interconnection pattern.

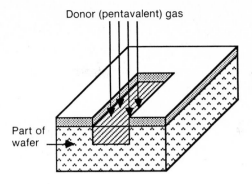

Figure 1-8 Diffusion process

It will be seen that the process revolves around the formation or deposition and patterning of three layers, separated by silicon dioxide insulation. The layers are diffusion within the substrate, polysilicon on oxide on the substrate, and metal insulated again by oxide.

To form depletion mode devices it is only necessary to introduce a masked ion implantation step between Steps 5 and 6 or 6 and 7 in Figure 1–7. Again, the thick oxide acts as a mask and this process stage is also self-aligning.

Consideration of the processing steps will reveal that relatively few masks are needed and the self-aligning aspects of the masking processes greatly ease the problems of mask registration. In practice, some extra process steps are necessary, including the overglassing of the whole wafer, except where contacts to the outside world are required. However, the process is basically straightforward to envisage and circuit design eventually comes down to the business of delineating the masks for each stage of the process. The essence of the process may be reiterated as follows.

1.7.1 Summary of an nMOS process

- Processing takes place on a p-doped silicon crystal wafer on which is grown a 'thick' layer of SiO_2.
- *Mask 1* — Pattern SiO_2 to expose the silicon surface in areas where paths in the diffusion layer or gate areas of transistors are required. Deposit thin oxide over all. For this reason, this mask is often known as the '*thinox*' *mask* but some texts refer to it as the *diffusion mask*.
- *Mask 2* — Pattern the ion implantation within the thinox region where depletion mode devices are to be produced — *self-aligning*.
- *Mask 3* — Deposit polysilicon over all (1.5 μm thick typically), then pattern using Mask 3. Using the same mask, remove thin oxide layer where it is not covered by polysilicon.
- Diffuse n^+ regions into areas where thin oxide has been removed. Transistor drains and sources are thus self-aligning with respect to the gate structures.

- *Mask 4* — Grow thick oxide over all and then etch for contact cuts.
- *Mask 5* — Deposit metal and pattern with Mask 5.
- *Mask 6* — Would be required for the overglassing process step.

1.8   CMOS fabrication

There are a number of approaches to CMOS fabrication, including the p-well, the n-well, the twin-tub, and the silicon-on-insulator processes. In order to introduce the reader to CMOS design we will be concerned mainly with p-well based circuits and, indeed, the p-well process is widely used in practice. However, the n-well process is also popular, particularly as it is an easy retrofit to existing nMOS lines, so we will also discuss it briefly.

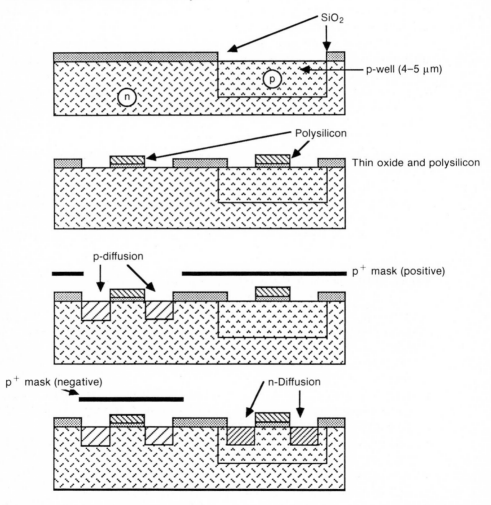

Figure 1-9   CMOS p-well process steps

1.8.1 The p-well process

A brief overview of the fabrication steps may be obtained with reference to Figure 1–9, noting that the basic processing steps are of the same nature as those used for nMOS.

In primitive terms, the structure consists of an n-type substrate in which p-devices may be formed by suitable masking and diffusion and, in order to accommodate n-type devices, a deep p-well is diffused into the n-type substrate as shown.

This diffusion must be carried out with special care since the p-well doping concentration and depth will affect the threshold voltages as well as the breakdown voltages of the n-transistors. To achieve low threshold voltages (0.6 to 1.0 V) we need either deep-well diffusion or high-well resistivity. However, deep wells require larger spacing between the n- and p-type transistors and wires due to lateral diffusion and therefore a larger chip area.

The p-wells act as substrates for the n-devices within the parent n-substrate and, provided that voltage polarity restrictions are observed, the two areas are electrically isolated. However, since there are now in effect two substrates, two substrate connections (V_{DD} and V_{SS}) are required, as shown in Figure 1–10.

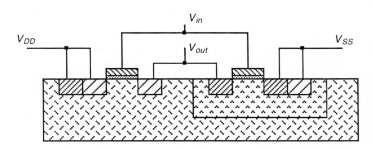

Figure 1–10   CMOS p-well inverter showing V_{DD} and V_{SS} substrate connections

In all other respects, masking, patterning, and diffusion, the process is similar to nMOS fabrication. In summary, typical processing steps are:

- *Mask 1* — defines the areas in which the deep p-well diffusions are to take place.
- *Mask 2* — defines the thinox regions, namely those areas where the thick oxide is to be stripped and thin oxide grown to accommodate p- and n-transistors and wires.
- *Mask 3* — used to pattern the polysilicon layer which is deposited after the thin oxide.
- *Mask 4* — A p-plus mask is now used (to be in effect '*And*ed' with mask 2) to define all areas where p-diffusion is to take place.
- *Mask 5* — This is usually performed using the negative form of the p-plus mask and defines those areas where n-type diffusion is to take place.

- *Mask 6* — Contact cuts are now defined.
- *Mask 7* — The metal layer pattern is defined by this mask.
- *Mask 8* — An overall passivation layer is now applied and this mask is required to define the openings for access to bonding pads.

1.8.2 The n-well process

As indicated earlier, although the p-well process is probably the most widely used, n-well fabrication has also gained wide acceptance particularly as a retrofit to nMOS lines.

N-well CMOS circuits are also superior to p-well because of the lower substrate bias effects on transistor threshold voltage and inherently lower parasitic capacitances associated with source and drain regions.

Typical n-well fabrication steps are illustrated in Figure 1–11. The first mask defines the n-well regions. This is followed by a low dose phosphorus implant driven in by a high temperature diffusion step to form the n-wells. The well depth is optimized to ensure against p-substrate to p^+ diffusion breakdown without compromising the n-well to n^+ mask separation. The next steps are to define the devices and diffusion paths, grow field oxide, deposit and pattern the polysilicon, carry out the diffusions, make contact cuts, and finally metalize as before. It will be

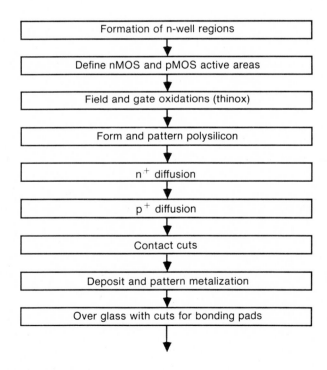

Figure 1–11 Main steps in a typical n-well process

seen that an n^+ mask and its complement may be used to define the n- and p-diffusion regions respectively. These same masks also include the V_{DD} and V_{SS} contacts (respectively). It should be noted that, alternatively, we could have used a p^+ mask and its complement, since the n^+ and p^+ masks are generally complementary.

By way of illustration, Figure 1–12 shows an inverter circuit fabricated by the n-well process, and this may be directly compared with Figure 1–10.

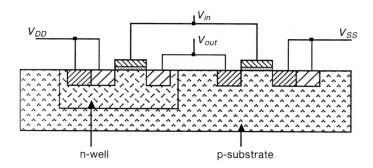

Figure 1–12 Cross-sectional view of n-well CMOS inverter

1.8.2.1 The Berkeley n-well process

There are a number of p-well and n-well fabrication processes and, in order to look more closely at typical fabrication steps, we will use the Berkeley n-well process as an example. This process is illustrated in Figure 1–13.

Owing to differences in charge carrier mobilities, the n-well process creates nonoptimum p-channel characteristics. However, in many CMOS designs (such as domino-logic and dynamic-logic structures), this is relatively unimportant since they contain a preponderance of n-channel devices. Thus the n-channel transistors are mainly those used to form logic elements, providing speed and high density of elements.

Latch-up problems can be considerably reduced by using a low-resistivity epitaxial p-type substrate as the starting material, which can subsequently act as a very low resistance ground-plane to collect substrate currents.

However, a notable factor of the n-well process is that the performance of the already poorly performing p-transistor is even further degraded.

1.8.3 The twin-tub process

A logical extension of the p-well and n-well approaches is the twin-tub fabrication process.

Here we start with a substrate of high resistivity n-type material and then create both n-well and p-well regions. Through this process it is possible to preserve the performance of n-transistors without compromising the p-transistors. Doping

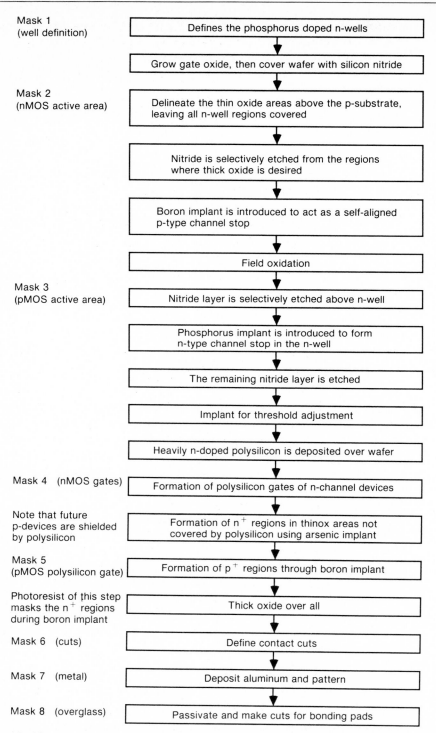

Figure 1-13 Flow diagram of Berkeley n-well fabrication

control is more readily achieved and some relaxation in manufacturing tolerances results. This is particularly important as far as latch-up is concerned.

In general, the twin-tub process allows separate optimization of the n- and p-transistors. The arrangement of an inverter is illustrated in Figure 1–14 which may, in turn, be compared with Figures 1–10 and 1–12.

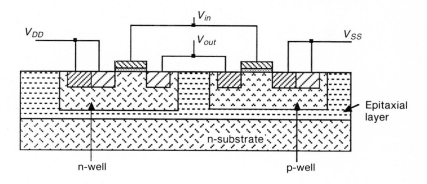

Figure 1–14 Twin-tub structure

1.9 Thermal aspects of processing

The processes involved in making nMOS and CMOS devices have differing high temperature sequences. This is illustrated in Figure 1–15.

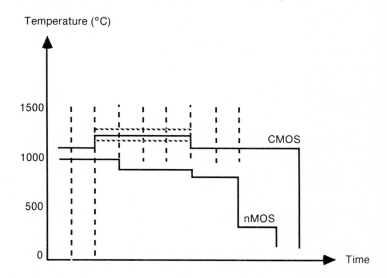

Figure 1–15 Thermal sequence difference between nMOS and CMOS processes

The CMOS p-well process, for example, has a high temperature p-well diffusion process (1100 to 1250°C), the nMOS process having no such requirement. Because of the simplicity, ease of fabrication, and high density per unit area of nMOS circuits, it is likely that nMOS and CMOS system designs will co-exist for some time to come.

1.10 Production of E-beam masks

All the processes discussed have made use of masks at various stages of fabrication. In many processes, the masks are produced by standard optical techniques and much has been written on the photolithographic processes involved. However, as geometric dimensions shrink and also to allow for the processing of a number of different chip designs on a single wafer, other techniques are evolving. One popular process used for this purpose uses an E-beam machine. A rough outline of this type of mask making follows:

1. The starting material consists of chrome-plated glass plates which are coated with an E-beam sensitive resist.
2. The E-beam machine is loaded with the mask description data (MEBES).
3. Plates are loaded into the E-beam machine, where they are exposed with the patterns specified by the customer's mask data.
4. After exposure to the E-beam, the plates are introduced into a developer to bring out the patterns left by the E-beam in the resist coating.
5. The cycle is followed by a bake cycle and a plasma de-summing, which removes the resist residue.
6. The chrome is then etched and the plate is stripped of the remaining E-beam resist.

The advantages of E-beam masks are:

- tighter layer to layer registration;
- smaller feature sizes.

There are two approaches to the design of E-beam machines:

- raster scanning;
- vector scanning.

In the first case, the electron beam scans all possible locations (in a similar fashion to a television display) and a bit map is used to turn the E-beam on and off depending on whether the particular location being scanned is to be exposed or not.

For vector scanning the beam is directed only to those locations which are to be exposed. Although this is inherently faster, the data handling involved is more complex.

1.11 Observations

This chapter has set the scene by introducing the very simple MOS transistor structures and the relatively straightforward fabrication processes used in the manufacture of nMOS and CMOS circuits. We have also attempted to emphasize the revolutionary spread of semiconductor-based technology which has, in the short space of 25 years, advanced from providing the system designer with individually packaged transistors, discrete resistors and capacitors to providing complete subsystems integrated on a single chip.

Although this text concentrates on digital circuits and systems, similar techniques can be applied to the design and fabrication of analog devices. Indeed, the trends are toward systems of VLSI (and beyond) complexity which will in future include, on single chips, significant analog interfaces and other appropriate circuitry. This higher level of integration will lead to fewer packages and interconnections and/or to more complex systems than today. There will be a marked beneficial effect on cost and reliability of the systems that will be available to all professions and disciplines and in most aspects of everyday life.

Our discussions of fabrication have simplified the processes used, to emphasize essential features. Indeed, the fabrication of similar devices by different fabricators may vary considerably in detail. This is also the case with the design rules used (to be dealt with in Chapter 3) but the main text here utilizes an almost universal set of 'lambda-based' rules based on the work of Mead and Conway and acceptable to many fabricators. However, alternative 'micron-based' real world rules are also given in Appendixes A and B for two particular fabrication houses which will allow the reader to utilize and assess the effect of tighter rules.

2 Basic electrical properties of MOS circuits

Having introduced the MOS transistor and the processes used to produce it, we are now in a position to gain some understanding of the electrical characteristics of the basic MOS circuits — enhancement and depletion mode transistors and inverters. Our considerations will be based on reasonable approximations so that the essential features can be evaluated and illustrated in a concise and easily absorbed manner. VLSI designers should have a good knowledge of the behavior of the circuits they are designing or designing with. Even if large systems are being designed, using computer-aided design processes, it is essential that the designs are based on a sound foundation of understanding, if those systems are to meet performance specifications.

The following expressions and discussion relate directly to nMOS transistors, but pMOS expressions are also given where appropriate and, generally, a reversal of voltage and current polarities of nMOS expressions and the exchange of μ_n for μ_p and electrons for holes will yield pMOS from nMOS expressions.

2.1 Drain-to-source current I_{ds} versus voltage V_{ds} relationships

The whole concept of the MOS transistor evolves from the use of a voltage on the gate to induce a charge in the channel between source and drain, which may then be caused to move from source to drain under the influence of an electric field created by voltage V_{ds} applied between drain and source. Since the charge induced is dependent on the gate to source voltage V_{gs}, then I_{ds} is dependent on both V_{gs} and V_{ds}. Consider a structure, as in Figure 2–1, in which electrons will flow source to drain:

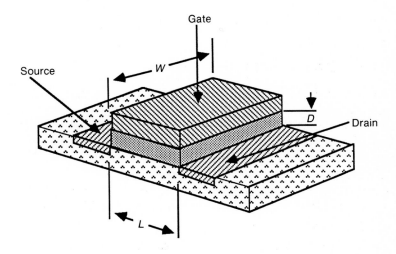

Figure 2–1 nMOS transistor

$$I_{ds} = -I_{sd} = \frac{\text{Charge induced in channel } (Q_c)}{\text{Electron transit time } (\tau)} \qquad \text{(2.1)}$$

First, transit time:

$$\tau_{sd} = \frac{\text{Length of channel } (L)}{\text{Velocity } (v)}$$

but velocity

$$v = \mu E_{ds}$$

where

$$\mu = \text{electron or hole mobility (surface)}$$
$$E_{ds} = \text{electric field (drain to source)}$$

Now

$$E_{ds} = \frac{V_{ds}}{L}$$

so that

$$v = \frac{\mu V_{ds}}{L}$$

Thus

$$\tau_{sd} = \frac{L^2}{\mu V_{ds}} \qquad \text{(2.2)}$$

Typical values of μ at room temperature are:

$$\mu_n \doteq 650 \text{ cm}^2/\text{Vsec (surface)}$$
$$\mu_p \doteq 240 \text{ cm}^2/\text{Vsec (surface)}$$

2.1.1   The nonsaturated region

Charge induced in channel due to gate voltage is due to the voltage difference between the gate and the channel, V_{gs} (assuming substrate connected to source).

Now note that the voltage along the channel varies linearly with distance x from the source due to the IR drop in the channel (see Figure 1–5) and assuming that the device is not saturated then the average value is $V_{ds}/2$. Furthermore, the effective gate voltage $V_g = V_{gs} - V_t$ where V_t is the threshold voltage needed to invert the charge under the gate and establish the channel.

Note that the charge/unit area $= E_g \varepsilon_{ins} \varepsilon_0$. Thus induced charge $Q_c = E_g \varepsilon_{ins} \varepsilon_0 WL$ where

$$E_g = \text{average electric field gate to channel}$$
$$\varepsilon_{ins} = \text{relative permittivity of insulation between gate and channel}$$
$$\varepsilon_0 = \text{permittivity of free space}$$

(*Note*: $\varepsilon_0 = 8.85 \times 10^{-14} \text{F cm}^{-1}$; $\varepsilon_{ins} \doteqdot 4.0$ for silicon dioxide.)

Now

$$E_g = \frac{\left((V_{gs} - V_t) - \dfrac{V_{ds}}{2}\right)}{D}$$

where $D =$ oxide thickness. Thus

$$Q_c = \frac{WL\varepsilon_{ins}\varepsilon_0}{D}\left((V_{gs} - V_t) - \frac{V_{ds}}{2}\right) \tag{2.3}$$

Now, combining equations (2.2) and (2.3) with equation (2.1) we have

$$I_{ds} = \frac{\varepsilon_{ins}\varepsilon_0\mu}{D}\frac{W}{L}\left((V_{gs} - V_t) - \frac{V_{ds}}{2}\right)V_{ds}$$

or

$$I_{ds} = K\frac{W}{L}\left((V_{gs} - V_t)V_{ds} - \frac{V_{ds}^2}{2}\right) \tag{2.4}$$

in the nonsaturated or resistive region where $V_{ds} < V_{gs} - V_t$ and

$$K = \frac{\varepsilon_{ins}\varepsilon_0\mu}{D}$$

Noting that gate/channel capacitance

$$C_g = \frac{\varepsilon_{ins}\varepsilon_0 WL}{D} \text{ (parallel plate)}$$

we have

$$K = \frac{C_g\mu}{WL}$$

so that

$$I_{ds} = \frac{C_g\mu}{L^2}\left((V_{gs} - V_t)V_{ds} - \frac{V_{ds}^2}{2}\right) \tag{2.4a}$$

which is an alternative form of equation 2.4.

2.1.2 The saturated region

Saturation commences when $V_{ds} = V_{gs} - V_t$ since at this point the IR drop in the channel equals the effective gate to channel voltage at the drain and we may assume that the current remains fairly constant as V_{ds} increases further. Thus

$$I_{ds} = K\frac{W}{L}\frac{(V_{gs} - V_t)^2}{2} \tag{2.5}$$

in saturation ($V_{ds} \geqslant V_{gs} - V_t$) or

$$I_{ds} = \frac{C_g \mu}{2L^2} (V_{gs} - V_t)^2 \tag{2.5a}$$

The expressions derived for I_{ds} hold for both enhancement and depletion mode devices, but it should be noted that the threshold voltage for the nMOS depletion mode device (denoted as V_{td}) is *negative*.

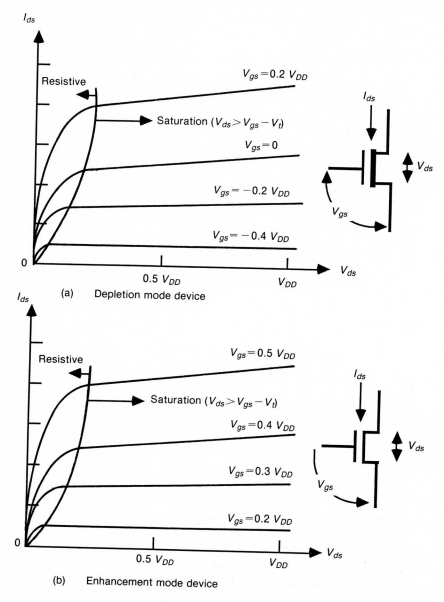

Figure 2-2 MOS transistor characteristics

Typical characteristics for nMOS transistors are given in Figure 2–2. pMOS transistor characteristics are similar, with suitable reversal of polarity.

2.2   Aspects of threshold voltage V_t

The gate structure of a MOS transistor consists, electrically, of charges stored in the dielectric layers and in the surface to surface interfaces as well as in the substrate itself.

Switching an enhancement mode MOS transistor from the off to the on state consists of applying sufficient gate voltage to neutralize these charges and enable the underlying silicon to undergo an inversion due to the electric field from the gate.

Switching a depletion mode nMOS transistor from the on to the off state consists of applying enough voltage to the gate to add to the stored charge and invert the 'n' implant region to 'p'.

The threshold voltage V_t may be expressed as:

$$V_t = \phi_{ms} + \frac{Q_B - Q_{SS}}{C_0} + 2\phi_{fN} \qquad (2.6)$$

where

Q_{SS} = charge density at Si:SiO$_2$ interface
Q_B = the charge per unit area in the depletion layer beneath the oxide
C_0 = capacitance per unit gate area
ϕ_{ms} = work function difference between gate and Si
ϕ_{fN} = Fermi level potential between inverted surface and bulk Si.

Now, for polysilicon gate and silicon substrate, the value of ϕ_{ms} is negative but negligible, and the magnitude and sign of V_t is thus determined by the balance between the remaining negative term $\dfrac{-Q_{SS}}{C_0}$ and the other two terms, both of which are positive. To evaluate V_t, each term is determined as follows:

$$Q_B = \sqrt{2\varepsilon_0\varepsilon_{Si}qN(2\phi_{fN} + V_{SB})} \text{ coulombs/m}^2$$
$$\phi_{fN} = \frac{kT}{q} \ln \frac{N}{n_i} \text{ volts}$$
$$Q_{SS} = (1.5 \text{ to } 8) \times 10^{-8} \text{ coulombs/m}^2$$

depending on crystal orientation, and where

V_{SB} = substrate bias voltage (negative w.r.t. source for nMOS, positive for pMOS)
$q = 1.6 \times 10^{-19}$ coulomb
N = impurity concentration in the substrate (N_A or N_D as appropriate)
ε_{Si} = relative permittivity of silicon ($\doteq 11.7$)
n_i = intrinsic electron concentration (1.6×10^{10}/cm^3 at 300°K)
k = Boltzmann's constant = 1.4×10^{-23} joule/°K

The *body effects* may also be taken into account since the substrate may be biased with respect to the source, as shown in Figure 2–3.

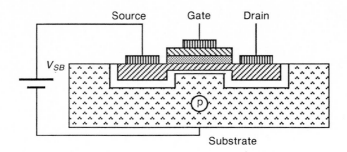

Figure 2–3   Body effect (nMOS device shown)

Increasing V_{SB} causes the channel to be depleted of charge carriers and, thus, the threshold voltage is raised.

Change in V_t is given by $\triangle V_t \doteq \gamma (V_{SB})^{\frac{1}{2}}$ where γ is a constant which depends on substrate doping such that the more lightly doped the substrate, the smaller will be the body effect.

Alternatively, we may write

$$V_t = V_t(0) + \left(\frac{D}{\varepsilon_{ins}\varepsilon_0}\right)\sqrt{2\varepsilon_0\varepsilon_{Si}qN}.(V_{SB})^{\frac{1}{2}}$$

where $V_t(0)$ is the threshold voltage for $V_{SB}=0$.

To establish the magnitude of such effects, typical figures for V_t are as follows:

For nMOS enhancement mode transistors:

$$V_{SB}=0 \text{ V}; \ V_t=0.2V_{DD} \ (= +1 \text{ V for } V_{DD}= +5 \text{ V})$$
$$V_{SB}=5 \text{ V}; \ V_t=0.3V_{DD} \ (= +1.5 \text{ V for } V_{DD}= +5 \text{ V})$$

$\left.\right\}$ Similar but negative values for pMOS

For nMOS depletion mode transistors:

$$V_{SB}=0 \text{ V}; \ V_{td}= -0.7V_{DD} \ (= -3.5 \text{ V for } V_{DD}= +5 \text{ V})$$
$$V_{SB}=5 \text{ V}; \ V_{td}= -0.6V_{DD} \ (= -3.0 \text{ V for } V_{DD}= +5 \text{ V})$$

2.3   Transistor transconductance g_m

Transconductance expresses the relationship between output current I_{ds} and the input voltage V_{gs} and is defined as

$$g_m = \left.\frac{\delta I_{ds}}{\delta V_{gs}}\right|_{V_{ds}=\text{constant}}$$

To find an expression for g_m in terms of circuit and transistor parameters, consider that the charge in channel Q_c is such that

$$\frac{Q_c}{I_{ds}} = \tau$$

where τ is transit time. Thus change in current

$$\delta I_{ds} = \frac{\delta Q_c}{\tau_{sd}}$$

Now

$$\tau_{sd} = \frac{L^2}{\mu V_{ds}} \qquad \text{(from 2.2)}$$

Thus

$$\delta I_{ds} = \frac{\delta Q_c V_{ds} \mu}{L^2}$$

but change in charge

$$\delta Q_c = C_g \delta V_{gs}$$

so that

$$\delta I_{ds} = \frac{C_g \delta V_{gs} \mu V_{ds}}{L^2}$$

Now

$$g_m = \frac{\delta I_{ds}}{\delta V_{gs}} = \frac{C_g \mu V_{ds}}{L^2}$$

In saturation

$$V_{ds} = V_{gs} - V_t$$

$$g_m = \frac{C_g \mu}{L^2} (V_{gs} - V_t) \qquad \textbf{(2.7)}$$

and substituting for $C_g = \dfrac{\varepsilon_{ins} \varepsilon_0 \, WL}{D}$

$$g_m = \frac{\mu \varepsilon_{ins} \varepsilon_0}{D} \frac{W}{L} (V_{gs} - V_t) \qquad \textbf{(2.7a)}$$

2.4 Figure of merit ω_0

An indication of frequency response may be obtained from the parameter ω_0 where

$$\omega_0 = \frac{g_m}{C_g} = \frac{\mu}{L^2}\,(V_{gs} - V_t)\,\left(= \frac{1}{\tau_{sd}}\right) \qquad (2.8)$$

This shows that switching speed depends on gate voltage above threshold and on carrier mobility and inversely as the square of channel length. A fast circuit requires that g_m be as high as possible.

Electron mobility on a (100) oriented n-type inversion layer surface (μ_n) is larger than that on a (111) oriented surface, and is, in fact, about three times as large as hole mobility on a (111) oriented p-type inversion layer. Surface mobility is also dependent on the effective gate voltage ($V_{gs} - V_t$).

For faster nMOS circuits, then, one would choose a (100) oriented p-type substrate in which the inversion layer will have a surface carrier mobility $\mu_n \doteqdot 650$ cm^2/V sec at room temperature.

Compare this with the typical bulk mobilities

$$\mu_n = 1250 \text{ cm}^2/\text{V sec}$$
$$\mu_p = 480 \text{ cm}^2 \text{ V sec}$$

from which it will be seen that $\dfrac{\mu_s}{\mu} \doteqdot 0.5$ (where μ_s = surface mobility).

2.5 The pass transistor

Unlike junction transistors, the isolated nature of the gate allows MOS transistors to be used as switches in series with lines carrying logic levels in a similar way to the use of relay contacts. This application of the MOS device is called the *pass transistor* and switching logic arrays can be formed — for example, an *And* array as in Figure 2–4.

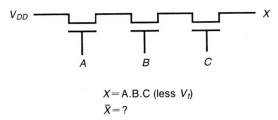

$$X = A.B.C \text{ (less } V_t)$$
$$\bar{X} = ?$$

Note: Means must exist such that X assumes ground potential when $A + B + C = 0$.

Figure 2–4 Pass transistor *And* gate

2.6 The nMOS inverter

A basic requirement for producing a complete range of logic circuits is the inverter. This is needed for restoring logic levels, for *Nand* and *Nor* gates, and for sequential and memory circuits of various forms. In the treatment of the inverter used in this section, the authors wish to acknowledge the influence of material previously published by Mead and Conway.

The basic inverter circuit requires a transistor with source connected to ground and a load resistor of some sort connected from the drain to the positive supply rail V_{DD}. The output is taken from the drain and the input applied between gate and ground.

Resistors are not conveniently produced on the silicon substrate; even modest values occupy excessively large areas so that some other form of load resistance is required.

A convenient way to solve this problem is to use a depletion mode transistor as the load, as shown in Figure 2–5.

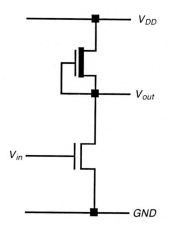

Figure 2–5 nMOS inverter

Now,

- With no current drawn from the output, the currents I_{ds} for both transistors must be equal.
- For the depletion mode transistor, the gate is connected to the source so it is always on and only the characteristic curve $V_{gs} = 0$ is relevant.
- In this configuration the depletion mode device is called the pull-up (p.u.) and the enhancement mode device the pull-down (p.d.) transistor.
- To obtain the inverter transfer characteristic we superimpose the $V_{gs} = 0$ depletion mode characteristic curve on the family of curves for the enhancement mode device, noting that maximum voltage across the enhancement mode device corresponds to minimum voltage across the depletion mode transistor.
- The points of intersection of the curves as in Figure 2–6 give points on the transfer characteristic, which is of the form shown in Figure 2–7.
- Note that as V_{in} ($= V_{gs}$ p.d. transistor) exceeds the p.d. threshold voltage current begins to flow. The output voltage V_{out} thus decreases and the subsequent

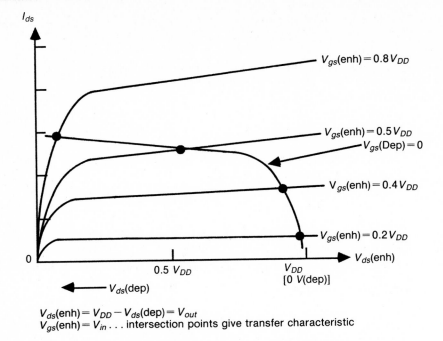

$V_{ds}(enh) = V_{DD} - V_{ds}(dep) = V_{out}$
$V_{gs}(enh) = V_{in}$ . . . intersection points give transfer characteristic

Figure 2-6 Derivation of nMOS inverter transfer characteristic

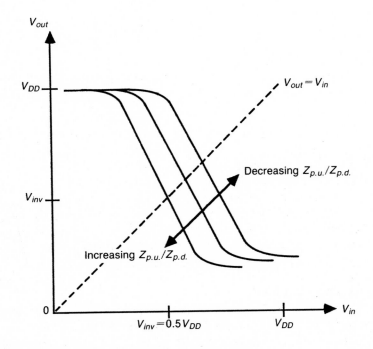

Figure 2-7 nMOS inverter transfer characteristic

increases in V_{in} will cause the p.d. transistor to come out of saturation and become resistive. Note that the p.u. transistor is initially resistive as the p.d. turns on.

- During transition, the slope of the transfer characteristic determines the gain:

$$\text{Gain} = \frac{\delta V_{out}}{\delta V_{in}}$$

- The point at which $V_{out} = V_{in}$ is denoted as V_{inv} and it will be noted that the transfer characteristics and V_{inv} can be shifted by variation of the ratio of pull-up to pull-down resistances (denoted $Z_{p.u.}/Z_{p.d.}$ where Z is determined by the length to width ratio of the transistor in question).

2.7 Determination of pull-up to pull-down ratio ($Z_{p.u.}/Z_{p.d.}$) for an nMOS inverter driven by another nMOS inverter

Consider the arrangement as in Figure 2–8 in which an inverter is driven from the output of another similar inverter. Consider the depletion mode transistor for which $V_{gs} = 0$ under all conditions, and further assume that in order to cascade inverters without degradation of levels we are aiming to meet the requirement

$$V_{in} = V_{out} = V_{inv}$$

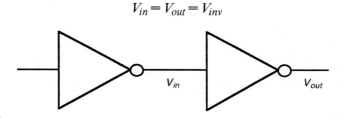

Figure 2–8   nMOS inverter driven directly from another inverter

For equal margins around the inverter threshold, we set $V_{inv} = 0.5 V_{DD}$. At this point both transistors are in saturation and

$$I_{ds} = K \frac{W}{L} \frac{(V_{gs} - V_t)^2}{2}$$

In the depletion mode

$$I_{ds} = K \frac{W_{p.u.}}{L_{p.u.}} \frac{(-V_{td})^2}{2} \quad \text{since } V_{gs} = 0$$

and in the enhancement mode

$$I_{ds} = K\frac{W_{p.d.}}{L_{p.d.}}\frac{(V_{inv} - V_t)^2}{2} \text{ since } V_{gs} = V_{inv}$$

Equating (since currents are the same) we have

$$\frac{W_{p.d.}}{L_{p.d.}}(V_{inv} - V_t)^2 = \frac{W_{p.u.}}{L_{p.u.}}(-V_{td})^2$$

where $W_{p.d.}$, $L_{p.d.}$, $W_{p.u.}$, and $L_{p.u.}$ are the widths and lengths of the pull-down and pull-up transistors respectively.

Now write

$$Z_{p.d.} = \frac{L_{p.d.}}{W_{p.d.}}; \; Z_{p.u.} = \frac{L_{p.u.}}{W_{p.u.}}$$

we have

$$\frac{1}{Z_{p.d.}}(V_{inv} - V_t)^2 = \frac{1}{Z_{p.u.}}(-V_{td})^2$$

whence

$$V_{inv} = V_t - \frac{V_{td}}{\sqrt{Z_{p.u.}/Z_{p.d.}}} \tag{2.9}$$

Now we can substitute typical values as follows

$$V_t = 0.2V_{DD}; \; V_{td} = -0.6V_{DD}$$

$$V_{inv} = 0.5V_{DD} \text{ (for equal margins)}$$

thus, from equation (2.9)

$$0.5 = 0.2 + \frac{0.6}{\sqrt{Z_{p.u.}/Z_{p.d.}}}$$

whence

$$\sqrt{Z_{p.u.}/Z_{p.d.}} = 2$$

and thus

$$Z_{p.u.}/Z_{p.d.} = 4/1$$

for an inverter directly driven from an inverter.

2.8 Pull-up to pull-down ratio for an nMOS inverter driven through one or more pass transistors

Now consider the arrangement of Figure 2–9 in which the input to inverter 2 comes from the output of inverter 1 but passes through one or more nMOS transistors used as switches in series (called *pass transistors*).

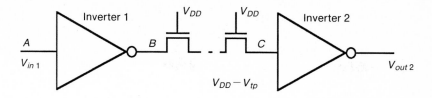

Figure 2-9   Pull-up to pull-down ratios for inverting logic coupled by pass transistors

We are concerned that connection of pass transistors in series will degrade the logic level into inverter 2 to a point where it will not give out proper logic levels. The critical condition is when point A is at 0 volts and B is thus at V_{DD}, *but* the voltage into inverter 2 at point C is now reduced from V_{DD} by the threshold voltage of the series pass transistor. With all pass transistor gates connected to V_{DD} (as shown in Figure 2-8), there is a loss of V_{tp}, however many are connected in series, since no static current flows through them and there can be no voltage drop in the channels. Therefore, the input voltage to inverter 2 is

$$V_{in2} = V_{DD} - V_{tp}$$

where

$$V_{tp} = \text{threshold voltage for a pass transistor}$$

We must now ensure that for this voltage we get out the same voltage as would be the case for inverter 1 driven with input $= V_{DD}$.

Consider inverter 1 (Figure 2-10(a)) with input $= V_{DD}$. If the input is at V_{DD}, then the p.d. transistor T_2 is conducting but with a low voltage across it; therefore, it

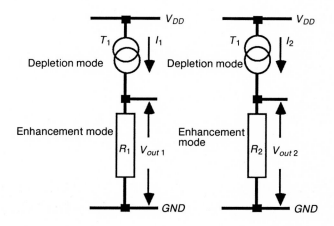

(a)   Inverter 1 with input $= V_{DD}$ (b)   Inverter 2 with input $= V_{DD} - V_{tp}$

Figure 2-10   Equivalent circuits of inverters 1 and 2

is in its resistive region represented by R_1 in Figure 2–10. Meanwhile, the p.u. transistor T_1 is in saturation and is represented as a current source.

For the p.d. transistor

$$I_{ds} = K \frac{W_{p.d.1}}{L_{p.d.1}} \left((V_{DD} - V_t) V_{ds1} - \frac{V_{ds1}^2}{2} \right) \qquad \text{(from 2.4)}$$

Therefore

$$R_1 = \frac{V_{ds1}}{I_{ds}} = \frac{1}{K} \frac{L_{p.d.1}}{W_{p.d.1}} \left(\frac{1}{V_{DD} - V_t - \dfrac{V_{ds1}}{2}} \right)$$

Note that V_{ds1} is small and $\dfrac{V_{ds1}}{2}$ may be ignored. Thus

$$R_1 \doteqdot \frac{1}{K} Z_{p.d.1} \left(\frac{1}{V_{DD} - V_t} \right)$$

Now, for depletion mode p.u. in saturation with $V_{gs} = 0$

$$I_1 = I_{ds} = K \frac{W_{p.u.1}}{L_{p.u.1}} \frac{(-V_{td})^2}{2} \qquad \text{(from 2.5)}$$

The product

$$I_1 R_1 = V_{out1}$$

Thus

$$V_{out1} = I_1 R_1 = \frac{Z_{p.d.1}}{Z_{p.u.1}} \left(\frac{1}{V_{DD} - V_t} \right) \frac{(-V_{td})^2}{2}$$

Consider inverter 2 (Figure 2–10(b)) when input $= V_{DD} - V_{tp}$. As for inverter 1

$$R_2 \doteqdot \frac{1}{K} Z_{p.u.2} \frac{1}{((V_{DD} - V_{tp}) - V_t)}$$

$$I_2 = K \frac{1}{Z_{p.u.2}} \frac{(-V_{td})^2}{2}$$

whence

$$V_{out2} = I_2 R_2 = \frac{Z_{p.d.2}}{Z_{p.u.2}} \left(\frac{1}{V_{DD} - V_{tp} - V_t} \right) \frac{(-V_{td})^2}{2}$$

If inverter 2 is to have the same output voltage under these conditions then $V_{out\,1} = V_{out\,2}$. That is

$$I_1 R_1 = I_2 R_2$$

Therefore

$$\frac{Z_{p.u.2}}{Z_{p.d.2}} = \frac{Z_{p.u.1}}{Z_{p.d.1}} \frac{(V_{DD} - V_t)}{(V_{DD} - V_{tp} - V_t)}$$

Taking typical values

$$V_t = 0.2 V_{DD}$$

$$V_{tp} = 0.3 V_{DD}*$$

$$\frac{Z_{p.u.2}}{Z_{p.d.2}} = \frac{Z_{p.u.1}}{Z_{p.d.1}} \frac{0.8}{0.5}$$

Therefore

$$\frac{Z_{p.u.2}}{Z_{p.d.2}} \doteq 2\frac{Z_{p.u.1}}{Z_{p.d.1}} = \frac{8}{1}$$

Summarizing for an nMOS inverter:

- An inverter driven directly from the output of another should have a $Z_{p.u.}/Z_{p.d.}$ ratio of $\geqslant 4/1$.
- An inverter driven through one or more pass transistors should have a $Z_{p.u.}/Z_{p.d.}$ ratio of $\geqslant 8/1$.

Note: It is the driven, *not* the driver, whose ratio is affected.

2.9 Alternative forms of pull-up

Up to now we have assumed that the inverter circuit has a depletion mode pull-up transistor as its load. There are, however, at least four possible arrangements:

1. *Load resistance* R_L (Figure 2–11). This arrangement is not practical due to the large space requirements of resistors produced in a silicon substrate.

2. *nMOS depletion mode transistor pull-up* (Figure 2–12).

    (a) Dissipation is high since current flows when V_{in} = logical 1.
    (b) Switching of output from 1 to 0 commences when V_{in} exceeds V_t of p.d.
    (c) When switching the output from 1 to 0 the p.u. device is nonsaturated initially and this presents lower resistance through which to charge capacitive loads.

---

* Larger than V_t since when pass transistor channel is at logical 1 (V_{DD}) the effective substrate bias with respect to source is 5 volts (V_{DD}) greater than conditions for which V_t applies.

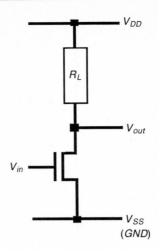

Figure 2-11   Resistor pull-up

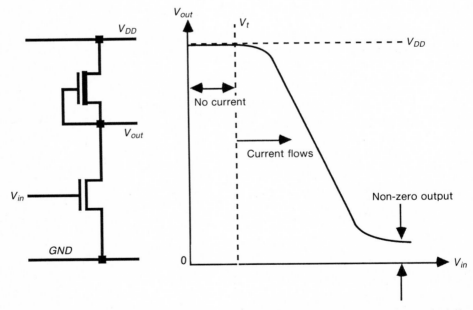

Figure 2-12   nMOS depletion mode transistor pull-up and transfer characteristic

3. *nMOS enhancement mode pull-up* (Figure 2-13).

    (a) Dissipation is high since current flows when V_{in} = logical 1 if V_{GG} is returned to V_{DD}.
    (b) V_{out} can never reach V_{DD} (logical 1) if $V_{GG} = V_{DD}$ as is normally the case.

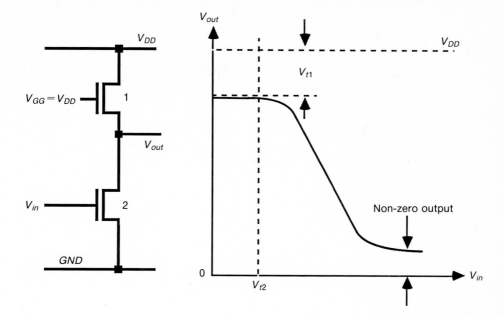

Figure 2–13 nMOS enhancement mode pull-up and transfer characteristic

(c) V_{GG} may be derived from a switching source, for example, one phase of the clock, so that dissipation can be greatly reduced.

(d) If V_{GG} is higher than V_{DD} then an extra supply rail is required.

4. *Complementary transistor pull-up (CMOS)* (Figure 2–14).

(a) No current flow either for logical 0 or for logical 1 inputs.

(b) Full logical 1 and 0 levels are presented at the output.

(c) For devices of similar dimensions the p-channel is slower than the n-channel device.

2.10 The CMOS inverter

The general arrangement and characteristics are illustrated in Figure 2–14.

We have seen (equations 2.4 and 2.5) that the current/voltage relationships for the MOS transistor may be written

$$I_{ds} = K\frac{W}{L}\left((V_{gs} - V_t)V_{ds} - \frac{V_{ds}^2}{2}\right)$$

in the resistive region or

$$I_{ds} = K\frac{W}{L}\frac{(V_{gs} - V_t)^2}{2}$$

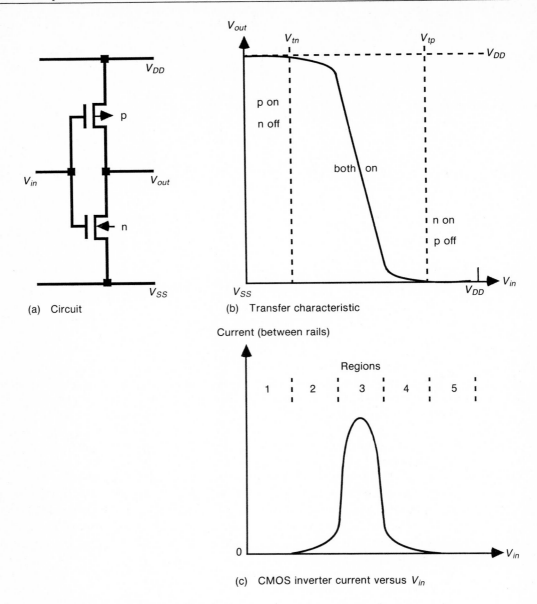

(a) Circuit

(b) Transfer characteristic

(c) CMOS inverter current versus V_{in}

Figure 2–14 Complementary transistor pull-up (CMOS)

in saturation. In both cases the factor K is a technology-dependent parameter such that

$$K = \frac{\varepsilon_{ins}\,\varepsilon_0\,\mu_n}{D}$$

The factor W/L is, of course, contributed by the geometry and it is common practice to write

$$\beta = K\frac{W}{L}$$

so that, for example

$$I_{ds} = \frac{\beta}{2}(V_{gs} - V_t)^2$$

in saturation, and where β may be applied to both nMOS and pMOS transistors as follows

$$\beta_n = \frac{\varepsilon_{ins}\varepsilon_0\mu_n}{D}\frac{W_n}{L_n}$$

$$\beta_p = \frac{\varepsilon_{ins}\varepsilon_0\mu_p}{D}\frac{W_p}{L_p}$$

where W_n and L_n, W_p and L_p are the n- and p-transistor dimensions respectively.

With regard to Figures 2–14(b) and 2–14(c), it may be seen that the CMOS inverter has five distinct regions of operation.

Considering the static conditions first, it may be seen that in *region 1* for which V_{in} = logic 0, we have the p-transistor fully turned on while the n-transistor is fully turned off. Thus no current flows through the inverter and the output is directly connected to V_{DD} through the p-transistor. A good logic 1 output voltage is thus present at the output.

In *region 5* V_{in} = logic 1, the n-transistor is fully on while the p-transistor is fully off. Again, no current flows and a good logic 0 appears at the output.

In *region 2* the input voltage has increased to a level which just exceeds the threshold voltage of the n-transistor. The n-transistor conducts and has a large voltage between source and drain; so it is in saturation. The p-transistor is also conducting but with only a small voltage across it, it operates in the unsaturated resistive region. A small current now flows through the inverter from V_{DD} to V_{SS}. If we wish to analyze the behavior in this region, we equate the p-device resistive region current with the n-device saturation current and thus obtain the voltage and current relationships.

Region 4 is similar to region 2 but with the roles of the p-and n-transistors reversed. However, the current magnitudes in regions 2 and 4 are small and most of the energy consumed in switching from one state to the other is due to the larger current which flows in region 3.

Region 3 is the region in which the inverter exhibits gain and in which *both* transistors are in saturation.

The currents (with regard to Figure 2–14(c)) in each device must be the same since the transistors are in series, so we may write

$$I_{dsp} = -I_{dsn}$$

where

$$I_{dsp} = -\frac{\beta_p}{2}(V_{in} - V_{DD} - V_{tp})^2$$

and

$$I_{dsn} = \frac{\beta_n}{2}(V_{in} - V_{tn})^2$$

from whence we can express V_{in} in terms of the β ratio and the other circuit voltages and currents

$$V_{in} = \frac{V_{DD} + V_{tp} + V_{tn}(\beta_n/\beta_p)^{1/2}}{1 + (\beta_n/\beta_p)^{1/2}} \tag{2.10}$$

Since both transistors are in saturation, they act as current sources so that the equivalent circuit in this region is two current sources in series between V_{DD} and V_{SS} with the output voltage coming from their common point. The region is inherently unstable in consequence and the changeover from one logic level to the other is rapid.

If $\beta_n = \beta_p$ and if $V_{tn} = -V_{tp}$, then from equation 2.10,

$$V_{in} = V_{DD}/2$$

This implies that the changeover between logic levels is symmetrically disposed about the point at which

$$V_{in} = V_{out} = V_{DD}/2$$

since only at this point will the two β factors be equal. But if $\beta_n = \beta_p$ then the device geometries must be such that

$$\mu_p W_p/L_p = \mu_n W_n/L_n$$

Now the mobilities are inherently unequal and thus it is necessary for the width to length ratio of the p-device to be two to three times that of the n-device, namely

$$W_p/L_p \doteq 2.5 \; W_n/L_n$$

However, it must be recognized that mobility μ is affected by the transverse electric field in the channel and is thus dependent on V_{gs} (and thus on V_{in} in this case). It has been shown empirically that the actual mobility is

$$\mu = \mu_z(1 - \phi(V_{gs} - V_t))^{-1}$$

ϕ is a constant approximately equal to 0.05, V_t includes any body effect, and μ_z is the mobility with zero transverse field. Thus a β ratio of 1 will only hold good around the point of symmetry when $V_{out} = V_{in} = V_{DD}/2$.

The β ratio is often unimportant in many configurations and in these cases minimum size transistor geometries are used for both n- and p-devices. Figure 2–15 indicates the trends in the transfer characteristic as the ratio is varied. The changes indicated in the figure would be for quite large variations in β ratio (e.g. up to 10:1) and the ratio is thus not too critical in this respect.

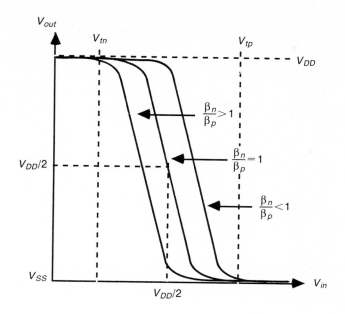

Figure 2–15 Trends in transfer characteristic with β ratio

2.11 MOS transistor circuit model

The MOS transistor can be modeled with varying degrees of complexity. However, a consideration of the actual physical construction of the device (as in Figure 2–16) leads to some understanding of the various components of the model.

Notes: C_{GC} = gate to channel capacitance

$\left. \begin{array}{l} C_{GS} = \text{gate to source capacitance} \\ G_{GD} = \text{gate to drain capacitance} \end{array} \right\}$ Small for self-aligning nMOS process.

Remaining capacitances are associated with the depletion layer and are voltage dependent. Note that C_{SS} indicates source-to-substrate, C_{DS} drain-to-substrate, and C_S channel-to-substrate capacitances.

2.12 Latch-up in CMOS circuits

A problem which is inherent in the p-well and n-well processes is due to the relatively large number of junctions which are formed in these structures and the

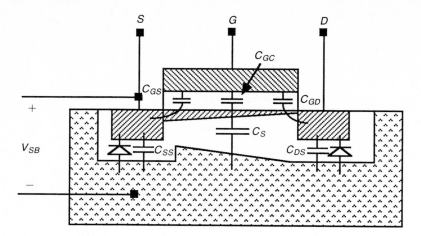

Figure 2–16   nMOS transistor model

presence, in consequence, of parasitic transistors and diodes. Latch-up is a condition in which the parasitic components give rise to the establishment of low-resistance conducting paths between V_{DD} and V_{SS} with consequent disastrous results. Careful control during fabrication is necessary to avoid this problem.

Latch-up may be induced by glitches on the supply rails or by incident radiation. The mechanism involved may be understood by referring to Figure 2–17 which shows the key parasitic components associated with a p-well structure in which an inverter circuit (for example) has been formed.

There are, in effect, two transistors and two resistances (associated with the p-well and with regions of the substrate) which form a path between V_{DD} and V_{SS}. If sufficient substrate current flows to generate enough voltage across R_s to turn on transistor T_1, this will then draw current through R_p and, if the voltage developed is

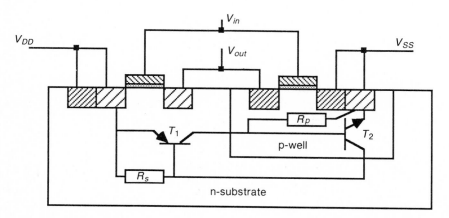

Figure 2–17   Latch-up effect in p-well structure

sufficient, T_2 will also turn on, establishing a self-sustaining low resistance path between the supply rails. If the current gains of the two transistors are such that $\beta_1 \times \beta_2 > 1$, latch-up may occur. Equivalent circuits are given in Figure 2–18.

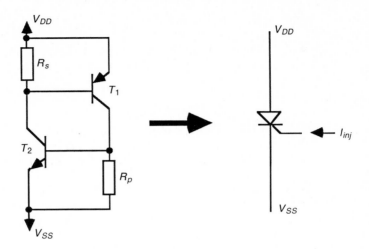

Figure 2–18 Latch-up circuit model

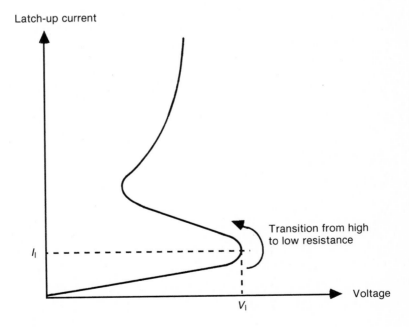

Figure 2–19 Latch-up current versus voltage

With no injected current the parasitic transistors will exhibit high resistance but sufficient substrate current flow will cause switching to the low-resistance state as already explained. The switching characteristic of the arrangement is outlined in Figure 2–19.

Once latched-up, this condition will be maintained until the latch-up current drops below I_l. It is thus essential for a CMOS process to ensure that V_l and I_l are not readily achieved in any normal mode of operation.

Remedies for the latch-up problem include:

1. an increase in substrate doping levels with a consequent drop in the value of R_s;
2. reducing R_p by control of fabrication parameters and by ensuring a low contact resistance to V_{SS};
3. other more elaborate measures such as the introduction of guard rings.

For completeness, the latch-up configuration for an n-well structure is given as Figure 2–20.

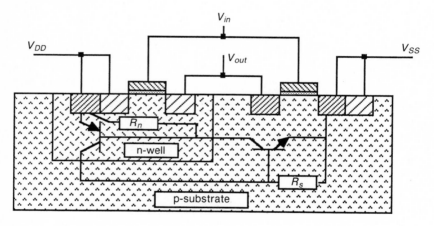

Figure 2–20   Latch-up circuit for n-well process

2.13 Exercises

1. Compare the relative merits of three different forms of pull-up for the inverter circuit. What is the best choice for realization in nMOS technology?
2. In the inverter circuit, what is meant by $Z_{p.u.}$ and $Z_{p.d.}$? Derive the required ratio between $Z_{p.u.}$ and $Z_{p.d.}$ if an nMOS inverter is to be driven from another inverter.
3. For a CMOS inverter calculate the shift in the transfer characteristic (Figure 2–15) when the β_n/β_p ratio is varied from 1/1 to 10/1.

3 | MOS circuit design processes

3.1   MOS layers

MOS design is aimed at turning a specification into masks for processing silicon to meet the specification. We have seen that nMOS circuits are formed on three layers — *diffusion*, *polysilicon*, and *metal*, which are isolated from one another by thick or thin (thinox) silicon dioxide insulating layers. The thin oxide (thinox) region includes n-diffusion, p-diffusion, and transistor channels. Polysilicon and thinox regions interact so that a transistor is formed where they cross one another. Layers may be deliberately joined together where contacts are formed. We have also seen that the basic MOS transistor properties can be modified by the use of an implant within the thinox region. We must find a way of capturing the topology of the actual layout in silicon so that we can set out simple circuit diagrams which convey both *layer* information and *topology*.

3.2   Stick diagrams

Stick diagrams are used to convey layer information through the use of a color code — green for n-diffusion, red for polysilicon, blue for metal, yellow for implant or p-diffusion, and black for contact areas. In this text the color coding has been complemented by monochrome encoding of the lines so that black and white copies of stick diagrams do not lose the layer information. The encodings chosen are shown in Figure 3–1, but when you are drawing your own stick diagrams you should use single lines in the appropriate colors, as in Color Plate 1. Note that mask layout information has also been monochrome encoded, as shown in Figure 3–1.

In this chapter we will see how basic circuits are represented in stick diagram form. We will also be using this type of representation quite widely throughout the text. The layout of stick diagrams faithfully reflects the topology of the actual layout in silicon. Two stick diagrams, one in nMOS and one CMOS, are included in Figure 3–1.

Having conveyed layer information and topology by using stick diagrams, the stick diagrams are relatively easily turned into mask layouts. For example, the transistor stick diagrams of Figure 3–2 are readily translated into mask layout form.

In order that the mask layouts produced during design will be compatible with the fabrication processes, a set of design rules are set out for layouts so that, if obeyed, the rules will produce layouts which will work in practice.

3.2.1   nMOS design style

A rational approach to stick diagram layout is readily adopted for nMOS circuits and the approach recommended here is both easy to use and easy to turn into a

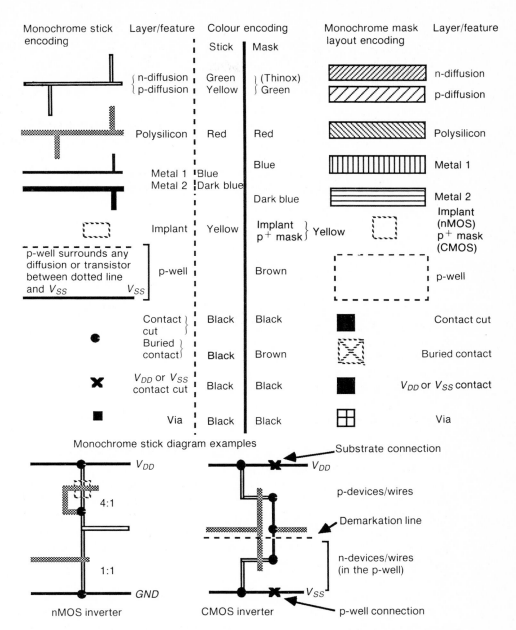

Figure 3–1   Layer/feature encoding schemes (see also Color Plate 1)

Notes: Layers are insulated from each other unless deliberately joined by a contact. However, wherever polysilicon crosses diffusion a transistor is formed.

Due to various complexities, we will allow buried contacts in nMOS processes only in the main text. Therefore there should not be any confusion with the brown color used to represent buried contacts and p-wells.

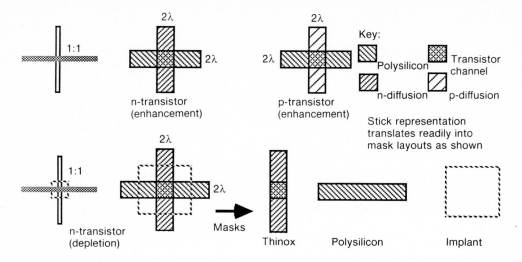

Figure 3–2 Stick diagrams and corresponding mask layout examples

mask layout. The layout of nMOS involves a subset of the layers and features set out in Figure 3–1; in fact, for nMOS we require:

- n-diffusion (green) and other thin oxide areas (green);
- polysilicon (red);
- metal (blue) + second metal — if any — (dark blue);
- implant (yellow);
- contacts (black or brown).

All transistors are formed by polysilicon crossing thinox (red over green) and all diffusion regions are n-type (green).

When starting a layout, the first step is normally to draw the metal (blue) V_{DD} and GND rails in parallel allowing enough space between them for the other circuit elements required. Next, thinox (green) paths are drawn between the rails for inverters and inverter-based logic, as shown in Figure 3–3(a), not forgetting to make the appropriate contacts. Inverters and inverter-based logic comprise a pull-up structure, usually a depletion mode transistor, connected from the output point to V_{DD} and a pull-down structure of enhancement mode transistors suitably interconnected between the output point and GND. This step in the process is illustrated in Figure 3–3(b). Do not forget the implants (yellow) for depletion mode transistors and do not forget to write in the length to width ($L:W$) ratio for each transistor.

Signal paths may also be switched by pass transistors and long signal paths may involve metal buses (blue) which are conveniently run in parallel with the power rails. Allowing for the fact that the stick diagram may well represent a small section of circuit which will be replicated many times, a convenient strategy is to run power rails and bus(es) in parallel in metal (blue) and then propagate control

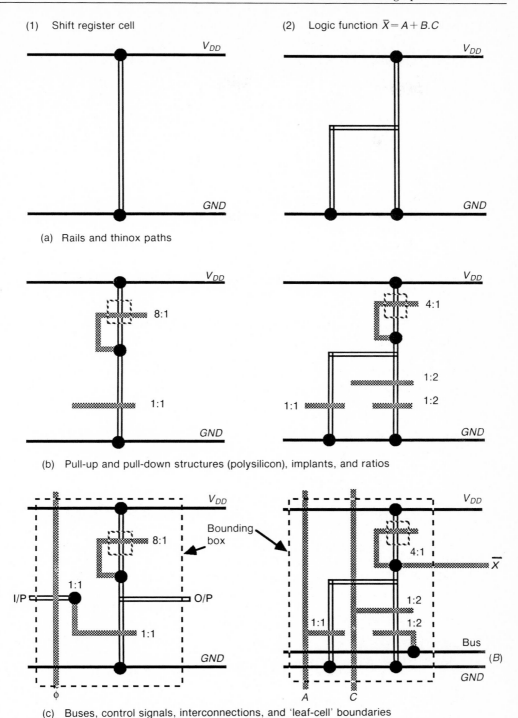

(1)   Shift register cell

(2)   Logic function $\bar{X} = A + B.C$

(a)   Rails and thinox paths

(b)   Pull-up and pull-down structures (polysilicon), implants, and ratios

(c)   Buses, control signals, interconnections, and 'leaf-cell' boundaries

Figure 3–3   Examples of nMOS stick layout design style

signals at right angles on polysilicon as shown. At this stage of design, 'leaf-cell' boundaries are conveniently shown in the stick diagram and these are placed so that replicated cells may be directly interconnected by direct abutment on a side-by-side or top-to-bottom basis. The aspects just discussed are illustrated in Figure 3–3(c).

From the very beginning a design style should encourage the concepts of regularity (replication) and generality so that design effort can be minimized and the interconnection of leaf cells, subsystems, and systems is facilitated.

3.2.2   CMOS design style

The stick and layout representations for CMOS used in this text are a logical extension of the nMOS approach and style already outlined. They are based on the widely accepted work of Mead and Conway.

All features and layers defined in Figure 3–1, with the exception of implant (yellow), are used in CMOS design. Yellow in CMOS design is now used to identify p-transistors and wires, as depletion mode devices are not utilized. As a result, no confusion results from the allocation of the same color to two different features.

The two types of transistor used, 'n' and 'p', are separated in the stick layout by the demarkation line above which all p-type devices are placed (transistors and wires (yellow)). The n-devices (green) are consequently placed below the demarkation line and are thus located in the p-well. These factors are emphasized by Figure 3–4.

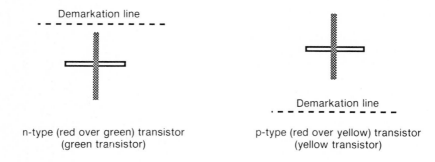

Figure 3–4   n- and p-type transistors in CMOS design

Diffusion paths must not cross the demarkation line and n- and p-diffusion wires must not join. The 'n' and 'p' features are normally joined by metal. Apart from the demarkation line, there is no indication of the actual p-well topology at this (stick diagram) level of abstraction; neither does the p^+ mask appear. Their geometry will appear when the stick diagram is translated to a mask layout. However, we must not forget to place crosses on V_{DD} and V_{SS} rails to represent the substrate and p-well connection respectively.

The design style is illustrated simply by taking as an example the design of a single bit of a shift register. The design commences with the drawing of the V_{DD} and

V_{SS} rails in parallel and in metal and the creation of an (imaginary) demarkation line in between, as in Figure 3–5(a). The n-transistors are then placed below this line and thus close to V_{SS}, while p-transistors are placed above the line and below V_{DD}. In both cases the transistors are placed with their diffusion paths parallel to the rails (horizontal in the diagram) as shown in Figure 3–5(b).

A sound approach is to now interconnect the n- with the p-transistors as required, using metal as shown in Figure 3–5(c). It must be remembered that only metal and polysilicon can cross the demarkation line but in the overall context wires can be run in diffusion also.

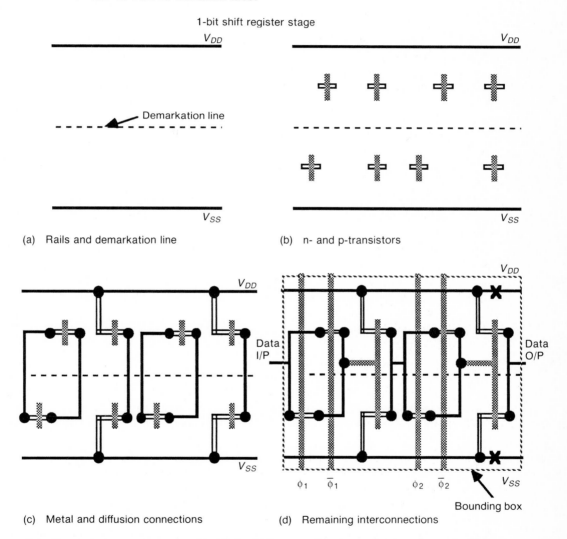

(a) Rails and demarkation line

(b) n- and p-transistors

(c) Metal and diffusion connections

(d) Remaining interconnections

Note: The contact crosses represented in (d) should have one V_{DD} contact for every four p-transistors and one V_{SS} contact for every four n-transistors.

Figure 3–5 Example of CMOS stick layout design style

Finally the remaining interconnections are made as appropriate and the control signals and data inputs are added. These steps are illustrated in Figure 3–5(d).

Although the circuit layout is now complete, we must not forget to represent the V_{SS} and V_{DD} contact crosses; one on the V_{DD} line for every four p-transistors and one on the V_{SS} line for every four n-transistors. The bounding box for the entire leaf-cell may also be shown if appropriate.

This design style is straightforward in application but later on we must recognize that sometimes transistors can be merged to advantage. We will also see how stick diagrams are turned into mask layouts, noting for CMOS layouts that the thinox mask includes all green features (n-devices) and all yellow features (p-devices).

3.3 Design rules and layout

The object of a set of design rules is to allow a ready translation of circuit design concepts, usually in stick diagram or symbolic form, into actual geometry in silicon. The design rules are the effective interface between the circuit/system designer and the fabrication engineer. Clearly, both sides of the interface have a vested interest in making their own particular tasks as easy as possible and design rules usually attempt to provide a workable and reliable compromise which is friendly to both sides.

Circuit designers in general want tighter, smaller layouts for improved performance and decreased silicon area. On the other hand, the process engineer wants design rules that result in a *controllable and reproducable* process. Generally we find that there has to be a compromise for a competitive circuit to be produced at a reasonable cost.

One of the important factors associated with design rules is the achievable definition of the process line. Definition is determined by process line equipment and process design. For example, it is found that if a 10:1 wafer stepper is used instead of a 1:1 projection mask aligner, the level-to-level registration will be closer. Design rules can be affected by the maturity of the process line. For example, if the process is mature, then one can be assured of the process line capability allowing tighter designs with less constraints on the designer.

The simple lambda (λ)-based design rules set out first in this text are based on the invaluable work of Mead and Conway and have been widely used, particularly in the context of the multiproject chips. The design rules are based on a single parameter λ which leads to a simple set of rules for the designer, wide acceptance of the rules by a large cross section of the fabrication houses and silicon brokers and allows for scaling of the designs to a limited extent. This latter feature helps to give designs a longer lifetime.

3.3.1 Lambda-based design rules

In general, design rules and layout methodology based on the concept of λ provide a process and feature size-independent way of setting out mask dimensions to scale.

All paths in all layers will be dimensioned in λ units and subsequently λ can be allocated an appropriate value compatible with the feature size of the fabrication process. This concept means that the actual mask layout design takes no account of the value subsequently allocated to the feature size, but the design rules are such that, if correctly obeyed, the mask layouts will produce working circuits for a range of values allocated to λ. For example, λ can be allocated a value of 2.5 μm so that minimum feature size on chip will be 5 μm (2λ). This is, in fact, the value allocated for multiproject chip designs which are discussed later in this text.

Design rules, also due to Mead and Conway, specify line widths, separations, and extensions in terms of λ, and are readily committed to memory. Design rules can be conveniently set out in diagrammatic form as in Figure 3–6 for the widths and separation of conducting paths, and in Figure 3–7 for extensions and separations associated with transistor layouts.

The design rules associated with contacts between layers are also set out in Figures 3–8 and 3–9 and it will be noted that connection can be made between any two or all three layers.*

In all cases, the use of the design rules will be illustrated in layouts resulting from exercises worked through in the text.

---

*It must be noted that Figures 3–6 to 3–8 apply to both nMOS and CMOS with any references to p-devices applying to CMOS only.

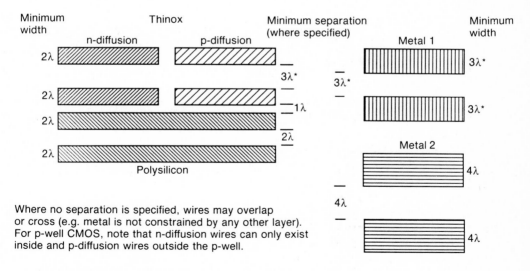

Where no separation is specified, wires may overlap or cross (e.g. metal is not constrained by any other layer). For p-well CMOS, note that n-diffusion wires can only exist inside and p-diffusion wires outside the p-well.

Note: Many fabrication houses now accept 2λ diffusion to diffusion separation and 2λ metal 1 width and separation.

Figure 3–6 Design rules for wires (nMOS and CMOS)

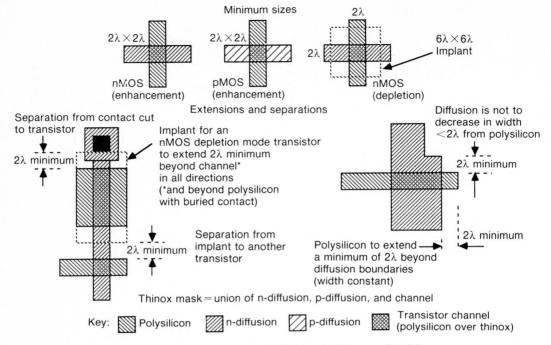

Figure 3–7   Transistor design rules (nMOS, pMOS, and CMOS)

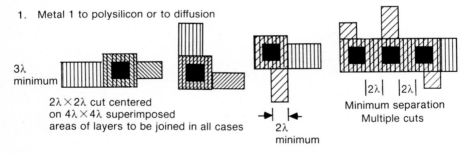

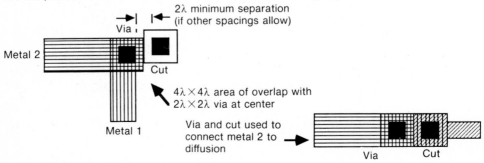

Figure 3–8   Contacts (nMOS and CMOS)

3.3.2 Contact cuts

In connection with contacts between polysilicon and diffusion in nMOS circuits it should be recognized that there are two possible approaches — the butting contact and the buried contact. The latter is generally less space-consuming and is held by many to be the more reliable contact. Designers should therefore consult the fabrication house where their designs are to be turned into silicon in order to decide on

1.   Buried contact: Basically, layers are joined over a $2\lambda \times 2\lambda$ area with the buried contact cut extending by 1λ in all directions around the contact area except that the contact cut extension is increased to 2λ in diffusion paths leaving the contact area. This is to avoid forming unwanted transistors (see following examples).

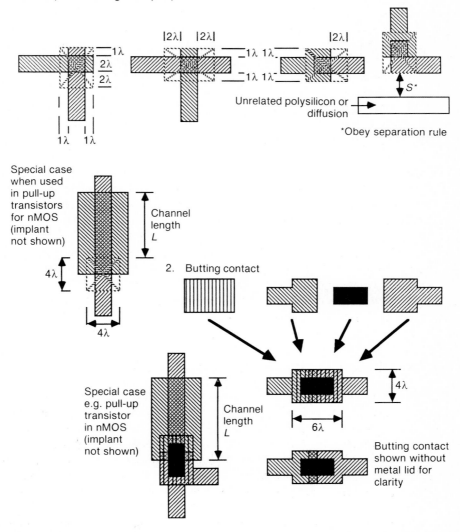

Figure 3–9 Contacts polysilicon to diffusion (nMOS only in the main text)

the best approach. In CMOS designs such contact is usually made by a metal wire and two contacts.

When making connections between metal and either of the other two layers (as in Figure 3–8), the process is quite simple. The $2\lambda \times 2\lambda$ contact cut indicates an area in which the oxide is to be removed down to the underlying polysilicon or diffusion surface. When deposition of the metal layer takes place the metal is deposited through the contact cut areas onto the underlying area so that contact is made between the layers.

When connecting diffusion to polysilicon using the butting contact approach (see Figure 3–9) the process is rather more complex. In effect, a $2\lambda \times 2\lambda$ contact cut is made down to each of the layers to be joined. The layers are butted together in such a way that these two contact cuts become contiguous. Since the polysilicon and diffusion outlines overlap and thin oxide under polysilicon acts as a mask in the diffusion process, the polysilicon and diffusion layers are also butted together. The contact between the two butting layers is then made by a metal overlay as shown in the figure. It is hoped that the cross-sectional view of the butting contact in Figure 3–10(b) helps to make the nature of the contact apparent.

The buried contact approach shown in Figures 3–9 and 3–10 is simpler, the contact cut (broken line) in this case indicating where the thin gate oxide is to be removed to reveal the surface of the silicon wafer before polysilicon is deposited. Thus, the polysilicon is deposited directly on the underlying crystalline wafer. When diffusion takes place, impurities will diffuse into the polysilicon as well as into the diffusion region within the contact area. Thus a satisfactory connection between polysilicon and diffusion is ensured. Buried contacts can be smaller in area than their butting contact counterparts and, since they use no metal layer, they are subject to fewer design rule restrictions in a layout.

The design rules in this case ensure that a reasonable contact area is achieved and that there will be no transistor formed unintentionally in series with the contact. The rules are such that they also avoid the formation of unwanted diffusion to polysilicon contacts and protect the gate oxide of any transistors in the vicinity of the buried contact cut area.

3.3.3   Double metal MOS process rules

A powerful extension to the process described in this text is provided by a second metal (or a second polysilicon) layer. The provision of a second metal layer gives a greater degree of freedom in distributing global V_{DD} and V_{SS} *(GND)* in a system.

Although not utilized in the examples used in the following chapters, the second metal layer in particular is becoming important and, although the use of such a layer is readily envisaged, its disposition relative to and connection with other layers can be readily established with reference to Figures 3–8 and 3–10(c).

As a rule, second-level metal layers are coarser than the first (conventional) layer and the isolation layer between the layers is also of relatively greater thick-

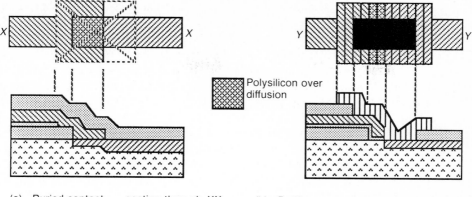

Polysilicon over diffusion

(a) Buried contact . . . section through *XX*

(b) Butting contact . . . section through *YY*

Contact from metal 2 to n-diffusion (not using minimum spacing via to cut)

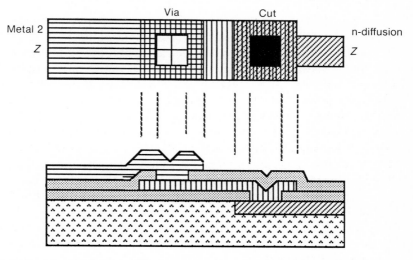

Metal 2   Via   Cut   n-diffusion

(c) Metal 2–via–metal 1–cut–n-diffusion connection . . . section through *ZZ*

Figure 3–10 Cross sections through some contact structures

ness. To distinguish contacts between first and second metal layers, they are known as *vias*. The second metal layer representation is color coded dark blue.

For the sake of completeness, the process steps for a two-metal layer process are briefly outlined as follows.

The oxide below the first metal layer is deposited by atmospheric chemical vapor deposition (CVD) and the oxide layer between the metal layers is applied in a similar manner. Depending on the process, removal of selected areas of the oxide is accomplished by plasma etching which is designed to have a high level of vertical ion bombardment to allow for high and uniform etch rates.

Similarly, the bulk of the process steps for a double polysilicon layer process are similar in nature to the process steps for the conventional MOS process. The main difference is that an additional oxide layer is grown on top of the first polysilicon layer to isolate it from the second polysilicon layer.

To revert to the double metal process it is convenient at this point to consider the layout strategy commonly used with this process. The approach taken may be summarized as follows:

1. Use the second level metal for the global distribution of power buses, that is, V_{DD} and GND (V_{SS}), and for clock lines.
2. Use the first level metal for local distribution of power and for signal lines.
3. The two metal layers are laid out so that the conductors are mutually orthogonal wherever possible.

3.3.4 CMOS lambda-based design rules

The CMOS fabrication process is much more complex than nMOS fabrication, which in turn has been simplified for ready presentation in this text. The new reader may well think that the design rules discussed here are quite complex enough, but in fact they constitute an abstract of the actual processing steps which are used to produce the chip. In a CMOS process, for example, the actual set of industrial design rules may well comprise more than one hundred separate rules, the documentation for which spans many pages of text and many diagrams. Two such rule sets are, in fact, given in the appendixes to this text.

However, extending the Mead and Conway concepts, which we have already set out for nMOS designs, and noting the exclusion of butting and buried contacts, it is possible to add rules peculiar to CMOS (Figure 3–11) to those already set out in Figures 3–6 to 3–10. The additional rules are concerned with those features unique to CMOS, such as the p-well and p^+ mask and the special 'substrate' contacts. We have already provided for the p-transistors and p-wires in Figures 3–6 to 3–10.

Although the CMOS rules in total may seem difficult to comprehend for the new designer, once use has been made of the simpler nMOS rules, the transition to CMOS is not hard to achieve. The real key to success in VLSI design is to put it into practice, and this text attempts to encourage the reader to do just that.

3.4 General observations on the design rules

Due to the microscopic nature of dimensions and features of silicon circuits, a major problem is presented by possible deviation in line widths and in interlayer registration.

If the line widths are too small, it is possible for lines thus defined to be discontinuous in places.

If paths in a layer are placed too close together, it is possible that they will merge in places.

V_{SS} and V_{DD} contacts

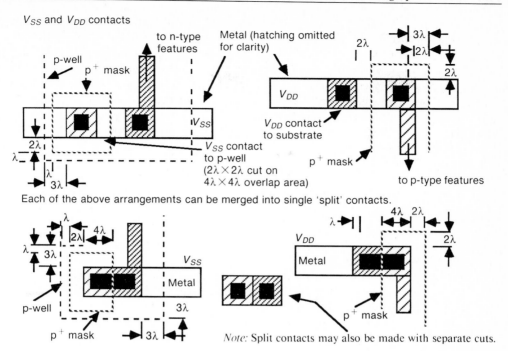

Each of the above arrangements can be merged into single 'split' contacts.

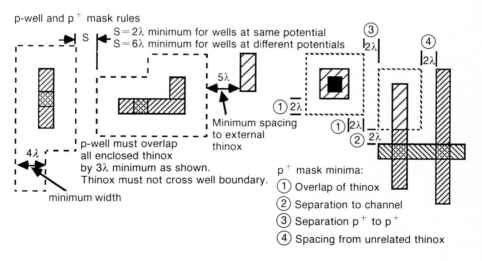

Note: Split contacts may also be made with separate cuts.

One V_{DD} contact for every four p-transistors and one V_{SS} contact for every four n-transistors are to be made.

p-well and p^+ mask rules

Figure 3-11 Particular rules for p-well CMOS process

The design rules given here are formulated in terms of λ which can subsequently be related to the resolution of the process. λ may be viewed as a bound on the width deviation of a feature from its ideal 'as drawn' size and as a bound on the maximum misalignment of any one mask level.

In the worst case, then, these effects may combine to cause feature edges on different mask levels to deviate by as much as 2λ in their interrelationship.

Layout rules, therefore, provide strict guidelines for preparing the photo mask layouts which provide the masks used in the fabrication process, and can be regarded as the communication link between the circuit designers and the process engineers engaged in manufacture.

The goal of any set of design rules should be to optimize yield while keeping the geometry as small as possible without compromising the reliability of the finished circuit.

On the questions of yield and reliability, even the conservative nature of the lambda-based rules can stand reevaluation when these two factors are of paramount importance. In particular, the rules associated with contacts can be improved upon in the light of experience. Figure 3–12 sets out aspects which need to be observed in high yield and reliability situations.

In our proposed scheme of events in creating stick layouts for CMOS, we have assumed that polysilicon and metal can both freely cross well boundaries and this is indeed the case, but we must be careful to try to exclude polysilicon from areas which lie within the p^+ mask. The reason for this is that the resistance of the polysilicon layer is reduced in current processes by doping it n-type. Clearly the p^+ doping which takes place inside the p^+ mask will also dope the polysilicon, which is already in place when the p^+ doping step takes place. This results in an increase in the polysilicon resistance which may be significant in certain parts of a system.

The 3λ metal width rule is a conservative one, but is implemented to allow for the fact that the metal layer is deposited after the others and on top of them and several layers of silicon dioxide, so the surface on which it sits is quite mountainous. This results in poor edge definition. In double metal the second layer of metal has an even more uneven terrain on which to be deposited and patterned. Hence the 4λ rule.

Separation for the metal layers is also large (3λ or 4λ respectively) and is brought about mainly by difficulties experienced in accurately defining metal edges during masking operations on the highly reflective metal.

All diffusion processes are such that lateral diffusion occurs as well as impurity penetration in from the surface. Hence the separation rules for diffusion allow for this and relatively large separations are specified. This is particularly the case for the p-well diffusions which are deep diffusions and thus have considerable lateral spread.

Transitions from thin gate oxide to thick field oxide in the oxidation process use up space and for this reason the minimum separation between thinox regions is 3λ. This implies that the minimum feature size for thick oxide is 3λ.

The simplicity of the lambda-based rules makes this approach to design a most appropriate one for the novice in chip design and also for those applications in which we are not trying to achieve the absolute minimum area and the absolute maximum performance. Because lambda-based rules try to be all things to all people, they do suffer from least common denominator effects and from the upward rounding of all process line dimension parameters into integer values of

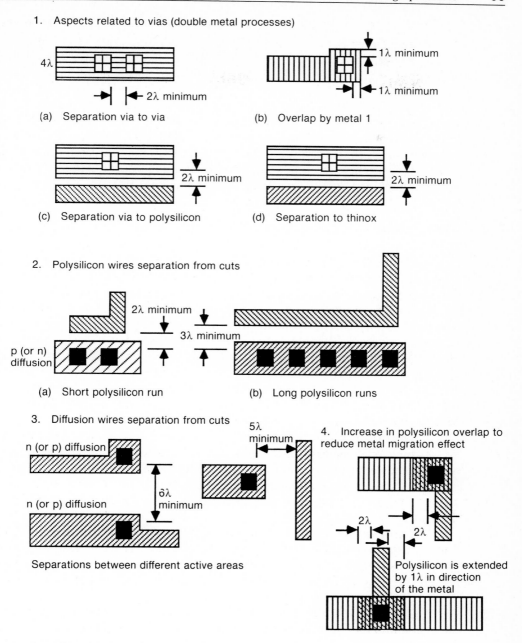

Figure 3-12 Further aspects of λ based design rules for contacts including some factors contributing to higher yield/reliability

lambda. The performance of any fabrication line in this respect clearly comes down to a matter of tolerances and definitions in terms of microns (or some other suitable unit of length). Thus expanded sets of rules, often referred to as micron-based rules, are available to the experienced designer to allow for the use of the full capability of any process.

In order to properly represent this important aspect, the next sections introduce CMOS processes as employed by Amalgamated Wireless (Australasia) Limited (AWA) and Orbit Semiconductors Inc. of California. We are indebted to both organizations for their permission to reproduce their micron-based rules. In order to avoid confusion with the lambda-based rules used throughout this text the sets of rules are included as Appendixes A (AWA) and B (Orbit).

3.5 The AWA OXCMOS process description

The starting material is 5 cm n-doped silicon. The wafer may be either n-doped bulk silicon or a 10 μm n-doped epitaxial layer on a 5 cm n^{++} substrate.

After an initial oxidation, the first photo step uses the p-well mask to open windows into the initial oxide wherever a p-well is required. Boron is implanted and diffused through the oxide openings to form p-wells. The resulting structure is shown in Figure 3–13(a).

The initial oxide is stripped and a layer of silicon nitride is deposited on a thin layer of oxide grown on the wafer. The purpose of this thin oxide layer is to provide a cushion between the silicon and the silicon nitride. The second mask (active area-nitride) is now used to define the nitride. The nitride is etched away wherever the isolating oxide will be needed.

The nitride remains wherever there is to be an active area. The third mask (p^-) step leaves openings in the photoresist that surround the p-well areas. The wafer is then exposed to a boron implant. This means that boron is implanted in those areas where there is no nitride and which extend somewhat beyond the p-well area. This will ultimately raise the threshold of parasitic n-channel field transistors.

The fourth mask (n^-) is opposite in polarity to the p^- mask and is used in the next step to mask against a phosphorus implant. This second implant ultimately raises the threshold of parasitic p-channel field transistors. The resultant wafer, after the active area definition and the two field implants, is shown in Figure 3–13(b).

The wafer is next put into an oxidizing furnace, where a thick layer (0.9 μm) of silicon dioxide is grown, using up some of the silicon, between the active areas covered by the silicon nitride. The resulting wafer structure is shown in Figure 3–13(c).

The nitride layer is now removed in an etching operation and gate oxide is grown in its place. Gate oxide thickness is 1000 Å. Using the fifth mask (V_{pt} adjust), the p-threshold adjust photoresist is defined. A boron implant is used to adjust the p-channel threshold value. This process step is optional, and is required only if a p-channel threshold of less than 1.4 V is required.

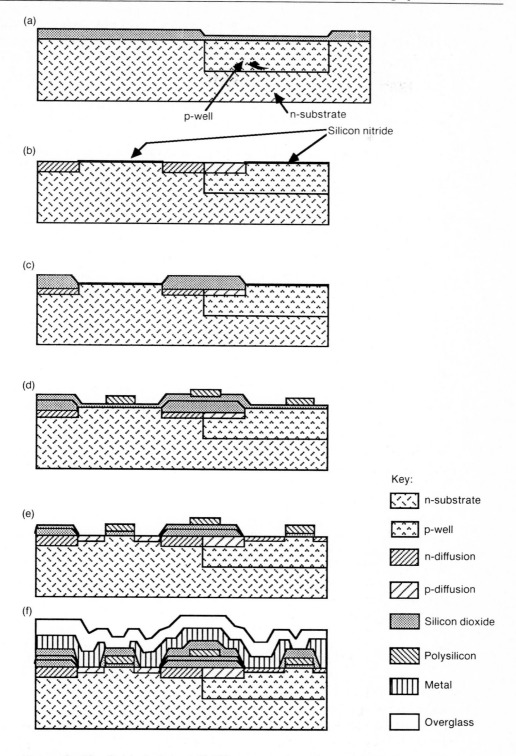

Figure 3–13 Oxide isolated CMOS process (courtesy of AWA Ltd)

The 5000 Å layer of polysilicon is then deposited and phosphorus (n-doping) doped over the entire wafer. This is etched using the sixth (polysilicon) mask in another photoresist — an etch–strip operation, using plasma etching. The resulting wafer, after polysilicon etch, is shown in Figure 3–13(d).

The seventh mask (p^+) is used in the next photo operation. Silicon dioxide is etched away from the inside of windows of photoresist exposing bare silicon. Boron is diffused into wafers forming p^+ doped active areas.

A similar process is performed using an eighth mask (n^+) to diffuse phosphorus into the wafer, creating n^+ doped active areas (Figure 3–13(e)).

The above diffusion steps form the transistor source and drain regions, and diffused interconnections. After the diffusion steps are complete, 2000 Å of low temperature oxide is deposited on the wafer and the ninth mask (contacts) is used in a photolithographic operation to etch the contacts down to the polysilicon or active areas. After this, 600 Å of silicon nitride followed by 8000 Å of BPSG is deposited on the wafer. In the tenth masking operation, the same contact mask is used to etch contact down to silicon nitride. BPSG glass is then reflowed to make the surface as smooth as possible. This step is important to ensure proper step coverage by subsequent aluminum metallization. After the reflow, silicon nitride is etched away and a 1 μm layer of aluminum is evaporated onto the wafer surface. The eleventh mask (metal) is used to define the aluminum interconnection pattern. After alloying the metal to the silicon in a short low temperature furnace operation, a layer of low temperature CVD silicon dioxide is deposited on the surface for passivation, and the twelfth mask level (silox) is used to remove silox over the bonding pad and test pad areas. A cross-section of completed wafer is shown in Figure 3–13(f).

3.6 A double metal, single polysilicon, micron-based CMOS process

More advanced CMOS processes use double metal technology and may also offer other facilities such as buried contacts. One such state-of-the-art process in 2 μm CMOS technology is offered by Orbit Semiconductor Inc. of Sunnyvale, California, and included in Appendix B with their design rules for this process are electrical parameters and other details.

A significant factor is that the rules cover both p-well and n-well CMOS processes and have been designed to facilitate incorporation in symbolic design tools for use with compaction. (See Chapter 12.)

3.7 Layout diagrams

Layout diagrams may be drawn on, say, 5 mm squared paper where the side of each square is taken to represent λ (for λ-based rules).

The layout diagrams which follow in Figures 3–14 to 3–16 inclusive illustrate the use of the design rules. The reader is also asked to study the butting contact

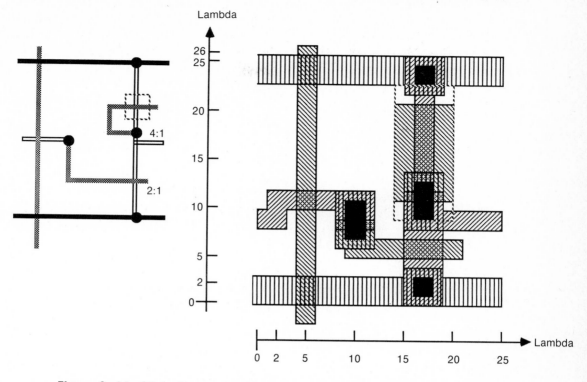

Figure 3-14 Stick diagram and layout for nMOS shift register cell

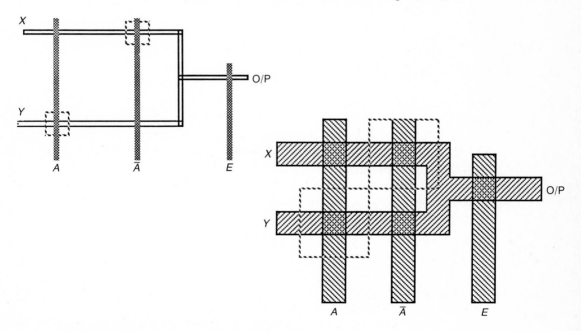

Figure 3-15 Two-way selector with enable

areas where departures from strict adherence to rules can take place. Those shown here are acceptable in practice.

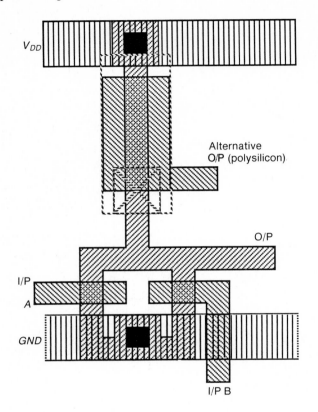

Figure 3–16   Two I/P nMOS *Nor* gate

3.8   Exercise

The reader is asked to draw the stick diagram(s) for any or all of Figures 3–14 to 3–16 inclusive and attempt to draw a layout for each circuit. These layouts may then be compared with those given in the book, although it must be recognized that lack of conformity in detail may not mean that a layout is incorrect.

3.9   Tutorial 1

Note: Use colors to represent layers.

1.   Draw the stick diagram and a mask layout for an 8:1 nMOS inverter circuit. Both the input and output points should be on the polysilicon layer.
2.   With regard to Figure 3–15, what will be the state of the output (O/P) when control line *E* is at 0 volts? Could you suggest any simple modification to this

circuit to improve its operation? If so, set out a modified stick diagram and corresponding mask layout.

3. With regard to Figure 3–14, determine suitable left-hand and right-hand boundary lines for this leaf cell, so that a series of such leaf cells can be butted directly together side by side without violating any design rules while occupying minimum area.

4. Can you reduce the area occupied by the leaf cell of Figure 3–14? Draw an alternative layout to illustrate your contention.

5. Figure 3–17 presents a simple CMOS layout. Study the layout, and from it produce a circuit diagram. Explain the nature and purpose of the circuit. Using this layout, explain how you could construct a four-way multiplexer (selector) circuit.

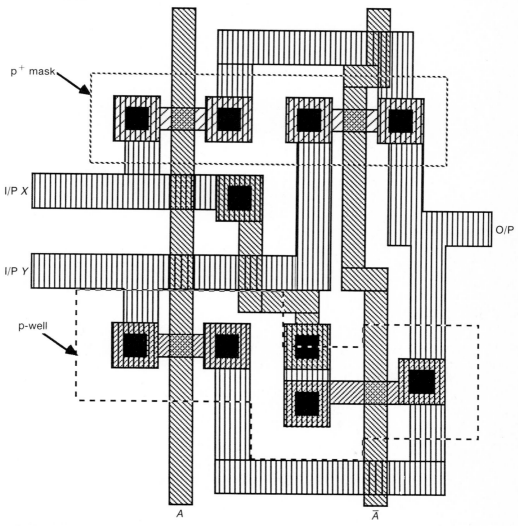

Figure 3–17 CMOS layout example

4 Basic circuit concepts

So far we have established equations (Chapter 2) which characterize the behavior of MOS transistors and the pull-up to pull-down ratios which must be observed when nMOS inverters and pass transistors are interconnected. However, as yet we have not considered the actual resistance and capacitance values associated with transistors, nor have we considered circuit wiring and parasitics. In order to simplify the treatment of such components, there are basic circuit concepts which will now be introduced, and for particular MOS processes we can set out approximate circuit parameters which greatly ease the design process in allowing straightforward calculations.

4.1 Sheet resistance R_s

Consider a uniform slab of conducting material of resistivity ρ, of width W, thickness t, and length between faces L. The arrangement is shown in Figure 4–1.

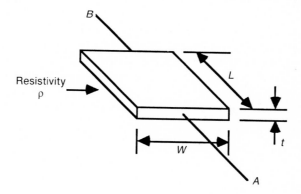

Figure 4–1 Sheet resistance model

With reference to Figure 4–1, consider the resistance R_{AB} between two opposite faces.

$$R_{AB} = \frac{\rho L}{A} \text{ ohm}$$

where

$$A = \text{cross section area}$$

Thus

$$R_{AB} = \frac{\rho L}{tW}$$

Now, consider the case in which $L = W$, that is, a square of resistive material, then

$$R_{AB} = \frac{\rho}{t} = R_s$$

where

$$R_s = \text{ohm per square or sheet resistance}$$

Thus

$$R_s = \frac{\rho}{t} \text{ ohm per square}$$

Note that R_s is completely independent of the area of the square; for example, a square slab of material of side 1 μm has exactly the same resistance as a square slab of the same material and thickness of side 1 cm.

The actual values associated with the layers in a MOS circuit depend on the thickness of the layer and the resistivity of the material forming the layer. For the metal and polysilicon layers, the thickness of a layer is easily envisaged and the resistivity of the material is known. For the diffusion layer, the depth of the diffusion regions contributes toward the effective thickness while the impurity concentration (or doping level) profile determines the resistivity.

For the MOS process considered here and for doping levels typical in 5 micron* technology, typical values of sheet resistance are given in Table 4–1.

Table 4–1   Typical sheet resistances R_s of MOS layers for 5 μm technology

Layer	R_s ohm per square
Metal	0.03
Diffusion	10→50
Silicide**	2→4
Polysilicon	15→100
n-transistor channel	10^4[†]
p-transistor channel	2.5×10^4[†]

** In some processes a silicide layer is used in place of polysilicon.
[†] These values are approximations only. Resistances may be calculated from a knowledge of V_{ds} and the expressions for I_{ds} given earlier.

4.2   Sheet resistance concept applied to MOS transistors and inverters

Consider the transistor structures of Figure 4–2 and note that the diagrams distinguish the actual diffusion regions from the channel regions. The thinox mask layout is the union of diffusion and channel regions and these regions have differing hatching patterns to stress the fact that the polysilicon and underlying silicon

---

* 5 micron (μm) technology implies minimum line width of 5 μm and in consequence that $\lambda = 2.5$ μm.

dioxide mask the substrate so that diffusion takes place only in the areas defined by the thinox mask which do not coincide with the polysilicon mask.

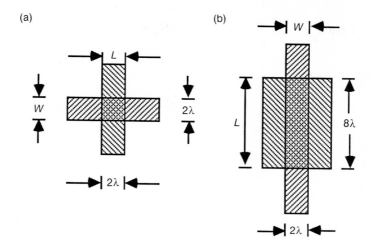

Figure 4-2 Resistance calculation for transistor channels

The simple n-type pass transistor of Figure 4–2(a) has a channel length $L = 2\lambda$ and a channel width $W = 2\lambda$. The channel is, therefore, square and channel resistance (with or without implant)

$$R = 1 \text{ square} \times R_s \frac{\text{ohm}}{\text{square}} = R_s = 10^4 \text{ ohm*}$$

The length to width ratio, denoted Z, is 1:1 in this case. The transistor structure of Figure 4–2(b) has a channel length $L = 8\lambda$ and width $W = 2\lambda$. Therefore,

$$Z = \frac{L}{W} = \frac{4}{1}$$

Thus, channel resistance

$$R = ZR_s = 4 \times 10^4 \text{ ohm}$$

Another way of looking at this is to recognize that this channel can be regarded as four $2\lambda \times 2\lambda$ squares in series, thus giving a resistance of $4R_s$. This particular way of approaching the calculation of resistance is often useful, particularly when dealing with shapes which are not simple rectangles.

Figure 4–3 takes these considerations one step further and shows how the pull-up to pull-down ratio of an inverter is determined. In the nMOS case a simple 4:1 $Z_{p.u.}:Z_{p.d.}$ ratio obviously applies. Note, for example, that a 4:1 ratio would also

---

* From Table 4–1.

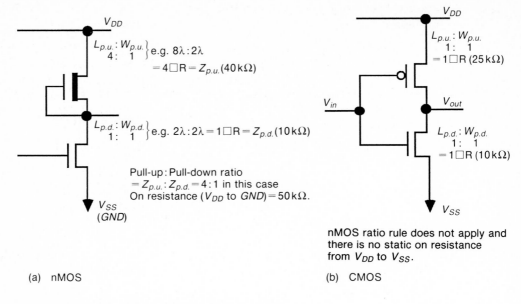

(a) nMOS

(b) CMOS

Figure 4–3 Inverter resistance calculation

be achieved if the upper channel (p.u.) length $L = 4\lambda$, and width $W = 2\lambda$ with lower channel (p.d.) length $L = 2\lambda$, and width $W = 4\lambda$.

For the CMOS case, note the different value of R_s which applies for the pull-up transistor.

4.2.1 Silicides

As the line width becomes smaller, the sheet resistance contribution to RC delay increases. With the currently available polysilicon sheet resistance ranging from 15–100 ohm it is becoming apparent that the advantages of scaling will be offset to a considerable extent by the interconnect resistance at the gate level. Therefore the low sheet resistances of refractory silicides (2–4 ohm), which are formed by depositing metal on polysilicon and then sintering, makes this type of material very attractive as an interconnecting medium.

Deposition of the metal or metal/silicon alloy prior to sintering may be done in any one of several ways:

- sputtering or evaporation;
- cosputtering metal and silicon in the desired ratio from two independent targets;
- coevaporation from the elements.

Clearly the properties of silicides make them attractive alternatives to polysilicon, but extra processing steps are implied.

4.3   Area capacitances of layers

From the diagrams we have used to illustrate the structure of transistors and from discussions of the fabrication processes, it will be apparent that conducting layers are separated from the substrate and each other by insulating (dielectric) layers, and thus parallel plate capacitive effects must be present and must be allowed for.

For any layer, knowing the dielectric (silicon dioxide) thickness, we can calculate area capacitance as follows:

$$C = \frac{\varepsilon_0 \varepsilon_{ins} A}{D} \text{ farads}$$

where

$$D = \text{thickness of silicon dioxide}$$
$$A = \text{area of plates}$$

(and it is assumed that ε_0, A, and D are in compatible units, for example, ε_0 in farads/cm, A in cm^2, D in cm).

$$\varepsilon_{ins} = \text{relative permittivity of SiO}_2 \doteqdot 4.0$$
$$\varepsilon_0 = 8.85 \times 10^{-14} \text{ F/cm (permittivity of free space)}$$

A normal approach is to give layer area capacitances in pF/μm^2 (where μm = micron = 10^{-6} meter = 10^{-4} cm). The appropriate figure may be calculated as follows:

$$C\left(\frac{\text{pF}}{\mu\text{m}^2}\right) = \frac{\varepsilon_0 \varepsilon_{ins}}{D} \frac{\text{F}}{\text{cm}^2} \times \frac{10^{12}\text{pF}}{\text{F}} \times \frac{\text{cm}^2}{10^8 \ \mu\text{m}^2}$$
$$(D \text{ in cm, } \varepsilon_0 \text{ in farads/cm})$$

For 5 μm MOS technology, typical values of area capacitance are set out in Table 4–2.

Table 4–2   Typical area capacitance values for 5 μm MOS circuits

Capacitance		*Value in pF/μm^2*	*Relative value*
Gate to channel		4×10^{-4}	1
Diffusion		1×10^{-4}	0.25
Polysilicon*		0.4×10^{-4}	0.1
Metal 1	to substrate	0.3×10^{-4}	0.075
Metal 2		0.2×10^{-4}	0.05
Metal 2 to metal 1		0.4×10^{-4}	0.1
Metal 2 to polysilicon		0.3×10^{-4}	0.075

Notes: Relative value = Specified value/gate to channel value.
 Double metal process parameters are included here for convenience.
 * Silicide layer similar.

4.4   Standard unit of capacitance $\square C_g$

It is convenient to employ a standard unit of capacitance which can be given a value appropriate to the technology but which can be used in calculations without associating it with an absolute value. The unit is denoted $\square C_g$ and is defined as the *gate-to-channel capacitance* of the minimum size ($2\lambda \times 2\lambda$) MOS transistor, as in Figure 4–2(a). (This concept was originated by VTI (USA) and has been adopted for this text.)

$\square C_g$ may be evaluated for any MOS process. For example, for 5 μm MOS circuits ($\lambda = 2.5$ μm):

Gate area $= 5$ μm $\times 5$ μm $= 25$ μm^2
Capacitance value (from Table 4–2) $= 4 \times 10^{-4}$ pF/μm^2
Standard value $\square C_g = 25$ μm$^2 \times 4 \times 10^{-4}$ pF/μm$^2 = .01$ pF

4.5   Some area capacitance calculations

The calculation of capacitance values may now be undertaken by establishing the ratio between the area of interest and the area of standard gate ($2\lambda \times 2\lambda$) and multiplying this ratio by the appropriate relative C value from Table 4–2. The product will give the required capacitance in $\square C_g$ units.

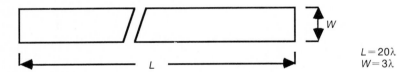

$L = 20\lambda$
$W = 3\lambda$

Figure 4–4   Simple area for capacitance calculation

Consider the area defined in Figure 4–4. First, we must calculate the area relative to that of a standard gate.

$$\text{Relative area} = \frac{20\lambda \times 3\lambda}{2\lambda \times 2\lambda} = 15$$

Now:

1. consider the area in metal

    Capacitance to substrate $=$ relative area $\times$ relative C value
    $= 15 \times 0.075 \square C_g$
    $= 1\tfrac{1}{8} \square C_g$

    That is, the defined area in metal has a capacitance to substrate $1\tfrac{1}{8}$ times that of a standard gate.

2. consider the same area in polysilicon

Capacitance to substrate $= 15 \times 0.1$
$$= 1.5 \square C_g$$

3. consider the same area in diffusion

Capacitance to substrate $= 15 \times 0.25$
$$= 3.75 \square C_g{}^*$$

Calculations of area capacitance values associated with structures occupying more than one layer are equally straightforward, as may be seen from Figure 4–5.

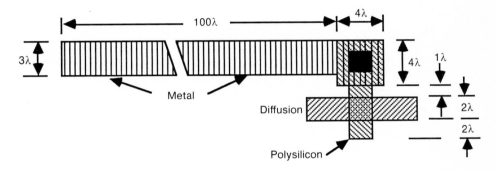

Figure 4–5 Capacitance calculation (multilayer)

Consider the metal area (less the contact region where the metal is connected to polysilicon and shielded from the substrate)

$$\text{Ratio} \ \frac{\text{Metal area}}{\text{Standard gate area}} = \frac{100\lambda \times 3\lambda}{4\lambda^2} = 75$$

Metal capacitance $C_m = 75 \times 0.075 = 5.625 \square C_g$

Consider the polysilicon area (excluding the gate region)

$$\text{Polysilicon area} = 4\lambda \times 4\lambda + 3\lambda \times 2\lambda = 22\lambda^2$$

Therefore

$$\text{Polysilicon capacitance} \ C_p = \frac{22}{4} \times 0.1 = .55 \square C_g$$

$$\text{Gate capacitance} \ C_g = 1 \square C_g$$

---

* Note the relatively high capacitance values of the diffusion layer even though peripheral capacitance (see Table 4–3) has not been allowed for. This may increase total diffusion capacitance to considerably more than the area capacitance calculated here.

Therefore

$$\text{Total capacitance } C_T = C_m + C_p + C_g \doteq 7.2 \square C_g$$

It is not unusual to find metal paths of uniform 4λ width but when taking this approach in design it must be borne in mind that, compared with 3λ width paths, the capacitance will be increased by one-third.

For example, if the metal width is increased to 4λ in Figure 4–5, the capacitance C_m is increased to $7.5 \square C_g$ and the capacitance of the complete structure will increase to $\doteq 9 \square C_g$.

4.6   The delay unit τ

We have developed the concept of sheet resistance R_s and standard gate capacitance unit $\square C_g$. If we consider the case of one standard gate capacitance being charged through one square of channel resistance (from a 2λ by 2λ nMOS pass transistor), as in Figure 4–6, we have:

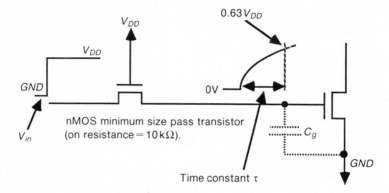

Figure 4–6 Model for derivation of τ

$$\text{Time constant } \tau = 1 R_s \text{ (channel)} \times 1 \square C_g \text{ seconds}$$

This can be evaluated for 5 μm technology so that

$$\text{Theoretical } \tau = 10^4 \text{ ohm} \times 0.01 \text{ pF} = 0.1 \text{ nsec}$$

However, in practice, circuit wiring and parasitic capacitances must be allowed for so that the figure taken for τ is normally increased by a factor of 2 or 3 so that for 5 μm circuit ($\lambda = 2.5$ μm)

$$\tau = 0.2 \rightarrow 0.3 \text{ nsec is a typical figure}$$

Note that τ thus obtained is not much different from transit time τ_{sd} calculated from equation 2.2

$$\tau_{sd} = \frac{L^2}{\mu_n V_{ds}}$$

Note that V_{ds} varies as C_g charges from 0 volts to 63 percent of V_{DD} in period τ in Figure 4–6, so that an appropriate value for V_{ds} in equation 2.2 is the average value = 3 volts. For 5 µm technology, then,

$$\tau_{sd} = \frac{25\ \mu m^2\ V\ sec}{650\ cm^2\ 3\ V} \times \frac{10^9\ nsec\ cm^2}{10^8\ sec\ \mu m^2}$$

$$= 0.13\ nsec$$

This is very close to the theoretical time constant τ calculated above.

Since the transition point of an inverter or gate is 0.5 V_{DD}, which is close to 0.63 V_{DD}, it appears to be common practice to use transit time and time constant (as defined for the delay unit τ) interchangeably and 'stray' capacitances are usually allowed for by doubling or more the theoretical values calculated.

In view of this, τ is used as the fundamental time unit and all timings in a system can be evaluated in relation to τ, which is associated once again with the basic minimum size $2\lambda \times 2\lambda$ transistor structure.

For 5 µm MOS technology $\tau = 0.3$ nsec is a reasonable figure to use.

4.7 Inverter delays

Consider the basic 4:1 ratio nMOS inverter. In order to achieve the 4:1 $Z_{p.u.}$ to $Z_{p.d.}$ ratio, $R_{p.u.}$ will be 4 $R_{p.d.}$, and if $R_{p.d.}$ is contributed by the minimum size transistor then, clearly, the resistance value associated with $R_{p.u.}$ is such

$$R_{p.u.} = 4\ R_s = 40\ k\Omega$$

Meanwhile, the $R_{p.d.}$ value is 1 $R_s = 10$ kΩ so that the delay associated with the inverter will depend on whether it is being turned on or off.

However, if we consider a pair of *cascaded inverters*, then the delay over the pair will be constant irrespective of the sense of the logic level transition of the input to the first. This is clearly seen from Figure 4–7 and, assuming $\tau = 0.3$ nsec and making no extra allowances for wiring capacitance, we have an overall delay of

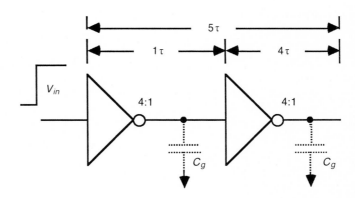

Figure 4–7 nMOS inverter pair delay

$\tau + 4\tau = 5\tau$. In general terms the delay through a pair of similar nMOS inverters is

$$T_d = (1 + Z_{p.u.}/Z_{p.d.})\tau$$

Thus, the inverter pair delay for inverters having 4:1 ratio is 5τ (which should be multiplied by a suitable factor to allow for wiring).

However, a single 4:1 inverter exhibits undesirable asymmetric delays since the delay in turning on is, for example, τ while the corresponding delay in turning off is 4τ. Quite obviously, the asymmetry is worse when considering an inverter with a ratio of 8:1.

When considering CMOS inverters, the nMOS ratio rule no longer applies, but we must allow for the natural asymmetry of the pull-up p-transistors compared with the n-type pull-down transistors. Figure 4–8 shows the theoretical delay associated with a pair of minimum size (both n- and p-transistors) inverters. Note that the gate capacitance ($2\square C_g$) is double that of the comparable nMOS inverter since the input to a CMOS inverter is connected to *both* transistor gates. Note also the allowance made for the differing channel resistances.

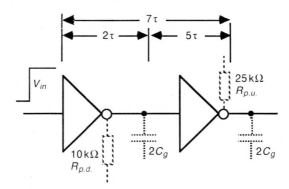

Figure 4–8 Minimum size CMOS inverter pair delay

The asymmetry of resistance values can be eliminated by increasing the width of the p-device channel by a factor of 2 or 3, but it should be noted that the gate input capacitance of the p-transistor is also increased by the same factor. This, to some extent, offsets the speed-up due to the drop in resistance but there is a small net gain since the wiring capacitance will be the same.

4.7.1 A more formal estimation of CMOS inverter delay

A CMOS inverter in general either charges or discharges a capacitive load C_L and rise time τ_r or fall time τ_f can be estimated from the following simple analysis.

4.7.1.1 Rise time estimation

In this analysis we assume that the p-device stays in saturation for the entire charging period of the load capacitor C_L. The circuit may then be modeled as in Figure 4–9.

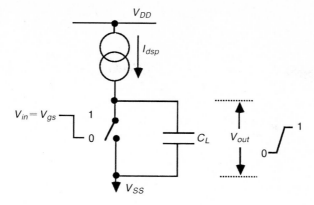

Figure 4-9 Rise time model

The saturation current for the p-transistor is given by

$$I_{dsp} = \frac{\beta_p \, (V_{gs} - |V_{tp}|)^2}{2}$$

This current charges C_L and, since its magnitude is approximately constant, we have

$$V_{out} = \frac{I_{dsp} \, t}{C_L}$$

Substituting for I_{dsp} and rearranging we have

$$t = \frac{2 \, C_L \, V_{out}}{\beta_p \, (V_{gs} - |V_{tp}|)^2}$$

We now assume that $t = \tau_r$ when $V_{out} = + V_{DD}$, so that

$$\tau_r = \frac{2 \, V_{DD} \, C_L}{\beta_p \, (V_{DD} - |V_{tp}|)^2}$$

with $|V_{tp}| = 0.2 V_{DD}$, then

$$\tau_r \doteqdot \frac{3 \, C_L}{\beta_p \, V_{DD}}$$

This result compares reasonably well with a more detailed analysis in which the charging of C_L is divided, more correctly, into two parts: (1) saturation and (2) resistive region of the transistor.

4.7.1.2 Fall-time estimation

Similar reasoning can be applied to the discharge of C_L through the p-transistor. The circuit model in this case is given as Figure 4–10.

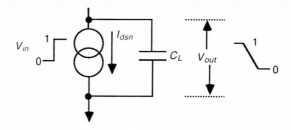

Figure 4–10 Fall time model

Making similar assumptions we may write, fall-time:

$$\tau_f \doteqdot \frac{3\,C_L}{\beta_n\,V_{DD}}$$

4.7.1.3 Summary of CMOS rise and fall factors
Using these expressions we may deduce that . . .

$$\frac{\tau_r}{\tau_f} = \frac{\beta_n}{\beta_p}$$

But, $\mu_n \doteqdot 2.5\,\mu_p$, and hence $\beta_n \doteqdot 2.5\,\beta_p$ so that the rise time is slower by a factor of 2.5 for minimum size devices for both 'n' and 'p'.

In order to achieve symmetrical operation we would need to make $W_p = 2.5\,W_n$ and for minimum geometries this would result in the inverter having an input capacitance of $1\square C_g$(n-device)$+ 2.5\square C_g$(p-device)$= 3.5\square C_g$ in total.

This simple model is quite adequate for most practical situations but it should be recognized that it gives optimistic results. However it does provide an insight into the factors which affect rise and fall times as follows:

1. τ_r and τ_f are proportional to $1/V_{DD}$;
2. τ_r and τ_f are proportional to C_L;
3. $\tau_r \doteqdot 2.5\tau_f$ for equal n- and p-transistor geometries.

4.8   Super buffers, HMOS, and native transistors

4.8.1   Super buffers

The asymmetry of the conventional inverter is clearly undesirable and gives rise to significant delay problems when an inverter is used to drive more significant capacitive loads.

A common approach used to alleviate this effect is to make use of super buffers as in Figure 4–11 and 4–12.

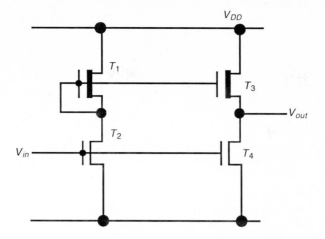

Figure 4–11   Inverting type nMOS super buffer

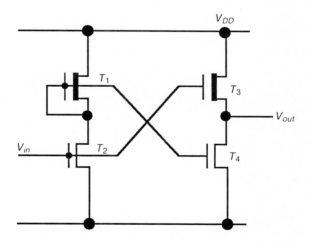

Figure 4–12   Noninverting type nMOS super buffer

The inverting type is shown as Figure 4–11; considering a positive going logic transition V_{in} at the input, it will be seen that the inverter formed by T_1 and T_2 is turned on and, thus, the gate of T_3 is pulled down toward 0 volt with a small delay. Thus, T_3 is cut off while T_4 (the gate of which is also connected to V_{in}) is turned on and the output is pulled down quickly.

Now consider the opposite transition: when V_{in} drops to 0 volt then the gate of T_3 is allowed to rise quickly to V_{DD}. Thus, as T_4 is also turned off by V_{in}, T_3 is caused to conduct with V_{DD} on its gate, that is, with twice the average voltage which would apply if the gate was tied to the source as in the conventional inverter. Now, since $I_{ds} \propto V_{gs}$ then clearly, doubling the effective V_{gs} will increase the current and, thus, reduce the delay in charging any capacitance on the output. Thus, more symmetrical transitions are achieved.

The corresponding noninverting buffer circuit is given as Figure 4–12 and, to put matters in perspective, the structures shown are capable of driving loads of 2 pF with 5 nsec risetime.

Finally, arrangements based on the native transistor and known as the native super buffer may be used.

4.8.2   Transistor types for HMOS*

In modern nMOS processes, enhancement and depletion thresholds are set by independent implant operations. Four transistor types are therefore available in this type of process, formed by the various combinations of the enhancement and depletion masks. With a minimum feature size of typically 3 μm, such processes are often called HMOS (Pashley, 1977).

One possible group of mask combinations for a positive resist process is shown in Table 4–3. Here, an entry 'yes' for a given mask means that it is required to generate the needed transistor type.

Table 4–3   Transistor types in advanced nMOS

Name	Typical V_t	Enhancement	Depletion	Use
Deep depletion	−3.0	No	Yes	Normal pull-up
Enhancement	+0.6	Yes	No	Normal pull-down
Native	0.0	No	No	Source follower, switch logic, chip enable circuits
Weak depletion	−1.5	Yes	Yes	Low power load, sustaining transistors in RAMs

The addition of an extra mask level complicates both the design and fabrication process in minor ways. However, use of these new transistors can shorten overall system design time, and improve system performance, as will be illustrated.

Color Plate 15(a) shows the contrast between a familiar nMOS static inverter in a 5 μm technology, and the HMOS equivalent. Physical size and performance are closely related in these technologies.

---

* The material in Section 4.8 (except Subsection 4.8.1) was contributed by M. L. Paltridge, formerly with the Commonwealth Scientific and Industrial Research Organisation (CSIRO) VLSI Program, Adelaide, South Australia.

4.8.3 The native transistor

The native, or natural, transistor ideally has a zero threshold voltage. When back gate bias effects and process tolerances are taken into account, this means that in source follower applications, only a small or zero gate to source voltage drop will be seen on logic highs. Conversely, on logic lows, power dissipation will be small or zero, with the transistor at or near cut off.

Therefore, the native transistor can replace conventional pull-ups in driven depletion transistor circuitry, such as super buffers, with appropriate power savings. Limiting power consumption is important in VLSI nMOS using a ratio logic design style. Native transistors are a useful way of limiting this power and easing the design problem.

4.8.4 Native super buffer

Color Plate 15(b) shows a possible circuit diagram and layout for a super buffer that is capable of driving a 2 pF load in typically 5 nsec.

Of note is the extra mask used to define the two enhancement transistors, the conventional pull-up, and the native enhancement output pair. In this configuration, the asymmetric drive capability, inherent in ratio logic, is minimized.

The best that the circuit designer can do is to equilibrate the internal delays at the logic threshold, in this case 1.8 volts.

Figure 4–13 shows the simulated performance of the super buffer. Approximately equal delays of 5 nsec have been achieved at the logic threshold of 1.8 volts.

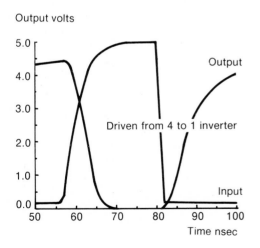

(a) Native super buffer with 2pF load

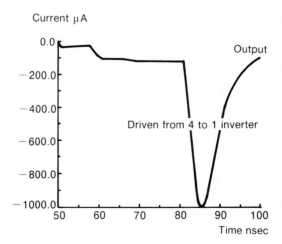

(b) Native super buffer with 2 pF load

Figure 4–13 Simulated performance

The output swing is from 0 to 4.5 volts. The power consumption for no load is that of a single inverter. Any attempt to increase the gate width of the output pair increases the delay time of the buffer. This is another illustration of the meaning of the concept of the speed power product for a technology.

This driver has been fabricated and its performance shows good agreement with this simulation.

The transient current performance is of considerable importance for the system designer. With the input low, only leakage current is drawn by the output pair. Driving the input high causes the driver pull-up to draw a current of about 100 µA. The output transition causes a large 1 mA transient current to flow as the 2 pF load capacitor is charged. At high clock speeds, such capacitive currents become the dominant term in the power consumption for any MOS technology.

A further extension of the drive capabilities of the arrangement can be effected by combining an inverting with a noninverting buffer.

4.8.5   Chip enable circuits

The native transistor can be used as a switch to power down sections of a system. Switches of low voltage drop can be made that turn off or on sections of the VLSI system as desired. This is found as a power conservation measure in many modern RAMs, for example (Chatterjee, 1982; Lee, 1979).

References

Palab K. Chatterjee et al., 'Enhanced Performances 4K × 1 High Speed SRAM Using Optically Defined Submicrometer Devices in Selected Circuits', *IEEE Journal of Solid-State Circuits*, Vol. SC–17, April 1982, pp. 330–44.

James M. Lee et al., 'A 80nS5V–Only Dynamic RAM', IEEE International Solid State Circuits Conference, Digest of Technical Papers, February 1979, pp. 142–3.

R. Pashley et al., 'H-MOS Scales Traditional Devices to Higher Performance Level', *Electronics*, August 1977, p. 94.

4.9   Driving large capacitive loads

The problem of driving comparatively large capacitive loads arises when signals must be propagated from the chip to off chip destinations. Generally, typical off chip capacitances may be several orders higher than on chip $\square C_g$ values. For example, if the off chip load is denoted C_L then

$$C_L \geqslant 10^4 \square C_g \text{ (typically)}$$

Clearly capacitances of this order must be driven through low resistances, otherwise excessively long delays will occur. Obviously, low resistance values for $Z_{p.d.}$ and $Z_{p.u.}$ imply low $L{:}W$ ratios; in other words, channels must be made very wide to reduce resistance value and, in consequence, an inverter to meet this need occupies a large area. Moreover, because of the large $L{:}W$ ratio and since L cannot be reduced below 2λ in length, the gate region area $L \times W$ becomes significant and a comparatively large capacitance is presented at the input, which, in turn, slows down the rates of change of voltage which can take place at input.

The remedy is to use cascaded inverters, each one of which is larger than the preceding stage by a width factor f as shown in Figure 4–14 (using nMOS inverters).

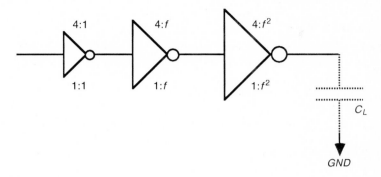

Figure 4–14 Driving large capacitive loads

Clearly, as the width factor increases, so the capacitive load presented at the inverter input increases, and the area occupied increases also. Equally clearly, the rate at which the width increases (i.e. the value of f) will influence the number N of stages which must be cascaded to drive a particular value of C_L. Thus, an optimum solution must be sought as follows (this treatment is attributed to Mead and Conway).

With large f, N decreases but delay per stage increases. For 4:1 nMOS inverters

$$\text{delay per stage} = f\tau \text{ for } \triangle V_{in}$$
$$\text{or} = 4f\tau \text{ for } \triangledown V_{in}$$

where $\triangle V_{in}$ indicates logic 0 to 1 transition and $\triangledown V_{in}$ indicates logic 1 to 0 transition of V_{in}

Therefore, total delay per nMOS pair $= 5f\tau$. A similar treatment yields delay per CMOS pair $= 7f\tau$. Now let

$$y = \frac{C_L}{\square C_g} = f^N$$

so that the choice of f and N are interdependent.

We now need to determine the value of f which will minimize the overall delay for a given value of y and from the definition of y

$$\ln(y) = N\ln(f)$$

That is

$$N = \frac{\ln(y)}{\ln(f)}$$

Thus, for N even

$$\text{total delay} = \frac{N}{2} 5f\tau = 2.5 \, Nf\tau \text{ (nMOS)}$$

$$\text{or} = \frac{N}{2} 7f\tau = 3.5 \, Nf\tau \text{ (CMOS)}$$

Thus, in all cases

$$\text{delay} \propto Nf\tau = \frac{\ln(y)}{\ln(f)} f\tau$$

It can be shown that total delay is minimized if f assumes the value e (base of natural logarithms); that is, each stage should be approximately* 2.7 times wider than its predecessor. This applies to CMOS as well as nMOS inverters.

Thus, assuming that $f = e$, we have

$$\text{Number of stages } N = \ln(y) \frac{C_L}{\Box C_g}$$

and overall delay t_d

N even: $t_d = 2.5eN\tau$ (nMOS)
or $t_d = 3.5eN\tau$ (CMOS)

N odd: $t_d = [2.5(N-1)+1]e\tau$ (nMOS) $\Big\}$ for $\triangle V_{in}$
or $t_d = [3.5(N-1)+2]e\tau$ (CMOS)

or

$t_d = [2.5(N-1)+4]e\tau$ (nMOS) $\Big\}$ for $\triangledown V_{in}$
or $t_d = [3.5(N-1)+5]e\tau$ (CMOS)

4.10 Propagation delays

4.10.1 Cascaded pass transistors

A degree of freedom offered by MOS technology is the use of pass transistors as series or parallel switches in logic arrays. Quite frequently, therefore, logic signals must pass through a number of pass transistors in series. A chain of four such transistors is shown in Figure 4–15(a) in which all gates have been shown connected to V_{DD} which would be the case for a signal to be propagated through to the output. The circuit thus formed may be modeled as in Figure 4–15(b) and it is then possible to evaluate the delay through the network.

---

* Approximately will do since the curve is fairly flat around its minimum.

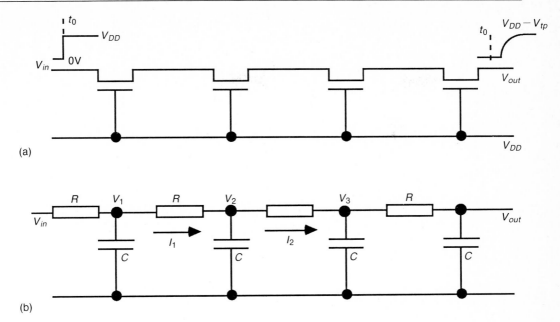

Figure 4-15 Propagation delays in pass transistor chain

The response at node V_2 with respect to time is given by

$$C \frac{dV_2}{dt} = (I_1 - I_2) = \frac{[(V_1 - V_2) - (V_2 - V_3)]}{R}$$

In the limit as the number of sections in such a network becomes large, this expression reduces to

$$RC \frac{dV}{dt} = \frac{d^2 V}{dx^2}$$

where

R = resistance per unit length
C = capacitance per unit length
x = distance along network from input.

The propagation time τ_p for a signal to propagate a distance x is such that

$$\tau_p \propto x^2$$

The analysis can be simplified if all Rs and Cs are lumped together, then

$$R_{total} = nr R_s$$
$$C_{total} = nc \Box C_g$$

where r gives the relative resistance per section in terms of R_s and c gives the relative capacitance per section in terms of $\Box C_g$.

Then, it may be shown that overall delay τ_d for n sections is given by

$$\tau_d \doteq n^2\, r\, c(\tau)$$

Thus, the overall delay increases rapidly as n increases and in practice no more than *four* pass transistors should be normally connected in series. However, this number *can* be exceeded if a buffer is inserted between each group of four pass transistors *or* if relatively long time delays are acceptable.

4.10.2   Design of long polysilicon wires

Long polysilicon wires also contribute distributed series R and C as was the case for cascaded pass transistors and, in consequence, signal propagation is slowed down. This would also be the case for wires in diffusion but the designer is discouraged from running signals in diffusion except over very short distances.

For long polysilicon runs, the use of buffers is recommended. In general, the use of buffers to drive long polysilicon runs has two desirable effects. Firstly, the signal propagation is speeded up and, secondly, there is a reduction in sensitivity to noise.

The reason why noise may be a problem with slowly rising signals may be deduced by considering Figure 4–16. In the diagram the slow rise time of the signal at the output of the inverter (to which the signal emerging from the long polysilicon line is connected) means that the input voltage to the inverter spends a relatively long time in the vicinity of V_{inv} so that small disturbances due to noise will switch the inverter state between '0' and '1' as shown at the output point.

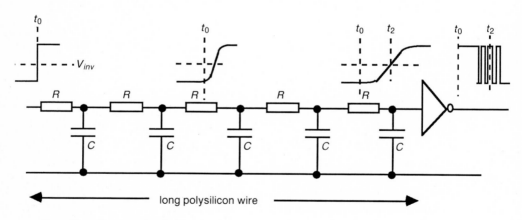

Note: V_{inv} = inverter threshold

Figure 4–16   Possible effects of delays in long polysilicon wires

Thus it is essential that long polysilicon wires be driven by suitable buffers to guard against the effects of noise and to speed up the rise time of propagated signal edges.

4.11 Wiring capacitances

In section 4.5 we considered the area capacitances associated with the layers to substrate and from gate to channel. However there are other significant courses of capacitance which contribute to the overall wiring capacitance.

Three such sources are discussed below.

4.11.1 Fringing fields

Capacitance due to fringing field effects can be a major component of the overall capacitance of interconnect wires. For fine line metalization the value of fringing field capacitance (C_{ff}) can be of the same order as that of the area capacitance. Thus, C_{ff} should be taken into account if accurate prediction of performance is needed.

$$C_{ff} = \frac{\varepsilon_{SiO_2}\varepsilon_0}{\pi} \, l \left[\frac{\pi}{\ln\left\{1 + \frac{2d}{t}\left(1 + \sqrt{(1 + \frac{t}{d})}\right)\right\}} - \frac{t}{4d} \right]$$

where

l = wire length
t = thickness of wire
d = wire to substrate separation

Then, total wire capacitance

$$C_w = C_{area} + C_{ff}$$

4.11.2 Interlayer capacitances

Quite obviously the parallel plate effects are present between one layer and another. For example, some thought on the matter will confirm the fact that, for a given area, metal to polysilicon capacitance must be higher than metal to substrate. The reason for not taking such effects into account for simple calculations is that the effects occur only where layers cross or when one layer underlies another, and in consequence interlayer capacitance is highly dependent on layout. However, for regular structures it is readily calculated and contributes significantly to the accuracy of circuit modeling and delay calculation.

4.11.3 Peripheral capacitance

The source and drain n-diffusion regions form junctions with the p-substrate or p-well at well-defined and uniform depths. Similarly for p-diffusion regions in n-substrates. The diode thus formed has associated with it a peripheral capacitance in picofarads per unit length which, in total, can be considerably greater than the area capacitance of the diffusion region to substrate; the smaller the source or drain area the greater becomes the relative value of the peripheral capacitance.

Thus, peripheral capacitance becomes particularly important as we shrink the device dimensions.

In order to calculate the total diffusion capacitance we must add the contributions of area and peripheral components.

$$C_{total} = C_{area} + C_{periph}$$

Typical values follow in Table 4–4.

For further considerations on capacitative effects the reader is referred to Arpad Barna, *VHSIC — Technologies and Tradeoffs* (Wiley, 1981).

Table 4–4   Typical values for diffusion capacitances

Diffusion capacitance	Typical values	
	Min	Max
Area (C_{area}) (as in Table 4–2)	0.8×10^{-4} pF/μm^2	1.2×10^{-4} pF/μm^2
Periphery (C_{periph})*	6.0×10^{-4} pF/μm	10×10^{-4} pF/μm

* The values given are for deep diffusion; implants will have significantly smaller values.

4.12 Choice of layers

Frequently, in designing an arrangement to meet given specifications, there are several possible ways in which the requirements may be met including the choice between the layers on which to route certain data and control signals. However, there are certain commonsense constraints which should be considered:

- V_{DD} and V_{SS} (*GND*) should be distributed on metal layers wherever possible and should only depart from metal for 'duck unders', etc., preferably on the diffusion layer when this is absolutely essential. A consideration of R_s values will reveal the reason for this.
- Long lengths of polysilicon should be used only after careful consideration because of the relatively high R_s value of the polysilicon layer. Polysilicon is unsuitable for routing V_{DD} or V_{SS} other than for very small distances.
- With these restrictions in mind it is generally the case that the resistances associated with transistors are much higher than any reasonable wiring resistance, so that there is no real danger of any problem due to voltage divider effects between wiring and transistor resistances.
- Capacitive effects must also be carefully considered, particularly where fast signal lines are required and particularly in relation to signals on wiring having relatively high values of R_s. Diffusion areas have relatively high values of

capacitance to substrate and are harder to drive in consequence. Charge sharing may also cause problems in certain circuits or architectures and must be carefully considered. Over small equipotential regions, the signal on a wire can be treated as being identical at all points. Within each region the delay associated with signal propagation is small in comparison with gate delays and with signal delays in systems connected by the wires.

Thus the wires in a MOS system can be modeled as simple capacitors. This concept leads to the establishment of electrical rules for communication paths (wires) as given in Table 4–5.

The factors set out in Tables 4–5 and 4–6 help to put matters in perspective.

Table 4–5   Electrical rules

Layer	Maximum length of communication wire
Metal	20,000λ
Silicide	2,000λ
Polysilicon	200λ
Diffusion	20λ*

* Taking account of peripheral and area capacitances.

Table 4–6   Choice of layers

Layer	R	C	Comments
Metal	Low	Low	Good current capability without large voltage drop . . . use for power distribution and global signals.
Silicide	Low	Moderate	Modest RC product. Reasonably long wires are possible. Silicide is used in place of polysilicon in some nMOS processes.
Polysilicon	High	Moderate	RC product is moderate; high IR drop.
Diffusion	Moderate	High	Moderate IR drop but high C. Hence hard to drive.

4.13 Exercises

1. A particular layer of MOS circuit has a resistivity $\rho = 1$ ohm cm. A section of this layer is 55 μm long and 5 μm wide and has a thickness of 1 μm. Calculate the resistance from one end of this section to the other (along the length). Use the concept of sheet resistance R_s. What is the value of R_s?

2. A particular section of a layout (as in Figure 4–17) includes a 3λ wide metal path which crosses a 2λ wide polysilicon path at right angles. Assuming that the layers are separated by a 0.5 μm thick layer of silicon dioxide, find the capacitance between the two layers.

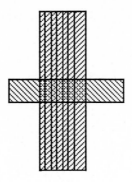

Figure 4–17 Layout detail for Question 2

The polysilicon layer in turn crosses a 4λ wide diffusion region at right angles to form a transistor. Using the tables provided in the text find the gate to channel capacitance. Compare it with the metal to polysilicon capacitance already calculated.

Assume λ = 2.5 μm in all cases.

3. Two nMOS inverters are cascaded to drive a capacitive load $C_L = 16\square C_g$ as shown in Figure 4–18. Calculate the pair delay (V_{in} to V_{out}) in terms of τ for the inverter geometry indicated in the figure. What are the ratios of each inverter?

If strays and wiring are allowed for, it would be reasonable to increase the capacitance to ground across the output of each inverter by $4\square C_g$. What is the pair delay allowing for strays?

Assume a suitable value for τ and calculate this delay.

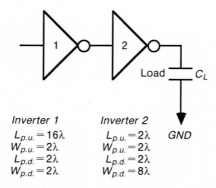

Inverter 1   Inverter 2

$L_{p.u.} = 16\lambda$ $L_{p.u.} = 2\lambda$ GND
$W_{p.u.} = 2\lambda$ $W_{p.u.} = 2\lambda$
$L_{p.d.} = 2\lambda$ $L_{p.d.} = 2\lambda$
$W_{p.d.} = 2\lambda$ $W_{p.d.} = 8\lambda$

Figure 4–18 Circuit for Question 3

4. An off chip capacitance load of 5 pF is to be driven from an arrangement of nMOS inverters. Set out a suitable arrangement giving appropriate channel *L:W* ratios and dimensions. Calculate the number of inverter stages needed together with the delay exhibited by the overall arrangement driving the 5 pF load.

5. *A worked example*: Using the parameters given in this chapter calculate the C_{in} and C_{out} values of capacitance for the structure represented in Figure 4–19.

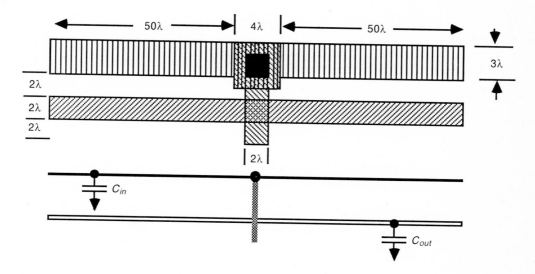

Figure 4–19 Structure for Question 5

Solution: The input capacitance C_{in} is made up of three components — metal bus capacitance C_m, polysilicon capacitance C_p, and the gate capacitance C_g. Thus

$$C_{in} = C_m + C_p + C_g$$

$$C_m = [2 \times (50 \times 3)\lambda^2 \times 6.25 \ \mu m^2/\lambda^2] \{0.3 \times 10^{-4} \ pF/\mu m^2\}$$
$$= .05625 \ pF$$

$$C_p = [(4 \times 4 + 2 \times 2 + 2 \times 1)\lambda^2 \times 6.25 \ \mu m^2/\lambda^2] \{0.4 \times 10^{-4} \ pF/\mu m^2\}$$
$$= .0055 \ pF$$

$$C_g = 1\Box C_g = .01 \ pF$$

Thus

$$C_{in} = .05625 + .0055 + .01 = .07175 \ pF \ (= > 7\Box C_g)$$

Now, the output capacitance C_{out} is contributed by the diffusion area C_{da} *and* peripheral C_{dp} capacitances so that (assuming transistor is off) we have

$$
\begin{aligned}
C_{out} &= C_{da} + C_{dp} \\
&= [(51 \times 2)\lambda^2 \times 6.25 \ \mu m^2/\lambda^2] \times 1 \times 10^{-4} \ pF/\mu m^2 + \\
&\quad [2 \times (51 + 2)\lambda \times 2.5 \ \mu m/\lambda] \times 8 \times 10^{-4} \ pF/\mu m
\end{aligned}
$$

$$
= .06375 + .212 = .27575 \ pF \ (\text{note significance of } C_{dp})
$$

5 | Subsystem design and layout

Having now covered the basic MOS technology, the behavior of components formed by MOS layers, the basic units which help to characterize behavior, and a set of design rules, we are in a position to undertake the design of some of the sub-systems (leaf cells) from which larger systems are composed.

5.1   Some architectural issues

In all design processes, a logical and systematic approach is essential. This is particularly so in the case of the design of a VLSI system which could otherwise take so long as to render the whole system obsolete before it is 'off the drawing board'. Take, for example, the case of a relatively straightforward MSI logic circuit comprising, say, 500 transistors. A reasonable time to allocate to the design and proving of such a circuit could be some two engineer-months. Consider now the design of a 500,000 transistor VLSI system. If a linear relationship exists between complexity and design time, the required design time would be 2000 engineer-months or 170 engineer-years. Obviously, then, we must adopt design methods which allow the handling of complexity in reasonable periods of time and with reasonable amounts of labor.

Certainly we are not about to tackle 500,000 transistor designs in this text, but some sensible concepts applied even at the subsystem (leaf cell) level can be most worthwhile and can also be directly compatible with larger system design requirements. Guidelines may be set out as follows:

1. Define the requirements (properly and carefully).
2. Partition the overall architecture into appropriate subsystems.
3. Consider communication paths carefully in order to develop sensible inter-relationships between subsystems.
4. Draw a floor plan of how the system is to map onto the silicon (and alternate between 2, 3, and 4 as necessary).
5. Aim for regular structures so that design is largely a matter of replication.
6. Draw suitable (stick) diagrams of the leaf cells of the subsystems.
7. Convert each cell to a layout.
8. Carefully and thoroughly carry out a design rule check on each cell.

The whole design process will be greatly assisted if considerable care is taken with:

1. the *partitioning* of the system so that there are clean and clear subsystems with the minimum interdependence and complexity of interconnection between them; and
2. the *design simplification* within subsystems so that architectures are adopted which allow the exploitation of a cellular design concept. This allows the system to be composed of relatively few standard cells which are replicated to form highly regular structures.

In designing digital systems in MOS technology, there are two basic ways of building logic circuits which will now be discussed.

5.2 Switch logic

Switch logic is based on the 'pass transistor' or on transmission gates.

This approach is fast for small arrays and takes no static current from the supply rails. Thus, power dissipation of such arrays is very small since current only flows on switching.

Switch logic is similar to logic arrays based on relay contacts in that the path through each switch is isolated from the signal activating the switch. In consequence, the designer has a considerable amount of freedom in implementing architectural features compared with bipolar logic-based designs.

A number of texts on switching theory, some dating from the 1950s and 1960s, have sections on relay/switch logic and the reader is referred to such

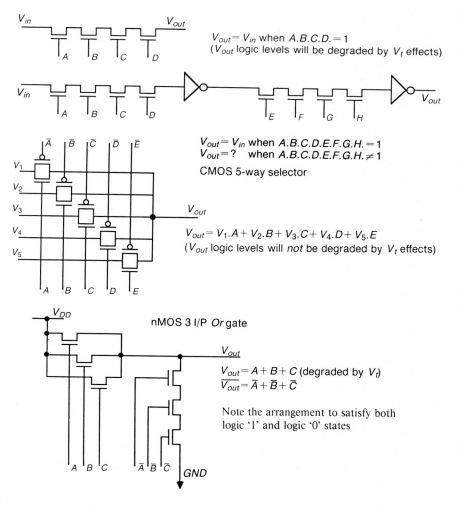

$V_{out} = V_{in}$ when $A.B.C.D. = 1$
(V_{out} logic levels will be degraded by V_t effects)

$V_{out} = V_{in}$ when $A.B.C.D.E.F.G.H. = 1$
$V_{out} = ?$ when $A.B.C.D.E.F.G.H. \neq 1$

CMOS 5-way selector

$V_{out} = V_1.A + V_2.B + V_3.C + V_4.D + V_5.E$
(V_{out} logic levels will *not* be degraded by V_t effects)

nMOS 3 I/P *Or* gate

$V_{out} = A + B + C$ (degraded by V_t)
$\overline{V_{out}} = \overline{A} + \overline{B} + \overline{C}$

Note the arrangement to satisfy both logic '1' and logic '0' states

Figure 5–1 Some switch logic arrangements

material for generating ideas for implementation in MOS switch logic. An example is Marcus, *Switching Circuits for Engineers* (Prentice-Hall, 1962, 3rd edn, 1975).

Basic *And* and *Or* connections are set out in Figure 5–1, but many combinations of switches are possible.

5.2.1   Pass transistors and transmission gates

Switches and switch logic may be formed from simple n- or p-pass transistors or from transmission gates (complementary switches) comprising an n- and a p-pass transistor in parallel as shown in Figure 5–2. The reason for adopting the apparent complexity of the transmission gate rather than using a simple n- or p-switch in most CMOS applications is to eliminate the undesirable threshold voltage effects which give rise to the loss of logic levels in pass transistors as indicated in Figure 5–2. No such degradation occurs with the transmission gate but more area is occupied and complementary signals are needed to drive it. 'On' resistance, however, is lower than that of the simple pass transistor switches.

In using nMOS switch logic, there is one restriction which must always be observed and that is that *no* pass transistor gate input may be driven through *one or more pass transistors* (see Figure 5–2). As shown, logic levels propagated through pass transistors are degraded by threshold voltage effects. Since the signal out of pass transistor T_1 does not reach a full logic 1, but rather a voltage one transistor threshold below a true logic 1, this degraded voltage would not permit the output of T_2 to reach an acceptable logic 1 level.

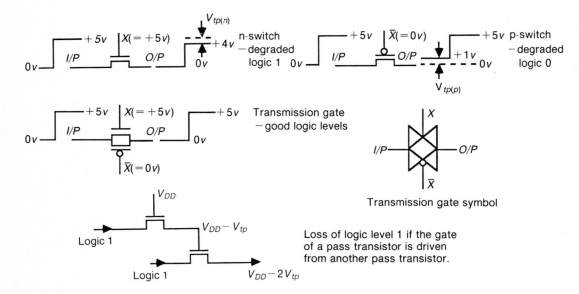

Figure 5–2   Some properties of pass transistors and Transmission gates

5.3 Gate (restoring) logic

Gate logic is based on adaptation of the inverter circuit.

Both *Nand* and *Nor* gate arrangements are available. Inverters are also employed which complement and restore logic signals which have been degraded (e.g. because they have passed through a number of pass transistors).

5.3.1 The inverter

The inverter circuit diagram, symbol, and stick diagram should all be familiar by now and are reproduced here as Figure 5–3. Note that it is often useful to indicate

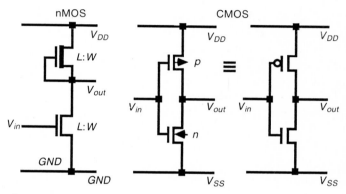

(a) Circuit symbols

Note: n- and p-transistors assumed to be minimum size unless stated otherwise.

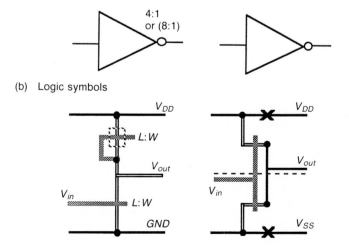

(b) Logic symbols

(c) Stick diagrams

Figure 5–3 nMOS and CMOS inverters

the nMOS inverter $Z_{p.u.}/Z_{p.d.}$ ratio and/or the channel length to width ratio as shown. In achieving the desired ratio several possibilities emerge, two of which are illustrated in Figures 5–4 and 5–5 for an 8 : 1 inverter. Note the effect that the different approaches have on power dissipation P_d and on the area occupied by the inverter. Also note the resistance and capacitance values.

The CMOS inverter carries no static current and thus has no power dissipation unless switching.

5.3.2 Two-input *Nand* gate

Two-input *Nand* gate arrangements are given in Figure 5–6; the nMOS $L:W$ ratios should be carefully noted since they must be chosen so as to achieve the desired overall $Z_{p.u.}/Z_{p.d.}$ ratio (where $Z_{p.d.}$ is contributed in this case by *both* input transistors in series).

In order to arrive at the required $L:W$ ratios for an nMOS *Nand* gate with n inputs, it is only necessary to consider the very simple circuit model of the *Nand* gate in the condition when all n pull-down transistors are conducting as in Figure 5–7. The critical factor here is that the output voltage V_{out} must be near enough to ground to turn off any following inverter-like stages, that is

$$V_{out} \leqslant V_t = 0.2 V_{DD}$$

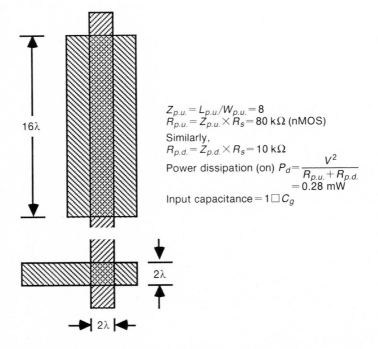

$Z_{p.u.} = L_{p.u.}/W_{p.u.} = 8$
$R_{p.u.} = Z_{p.u.} \times R_s = 80\ \text{k}\Omega\ \text{(nMOS)}$
Similarly,
$R_{p.d.} = Z_{p.d.} \times R_s = 10\ \text{k}\Omega$
Power dissipation (on) $P_d = \dfrac{V^2}{R_{p.u.} + R_{p.d.}}$
$= 0.28\ \text{mW}$
Input capacitance $= 1\square C_g$

Figure 5–4 8:1 nMOS inverter (minimum size p.d.)

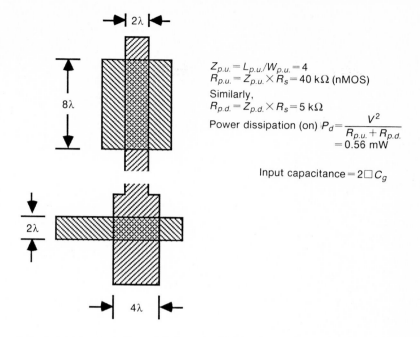

$Z_{p.u.} = L_{p.u.}/W_{p.u.} = 4$
$R_{p.u.} = Z_{p.u.} \times R_s = 40 \text{ k}\Omega \text{ (nMOS)}$
Similarly,
$R_{p.d.} = Z_{p.d.} \times R_s = 5 \text{ k}\Omega$
Power dissipation (on) $P_d = \dfrac{V^2}{R_{p.u.} + R_{p.d.}}$
$= 0.56 \text{ mW}$

Input capacitance $= 2\square C_g$

Note: A 4:1 inverter is formed if the p.d. width is halved.

Figure 5-5   An alternative 8:1 nMOS inverter

Thus

$$\frac{V_{DD} \times nZ_{p.d.}}{nZ_{p.d.} + Z_{p.u.}} \leqslant 0.2 V_{DD}$$

where $Z_{p.d.}$ applies for any one pull-down transistor. The boundary condition then is

$$\frac{nZ_{p.d.}}{nZ_{p.d.} + Z_{p.u.}} = 0.2$$

whence nMOS *Nand* ratio $= \dfrac{Z_{p.u.}}{nZ_{p.d.}} = \dfrac{4}{1}$

that is, the ratio between $Z_{p.u.}$ and the sum of all the pull-down $Z_{p.d.}$s must be 4:1 (as for the nMOS inverter).

This ratio must be adjusted appropriately if input signals are derived through pass transistors.

Further consideration of the nMOS *Nand* gate geometry reveals two significant factors:

1.   nMOS *Nand* gate *area requirements* are considerably greater than those of a corresponding nMOS inverter since not only must pull-down transistors be

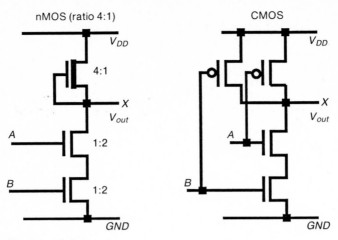

(a)   Circuit symbols

Note: n- and p-transistors assumed to be minimum size unless stated otherwise.

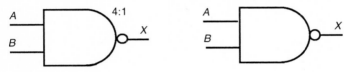

(b)   Logic symbols

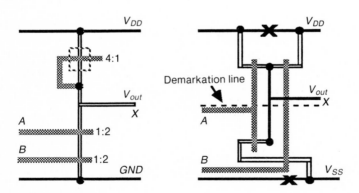

(c)   Stick diagrams

Note: The natural 2.5:1 asymmetry of the CMOS inverter is improved to 1.25:1 (or better) due to the 2 n-pull-down transistors in series.

Figure 5–6   nMOS and CMOS 2 I/P *Nand* gate

added in series to provide the desired number of inputs, but as inputs are added so must there be a corresponding adjustment of the length of the pull-up transistor channel to maintain the required overall ratio.

2.   nMOS *Nand* gate *delays* are also increased in direct proportion to the number of inputs added. If each pull-down transistor is kept to minimum size $(2\lambda \times 2\lambda)$, then each will present $1\Box C_g$ at its input, but if there are n such inputs

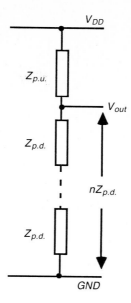

Figure 5–7 nMOS *Nand* ratio determination

then the length and *resistance* of the pull-up transistor must be increased by a factor of n to keep the correct ratio. Thus, delays associated with the nMOS *Nand* are:

$$\tau_{Nand} = n\,\tau_{inv}$$

where n is the number of inputs and τ_{inv} is the corresponding nMOS inverter delay. (The alternative approach of keeping $Z_{p.u.}$ constant and widening the pull-down channels has the same effect, since in this case C_g for each pull-down transistor will be increased to $n\Box C_g$.)

Furthermore, the rise time of the nMOS *Nand* output is dependent on the actual input(s) on which the $\triangledown$ transition takes place.

In consequence of these properties, the nMOS *Nand* gate is only used where absolutely necessary and the number of inputs is restricted.

The CMOS *Nand* gate has no such restrictions but, bearing in mind the remarks on asymmetry (Figure 5–6), it is necessary to allow for extended fall times on capacitive loads due to the number of n-transistors in series forming the pull-down.

Some adjustment of transistor geometry may be necessary for this reason and to keep the transfer characteristic symmetrical about $V_{DD}/2$.

5.3.3 Two-input *Nor* gate

Two-input *Nor* gate arrangements are given in Figure 5–8; it will be noted here that the *Nor* gate can be expanded to accommodate a reasonably large number of inputs (see Color Plate 3) and, for nMOS designs, is preferred to the *Nand* gate where there

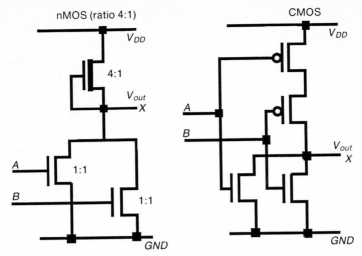

(a) Circuit symbols

Note: n- and p-transistors assumed to be minimum size unless stated otherwise.

(b) Logic symbols

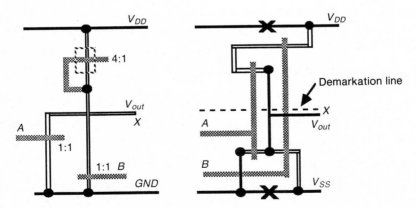

(c) Stick diagrams

Note: The natural 2.5:1 asymmetry of a CMOS inverter driving a capacitive load is aggravated to 5:1 (or more) for the 2 I/P *Nor* gate due to the 2 p-pull-up transistors in series.

Figure 5–8 nMOS and CMOS 2 I/P *Nor* gate

is a choice (which is usually the case if logical expressions are suitably manipulated).

Since both 'legs' of the nMOS *Nor* gate provide a path to ground from the pull-up transistor, the ratios must be such that any one conducting pull-down leg will give the appropriate inverter-like transfer characteristic. Thus each leg has the same ratio as would be the case for an nMOS inverter, irrespective of the number of inputs accommodated.

The area occupied by the nMOS *Nor* gate is reasonable since the pull-up transistor dimensions are unaffected by the number of inputs accommodated. In consequence, the *Nor* gate is as fast as the corresponding inverter and is the preferred inverter-based nMOS logic gate when a choice is possible.

Obviously, the ratio between $Z_{p.u.}$ and $Z_{p.d.}$ of any one leg must be appropriate to the source from which that input is driven for nMOS designs (namely 4:1 driven from another inverter-based circuit or 8:1 if driven via one or more pass transistors).

The CMOS *Nor* gate (see also Color Plate 3) consists of a pull-up p-transistor-based structure, which implements the logic 1 conditions and a complementary n-transistor arrangement to implement the logic 0 conditions at the output. In the case of the *Nor* gate, the p-structure consists of transistors in series, one for each input, while the n-pull-down arrangement has as many transistors in parallel as there are inputs to the *Nor* gate. Thus the already predominant resistance of the p-devices is aggravated in its effect by the number connected in series. Rise and fall time asymmetry on capacitive loads is thus increased and there will also be a shift in the transfer (V_{in} vs. V_{out}) characteristic which will reduce noise immunity. For these reasons, *Nor* gates with a significant number of inputs may require adjustment of the p- and/or n-transistor geometries ($L:W$ ratios).

The CMOS *Nand* gate, on the other hand, benefits from the connection of p-transistors in parallel but once again the geometries may require thought when several inputs are required.

5.3.4 Other forms of CMOS logic

The availability of both n- and p-transistors makes it possible for the CMOS designer to explore and exploit various alternatives to inverter-based CMOS logic.

5.3.4.1 Pseudo-nMOS logic

Clearly, if we replace the depletion mode pull-up transistor of the standard nMOS circuits with a p-transistor with gate connected to V_{SS}, we have a structure similar to the nMOS equivalent. This approach to logic design is illustrated by the 3 I/P *Nand* gate in Figure 5–9. Because the circuit arrangements look and behave much like nMOS circuits, *ratio rules must be applied*.

In order to determine the required ratio we consider the arrangement of Figure 5–10 in which a pseudo-nMOS inverter is being driven by another similar inverter and we consider the conditions necessary to produce an output voltage of

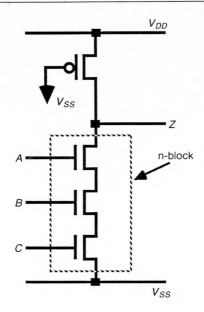

Figure 5-9 Pseudo-nMOS logic 3 I/P *Nand* gate

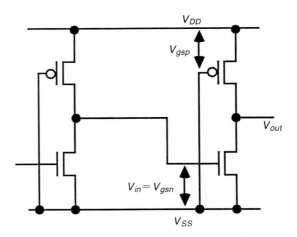

Figure 5-10 Pseudo-nMOS inverter when driven from a similar inverter

V_{inv} for an identical input voltage. As for the nMOS analysis we consider the conditions for which $V_{inv} = V_{DD}/2$.

At this point the n-device is in saturation (i.e. $0 < V_{gsn} - V_{tn} < V_{dsn}$) and the p-device is operating in the resistive region (i.e. $0 < V_{dsp} < V_{gsp} - V_{tp}$). Equating currents of the n-transistor and the p-transistor, and by suitable rearrangement of the resultant expression, we obtain

$$V_{inv} = V_{tn} + \frac{(2\mu_p/\mu_n)^{1/2}[(-V_{DD} - V_{tn}) V_{dsp} - V_{dsp}^2]^{1/2}}{(Z_{p.u.}/Z_{p.d.})^{1/2}}$$

where

$$Z_{p.u.} = L_p/W_p$$

and

$$Z_{p.d.} = L_n/W_n$$

With

$$V_{inv} = 0.5 V_{DD}$$

$$V_{tn} = |V_{tp}| = 0.2 V_{DD}$$

$$V_{DD} = 5 \text{ V}$$

$$\mu_n = 2.5 \mu_p$$

we obtain

$$\frac{Z_{p.u.}}{Z_{p.d.}} = \frac{3}{1}$$

A transfer characteristic, V_{out} vs. V_{in}, can be drawn and, as for the nMOS case, the characteristic will shift with changes of $Z_{p.u.}/Z_{p.d.}$ ratio.

Two points are worthy of comment:
1. Since the channel sheet resistance of the p-pull-up is about 2.5 times that of the n-pull-down, and allowing for the ratio of 3:1, the pseudo-nMOS inverter presents a resistance between V_{DD} and V_{SS} which is, say, 85 kΩ compared with 50 kΩ for a comparable 4:1 nMOS device. Thus, power dissipation is reduced to about 60 percent of that associated with a comparable nMOS device.
2. Due to the higher pull-up resistance the inverter pair delay is larger by a factor of 8.5:5 than the 4:1 minimum size nMOS inverter.

5.3.4.2 Dynamic CMOS logic
The actual logic (see Figure 5–11(a) for the schematic arrangement) is implemented in the inherently faster nMOS logic (the n-block); a p-transistor is used for the non-time-critical precharging of the output line 'Z' so that the output capacitance is charged to V_{DD} during the off period of the clock signal ϕ. During this same period the inputs are applied to the n-block and the state of the logic is then evaluated during the on period of the clock when the bottom n-transistor is turned on. The following remarks are relevant:

1. Charge sharing may be a problem unless the inputs are constrained not to change during the on period of the clock.

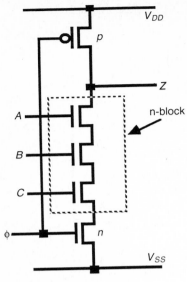

(a) Schematic

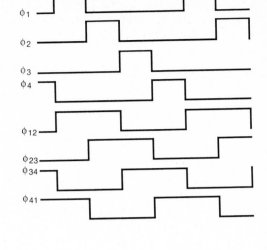

(b) Possible 4φ and derived clocks

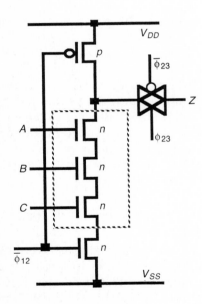

(c) Type 3 arrangement

Figure 5–11 Dynamic CMOS logic 3 I/P *Nand* gate

2. *Single phase dynamic logic structures cannot be cascaded* since, due to circuit delays, an incorrect input to the next stage may be present when evaluation commences, causing its output to be inadvertently discharged and the wrong output resulting.

One remedy is to employ a four-phase clock in which the actual signals used are the derived clocks ϕ_{12}, ϕ_{23}, ϕ_{34}, and ϕ_{41}, as illustrated in Figure 5–11(b).

The basic circuit of Figure 5–11(a) is modified by the inclusion of a transmission gate as in Figure 5–11(c), the function of which is to sample the output during the 'evaluate' period and to hold the output state while the next stage logic evaluates. For this strategy to work, the next stage must operate on overlapping but later clock signals. Clearly, since there are four different derived clock signals which are used in sequential pairs (e.g. $\bar{\phi}_{12}$ and ϕ_{23} in Figure 5–11(c)), there are four different gate clocking configurations. These configurations are usually identified by a type number which reflects the last of the clock periods activating the gate. For example, the gate shown would be identified as 'type 3' since the output Z is precharged during ϕ_2 and is evaluated during ϕ_3 (the transmission gate is clocked by ϕ_{23}). In order to avoid erroneous evaluations, the gates must be connected in allowable sequences as set out in Table 5–1.

Table 5–1 Dynamic logic types and sequences

Gate type	Evaluate clock	Transmission gate clock	Allowable next types
Type 1	$\bar{\phi}_{34}$	ϕ_{41}	Types 2 or 3
Type 2	$\bar{\phi}_{41}$	ϕ_{12}	Types 3 or 4
Type 3	$\bar{\phi}_{12}$	ϕ_{23}	Types 4 or 1
Type 4	$\bar{\phi}_{23}$	ϕ_{34}	Types 1 or 2

5.3.4.3 Clocked CMOS (C² MOS) logic

The general arrangement may be appreciated by inspection of Figure 5–12. The logic is implemented in both n- and p-transistors in the form of a pull-up p-block and a complementary n-block pull-down structure (Figure 5–12(a)), as for the inverter-based CMOS logic discussed earlier. However, the logic in this case is evaluated (connected to the output) only during the on period of the clock. As might be expected, a clocked inverter circuit forms part of this family of logic as shown in Figure 5–12(b). Owing to the extra transistors in series with the output, slower rise and fall times can be expected.

5.3.4.4 CMOS domino logic

An extension to the dynamic CMOS logic discussed earlier is set out in Figure 5–13. This modified arrangement allows for the cascading of logic structures using only a single phase clock. This requires a static CMOS buffer in each logic gate.

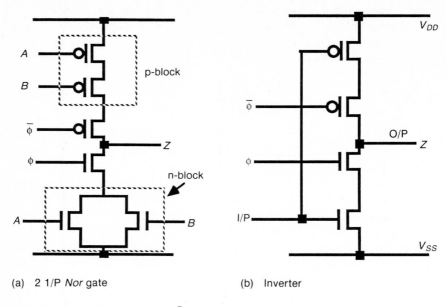

(a)   2 1/P *Nor* gate   (b)   Inverter

Figure 5–12   Clocked CMOS (C²MOS) logic

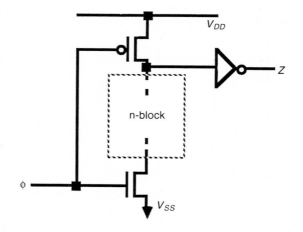

Figure 5-13   CMOS domino logic

The following remarks will help to place this type of logic in the scheme of things:

1. Such logic structures can have smaller areas than conventional CMOS logic.
2. Parasitic capacitances are smaller so that higher operating speeds are possible.
3. Operation is free of glitches since each gate can make only one '1' to '0' transition.

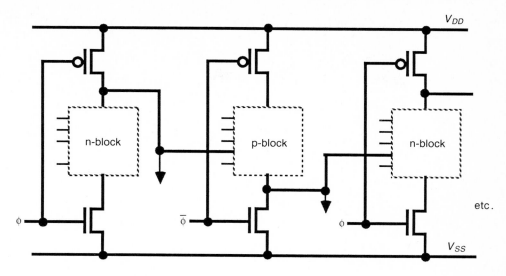

Figure 5–14 n-p CMOS logic

4. Only noninverting structures are possible due to the presence of the inverting buffer.
5. Charge distribution may be a problem and must be considered.

5.3.4.5 *n–p CMOS logic*

This is another variation of basic dynamic logic arrangement in which the actual logic blocks are alternately 'n' and 'p' in a cascaded structure as in Figure 5–14. The precharge and evaluate transistors are fed from the clock ϕ and clockbar $\bar{\phi}$ alternately and clearly the functions of the top and bottom transistors also alternate between precharge and evaluate.

Other forms of CMOS logic are also possible, but this text does not attempt to give an exhaustive treatment.

5.4 Examples of structured design (combinational logic)

The best way to illustrate an approach to structured design is to work through some examples.

5.4.1 A parity generator

A circuit is to be designed to indicate the parity of a binary number or word. The requirement is indicated in Figure 5–15 for an $n+1$-bit input.

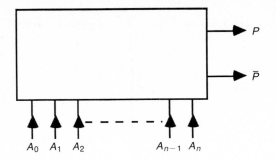

Figure 5-15 Parity generator basic block diagram

Note: $P = \begin{cases} 1 & \text{Even number of 1s at input} \\ 0 & \text{Odd number of 1s at input} \end{cases}$

Since the number of bits is undefined we must find a general solution on a cascadable bit-wise basis so that n can have any value.

A suitably regular structure is set out in Figure 5–16. From this, we may recognize a standard or basic one-bit cell from which an n-bit parity generator may be formed. Such a cell is shown as Figure 5–17.

It will be seen that parity information is passed from one cell to the next and is modified or not by a cell depending on the state of the input lines A_i and $\bar{A}_i$.

A little reflection will readily reveal that the requirements are

$$A_i = 1 \text{ parity is changed, } P_i = \bar{P}_{i-1}$$
$$A_i = 0 \text{ parity is unchanged, } P_i = P_{i-1}$$

A suitable arrangement for such a cell is given in stick diagram form in Figure 5–18(a) (nMOS) and 5–18(b) (CMOS). The circuit implements the function

$$P_i = \bar{P}_{i-1} \cdot A_i + P_{i-1} \cdot \bar{A}_i$$

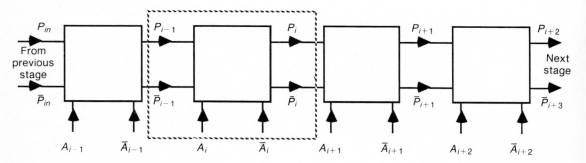

Note: Parity requirements are set at the left-most cell where $P_{in} = 1$ sets even and $P_{in} = 0$ sets odd parity.

Figure 5-16 Parity generator — structured design approach

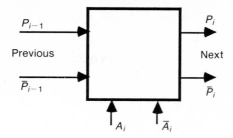

Figure 5–17 Basic one-bit cell

Note that a cell boundary may be chosen in each case such that cells may be cascaded at will.

When converting stick diagrams to layouts, care must be taken that the boundary is set so that no design rule violations occur when cells are *butted together*. Obviously, the boundary must also be chosen so that wastage of area is avoided and so that design rule errors are not present when a cell is checked *in isolation*, although this may not always be possible.

Also, note that inlet and corresponding outlet points should match up both in *layer* and *position*, so that direct interconnection between cells is achieved when cells are butted.

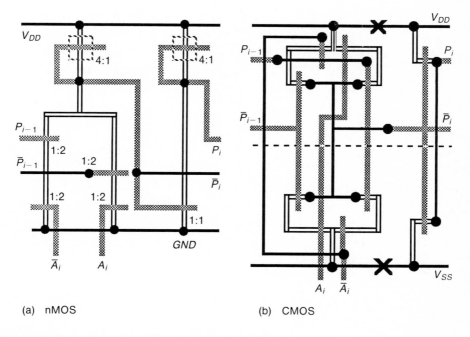

(a) nMOS

(b) CMOS

Figure 5–18 Stick diagrams (parity generator)

5.4.2 Bus arbitration logic for *n* line bus

(This example and its solutions are similar to an example accredited to Professor John Newkirk in VTI course material.)

The functional requirements of this circuit may be ascertained with reference to Figure 5–19 and associated truth table. If the highest priority line A_n is Hi (Logic 1) then output line A_n^p will be Hi and all other output lines Lo (Logic 0), irrespective of the state of the other input lines A_1---A_{n-1}. Similarly, A_{n-1}^p will be Hi only when A_{n-1} is Hi and A_n is Lo; again the state of all input lines of lower priority (A_1----A_{n-2}) will have no effect and all other output lines will be Lo.

This requirement can be expressed algebraically as follows:

$$A_n^p = A_n$$
$$A_{n-1}^p = \overline{A}_n . A_{n-1} \qquad\qquad [\overline{A}_{n-1}^p = A_n + \overline{A}_{n-1}]$$
$$A_{n-2}^p = \overline{A}_n . \overline{A}_{n-1} . A_{n-2} \qquad\qquad [\overline{A}_{n-2}^p = A_n + A_{n-1} + \overline{A}_{n-2}]$$

$$A_1^p = \overline{A}_n . \overline{A}_{n-1} . \overline{A}_{n-2}\text{----------}\overline{A}_3 . \overline{A}_2 . A_1 \qquad\qquad \text{(etc)}$$

A direct implementation of these expressions may be readily envisaged and a suitable arrangement of switch logic is given in Figure 5-20.

Truth table

A_n	. . . . .	A_3	A_2	A_1	A_n^p	. . . . .	A_3^p	A_2^p	A_1^p
0	. . . . .	0	0	0	0	. . . . .	0	0	0
0		0	0	1	0		0	0	1
0		0	1	X	0		0	1	0
0		1	X	X	0		1	0	0
.		.	.	.	.		.	.	.
.		.	.	.	.		.	.	.
.		.	.	.	.		.	.	.
1	. . . . .	X	X	X	1	. . . . .	0	0	0

X = Don't care

Figure 5–19 Bus arbitration logic and truth table

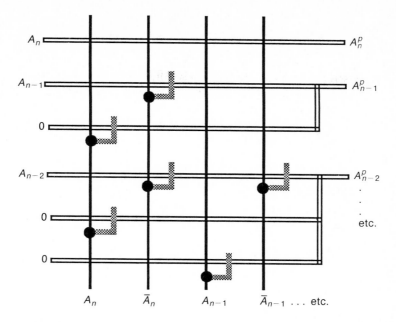

Figure 5–20 Stick diagram — bus arbitration logic

This implementation seems the obvious one but it does suffer from the fact that as the input line under consideration moves down in significance so the complexity of the logic grows. For example, we have shown only the top three lines in Figure 5–20 but it will be seen that:

A_n requires one diffusion path and no switches

A_{n-1} requires two diffusion paths and two switches

A_{n-2} requires three diffusion paths and four switches

and so on.

This is not a regular structure and is not well suited for VLSI implementation. Therefore, we must take a cellular approach by setting out the requirements in alternative fashion as in Figure 5–21.

Having arrived at a regular structure the requirements for each cell may be expressed as follows:

$$A_i^p \begin{cases} = g_{i+1} \text{ if } A_i = 1 \\ \text{or } 0 \text{ otherwise} \end{cases}$$

$$g_i \begin{cases} = 0 \quad\ \text{ if } A_i = 1 \\ \text{or } g_{i+1} \text{ otherwise} \end{cases}$$

These requirements may be met by the circuit of Figure 5–22 but care must be taken not to cascade more than four cells without buffering the grant line.

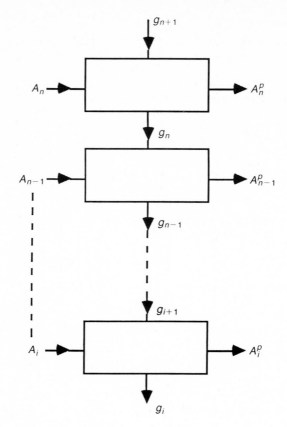

Notes: 1. g = grant line.
2. If grant line is 1, none of the lines above it wants priority.
3. If $A_i = 0$, pass grant.

Figure 5-21 Bus arbitration logic — structured design

The art of arriving at conveniently expressed relationships is one which must be cultivated and it is often helped by adopting an 'if, then, else (or otherwise)' approach. The solution to the problem under consideration can be formulated after expressing the need of each cell in words:

If $A_i = 1$ then $A_i^p = g_{i+1}$,
else $A_i^p = 0$ (if $A_i = 0$)

If $A_i = 0$ then $g_i = g_{i+1}$
else $g_i = 0$ (if $A_i = 1$)

both A_i^p and g_i can be derived from g_{i+1}

From which we could deduce

$$A_i^p = A_i \cdot g_{i+1}$$

$$g_i = \bar{A}_i \cdot g_{i+1}$$

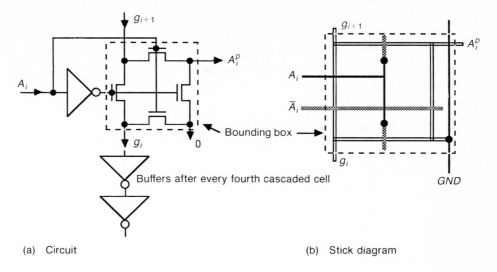

(a) Circuit

(b) Stick diagram

Figure 5–22 Bus arbitration logic — structured design

However, there is a danger with expressions of the conventional Boolean type — a tendency to ignore the fact that MOS *switch* logic is such that not only must the logic 1 condition be satisfied but it is also necessary to deliberately *satisfy* the logic 0 conditions. The TTL logic designer is used to working with logic circuits in which the output must be logic 0 if the logic 1 output conditions are not satisfied. However, some MOS switch-based logic circuits have the property that if the logic 1 output conditions are not met, then the output can be indeterminate, or if some storage capacitance is present (e.g. input capacitance C_g of an inverter) then the output can remain at logic 1 even after the conditions which caused it no longer exist. Thus, it is necessary to deliberately implement the 'else' conditions. We must, therefore, write expressions for both the logic 1 and logic 0 conditions of the output lines, thus

$$A_i^p = A_i . g_{i+1}; \ \overline{A}_i^p = \overline{A}_i + \overline{g}_{i+1}$$
$$g_i = \overline{A}_i g_{i+1}; \overline{g}_i = A_i + \overline{g}_{i+1}$$

which is the circuit realized in Figure 5–22.

5.4.3 Multiplexers (data selectors)

Multiplexers are widely used and have many applications. They are also commonly available in a number of standard configurations in TTL and other logic families.

In order to arrive at a standard cell for multiplexers, we will consider a commonly used circuit, the four-way multiplexer.

The requirements and general arrangement of a four-way multiplexer are set out in Figure 5–23, from which we may write

$$Z = I_0 . \overline{S}_1 . \overline{S}_0 + I_1 . \overline{S}_1 . S_0 + I_2 . S_1 . \overline{S}_0 + I_3 . S_1 . S_0$$

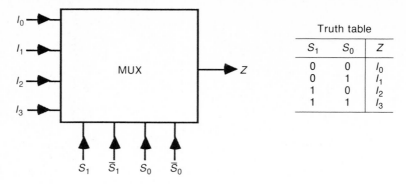

Truth table

S_1	S_0	Z
0	0	I_0
0	1	I_1
1	0	I_2
1	1	I_3

Notes: 1. $Z = I_S$; $0 \leqslant S \leqslant 3$ where S = selected inputs.
2. The availability of the complement of the select signals is assumed.

Figure 5–23   Selector logic circuit

where S_1 and S_0 are the selector inputs. Note that in this case we do not need to be concerned about undefined ouput conditions since, if S_1 and S_0 have defined logic states, output Z must always be connected to one of I_0 to I_3.

Thus a direct nMOS switch logic implementation follows which is given as Figure 5–24(a) in stick diagram form with a standard-cell-based mask layout following as Figure 5–25.

A transmission-gate-based CMOS stick diagram is given as Figure 5–24(b). A mask layout of this figure appears as Color Plate 5 and it can be seen that all n-transistors are placed below the demarkation line and close to the V_{SS} rail to allow ready configuration of the p-well and V_{SS} contacts. The p-transistors are similarly placed above the notional demarkation line and close to V_{DD}. Note that logic 1 levels will not be degraded by this arrangement as are those in the nMOS version.

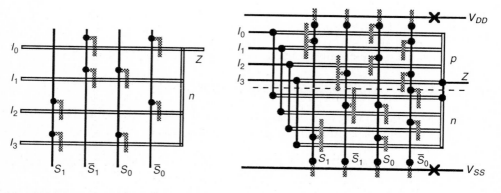

(a)   nMOS switches (See Color Plate 4)   (b)   Transmission gates (CMOS) (See Color Plate 5)

Figure 5–24   Switch logic implementations of a four-way multiplexer

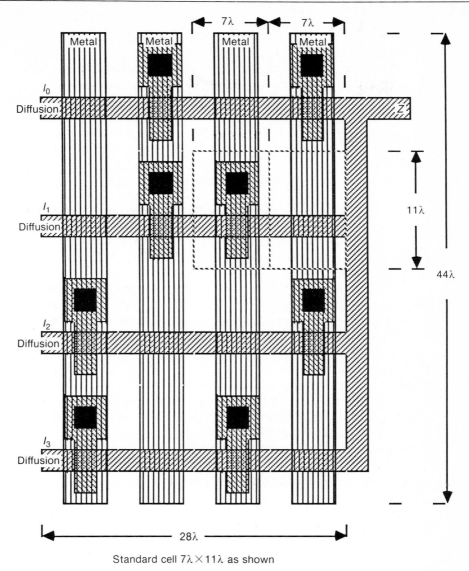

Standard cell $7\lambda \times 11\lambda$ as shown

Figure 5–25 Four-way multiplexer (MUX) layout (see Color Plate 4)

Now if we can establish standard cells from which a four-way multiplexer can be composed then we will also cover the case of the two-way multiplexer. Such a cell will, by inference, also be suitable for constructing an eight-way or a sixteen-way multiplexer.

For the nMOS case a standard cell is illustrated in Figure 5–25. The standard cell in this case measured $7\lambda \times 11\lambda$ and is shown in the dotted outline. Note that two versions of the cell are needed to complete the network, one version with a pass transistor as shown and the other version without. If computer-aided design tools are used, the two versions may be designed as one cell suitably parameterized to include or exclude the pass transistor. Note that in Figure 5–25 the dimensions do not include the end connection to Z.

Note also that this layout places the metal select lines over the top of pass transistors. This practice is acceptable in this situation where a transistor gate is actually driven from and connected to the particular metal line which runs across it. This method of economizing in area must be used with caution when locating transistors under metal layers to which they are not connected, and is not acceptable when the underlying transistors are used as storage points to hold a charge and retain a logic level. It is also possible to implement a two- or four-way nMOS multiplexer as a red–green function block.

5.4.4 The red–green (polysilicon–diffusion) function block

A stick diagram for the red–green function block implementation of an nMOS four-way multiplexer is given as Figure 5–26 with a corresponding layout and a standard cell identified in Figure 5–27.

The red–green block relies on using the implant to form permanently turned on depletion mode transistors in the diffusion path. This type of arrangement depends then on the threshold voltages of the depletion mode transistors being such that they will conduct even when the gate is at 0 volts and the channel is at V_{DD}. Care must be taken to ensure that the process to be used in manufacturing produces the desired *threshold voltages* if the red–green block is to be used. Its main attraction is simplicity and small area, as can be appreciated by comparing the layout of Figure 5–27 with that of Figure 5–25. Note that the red–green function block should not be extended to more than a four-way multiplexer because of the number of pass transistors which would be needed in series in each line. In all cases, the multiplexer arrangement of Figure 5–24 (etc.) is both safer and faster.

5.4.5 A general logic function block

An arrangement to generate any function of two variables (A, B) is readily formed from any form of four-way multiplexer.

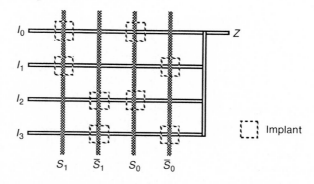

Figure 5–26 Stick diagram — red–green function block

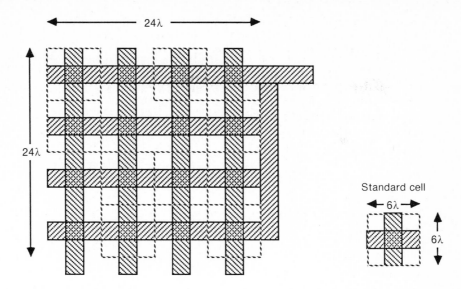

Figure 5–27   Mask layout red–green block version of four-way multiplexer

The general approach is indicated in Figure 5–28 (using a red–green function block in this case). It will be seen that the required function is generated by replacing the select inputs by the required two variables A and B and by 'programming' the inputs I_0–I_3 appropriately with 0s and 1s, as indicated in the figure. The switch-based multiplexer may also be similarly employed to generate any function of up to four variables. The red–green function block is not suited to cope with more than two variable situations because of the restriction indicated at the end of section 5.4.4.

5.4.6   A four-line Gray code to binary code converter

As a further exercise, and to utilize a very widely used logic arrangement (the *Exclusive-Or* gate), let us consider the requirement for code conversion from Gray to binary as set out in Table 5–2.

By inspection of (or mapping from) Table 5.2, it will be seen that the following expressions relate the two codes:

$$\left.\begin{array}{l} A_0 = \overline{G}_0.A_1 + G_0.\overline{A}_1 \\ A_1 = \overline{G}_1.A_2 + G_1.\overline{A}_2 \\ A_2 = \overline{G}_2.A_3 + G_2.\overline{A}_3 \end{array}\right\} \quad \textit{Exclusive-Or operations}$$

$$A_3 = G_3$$

A suitable arrangement is set out in Figure 5–29 and the only detailed design required is that of a two input *Exclusive-Or* gate. Many arrangements are possible to implement this operation but let us consider an *Exclusive-Or* gate made up of standard logic gates, as in Figure 5–30.

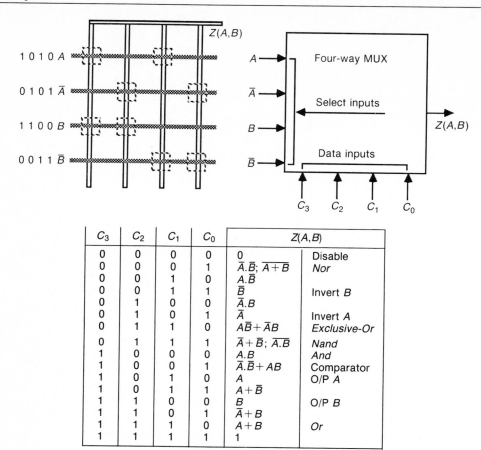

C_3	C_2	C_1	C_0	$Z(A,B)$	
0	0	0	0	0	Disable
0	0	0	1	$\overline{A}.\overline{B}$; $\overline{A+B}$	Nor
0	0	1	0	$A.\overline{B}$	
0	0	1	1	$\overline{B}$	Invert B
0	1	0	0	$\overline{A}.B$	
0	1	0	1	$\overline{A}$	Invert A
0	1	1	0	$A\overline{B}+\overline{A}B$	Exclusive-Or
0	1	1	1	$\overline{A}+\overline{B}$; $\overline{A.B}$	Nand
1	0	0	0	$A.B$	And
1	0	0	1	$\overline{A}.\overline{B}+AB$	Comparator
1	0	1	0	A	O/P A
1	0	1	1	$A+\overline{B}$	
1	1	0	0	B	O/P B
1	1	0	1	$\overline{A}+B$	
1	1	1	0	$A+B$	Or
1	1	1	1	1	

Figure 5–28 General logic function block

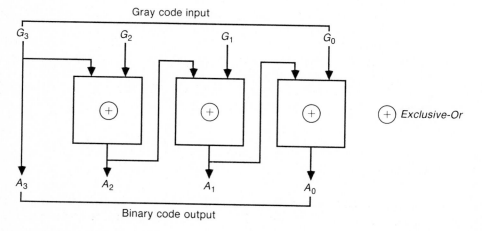

Figure 5–29 Gray to binary code converter

Table 5-2 Conversion from Gray to binary code

Gray code				Binary code			
G_3	G_2	G_1	G_0	A_3	A_2	A_1	A_0
0	0	0	0	0	0	0	0
0	0	0	1	0	0	0	1
0	0	1	1	0	0	1	0
0	0	1	0	0	0	1	1
0	1	1	0	0	1	0	0
0	1	1	1	0	1	0	1
0	1	0	1	0	1	1	0
0	1	0	0	0	1	1	1
1	1	0	0	1	0	0	0
1	1	0	1	1	0	0	1
1	1	1	1	1	0	1	0
1	1	1	0	1	0	1	1
1	0	1	0	1	1	0	0
1	0	1	1	1	1	0	1
1	0	0	1	1	1	1	0
1	0	0	0	1	1	1	1

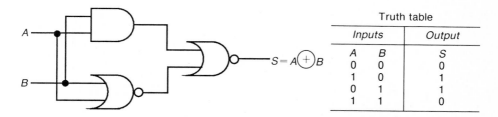

	Truth table	
Inputs		Output
A	B	S
0	0	0
1	0	1
0	1	1
1	1	0

Figure 5-30 One possible arrangement for an *Exclusive-Or* gate

A mask layout for this arrangement is presented in Figure 5–31 and it will be noted that the p-well and p$^+$ mask outlines are included in the layout together with the two substrate connections. Simulation of the design yields the results given in Figure 5–32. The simulator used was the ISD program PROBE and the circuit extractor NET. Likely circuit delays can be seen quite plainly.

5.5   Some clocked sequential circuits

5.5.1   Two-phase clocking

The clocked circuits to be considered here will be based on a two-phase non-overlapping clock signal as defined in essence in Figure 5–33.

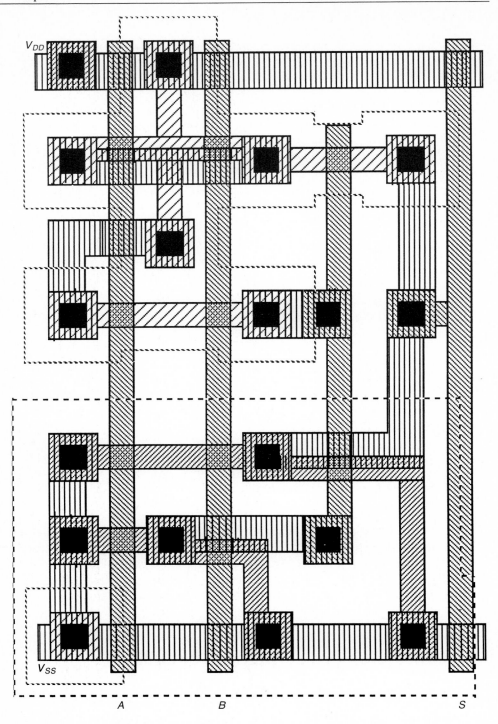

Figure 5–31 Mask layout for *Exclusive-Or* gate of figure 5–30

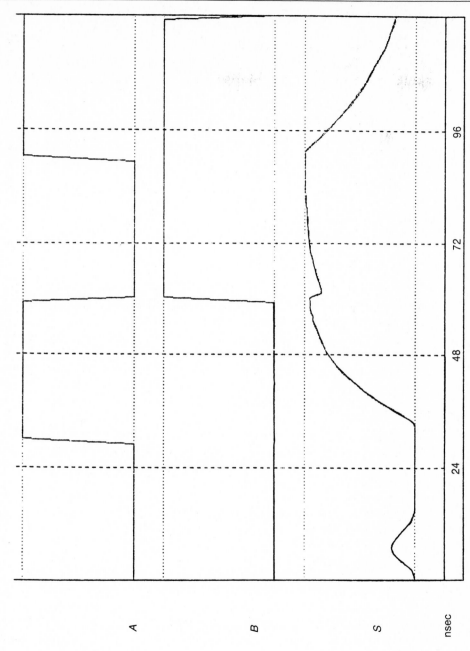

Figure 5-32 Simulation results

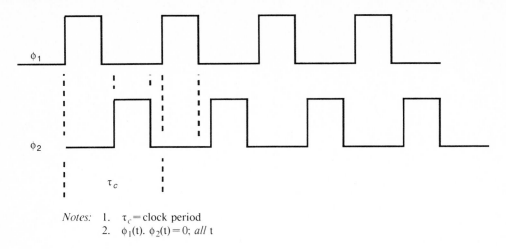

Notes: 1. τ_c = clock period
2. $\phi_1(t). \; \phi_2(t) = 0; \; all \; t$

Figure 5–33 Two-phase clocking

A two-phase clock offers a great deal of freedom in design if the clock period and the duration of the signals ϕ_1 and ϕ_2 are correctly chosen. If this is the case, data is allowed to become stable before any further transfer takes place and there is no chance of race conditions occurring.

Clocked circuitry is considerably easier to design than the corresponding asynchronous sequential circuitry. It does, however, pay the penalty of being slower. However, at this stage of learning VLSI design we will concentrate on two-phase clocked circuits alone and thus simplify design procedures.

When studying Figure 5–33 it is necessary to recognize the fact that ϕ_1 and ϕ_2 do not need to be symmetrical as shown. For a given clock period, each clock phase period and its associated underlap period can be varied if the need arises in optimizing a design.

A number of techniques are used to generate the two clock phases. One popular method is illustrated in Figure 5–34 and it will be seen that the output frequency is one-quarter of that of the input clock.

5.5.2 Charge storage

A necessary feature of sequential circuits is a facility to remember or take account of previous conditions. An obvious area of application of such a facility is in memory elements, registers, finite state machines, etc.

MOS technology takes advantage of the excellent insulating properties of silicon dioxide layers on integrated circuits to store charges in capacitors, including the gate-channel capacitance of transistors. Such storage is known as *dynamic storage* since, in a reasonably short time, charges stored will leak away and have to be refreshed if data/conditions are to be retained.

Considering charges on the gate capacitance, the leaking away of the charge is mainly due to leakage currents I_s across the channel to substrate reversed biased

Input clock

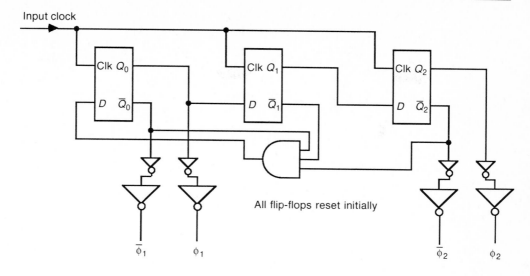

Figure 5–34 Two-phase clock generator using D flip-flops

diode. At room temperature and for typical 5 μm dimensions and voltages, this current is in the order of 0.1 nA, and so an approximate idea of holding time can be obtained from the simple circuit model of Figure 5–35 which considers $1 \square C_g$ initially charged to 5 volts.

This simple model indicates storage times of up to, say, 0.25 milliseconds to discharge from V_{DD} to V_{inv} ($=0.5V_{DD}$), but it should be noted that current I_s doubles for every 10°C rise in temperature so that the storage time is halved.

5.5.3 Dynamic register element

The basic dynamic register element is shown in Figure 5–36 in mixed stick/circuit notation and may be seen to consist of three transistors for nMOS and four for CMOS to store one bit in complemented form. The element's operation is simple to appreciate. $(V_{in})_t$ is clocked in by ϕ_1 (or ϕ_2) of the clock and charges the gate capacitance C_g of the inverter to V_{in}. If subscript t is taken to represent the time during which ϕ_1 (say) is at logic 1 and subscript $t+1$ is taken to indicate the period during

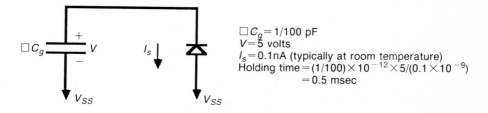

$\square C_g = 1/100$ pF
$V = 5$ volts
$I_s = 0.1$nA (typically at room temperature)
Holding time $= (1/100) \times 10^{-12} \times 5/(0.1 \times 10^{-9})$
$= 0.5$ msec

Figure 5–35 Simple stored charge model

which ϕ_1 is at logic 0, then the output available will be $(\overline{V}_{in})_{t+1}$ which will persist due to the stored charge until C_g discharges or until the next ϕ_1 signal occurs.

If uncomplemented storage is essential, the basic element is modified as indicated in Figure 5–37 and will be seen to consist of six transistors for nMOS and eight for CMOS. Data clocked in on ϕ_1 is stored on C_{g1} and the corresponding output appears at the output of inverter 1. On ϕ_2 this value is clocked in and stored on C_{g2} where the output of inverter 2 then presents the 'true' data. Note that data read in on ϕ_1 is not available at the output until after the next ϕ_2 of the clock.

Dynamic storage elements and the corresponding registers are used in situations where signals are updated frequently (i.e. at <0.25 msec intervals).

5.5.4 A dynamic shift register

Cascading the basic elements of Figure 5–37 gives a serial shift register arrangement which may be extended to n bits. A four-bit serial shift register is illustrated in Figure 5–38. Data bits are shifted in when $\phi_1.LD$ is present, one bit being entered into the register on each ϕ_1 signal (while LD is logic 1). Each bit is stored in C_{g1} as it is entered and then transferred complemented to C_{g2} on the next ϕ_2. Thus, after ϕ_1 and following ϕ_2 signals the bit is present uncomplemented on the output of inverter 2. On the next ϕ_1 the next input bit is stored in C_{g1} and simultaneously the first bit is passed into inverter pair 3 and 4 by being stored in C_{g3}, and so on. It will be seen that bits are clocked to the right along the shift register on each pair of ϕ_1 and following ϕ_2 signals. Once four bits are stored, the data is present in parallel form if desired on the inverter outputs and is available for further serial transfers from the inverter 8 if $\phi_1.RD$ is high (where RD is the read signal).

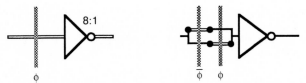

(a) nMOS pass transistor switched (b) CMOS transmission gate switched

Figure 5–36 Basic inverting dynamic storage cells

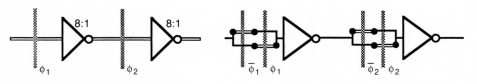

(a) nMOS pass transistor switched   (b) CMOS transmission gate switched

Figure 5–37 Non-inverting dynamic storage cells

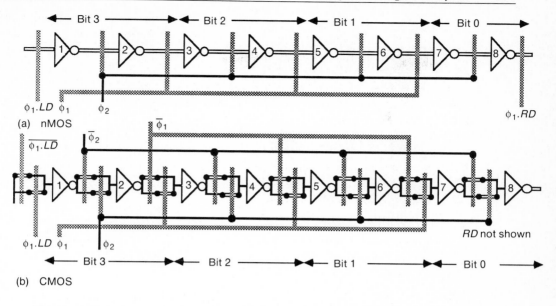

Figure 5–38 Four-bit dynamic shift registers (nMOS and CMOS)

Many variations of this basic arrangement are possible, but in general they are all based on the basic cell consisting of an inverter and a pass transistor or a transmission gate. Suitable standard cells are shown in stick diagram form in Figure 5–39 with the corresponding mask layouts as Figure 5–40. Note that two nMOS layouts are given (using butting and buried contacts respectively) and one possible CMOS layout is suggested.

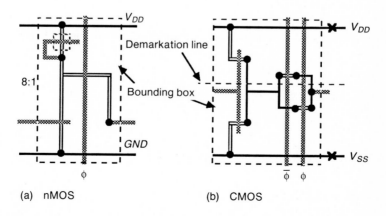

Figure 5–39 Stick diagrams for shift register cells

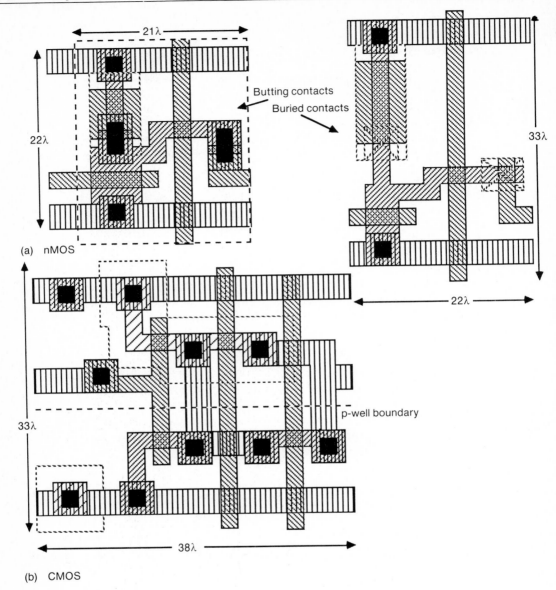

Butting contacts
Buried contacts

(a) nMOS

p-well boundary

(b) CMOS

Figure 5–40 Mask layouts for nMOS and CMOS shift register cells
(See also Color Plate 2)

5.6 Other system considerations

When designing at leaf cell level it is easy to lose sight of overall system requirements and restrictions. In particular, the use of buses to interconnect subsystems and circuits must always be most carefully considered; such matters and the current-carrying capacity of aluminum wiring used for V_{DD} and *GND* or V_{SS} rails are often overlooked completely.

5.6.1 The precharged bus concept

Bus structures carrying data or control signals are generally long and connected to and through a significant number of circuits and subsystems. Thus, the bus capacitances are appreciable and thought must be given to the manner in which any bus line is to be driven. Otherwise, the propagation of signals may be a slow process.

There are three classes of bus — passive, active, and precharged. A *passive* bus rail is a floating rail to which signals may be connected from drivers through pass transistors to propagate along the bus and from which signals may be taken also through pass transistors (see Figure 5–41).

A form of *active* bus is to treat the bus rail as a wired *Nor* connection which has a common pull-up $R_{p.u.}$ and pull-down transistor or transistor pairs where there are circuits which can be selected to drive the bus. Signals are taken off the bus through pass transistors and the general arrangement is given as Figure 5–42. This arrangement is not suited to CMOS designs.

The passive bus suffers from ratio problems in that for reasonable area restrictions on the bus drivers the bus will be slow to respond, particularly for the $\triangle V$(logic 0 to 1) transitions, due to the relatively high value pull-up resistance of the drivers and the associated series pass transistor or transmission gate.

The active bus is better in that more time is available for the bus to charge to V_{DD}, since $R_{p.u.}$ is always connected to the bus and there are no series pass transistors between $R_{p.u.}$ and the bus. However, there are still ratio problems which limit the speed of the bus if reasonable area is to be occupied.

The *precharged* bus approach limits the effects of bus capacitance in that a single pull-up transistor which is turned on only during ϕ_2 (say) provides for the bus

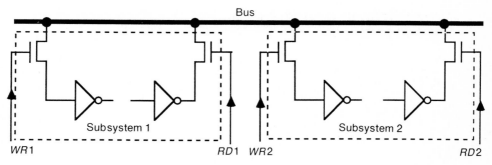

Note: For CMOS the pass transistors could become transmission gates.

Figure 5–41 Passive bus — nMOS or CMOS

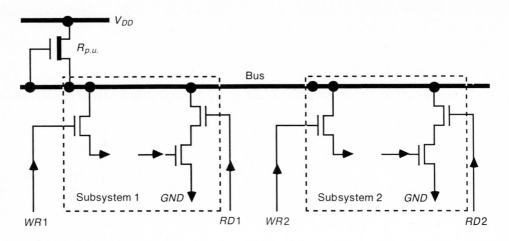

Figure 5-42 Active bus (not CMOS)

to charge during the ϕ_2 on period; the size of this transistor can be made relatively large (i.e. a low $L{:}W$ ratio) and, therefore, have a low resistance. There are no ratio problems between it and the drivers since they are never turned on at the same time. The drivers merely pull down or not the precharged bus by discharging C_{Bus}. The arrangement is given as Figure 5-43 and, in effect, a ratioless precharged wired *Nor* circuit is formed by the bus system. However, care must be taken in nMOS

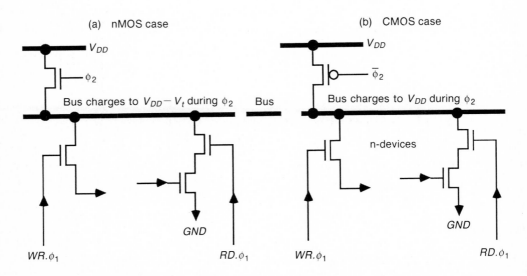

Figure 5-43 Precharged bus — nMOS and CMOS

systems in using logic 1 levels from the bus in that the bus never reaches V_{DD}, due to threshold voltage effects in the precharging transistor.

Bus structures are widely used and will be further discussed in following sections of this text.

5.6.2 Power dissipation and current calculation for CMOS circuits

For pseudo-nMOS type circuitry current and power are readily determined in a manner similar to nMOS. However, for complementary inverter-based circuits we may proceed by first recognizing that the very short current pulses which flow when circuits of this type are switching between states are negligible in comparison with charge and discharge currents of circuit capacitances. Then we may see that overall dissipation is composed of two terms:

1. P_1 the dissipation due to leakage current I_1 through 'off' transistors. Consequently, for n devices we have

$$P_1 = nI_1 V_{DD}$$

where $i_1 = 0.1$ nA, typically at room temperature

2. P_s the dissipation due to energy supplied to charge and discharge the capacitances associated with each switching circuit. Assuming that the output capacitance of a stage can be combined with the input capacitance(s) of the stage(s) it is driving and represented as C_L then, for n identical circuits switched by a square wave at frequency f it may be shown that

$$P_s = C_L V_{DD}^2 f$$

The total power dissipation P_T is thus

$$P_T = P_1 + P_s$$

from which the average current may be deduced.

5.6.3 Current limitations for V_{DD} and GND (V_{SS}) rails

A problem often ignored is that of metal migration for high current densities in metal conductors. If the current density exceeds a threshold value J_{th} then one finds that metal atoms begin to move in the direction of the current. For aluminum conductors this threshold value is

$$J_{th} \doteq 1 \text{ to } 2 \text{ mA/}\mu\text{m}^2$$

The danger points occur where there is a narrowing of or constriction in the conductor. At these points the current density is at its highest and metal is transported from the constricted regions which, in consequence, become even more constricted and eventually may blow like a fuse. The actual mechanism of atomic

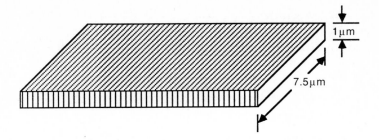

Figure 5-44 A minimum size metal path or wire

transport of metal in a thin film carrying relatively high currents is well understood, but the science of predicting the location and the time of such occurrences is not well-developed.

By way of example we may consider the question of how many nMOS 8:1 inverters (as in a dynamic S/R) can be driven by a minimum size conductor. From design rules, the metal is 3λ wide which corresponds to 7.5 μm. The thickness of the conductor is about 1 μm as shown in Figure 5–44.

For 8:1 inverter (8:1; 1:1):

$$R = (8 + 1) \times 10^4$$
$$= 90 \text{ k}\Omega$$

Therefore

$$I = \frac{5}{90} = 0.06 \text{ mA per inverter}$$

and with a wire cross-section of 7.5 μm², a current of 7.5 mA can be supplied. Thus ~ 125 inverters can be driven.

An approach that may be pursued to increase the current density above the specified critical limit is by taking advantage of the 'Relaxation Effect' that occurs in the metal when electron flow occurs in short pulses rather than at a steady state level.

The important factor to be illustrated here is that the standard width metal conductors can only support a subsystem of *modest* size. Thus, in a design of any complexity we must ensure that this fact is not overlooked.

5.7 Tutorial 2

1. (a) Construct a color-coded stick diagram to represent the design of the following integrated nMOS and CMOS structures *and* indicate pull-up/pull-down ratios in each case:
    (i)   three-input *Nand* gate;
    (ii) three-input *Nor* gate;

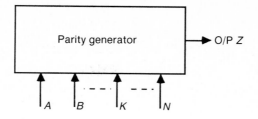

Figure 5–45 Parity generator outline

   (iii)   8:1 multiplexer circuit incorporating an enable control line;
   (iv)   a dual-serial shift register capable of holding and shifting (right) two four-bit words;
   (v)   a selectively loadable dynamic register to hold one four-bit word (parallel).

  (b) For question 1(a)(iv) draw the corresponding *transistor* circuit diagram.

2. Construct a stick diagram for an nMOS or CMOS parity generator as in Figure 5–45. The required response is such that $Z = 1$ if there is an *even* number (including zero) of 1s on the inputs and $Z = 0$ if there is an odd number. (Use simple color coding for stick diagrams.)

     Configure your design in a modular expandable fashion so that the inputs could be increased to five or more quite readily using the basic cell suggested in Figure 5–46.

3. (a) Construct a color-coded stick diagram to represent the design of an integrated nMOS structure to decode the three input lines E_0, E_1, and E_2 into eight output lines Z_0, Z_1, ... Z_7, in accordance with the following truth table.

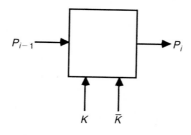

Figure 5–46 Parity generator cell

Truth table

E_2	E_1	E_0	Z_0	Z_1	Z_2	Z_3	Z_4	Z_5	Z_6	Z_7
0	0	0	0	1	1	1	1	1	1	1
0	0	1	1	0	1	1	1	1	1	1
0	1	0	1	1	0	1	1	1	1	1
0	1	1	1	1	1	0	1	1	1	1
1	0	0	1	1	1	1	0	1	1	1
1	0	1	1	1	1	1	1	0	1	1
1	1	0	1	1	1	1	1	1	0	1
1	1	1	1	1	1	1	1	1	1	0

(b)   Discuss the expandability or otherwise of your structure and the ease with which it would translate to CMOS.

4.   A priority encoder is a combinational circuit in which each input is assigned a priority with respect to the other inputs, and the output code generated at any time is that associated with the highest priority input then present.

   Construct a color-coded stick diagram to implement such a structure as in the following table with Figure 5–47.

Truth table

E_2	E_1	E_0	P_1	P_0
0	0	0	0	0
0	0	1	1	1
0	1	0	1	0
0	1	1	1	0
1	0	0	0	1
1	0	1	0	1
1	1	0	0	1
1	1	1	0	1

5.   Referring to section 5.4.6 and to the development of an *Exclusive-Or* gate, design an alternative form of two I/P *Exclusive-Or* using transmission gates and inverters only. Your design should include a stick diagram and a mask layout.

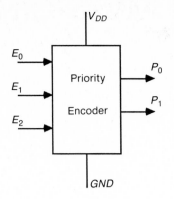

Truth table				
E_2	E_1	E_0	P_1	P_0
0	0	0	0	0
0	0	1	1	1
0	1	0	1	0
0	1	1	1	0
1	0	0	0	1
1	0	1	0	1
1	1	0	0	1
1	1	1	0	1

Figure 5–47   Priority encoder

6 | Scaling of MOS circuits

In the design processes postulated by Mead and Conway and used in this text, it has been the practice to dimension all layouts in terms of λ. A value may then be allocated to λ, prior to manufacture, which is in line with the capabilities of the silicon foundry or is determined by current technology and/or meets the specifications which have been set out for the circuit. The elegance of this approach lies in the fact that the design rules have been formulated in such a way as to allow limited direct scaling of the dimensions of circuits, so that today's design is not automatically outdated when line widths are reduced (i.e. the value allocated to λ is reduced), by advances in tomorrow's technology. This chapter discusses scaling and its effect on performance and indicates some problems and ultimate limitations.

6.1   Scaling factor α

First-order scaling theory indicates that, over a relatively wide range of scaling factor α, the characteristics of a MOS transistor can be maintained and the desired operation achieved if parameters of the device are all scaled by the same factor α. For example, all dimensions, including those *vertical* to the silicon surface, can be scaled by factor α as indicated in Figure 6–1. It should be noted that *substrate doping* is also adjusted by factor α so that depletion region widths and so on scale accordingly. It is also necessary to scale supply rail voltages to keep electric field strengths constant. The effects of scaling transistors between one value for λ and another are indicated in Table 6–1.

The entries under 'Effects' in Table 6–1 are mostly indicative of beneficial results as a consequence of scaling to reduce device dimensions. For example, if direct scaling is possible over a wide range of values for α, say 10:1, then the components/unit area will increase by a factor of 100 (50,000 transistors per chip now will become 5,000,000 per chip if 10:1 scaling is possible in the future). From

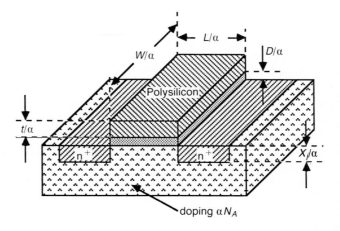

Figure 6–1   Scaled nMOS transistor (pMOS similar)

Table 6-1 Effects of scaling the value allocated to λ for transistors

Parameters		Scaling	Effects
Length	L		Channel length to width ratio ... unchanged
Width	W		Gate area ... reduced by $1/\alpha^2$
Gate oxide thickness	D	$1/\alpha$	Gate dielectric thickness reduced by $1/\alpha$
Junction depth	X_j		Gate capacitance $\square C_g$ reduced by $1/\alpha$
Layer thickness	t		Parasitic capacitances (fX_j) reduced by $1/\alpha$
			Resistance layer thickness reduced by $1/\alpha$
Substrate doping	N	α	Resistivity ρ reduced by $1/\alpha$
			Sheet resistance $R_s = \dfrac{\rho}{t}$ ... unchanged
			Time delay $\tau = R_s \square C_g$ reduced by $1/\alpha$
			Inverter/gate delay ... reduced by $1/\alpha$
Supply voltage	V_{DD}	$1/\alpha$	Current I reduced by $1/\alpha$
			Cross-section of conductors reduced by $1/\alpha^2$
			Current density increased by α
			Logic levels reduced by $1/\alpha$
			Power dissipation P_d reduced by $1/\alpha^2$
			Power–speed product reduced by $1/\alpha^3$
			Switching energy/circuit $f\square C_g(V_{DD})^2$ reduced by $1/\alpha^3$
			Components/unit area ⎫ increased by α^2
			Complexity/chip ⎭
			Power dissipated/unit area ... unchanged

Note: α is assumed to be an integer. *f* is used to indicate 'function of'.

the table, we can also see that the power dissipation of such a chip will not be increased over present designs if direct scaling of all parameters as suggested is effected. However, circuit designs scaled by 10:1 should be 10 times faster and since power dissipation per circuit is reduced by 100:1, the power speed product is reduced by 1000:1. The same factor of 1000:1 reduction also applies to switching energy.

Engineering is a field of endeavor where one never expects something for nothing and the area of VLSI system design is no exception. Scaling does have some serious problems, one of which is the increased current density in conductors. This will be a particular problem for V_{DD} and GND or V_{SS} rails where on scaling by say 10:1 the consequent 10:1 increase in current density can cause failures of designs which are directly scaled down. A second serious problem concerns the loss of a marked distinction between the logic 1 and logic 0 voltage levels which results from scaled down supply voltage. For example, if the 5-volt supply rail voltage of present

IC designs is scaled by 10:1, the corresponding supply rail will be 0.5 volt with consequent narrow voltage margin and susceptibility to noise, sensitivity to IR drops, etc.

6.2 Some functional limitations to scaling

We have already seen that direct scaling is not possible where current densities in the unscaled circuit are already near the maximum allowable limit. If such a circuit is scaled, current densities are increased by the scaling factor and metal migration and subsequent 'blowing' of conducting paths is likely. This problem has a solution at the design stage; it is possible to overspecify conducting path widths and/or arrange the current distribution paths in such a way as to allow for limited future scaling by keeping unscaled current densities below the maximum allowable by a factor equal to or in excess of the likely scaling factor. The solution will be at the expense of area and some increased complexity in the unscaled circuit.

Other limitations arise due to the scaling of supply voltage V_{DD}. We have already discussed the consequent loss of a 'healthy' voltage difference between logic levels 1 and 0. A further voltage scaling-induced problem results from the scaling of threshold voltages, and in particular V_{tp}, which results in significant reductions in the voltage which is turning off a pass transistor in the nonconducting state. In other words, the voltage which is turning off the pass transistor is the difference between the gate voltage and the threshold voltage, that is, $V_{gs} - V_{tp}$. Up to now we have tacitly assumed that for voltages below the threshold, a pass transistor presents a very high resistance between source and drain. However, it may be shown that the off resistance R_{off} is such that

$$R_{off} \propto \frac{1}{e^{(V_{gs} - V_{tp})/(kT/q)}}$$

where

k is Boltzmann's constant

$$\left\{ \begin{matrix} 1.38 \times 10^{-23} \text{ joule/}°K \\ \text{or } 8.63 \times 10^{-5} \text{ eV/}°K \end{matrix} \right\}$$

q is electron charge ($= 1.6 \times 10^{-19}$ coulomb)
T is temperature (°K) (300°K $\doteqdot$ room temperature)
kT/q evaluates to just under 26 millivolt at 300°K

Thus for R_{off} to be high $(V_{gs} - V_{tp})/(kT/q)$ must be as large as possible and negative. The effects of scaling on threshold voltage may thus be readily assessed, assuming that $V_{gs} = 0$ and that V_{tp} unscaled $\geqslant 1.0$ volt and that V_{tp} scaled (5:1, say) is consequently about one-fifth of this. In the unscaled case, there will be a ratio of 38:1 between $V_{gs} - V_{tp}$ and kT/q. In the scaled case, this ratio drops to $\doteqdot 8:1$.

Thus a very significant decrease in off resistance is likely on scaling. This can present problems where storage nodes are charged through and then isolated by pass transistors. Quite obviously the allowable refresh intervals must be greatly reduced in such circumstances.

A remedy for these problems lies in *not* fully scaling the supply rails by factor α. However, this results in increased electric field strengths and the consequent widening of depletion regions. Thus, the behavior of scaled devices in which V_{DD} is not fully scaled will not necessarily be that which is prediced for a fully scaled circuit. This may lead to difficulties including, perhaps, a failure to function at all. Therefore, such matters as are raised here should be considered most carefully when design scaling is contemplated.

As the channel length L is reduced, so the depletion regions around the source/substrate and drain/substrate junctions are brought closer together and, thus, depletion regions will occupy comparatively more of the total channel length. Eventually, further shortening of L will cause the depletion regions to meet and it will then be impossible to establish the channel between source and drain. Obviously, transistor action will then cease.

Depletion region width d for the junctions is given by

$$d = \sqrt{\frac{2\varepsilon_{Si}\varepsilon_0 V}{qN}}$$

where

ε_{Si} = relative permittivity of silicon ($\doteq 12$)
ε_0 = permittivity of free space ($= 8.85 \times 10^{-14}$ F/cm)
V = effective voltage across the junction = $V_a + V_B$
q = electron charge
N = doping level of substrate

Obviously, scaling the applied voltage V_a will help to reduce V in this expression, but as voltages are scaled down an increasingly large proportion of V is contributed by the junction potential V_B. Note that

$$V_B = \frac{kT}{q} \ln \frac{N_A N_D}{n_i}$$

where N_D is the doping level in the source or drain diffusion regions and N_A is the substrate doping, or vice versa, and n_i is the intrinsic carrier concentration in silicon.

Thus depletion region widths do not scale directly when V_a is small. However, when $V_a > V_B$, the substrate doping can be increased to reduce depletion region width. Also, the electric fields in the depletion regions will be increased for any applied voltage and, thus, voltage restrictions will apply on scaling to avoid breakdown. Similarly, there is an increase in electric field strength in the oxide adjacent to the depletion layers at the surface of the silicon. Thus, a voltage restriction is necessary to avoid both junction and oxide breakdown.

The breakdown of silicon and silicon dioxide is a well-studied subject and it is possible at any voltage to calculate the maximum doping level that can be used

Channel length L (μm)

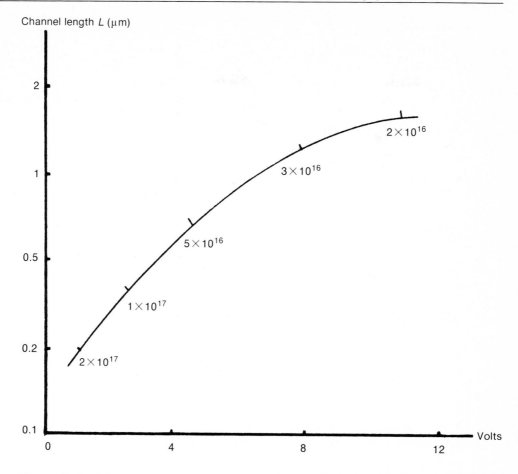

Figure 6-2 Substrate doping levels versus channel length and applied voltages

for a particular channel length L. This information is presented graphically as Figure 6-2. However, it should be noted that nonuniform doping profiles and junction curvature will affect the relationship.

An ultimate physical limitation can be calculated for L and this is in the region of 0.25 μm. Below this value transistors will no longer function. This corresponds to a value of $\lambda = 0.125$ μm which is well below current values of around 1 to 2 μm used in commercial processing.

The practice in the industry is some guide to scaling factors which have been used as technology advances. Some typical nMOS device parameters over a period of eight years have been set out in Table 6-2. Contemporary CMOS parameters are given for comparison.

Table 6–2 Scaling as a function of time for nMOS

Parameters	Enhancement type 1972	Depletion type 1976	HMOS 1980	CMOS 1985
Length; L	6 µm	6 µm	2 µm	2 µm
Gate oxide thickness; D	1200 Å	1200 Å	400 Å	400Å
Junction depth; X_j	2 µm	2 µm	0.8 µm	0.25 µm
Supply voltage; V_{DD}	4–15 volts	4–8 volts	2–4 volts	2–5 volts
Gate delay	12–15 nsec	4 nsec	0.4 nsec	1 nsec
Power dissipation; P_d	1.5 mW	1 mW	0.4 mW	0.2 mW ⎫
Power–speed product	18 pJ	4 pJ	0.2 pJ	0.2pJ ⎬ @ 1 MHz

6.3 Scaling of wires and interconnections

So far we have considered scaling factors as they affect MOS transistor structures. Quite obviously, circuit 'wiring' and contacts are also scaled as dimensions allocated to λ are reduced, but resistivity is not.

Consider a conductor (wire) of length L, width W, thickness t, and resistivity ρ

Resistance unscaled $R_u = \dfrac{\rho L}{Wt}$

Resistance scaled $R_{sc} = \dfrac{\rho L/\alpha}{Wt/\alpha^2}$

that is

$$R_{sc} = \alpha R_u$$

Another way of looking at this is that sheet resistance $R_s = \rho/t$ must increase by α when t is scaled by $1/\alpha$. Since currents are reduced by factor α, IR drops in wires remain *constant*.

However, when viewed relative to the circuit voltages, which are also scaled down by α, this represents a *relative increase* by factor α.

Similarly, the time response of scaled wires

$$\tau_{sc} = (\alpha R)(C/\alpha) = RC = constant = \tau$$

Thus time delays of wires and IR drops do *not* scale. Another factor is current density

$$J = \frac{I}{Wt}$$

When scaling takes place

$$J_{sc} = \frac{I/\alpha}{Wt/\alpha^2} = \alpha J$$

Thus, current density in wires increases by the scaling factor.

Similar reasoning can be applied to the voltage drops in contacts which will scale up by α^2 relative to the scaled circuit voltages.

These results are summarized in Table 6–3.

Table 6–3   Scaling of interconnects

Parameters	Scaling factor
Line resistance; R	α
Line voltage drop; V_d	1
Normalized line voltage drop $\dfrac{V_d}{V}$	α
Current density; J	α
Normalized contact; voltage drop; V_c/V	α^2

6.4   Latch-up in scaled CMOS circuits

A significant factor in determining the absolute spacing between p-regions and n-regions in CMOS circuits is the susceptibility to latch-up.

Although nMOS and pMOS structures can be individually scaled into the submicron range, the spacing between nMOS and pMOS devices cannot be arbitrarily scaled down without the danger of inducing latch-up conditions. Care must be taken in scaling.

6.5   Some aspects of fabrication

Silicon wafers from three inches (75 mm) to six inches in diameter are usually patterned through a series of masks, each of which represents a layer and each of which exposes the entire wafer area. Masks must be registered with respect to each other to close tolerance limits.

Each wafer mask representing the pattern for one layer is formed from a chip mask representing that layer for one chip, which is then stepped and repeated over the entire wafer mask area. In general, then, each wafer mask represents a particular layer for a large number of chips. As each subsequent layer is to be patterned, a different mask is required which has then to be positioned and aligned.

Two major problems are experienced in this process:

1. *Runout* which occurs for $\lambda < 0.5$ μm and has the effect of causing successive patterning steps to misalign over a significant area of the wafer. The usual remedy for runout problems is to deliberately expose less than the full wafer area.

2. *Resolution* of photolithographic processes becomes a serious problem when $\lambda < 0.5$ μm.

A remedy for the resolution problems of photolithography is to be had in the newer technologies of electron beam lithography and ion implantation. For example, rather than exposing photo resists through photographic masks, it is possible to 'expose' suitable resists by guided electron beams. There appears to be no significant practical limit to the resolution of electron beam-based processing, although achieving the required current density in the beam to allow the patterning of large numbers (e.g. 10^7) of resolution elements in a reasonable time presents some practical problems. As one might expect, large beam currents and small spot diameters are in conflict. However, the limits of particle beam lithography are not fundamental but are of practical and economic origin.

7 | PLAs and finite state machines

7.1   Some thoughts on combinational logic

It is hard to envisage a digital system of any complexity that will not need combinational logic as part of its architecture. MOS VLSI circuitry includes pass transistor and transmisstion gate switches, inverters, and *Nand* and *Nor* gate arrangements from which it is possible to realize any combinational logic requirements.

A well-established body of theory and procedures is available for expressing, manipulating, and simplifying combinational logic requirements. When realizing such requirements it is frequently convenient to manipulate logical expressions into their sum of products (SOP) form. This form is easily turned into two-level *And–Or* logic or, alternatively, into the equivalent *Nand–Nand* logic. Logic circuits for a multiple output function of five variables are given as Figure 7–1 by way of illustration. Figure 7–1(a) presents an arrangement in *And–Or* form while Figure 7–1(b) suggests an equivalent *Nand–Nand* circuit.

Conventional switching theory minimization processes can be applied to both single and multiple output functions; the arrangements arrived at generally provide the minimum number of logic gates with the minimum number of inputs but do not result in structures which are regular. The minimization processes also impose the interconnection topology since the connections are specified in the minimized expressions.

A regular structure or structures to realize combinational logic expressions and suitable for implementation in silicon must therefore be sought.

7.2   Some alternatives to simple combinational logic

In seeking regular structures to realize the requirements of combinational logic, we can consider the use of memory arrays or multiplexers

7.2.1   Read-only memory (ROM) or programmable read-only memory (PROM) realizations of combinational logic

Considering the multiple output function realized in gate logic in Figure 7–1, the same functions can be readily 'programmed in' to a ROM (or PROM), as shown in Figure 7–2. Here the variables a to e are connected to the PROM address lines A_4 to A_0 respectively, so that a is given the weight 16, b the weight 8, c the weight 4, d the weight 2, and e weight 1. Thus any particular combination of the variables a to e will select a given location in memory and, in fact, this will be the location, the address of which is equal to the minterm number for that combination of variables specified. Thus a simple conversion of each output function into minterm form, as shown in Figure 7–2, will indicate those locations to be programmed with 1s, the particular bits in each location being determined by the allocation of data lines to particular output function. For example, we have allocated data bit D_1 to function

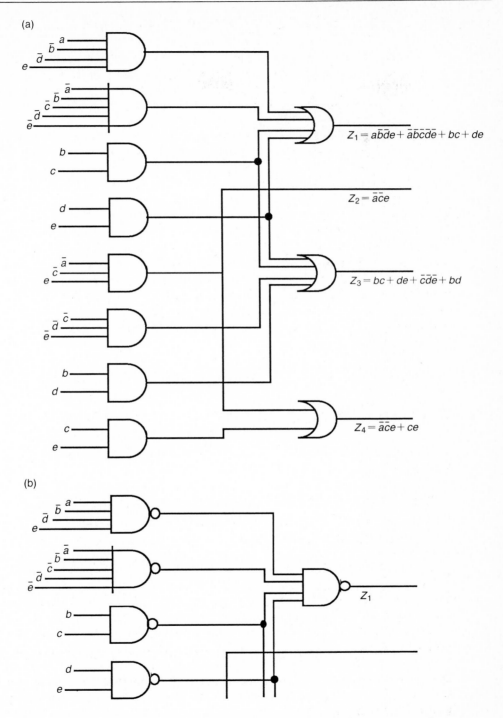

Figure 7-1   Logic gate realization of multioutput combinational functions

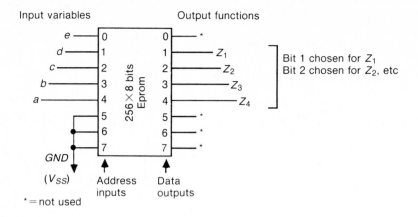

Output functions

$Z_1 = a\bar{b}\bar{d}e + \bar{a}\bar{b}\bar{c}\bar{d}\bar{e} + bc + de = \Sigma\, m\,(0,3,7,11,12,13,14,15,17,19,$
$\qquad\qquad\qquad\qquad\qquad\qquad\qquad 21,23,27,28,29,30,31)$

$Z_2 = \bar{a}\bar{c}e \qquad\qquad\qquad\quad = \Sigma\, m\,(1,3,9,11)$

$Z_3 = bc + de + \bar{c}\bar{d}\bar{e} + bd \quad = \Sigma\, m\,(0,3,7,8,10,11,12,13,14,15,$
$\qquad\qquad\qquad\qquad\qquad\qquad\qquad 16,19,23,24,26,27,28,29,30,31)$

$Z_4 = \bar{a}\bar{c}e + ce \qquad\qquad\quad = \Sigma\, m\,(1,3,5,7,9,11,13,15,21,23,29,31)$

Location/address

	0	1	2	3	4	5	6	7	8	9	10	11	12	13	14	15	16	17	18	19	20	21	22	23	24	25	26	27	28	29	30	31
Bit 1	1	0	0	1	0	0	0	1	0	0	0	1	1	1	1	1	0	1	0	1	0	1	0	1	0	0	0	1	1	1	1	1
Bit 2	0	1	0	1	0	0	0	0	0	1	0	1	0	0	0	0	0	0	0	0	0	0	0	0	0	0	0	0	0	0	0	0
Bit 3	1	0	0	1	0	0	0	1	1	0	1	1	1	1	1	1	1	0	0	1	0	0	0	1	1	0	1	1	1	1	1	1
Bit 4	0	1	0	1	0	1	0	1	0	1	0	1	0	1	0	1	0	0	0	0	0	1	0	1	0	0	0	0	0	1	0	1

All other locations and bits may be left clear

Figure 7-2 ROM realization of combinational functions

Z_1, D_2 to function Z_2, etc. Since five variables cannot generate an address higher than 31, only the first 32 locations of the PROM are programmed, as shown in Figure 7-2.

Thus a memory array provides a regular structure which is often used for combinational logic but suffers from the disadvantages that it is often wasteful of space and access times can be slow.

7.2.2 Multiplexer-based realization of combinational logic

Another regular structure which can be used is the multiplexer. Consider just one of the output functions introduced in Figure 7-1 and expanded into mintern form in Figure 7-2. The function is

$$Z_1 = a\bar{b}\bar{d}e + \bar{a}\bar{b}\bar{c}\bar{d}\bar{e} + bc + de$$
$$= \Sigma m(0,3,7,11,12,13,14,15,17,19,21,23,27,28,29,30,31)$$

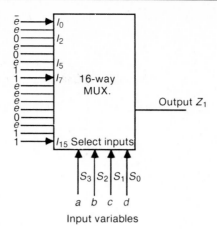

To realize function Z_1 the MUX input connections are:

Mux I/P	I_0	I_1	I_2	I_3	I_4	I_5	I_6	I_7	I_8	I_9	I_{10}	I_{11}	I_{12}	I_{13}	I_{14}	I_{15}
Minterms	0,1	2,3	4,5	6,7	8,9	10,11	12,13	14,15	16,17	18,19	20,21	22,23	24,25	26,27	28,29	30,31
Connection	$\bar{e}$	e	0	e	0	e	1	1	e	e	e	e	0	e	1	1

Figure 7–3 16-way multiplexer realization of combinational function (Z_1)

A 16-way (16:1) multiplexer circuit can be used to realize this function by, for example, connecting the select inputs to variables a, b, c, and d, as shown in Figure 7–3. With the connections given, multiplexer input I_0 will be selected when $abcd = 0000$, input I_1 will be selected when $abcd = 0001$, and so on; input I_{15} will be selected when $abcd = 1111$. Thus, input I_0 must cover minterms 0 and 1, I_1 minterms 2 and 3, etc., and I_{15} minterms 30 and 31. Thus, each input can be programmed as shown in the figure and function Z_1 will be realized. A similar approach can be taken to functions Z_2, Z_3, and Z_4.

The multiplexer provides a ready and regular solution to problems in up to five variables, but larger problems require cascaded multiplexers and buffers to avoid having large numbers of pass transistors or transmission gates in series.

Therefore, the multiplexer is not the general solution we would like but it is one which is useful for small problems and should, therefore, be borne in mind by the designer. A more general solution is an arrangement called a programmable logic array (PLA).

7.3   The programmable logic array (PLA)

Another solution to the mapping of irregular combinational logic functions into regular structures is provided by the PLA. The PLA provides the designer with a systematic and regular way of implementing multiple output functions of n variables in sum of products (SOP) form. The general arrangement of a PLA is given as

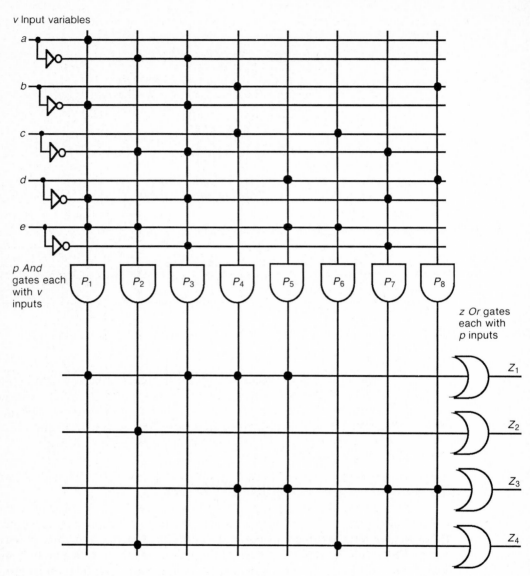

v Input variables

Note: $5 \times 8 \times 4$ PLA shown symbolically and programmed for:
$Z_1 = p_1 + p_3 + p_4 + p_5 \therefore Z_1 = a\bar{b}\bar{d}e + \bar{a}\bar{b}\bar{c}\bar{d}\bar{e} + bc + de$
$Z_2 = p_2 \qquad\qquad\quad \therefore Z_2 = \bar{a}\bar{c}e$
$Z_3 = p_4 + p_5 + p_7 + p_8 \therefore Z_3 = bc + de + \bar{c}\bar{d}\bar{e} + bd$
$Z_4 = p_2 + p_6 \qquad\quad \therefore Z_4 = \bar{a}\bar{c}e + ce$

Figure 7–4 $v \times p \times z$ PLA

Figure 7-4 and it may be seen to consist of a programmable two-level *And/Or* structure. Clearly, the structure is regular and may be expanded in any of its dimensions — the number of input variables v, the number of product (*And*) terms p, and the number of output functions (*Or* terms) z. It will also be noted that if there are v input variables, then for complete generality each of the product forming *And* gates must have v inputs, and if there are p product terms, each output *Or* gate must have p inputs if the PLA is to maintain generality within the constraints of its dimensions.

In practice, a range of 'off-the-shelf' PLAs is available to the TTL-based system designer. Typically, PLAs with 14 variable inputs, 96 product terms, and eight output functions are readily obtained, and much larger PLAs (e.g. with more than 200 product terms) are also available. Such elements are programmed by the manufacturer or by the user to meet requirements.

In VLSI, design, however, PLAs can be readily designed and must be 'programmed' during the design process. Thus for the VLSI designer PLAs are tailored to specific tasks with little wastage of functions or space. However, the PLA structure is regular and readily expanded, contracted, or modified during design. This contrasts sharply with the attributes of random logic.

In VLSI design our objective is to map circuits onto silicon to meet particular specifications. The way in which a PLA maps onto the chip may be indicated by a 'floor plan' which gives the notional areas and relative disposition of the particular circuits and subsystems. A floor plan for a PLA is given in Figure 7–5(a).

For MOS fabrication, *And* and *Or* gates are neither as simple nor as satisfactory as the *Nor* gate. Thus, we look to De Morgan's theorem to manipulate *And–Or* combinational logic requirements into *Nor* form.

For an n input *Nor* gate, we may write

$$\bar{X} = A + B + C + \ldots + N$$

where X is the output and A to N the inputs.

By De Morgan's theorem

$$X = \bar{A}.\bar{B}.\bar{C}.\ldots\bar{N}$$

In other words, the *Nor* gate is an *And* gate to inverted input levels.

Obviously, the output *Or* functions of the PLA can be realized with *Nor* gates each followed by an inverter. Thus, the requirements and floor plan of the PLA may be adapted to *Nor* gate form as in Figure 7–5(b). A MOS PLA realization for the multiple output functions used as an example in this chapter is presented in Figure 7–6.

It will be noted that Figure 7–6 is a PLA, tailored to meet the particular need and drawn in mixed circuit and logic symbol notation. Although not in mask layout form, it can be clearly seen how the factors v, p, and z affect the dimensions of the PLA. It will be shown, later in this chapter, how readily a PLA layout may be turned into stick diagram and then mask layout form. The PLA is drawn as an nMOS

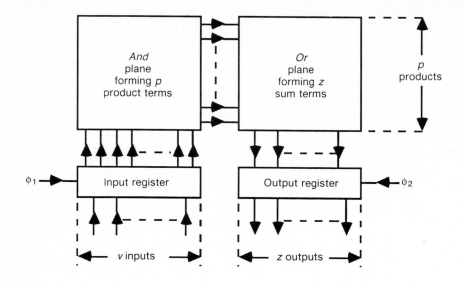

(a)   *And Or* based

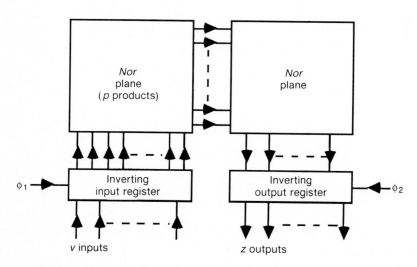

(b)   *Nor* based

Note: Dimensions are determined by v, p, and z as shown.

Figure 7–5   PLA floor plan

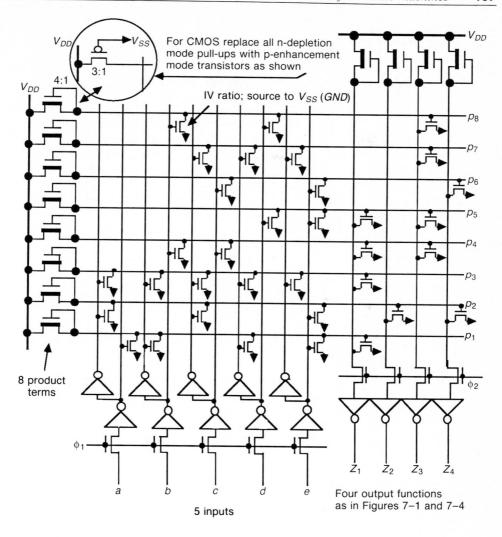

Figure 7–6 PLA arrangement for multiple output function

arrangement but converts readily to CMOS. One form of CMOS PLA is based on the pseudo nMOS *Nor* gate as indicated.

7.4 Finite state machines

The finite state machine is an important element in digital systems design and in the design of VLSI systems. Indeed, an entire digital system may be viewed as a hierarchy of nested finite state machines. In any digital system which is not purely combinational, sequential circuit or finite state machine design is essential.

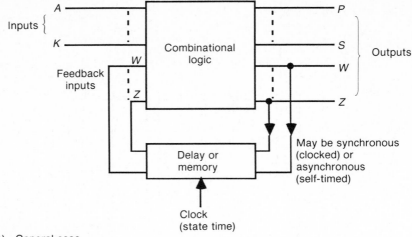

(a) General case

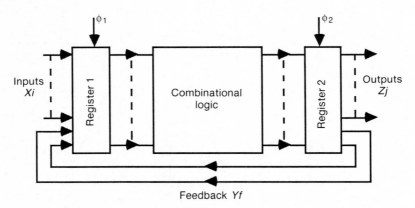

Feedback in a register transfer path implementing a finite state machine (synchronous)

(b) PLA form

Figure 7-7 State machine models

The general model of a state machine is given as Figure 7–7(a) and will be seen to comprise combinational logic with both independent and output dependent inputs. Enough outputs from the combinational logic must be fed back as input in order to generate the required number of finite states. For example, if n outputs are fed back, a maximum of 2^n states may be generated. There may also be outputs which are not fed back. In the general model shown there is a delay or memory interposed between the outputs fed back and the corresponding inputs. In general, this delay path may be clocked or unclocked and, in fact, the feedback may be direct and the delay, which is essential for the operation of the state machine, may be the delay contributed by the combinational logic itself so that no separate delay element is needed. A particular form of the general model is given in Figure 7–7(b) where the feedback path is via two clocked registers as shown. It will be seen quite clearly that this model is the PLA with some of the outputs fed back to the input register. Thus, the PLA with feedback links can be used to realize any finite state machine requirements. Referring to Figure 7–7(b), we can see that the feedback signal Yf (known as the state vector) is a binary number that may be regarded as identifying the present state of the machine. Yf together with the externally derived input(s) Xi is stored in Register 1 during ϕ_1 of the clock. Together, the combined inputs then propagate through the combinational logic to form the next state vector which is then clocked into register 2 on ϕ_2 of the clock. Register 2 provides both outputs Zj (which are not fed back) and a new state vector Yf. Clearly, this arrangement implements the requirements of a finite state machine, provided that the interval between the leading edges of the ϕ_1 and ϕ_2 clock signals is greater than the delay through the combinational logic (the *And* and *Or* planes of the PLA).

Thus the PLA is a straightforward and regular way of implementing finite state machines, the required transfer function being programmed into the combinational logic of the PLA during design. The easiest and most effective way to illustrate the design process for a finite state machine is by way of an example.

7.4.1 A PLA-based finite state machine design example

7.4.1.1 Specification

We are to design a circuit, the input to which are serial binary digits clocked by ϕ_2 and presented at an input W. The circuit is to produce an output $Z = 1$ when the circuit has detected an odd number of 1s in groups of three bits arriving at input W. Otherwise, Z is to be 0. Groups of three bits arriving at W do not overlap, that is, bits 1, 2, and 3 form the first group, bits 4, 5, and 6 the second, bits 7, 8, and 9 the third group of three, etc. Z is to be clocked by ϕ_2 and W can be clocked into the PLA by ϕ_1 since it is available following the preceding ϕ_2.

7.4.1.2 Procedure

Standard sequential circuit (finite state machine) design procedures may be followed in which the circuit requirements are set out as a state diagram which, in this case, may be merged to the form given as Figure 7–8. Secondary variables A, B, and C are allocated to identify each state.

From the state diagram it is then possible to draw up a state transition table (Table 7–1) which for any of the used combinations of A, B, C, and W shows the next state vector which is to be generated. The subscripts p and n are used to denote 'present' and 'next' states respectively. The only addition to this table for PLA implementation is the *And* term column, which identifies the product terms R_1 to R_{10} inclusive, which are formed from the present state vectors $A_pB_pC_p$ together with input W. At this stage, we can list these product terms (which are to be formed in the *And* plane) as indicated in Table 7–2. However, in allocating state vector conditions (secondary variables) to the five states of the circuit (Figure 7–8), not all combinations of A, B, and C were used. Thus these unused or 'don't care' conditions may be tested with each of the product terms in turn to see if any grouping and consequent simplification is possible. In this case, simplification is possible for all but two of the terms.

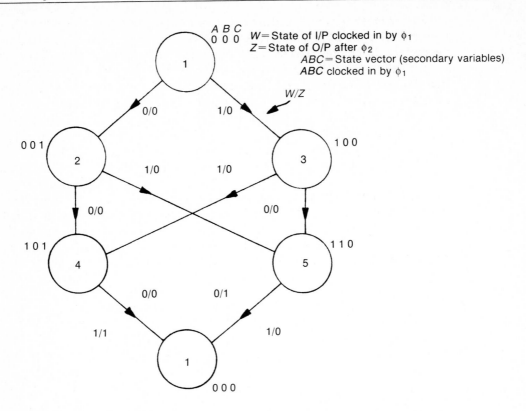

Figure 7–8 Merged state diagram (Mealy model) for design example

Table 7–1 State transition table for example

State number	Inputs				And term	Outputs			
	W	State vector				Next vector			Z
		A_p	B_p	C_p		A_n	B_n	C_n	
①	0	0	0	0	R_1	0	0	1	0
	1	0	0	0	R_2	1	0	0	0
②	0	0	0	1	R_3	1	0	1	0
	1	0	0	1	R_4	1	1	0	0
③	0	1	0	0	R_5	1	1	0	0
	1	1	0	0	R_6	1	0	1	0
④	0	1	0	1	R_7	0	0	0	0
	1	1	0	1	R_8	0	0	0	1
⑤	0	1	1	0	R_9	0	0	0	1
	1	1	1	0	R_{10}	0	0	0	0

Using the abbreviated identification ($R_1 - R_{10}$) for each product term and referring to Table 7–1, it is now possible to write expressions for the next state vectors A_n, B_n, C_n, and output Z. This is done by including in the expression for A_n, say, all those product (*And*) terms which are associated with a '1' entry under the next vector A_n (or output) column. Thus, applying the same procedure to each column

$$A_n = R_2 + R_3 + R_4 + R_5 + R_6$$
$$B_n = R_4 + R_5$$
$$C_n = R_1 + R_3 + R_6$$
$$Z = R_8 + R_9$$

In realizing these expressions we may use the simplified product terms, as shown in Table 7–2.

Table 7–2 Product terms for design example

Product term	Minterm form	Simplified form
R_1	$\overline{W}\overline{A}B\overline{C}$	$\overline{W}\overline{A}\overline{C}$
R_2	$W\overline{A}\overline{B}\overline{C}$	$W\overline{A}\overline{C}$
R_3	$\overline{W}\overline{A}\overline{B}C$	$\overline{W}\overline{A}C$
R_4	$W\overline{A}\overline{B}C$	$W\overline{A}C$
R_5	$\overline{W}A\overline{B}\overline{C}$	$\overline{W}AB\overline{C}$
R_6	$WA\overline{B}\overline{C}$	$WAB\overline{C}$
R_7	$\overline{W}A\overline{B}C$	$\overline{W}AC$
R_8	$WA\overline{B}C$	WAC
R_9	$\overline{W}AB\overline{C}$	$\overline{W}B$
R_{10}	$WAB\overline{C}$	WB

We have now fully defined the PLA *And* and *Or* plane configurations which are readily translated to the *Nor* form convenient for nMOS realization:

And plane (*Nor* form)

$$\overline{R}_1 = W + A + C \qquad \text{that is, } R_1 = \overline{W}\overline{A}\overline{C}$$
$$\overline{R}_2 = \overline{W} + A + C \qquad \qquad \text{-}etc.\text{ --}$$
$$\overline{R}_3 = W + A + \overline{C} \qquad \qquad \text{---}$$
$$\overline{R}_4 = \overline{W} + A + \overline{C} \qquad \qquad \text{-}$$
$$\overline{R}_5 = W + \overline{A} + B + C \qquad \text{-}$$
$$\overline{R}_6 = \overline{W} + \overline{A} + B + C \qquad \text{-}$$
$$\overline{R}_8 = \overline{W} + \overline{A} + \overline{C} \qquad \qquad \text{-}$$
$$\overline{R}_9 = W + \overline{B} \qquad \qquad R_9 = \overline{W}B$$

Note that R_7 and R_{10} are not used in forming the next state vector or output so they need not be formed in the *And* plane.

Or plane (*Nor* form)

$$\left.\begin{array}{l} \overline{A}_n = R_2 + R_3 + R_4 + R_5 + R_6 \\ \overline{B}_n = R_4 + R_5 \\ \overline{C}_n = R_1 + R_3 + R_6 \\ \overline{Z} = R_8 + R_9 \end{array}\right\} \quad \text{A total of eight product terms needed.}$$

The output inverting register will clearly convert these to the desired *Or* function.

     The general arrangement and dimensions of the PLA to realize this finite state machine are set out in Figure 7–9. Note that it requires the *And* plane to form eight product terms.

7.4.1.3 *Some cautionary remarks*

Before proceeding to the implementation of the PLA for this example, it is appropriate to examine two issues which may cause confusion in the first case or failure to operate correctly in the second case.

     The first issue is that of the possible simplification of the output *Or* expressions for this, or any other, PLA.

     We have the following ouput expression for A_n, for example

$$A_n = R_2 + R_3 + R_4 + R_5 + R_6$$

and, with subscripts omitted for the present states

$$A_n = W\overline{A}\overline{C} + \overline{W}\overline{A}C + W\overline{A}C + \overline{W}A\overline{B}\overline{C} + WA\overline{B}\overline{C}$$

This can be mapped to look for possible simplification as in Figure 7–10. From the map

$$A_n = W\overline{A} + \overline{A}C + A\overline{B}\overline{C}$$
$$= r_1 + r_2 + r_3$$

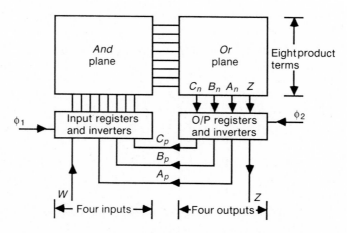

Figure 7-9 Floor plan/arrangement of PLA for design example

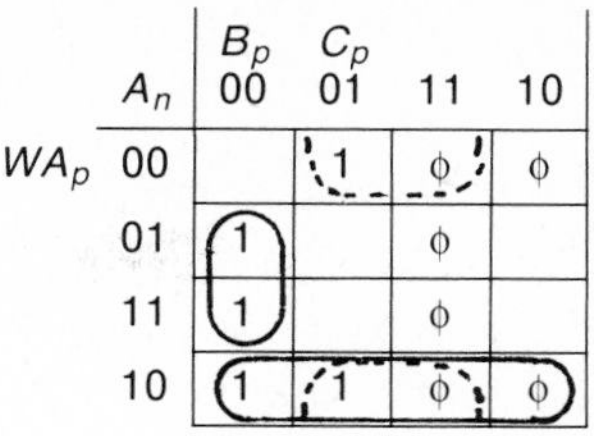

Note the inclusion of the unused combinations of $(A\,B\,C)_p$, that is $(\overline{A}B\overline{C},\ \overline{A}BC,$ and $ABC)$ as 'don't cares'.

Figure 7–10 Map for A_n

which is a simpler form of expression requiring the formation of three simplified *And* terms r_1, r_2, r_3 as defined above. Similar treatment of B_n, C_n, and Z yields the following:

$$B_n = W\overline{A}C + \overline{W}A\overline{B}\overline{C} = R_4 + R_5 \text{ (as before)}$$
$$C_n = \overline{W}\overline{A} + WA\overline{B}\overline{C} = r_4 + R_6 \text{ (one term as before)}$$
$$Z = WAC + \overline{W}B = R_8 + R_9 \text{ (as before)}$$

Thus, simplification of *individual* output expressions has resulted in a need to form the following product terms:

$$R_4,\ R_5,\ R_6,\ R_8,\ R_9 \text{ (as before)}$$

together with

$$r_1,\ r_2,\ r_3,\ r_4 \text{ (new simplified terms)}$$

The simplification has resulted in a need to form nine product terms rather than the eight needed in the unsimplified case.

Since one of the PLA dimensions depends on the number of product terms, then a larger-than-necessary structure may well result from such simplification, as it has done in this case.

The reason for this is that simplification must be done on a multi-output rather than individual-output basis for results to be in the direction of reducing PLA dimensions. However, multi-output reduction techniques are not as widely known or as readily applied, so that the reader of this text may not be aware of the necessary processes. Therefore, the PLA we will realize here will be based on the expressions derived in section 7.4.1.2 without any further simplification.

A second issue of concern arises from our earlier use of 'don't care' states in arriving at these expressions. Our use of 'don't cares' is based on the assumption that the circuit never gets into one of the unused states of variables A, B and C. The reader will be aware that the effects of Murphy's Law cannot be scaled by $1/\alpha$ and that it is inevitable that our design will get into one of the unused states on power up (or as a result of a glitch). We could rework the design so that if any unused state is entered then the circuit will be forced into a 'legal' state on the next clock pulse, but in this case we will provide an initialization signal INIT which forces the circuit into state 1.

7.4.1.4 PLA realization of the example

The points raised in the preceding section have been taken into account and the PLA design given in circuit form as Figure 7–11. The stick diagram of the PLA follows as Figure 7–12, and a standard cell mask layout derived from the stick diagram is set out in Figure 7-13. The regularity of the PLA structure is clearly demonstrated and it will be seen that both the *And* and the *Or* planes are constructed from the same standard cell.

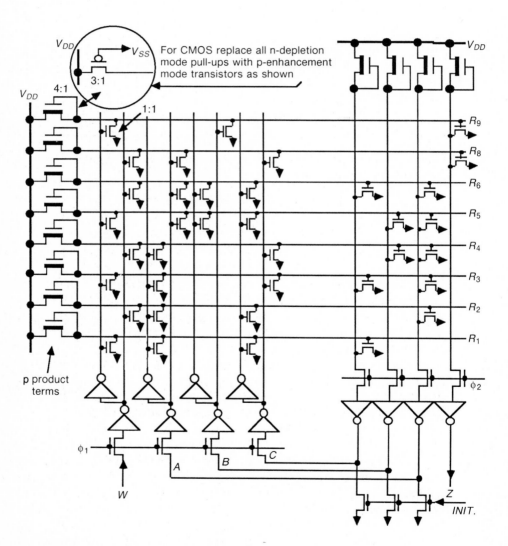

Figure 7–11 PLA arrangement for design example

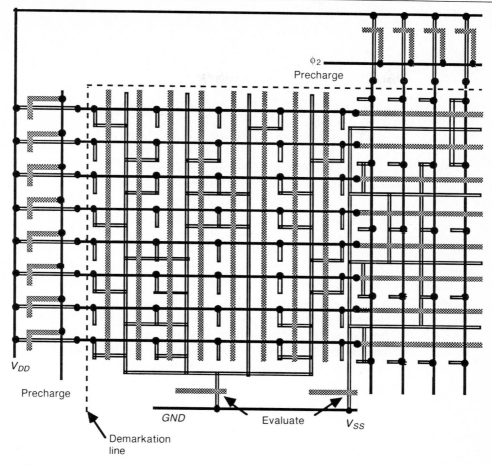

ϕ_2
Precharge

V_{DD}

Precharge

GND   Evaluate V_{SS}

Demarkation
line

Depending on clocking strategy, there may be clocked buffers between *And* and *Or* planes.

Figure 7–12 CMOS (dynamic logic) stick diagram for *And–Or* planes for design example

Figure 7–11 indicates the easy transition between an nMOS and a pseudo-nMOS CMOS arrangement, while the stick diagram of Figure 7–12 shows an arrangement based on Figure 7–11 but realized with clocked dynamic CMOS logic (care must be taken to consider charge sharing).

7.5 Tutorial 3

PLA-finite state machines

1. Either:
    (a) *Serial code detector*
         Design (up to stick diagram level) a circuit which will detect *any* occurrence of the six-bit sequence $\underset{\text{time}}{\underrightarrow{011010}}$ on a single line *W*.

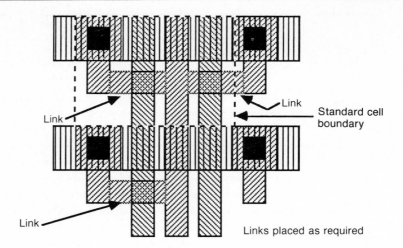

Link

Link

Link

Link

Standard cell boundary

Links placed as required

Figure 7-13 Possible PLA cell

Bits are clocked on W by ϕ_2 and are, therefore, available on clock ϕ_1. Correct sequences must not overlap, that is, the last 0 of a correct sequence cannot be the first 0 of the next sequence.

The circuit is to produce two outputs: $Y=1$ (Hi) when the first three or more bits or a correct sequence have been detected. $Z=1$ (Hi) whenever a complete correct sequence is detected. Use a PLA.

Or:

(b) *BCD 'special' purpose decoder (serial BCD)*

Design (up to stick diagram level) a circuit which will detect occurrence of either BCD 6 *or* BCD 3 in groups of four-input bits on a single input line A. The circuit is to produce an output $B=1$ (Hi) when either 6 or 3 is detected. Digits on A are clocked by ϕ_2 and are therefore available on ϕ_1 of the clock. Use a PLA.

2. In either case, produce layout(s) for standard PLA cell(s) from which the necessary IC design could be built up. (Exclude inverters. Use 5 mm grid for λ and color coding for the layers.)

8 | Aspects of system design

8.1 Some general considerations

The first question to ask about any design methodology is the time-honored 'What's in it for me? Is it going to be worthwhile investing the time to learn?'

To answer the second part first, remarkably little time is needed to learn VLSI design, thanks to the Mead and Conway methodology. In fact, the average undergraduate student of electrical or electronic engineering can acquire an acceptable level of competence in VLSI design for an investment of between 40 and 45 hours spread over one academic term or semester. Similarly, a ten-day full-time continuing education course can quite readily bring practicing professional engineers or computer scientists up to a similar standard. An acceptable level of competence is taken as the ability to apply the design methodology and make use of design tools and procedures to the point where a chip design of several hundred transistors (or higher for regular structures) can be tackled.

The answer to the first part of the question may be quite simply expressed as providing better ways of tackling some problems, and providing a way of designing and realizing systems which are too large, too complex, or just not suited to 'off-the-shelf' components.

'Better' may include:

1. *Lower unit cost* compared with other approaches to the same requirement. Quantity plays a part here but even small quantities, if realized through cooperative ventures such as the multiproject chip or multiproduct wafer, can be fabricated for as little as $200 per square millimetre of silicon, including bonding and packaging of five or six chips per customer.
2. *Higher reliability.* High levels of system integration usually greatly reduce interconnections — a weak spot in any system.
3. *Lower power dissipation, lower weight, and lower volume* compared with most other approaches to a given system.
4. *Better performance* — particularly in terms of speed power product.
5. *Enhanced repeatability.* There are fewer processes to control if the whole system or a very large part of it is realized on a single chip.
6. *The possibility of reduced design/development periods* (particularly for more complex systems) if suitable design procedures and design aids are available.

8.1.1 Some problems

Some of the problems associated with VLSI design are:

1. How to design large complex systems in a reasonable time and with reasonable effort. This is a problem shared with other approaches to system design.
2. The nature of architectures best suited to take full advantage of VLSI and the technology.
3. The testability of large/complex systems once implemented in silicon.

Problems 1 and 3 are greatly reduced if two aspects of standard practice are accepted.

- Approach design in a top-down manner and with adequate computer-aided tools to do the job. Partition the system sensibly and aim at high regularity. Generate and then verify each section of the design.
- Design testability into the system from the outset and be prepared to devote a significant proportion (e.g. up to 30 percent) of the total chip area to test and diagnostic facilities.

These problems are the subject of considerable research and development activity at this time.

In tackling the design of a system, we must bear in mind that topological properties are generally far more significant than the logical operations being performed. It may be said that it is better to duplicate (or triplicate, etc.) rather than communicate. This is indeed the case, and it is an approach which seems wrong to more traditional designers. In fact, even in relatively straightforward designs, there may be as much as 40 percent of the chip taken up with interconnections, and it is true to say that interconnections generally pose the most acute problems in the design of large systems. Communications must, therefore, be given the highest priority early in the design process and a *communications strategy* should be evolved and adhered to throughout the design process.

Allied to this, the architecture should be carefully chosen to allow the design objectives to be realized *and* to allow high regularity in realization.

8.2   An illustration of design processes

- Structured design begins with the concept of hierarchy.
- It is possible to divide any complex function into less complex subfunctions; these may be subdivided further into even simpler subfunctions.
- This process is known as top-down design.
- As a system's complexity increases, its organization changes as different factors become relevant to its creation.
- Coupling can be used as a measure of how much submodules interact. Clever systems partitioning aims at reducing implicit complexity by minimizing the amount of interaction between subparts; thus independence of design becomes a reality.
- It is crucial that components interacting with high frequency are physically proximate, since one may pay severe penalties for long, high-bandwidth interconnects.
- Concurrency needs to be exploited — it is desirable that all gates on the chip do useful work most of the time.
- Because technology changes so fast, the adaption to a new process must occur in a short time. Thus a technology-independent description becomes important.

In representing a design there are several approaches which may be used at different stages of the design process:

- conventional circuit symbols;
- logic symbols;
- stick diagrams;
- any mixture of logic symbols and stick diagrams that is convenient at a particular stage;
- mask layouts;
- architectural block diagrams;
- floor plans.

We will illustrate the various representations during the course of a design exercise which will now be undertaken to illustrate design processes.

8.2.1 The general arrangement of a four-bit arithmetic processor

The four-bit microprocessor has been chosen as a design example because it is particularly suitable for illustrating the design and interconnection of common architectural blocks.

Figure 8–1 sets out the basic architecture of most, if not all, microprocessors. At this stage we will consider the design of the data path only, but matters relevant to other blocks will follow in later chapters.

The data path has been separated out in Figure 8–2 and it will be seen that the structure comprises a unit which processes data applied at one port and presents its output at a second port. Alternatively, the two data ports may be combined as a single bidirectional port if storage facilities exist in the data path. Control over the functions to be performed is effected by control signals as indicated.

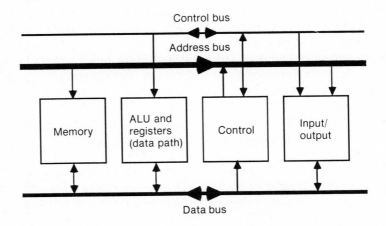

Figure 8–1 Basic digital processor structure

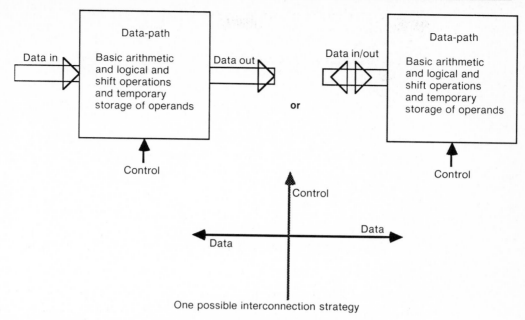

Figure 8-2 Communications strategy for data path

At this early stage it is essential to evolve an interconnections strategy (as shown) to which we will then adhere.

Now we will decompose the data path into a block diagram showing the main subunits. Later we will work out a possible *floor plan* showing a planned relative disposition of the subunits on the chip and thus on the mask layouts. This information is presented in Figure 8–3.

A further decision must then be made as to the nature of the bus architecture linking the subunits. The choices in this case range from one-bus, to two-bus or three-bus architecture. Some of the possibilities are shown in Figure 8–4.

In pursuing this particular design exercise it was decided to implement the structure with a two-bus architecture. In our planning we can now extend on our interconnections strategy by planning for power rails and notionally making some

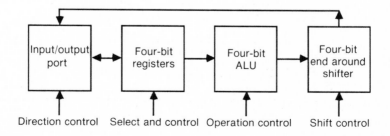

Figure 8-3 Subunits and basic interconnections for data path

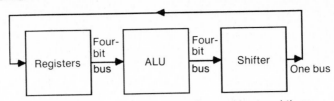

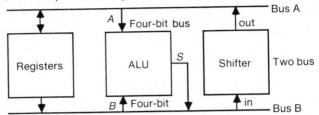

Sequence: (i) First operand from registers to ALU. Operand is stored there.
  (ii) Second operand from registers to ALU. Operands are added (etc.) and the result is, say, stored in the ALU.
  (iii) The result is passed through the shifter and stored in the registers.

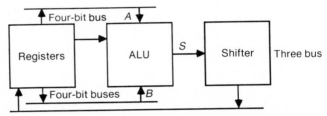

Sequence: (i) Two operands (*A* and *B*) are sent from register(s) to ALU and are operated upon and the result (*S*) stored in ALU.
  (ii) Result is passed through the shifter and stored in the registers.

Sequence: The two operands (*A* and *B*) are sent from the registers, operated upon, and the shifted result (*S*) returned to another register *all in the same clock period*.

Figure 8-4 Basic bus architectures

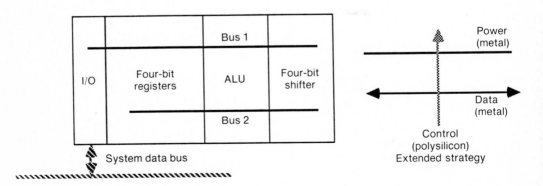

Figure 8-5 Tentative floor plan for four-bit data path

basic allocation of layers on which the various signal paths will be predominantly run. These additional features are illustrated in Figure 8–5, together with a tentative floor plan of the proposed design which includes some form of interface (I/O) to the parent system data bus (see Figure 8–1).

The proposed processor will be seen to comprise a register array in which four-bit numbers can be stored, either from an input/output port or from the output of the ALU via a shifter. Numbers from the register array can be fed in pairs to the ALU to be added (or subtracted, etc.) and the result can be shifted or not, before being returned to the register array or possibly out through the I/O port. Obviously, data connections between the I/O port, ALU, and shifter must be in the form of four-bit buses. Simultaneously, we must recognize that each of the blocks must be suitably connected to control lines so that its function may be defined for any of a range of possible operations.

The required arrangement has been turned into a very tentative floor plan, as in Figure 8–5, which indicates a possible relative disposition of the blocks and also indicates an acceptable and sensible interconnection strategy indicated by the lines showing the preferred direction of data flow and control signal distribution. At this stage of learning, floor plans will be very tentative since we will not as yet have a good feel for the area requirements, say for a four-bit register or a four-bit adder.

Having determined overall interconnection strategy, stick diagrams for the circuits comprising sections of the various blocks may be developed, conforming to the required strategy.

An interactive process of modification may well then take place between the various stages as the design progresses. During the design process, and in particular when defining the interconnection strategy and designing the stick diagrams, care must be taken in allocating the layers to the various data or control paths. We must remember that:

1. Metal can cross polysilicon or diffusion without any significant effect (with some reservations to be discussed later).
2. Wherever polysilicon crosses diffusion a transistor will be formed.
3. Wherever lines cross on the same level an interconnection is formed.
4. Simple contacts ($4\lambda \times 4\lambda$) can be used to join diffusion or polysilicon to metal.
5. To join diffusion and polysilicon we must either use a buried contact or a butting contact (in which case all three layers are joined together at the contact) or two contacts, diffusion to metal then metal to polysilicon.
6. Each layer has particular electrical properties which must be taken into account.
7. For CMOS layouts, p- and n-diffusion wires must not directly join each other nor may either cross the p-well boundary.

With these factors in mind, we may now adopt suitable tactics to meet the strategic requirements when we approach the design of each subunit in turn.

8.2.2   The design of a four-bit shifter

Any general purpose n-bit shifter should be able to shift incoming data by up to $n-1$ places in a right-shift or left-shift direction.

If we now further specify that all shifts should be on an 'end-around' basis, such that any bit shifted out at one end of a data word will be shifted in at the other end of the word, then the problem of right shift or left shift is greatly eased. In fact, a moment's consideration will reveal, for a four-bit word, that a one-bit shift right is equivalent to a three-bit shift left and a two-bit shift right is equivalent to a two-bit shift left, etc. Thus we can achieve a capability to shift left or right by zero, one, two, or three places by designing a circuit which will shift right only (say) by zero, one, two, or three places.

Having decided on the nature of the shifter, its implementation must then be considered. Obviously, the first circuit which comes to mind is that of the shift register in Figures 5–38, 5–39, and 5–40. Data could be loaded from the output of the ALU, shifting effected, then the outputs of each stage of the shift register would provide the required parallel output to be returned to the register array (or elsewhere in the general case).

However, there is danger in accepting the obvious without question. Many designers, used to the constraints of TTL, MSI, and SSI logic, would be conditioned to think in terms of such standard arrangements. When designing VLSI systems, it pays to set out exactly what is required in order to assess the best approach.

In this case, the shifter must have:

- input from a four-line parallel data bus;
- four output lines for the shifted data;
- means of transferring input data to output lines with any shift from zero to three bits inclusive.

In looking for a way of meeting these requirements, we should also attempt to take best advantage of the technology, for example, the availability of the switch-like MOS pass transistor and transmission gate.

We must also observe the strategy decided on earlier for the direction of data and control signal flow and the approach adopted should be such that this can be done. The reader will recall that the overall strategy in this case is for data to flow horizontally and control signals vertically.

A solution which meets these requirements emerges from the days of switch and relay contact based switching networks — the *crossbar switch*. Consider a direct MOS switch implementation of a 4×4 crossbar switch, as in Figure 8–6. The arrangement is quite general and may be readily expanded to accommodate n-bit inputs/outputs. In fact, this arrangement is an overkill, in that any input line can be connected to any or all output lines — if all switches are closed then all inputs are connected to all outputs in one glorious short circuit. Furthermore, 16 control signals (sw_{nm}), one for each transistor switch, must be provided to drive the crossbar switch, and such complexity is highly undesirable. An adaptation of this arrangement recognizes the fact that we can couple the switch gates together in groups of

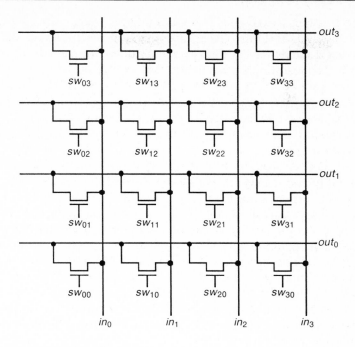

Figure 8-6   4×4 crossbar switch

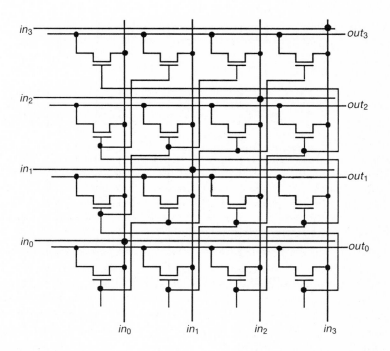

Figure 8-7   4×4 barrel shifter

four (in this case) and also form four separate groups corresponding to shifts of zero, one, two and three bits. The arrangement is readily adapted so that the in-lines also run horizontally (to conform to the required strategy).

The resulting arrangement is known as a *barrel shifter* and a 4×4-bit barrel shifter circuit diagram is given as Figure 8–7. The interbus switches have their gate inputs connected in a staircase fashion in groups of four and there are now four shift control inputs which must be mutually exclusive in the active state. CMOS transmission gates may be used in place of the simple pass transistor switches if appropriate.

The structure of the barrel shifter is clearly one of high regularity and generality and it may be readily represented in stick diagram form, one possible implementation being given in Figure 8–8. The stick diagram clearly conveys regular topology and allows the choice of a standard cell from which complete barrel shifters of any size may be formed by replication of the standard cell. It should be noted that standard cell boundaries must be carefully chosen to allow for butting together side by side and top to bottom to retain the overall topology. The mask layout for standard cell number 2 (arbitrary choice) of Figure 8–8 may then be set out as in Figure 8–9. Once the standard cell dimensions have been determined, then any $n \times n$ barrel shifter may be configured and its outline, or bounding box, arrived at by summing up the dimensions of the replicated standard cell.

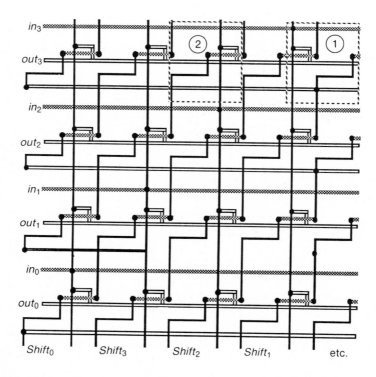

Figure 8–8   One possible stick diagram for a 4×4 barrel shifter

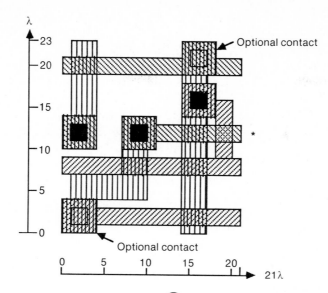

Figure 8–9 Barrel shifter standard cell ② — mask layout (See also Color Plate 7)

*If this particular cell is checked for design rule errors in isolation then an error will be generated due to insufficient extension of polysilicon over thinox where shown. This error will *not* be present when cells are butted together. This effect is caused by the particular choice of cell boundaries and care must be taken when making such choices.

The *bounding box* outline for the 4×4-way barrel shifter is given in Figure 8–10 and it is necessary to indicate all inlet and outlet points around the periphery together with the layer on which each is located. This allows ready placing of the shifter within the floor plan and its interconnection with other subsystems on the chip. It also emphasizes the fact, as in this case, that many subsystems need external links to complete their architecture. In this case, the links shown on the right of the bounding box must be made and must be allowed for in interconnections and overall dimensions. It also allows the subsystem characterization to be that of the bounding box alone for composing higher levels of the system hierarchy.

8.3 Summary of design processes

At this stage it is convenient to examine the way we have approached the design of a system and of a particular subsystem in detail. The steps involved may be set out as follows:

1. Set out a specification together with an architectural block diagram.
2. Suitably partition the architecture into subsystems which are, as far as possible, self-contained and which give as simple interconnection requirements as possible.

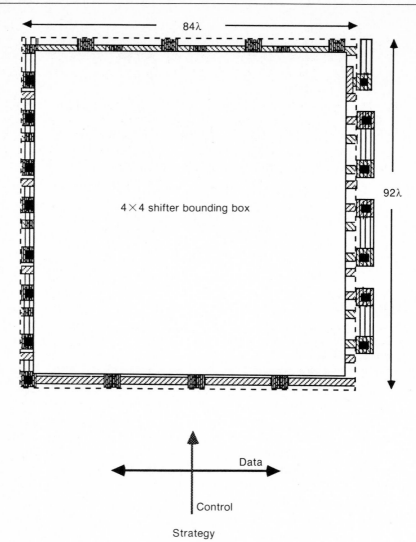

Figure 8–10 Bounding box for 4×4 barrel shifter

3. Set out a tentative floor plan showing the proposed physical disposition of subsystems on the chip.
4. Determine interconnection strategy.
5. Revise 2, 3 and 4 interactively as necessary.
6. Choose layers on which to run buses and the main control signals.
7. Take each subsystem in turn and conceive a regular architecture to conform to the strategy set out in 4. Set out circuit and/or logic diagrams as appropriate. Remember that MOS switch-based logic is such that both the logic 1 and logic 0 conditions of an output *must* be deliberately satisfied (not as in

TTL logic, where if logic 1 conditions are satisfied then logic 0 conditions follow automatically).

8. Develop stick diagrams adopting suitable tactics to observe the overall strategy (4) and choice of layers (6). Determine suitable *standard cell(s)* from which the subsystem may be formed.

9. Produce mask layouts for the standard cell(s) making sure that cells can be butted together, side by side and top to bottom, without design rule violation or waste of space. Determine overall dimension of the standard cell(s).

10. Cascade and replicate standard cells as necessary to complete the desired subsystem. This may now be characterized in *bounding box* form with positions and layers of inlets and outlets. External links, etc. *must* be allowed for.

9 | Further consideration and illustration of the design process

9.1   Some observations on the design process

The design of the shifter, as the first subsystem of the proposed four-bit data path, has illustrated some important features:

1. First and foremost, try to put requirements into words (often, an *if, then, else* approach helps to do this) so that the most appropriate architecture or logic can be evolved.
2. If a standard cell (or cells) can be arrived at then the actual detailed design work is confined to relatively small areas of simple circuitry. Such cells can usually have their performance simulated with relative ease and, thus, an idea of the performance of the complete subsystem may be obtained.
3. If generality as well as regularity is achieved then, for example, any size of shifter can be built up by simple replication and butting together of the standard cell(s).
4. Design is largely a matter of the topology of communications rather than detailed logic circuit design.
5. Once standard cell layouts are designed then overall area calculations can be precisely made (*not* forgetting to allow for any necessary links or other external terminations). Thus accurate floor plan areas may be allocated.
6. VLSI design methodology for MOS circuits is not hard to learn.
7. The Mead and Conway-based design rules are simple and straightforward in application.
8. A structured and orderly approach to system design is highly beneficial and becomes essential for large systems.

9.2   Regularity

So far we have used regularity as a qualitative parameter. Regularity should be as high as possible to minimize the design effort required for any system.

The level of any particular design as far as this aspect is concerned may be measured by quantifying regularity as follows

$$\text{Regularity} = \frac{\text{Total number of transistors on the chip}}{\text{Number of transistor circuits which must be designed in detail}}$$

The denominator of this expression will obviously be greatly reduced if the whole chip, or large parts of it, can be fabricated from a few standard cells, each of which is relatively simple in structure.

For the 4×4-bit barrel shifter just designed, the regularity factor is given by

$$\text{Regularity} = \frac{16}{1} = 16$$

However, an 8×8-bit shifter would require no more detailed design and would have a regularity factor of 64.

Good system design can achieve regularity factors of 50 or 100 or more and structures which are inherently regular, such as memories, achieve very high figures indeed.

9.3   Design of an ALU subsystem

Having designed the shifter, we may now turn our attention to another subsystem of the four-bit data path (as in Figure 9–1). A convenient and appropriate choice is the ALU.

The heart of the ALU is a four-bit adder circuit and it is this which we will actually design, indicating later how it may be readily adapted to subtract and perform logical operations.

Obviously, a four-bit adder must take the sum of two four-bit numbers, and it will be seen we have assumed that all four-bit quantities are presented in parallel form and that the shifter circuit has been designed to accept and shift a four-bit parallel sum from the ALU.

Let us now specify that the sum is to be *stored* in parallel at the output of the adder from whence it may be fed through the shifter and back to the register array. Thus, a single four-bit data bus is needed from the adder to the shifter and another four-bit bus is required from the shifted output back to the register array (since the shifter is merely a switch array with no storage capability). As far as the input to the adder is concerned, the two four-bit parallel numbers to be added are to be presented in parallel on two four-bit buses. We can also decide on some of the basic aspects of system timing at this stage and will assume clock phase ϕ_1 as being the phase in which signals are fed along buses to the adder input and during which their sum is stored at the adder output. Thus clock signals are required by the ALU as shown. The shifter is unclocked but must be connected to four shift control lines as shown. It is also necessary to provide a 'carry out', signal from the adder and, in the general case, to provide for a possible 'carry in' signal, as shown in the figure.

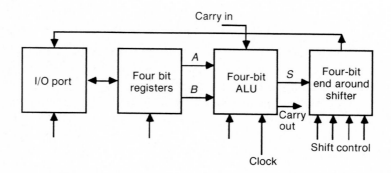

Figure 9–1   Four-bit data path for processor (block diagram)

9.3.1 Design of a four-bit adder

In order to derive the requirements for an *n*-bit adder, let us first consider the addition of two binary numbers $A + B$ as follows:

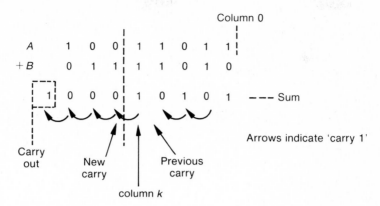

It will be seen that for any column *k* there will be *three* inputs — the corresponding bits of the input numbers, A_k and B_k, and the 'previous carry' (C_{k-1}). It will also be seen that there are *two* outputs, the *sum* (S_k) and a *new carry* (C_k).

We may, thus, set out a truth table for the *k* column of any adder, as in Table 9–1.

Table 9–1 Truth table for binary adder

	Inputs		*Outputs*	
A_k	B_k	*Previous carry* C_{k-1}	*Sum* S_k	*New carry* C_k
0	0	0	0	0
0	1	0	1	0
1	0	0	1	0
1	1	0	0	1
0	0	1	1	0
0	1	1	0	1
1	0	1	0	1
1	1	1	1	1

Conventionally, and assuming that we are not implementing a 'carry look ahead' facility, we may write the *standard adder equations* which fully describe the entries in Table 9–1 in the form

$$\text{Sum} \qquad S_k = H_k \overline{C}_{k-1} + \overline{H}_k C_{k-1}$$
$$\text{New carry} \qquad C_k = A_k B_k + H_k C_{k-1}$$

where

$$\text{Half sum} \qquad H_k = \bar{A}_k B_k + A_k \bar{B}_k$$

Previous carry is indicated as C_{k-1} and $0 \leqslant k \leqslant n-1$ for n-bit numbers.

These equations may be directly implemented as *And–Or* functions or, most economically, S_k and H_k can be directly implemented with *Exclusive–Or* gates. However, for VLSI implementation there are none of the standard logic packages which are the delight of the TTL logic designer. It may be advantageous, then, to restate the requirements in another way.

9.3.1.1 Adder element requirements

Inspection of Table 9–1 reveals that the *adder requirements* may be stated thus:

$$\begin{aligned} \text{If} \quad & A_k = B_k \quad \text{then} \quad S_k = C_{k-1} \\ \text{else,} \quad & S_k = \bar{C}_{k-1} \end{aligned}$$

and for the carry C_k

$$\begin{aligned} \text{If} \quad & A_k = B_k \quad \text{then} \quad C_k = A_k = B_k{}^* \\ \text{else,} \quad & C_k = C_{k-1} \end{aligned}$$

*This relationship could also have been stated as:

$$\text{Carry} \quad C_k = 1 \quad \text{when} \quad A_k = B_k = 1$$

or

$$C_k = 0 \quad \text{when} \quad A_k = B_k = 0$$

9.3.1.2 A standard adder element

A one-bit adder element may now be represented as in Figure 9–2.

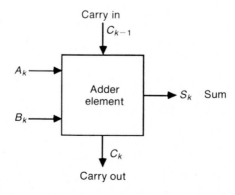

n such elements would be cascaded to form an n-bit adder.

Figure 9–2 Adder element

Note that any number of such elements may be cascaded to form any size of adder and that the element is quite general.

It should be noted that this standard adder element may itself be composed from a number of standard cells and that regularity and generality must be aimed at in all levels of the architecture.

One implementation of the logic circuitry for the adder element which is easy to follow is to use two red–green function blocks, one to generate the sum and the other the carry, as shown in Figure 9–3 indicating the connections resulting from the way in which the requirements are stated in words. (See section 9.3.1.1– Adder element requirements.) An alternative approach is to use multiplexers rather than red–green function blocks and this approach is illustrated in Figures 9–4 and 9–5. In these figures the multiplexers form C_k and $\bar{S}_k$ (not S_k) to allow single inverter storage or buffering of S_k if this is needed. Although the adder design to be pursued in this chapter is based on the nMOS red–green function block, the reader is given the opportunity to actually design the multiplexer version as part of the tutorial at the end of this chapter. In fact, the design actually implemented in silicon (see Figure 11–9) uses the nMOS multiplexer-based version of the adder. The logic requirements of the adder element are thus readily met but practical factors must now be taken into account.

In order to form an *n*-bit adder, *n* of these elements must be cascaded with 'carry out' of one element connecting to 'carry in' of the next more significant element. Thus, the carry chain as a whole will consist of many pass transistors in series. This will give a very slow response and the carry line must therefore be suitably buffered after or before each adder element. (Remember, no more than four pass transistors in series — see section 4.10 of this text.) Also, we have assumed

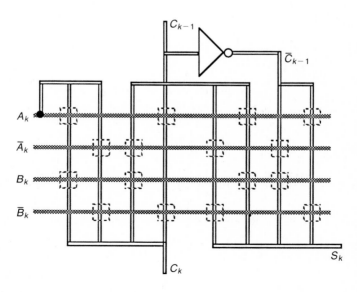

Figure 9–3 Stick diagram for adder logic (function block)

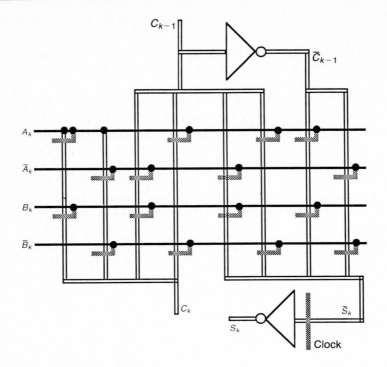

Figure 9-4 Multiplexer (n-switches)-based adder logic with stored and buffered sum output

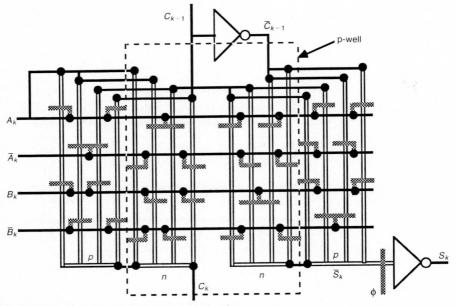

Figure 9-5 CMOS version of adder logic

that both complements, $\bar{A}_k$ and $\bar{B}_k$, of the incoming bits are available. This may not be the case. Furthermore, signals A_k and B_k are to be derived from buses interconnecting the register with the ALU and may thus be taken off the bus through pass transistors. If this is the case, then these signals could not be used directly to drive the pass transistors of the function blocks. Finally, we must allow for storing the sum at the output of the adder, as discussed early in this section.

More practical and general arrangements are shown in Color Plate 10 and Figure 9–6. It will be seen that the adder element now contains all necessary buffering (at the expense of increased area). Seven inverter stages are required, deployed as follows (from top to bottom of Color Plate 10 or Figure 9–6):

- Two inverters to form $\bar{C}_{k-1}$ and C_{k-1} (buffered)
- Two inverters to form $\bar{A}_k$ and A_k (buffered)
- Two inverters to form $\bar{B}_k$ and B_k (buffered)
- One inverter to act as a dynamic store for S_k.

Note that only one inverter needs to be used to store the sum digit S_k *provided* that $\bar{S}_k$ rather than S_k is formed by the function block. Thus, the observant reader will note that the logic forming the sum has had its configuration modified to com-

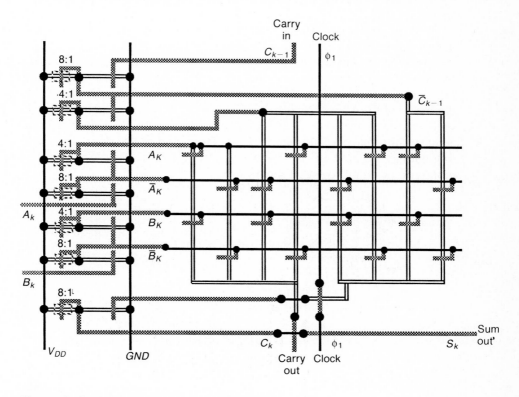

Figure 9–6   Adder element — stick diagram
(See Color Plate 10 for function block version.)

plement S_k (compared with Figure 9–3). The ratio appropriate to each inverter is given beside it in Figure 9–6, since this particular example is implemented with nMOS circuits.

9.3.1.3 Standard cells required to be designed for the adder element

The stick diagrams of Color Plate 10 and Figure 9–6 consist basically of three parts:

1. the red–green function blocks (or multiplexers);
2. the inverter circuits (4:1 and 8:1 ratios);
3. the communication paths.

The first choice to be made is between the red–green function block and the multiplexer, both of which lend themselves well to a replicated standard cell approach. Then only two standard cells are required for the complete adder element — the very simple cells from which the red–green function block or multiplexer is formed (given as Figure 9–7), and secondly an inverter.

Two versions of a standard inverter are needed — one for an 8:1 ratio as in Figure 9–8 and a second version for a 4:1 ratio as in Figure 9–9. However, only one standard cell design is needed with a choice of widths for the pull-down channel as shown.

The same approach to a standard inverter can be taken using a buried rather than a butting contact, as shown for a 4:1 ratio in Figure 9–10. In this case the vertical dimension is larger than that of Figure 9–9, but there are occasions where the lack of any metal regions in the center of the inverter is a positive advantage. For the layout shown two metal bus lines could be run through the cell and across the inverter from side to side. This might provide a considerable advantage in saving space in certain layouts, such as register or memory arrays where data buses must run through each storage element. This could not be done when using a butting contact because of the metal layer 'cover' on the contact and the need to maintain 3λ metal to metal separation.

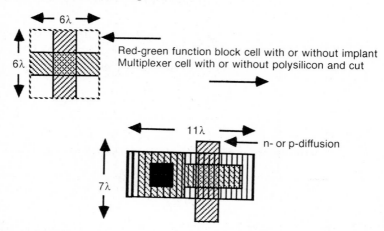

Figure 9–7   Function block and multiplexer cells (See Colour Plate 9(d))

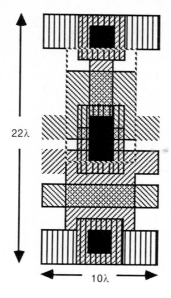

Figure 9-8   Inverter 8:1 version mask layout (See also Color Plate 9(b))

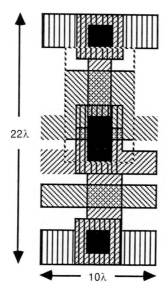

Figure 9-9   Inverter 4:1 version mask layout (See also Color Plate 9(c))

The use of a standard nMOS inverter with choice of width for the pull-down channel is a common practice. However, note that the narrow channel for the 4:1 configuration has been placed so that its edges are on *whole λ boundaries*, not half λ boundaries as would be the case if narrowing had been carried out symmetrically.

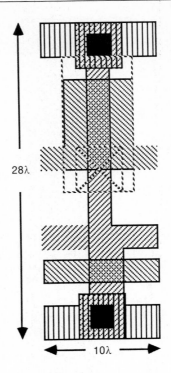

28λ

10λ

Figure 9–10 Inverter 4:1 — buried contact version (8:1 formed by doubling p.d. width)

Always aim at designing mask layouts to have edges on whole λ boundaries. Some design rule checking software and some fabrication processes might not accept half λ edges.

9.3.1.4 Adder element bounding box

Referring now to Color Plate 10 we may first draw up a bounding box for the function block area of the adder. Each standard cell is $6λ \times 6λ$ and there are eight such elements horizontally and four vertically. We must also allow 3λ for the metal bus passing through the center and carrying the $φ_1$ clock signal. Thus, the bounding box must be $8 \times 6λ + 3λ = 51λ$ 'wide' and $4 \times 6λ = 24λ$ in 'height', as shown in Figure 9–11.

To complete the adder element we need the inverters shown in Figure 9–6 and Color Plate 10. We have already determined a bounding box outline for an inverter circuit (see Figures 9–8 and 9–9 (or 9–10 if buried contacts are to be used)) and it will be seen that each inverter occupies a rectangle measuring at least 10λ 'wide' and 22λ 'high'. Thus, seven inverters alone will occupy an area of $70λ \times 22λ$ and, allowing, say, a 5λ space between each on average for connections, we have an overall area requirement of $100λ \times 22λ$ for the inverters. The overall bounding box *outline* for a complete adder element will be approximately that given as

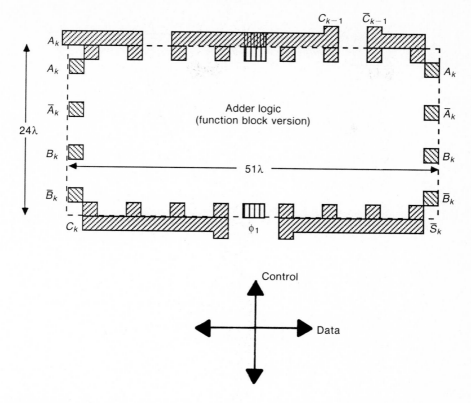

Figure 9–11 Bounding box and connections for adder logic (function block)

Figure 9–12. Note that vertical distribution of power has been assumed and has been added to the data and control distribution strategy which is being observed, but the direction of power distribution may be reviewed as the design of the complete processor progresses. Details of inlet/outlet points on the inverter block and overall adder element bounding boxes will be worked out as part of the next tutorial exercise.

The four-bit adder is then formed by cascading four adder elements as indicated in Figure 9–13. The mask layout detail may be examined in Color Plate 11, which shows two cascaded adder elements.

9.3.2 Implementing ALU functions with an adder

An arithmetic and logical operations unit (ALU) must, obviously, be able to *add* two binary numbers ($A + B$), and must also be able to *subtract* ($A - B$).

From the point of view of logical operations it is essential to be able to *And* two binary words ($A.B$). It is also desirable to *Exclusively-Or* ($A \oplus B$) and perhaps also detect *Equality* ($\overline{A \oplus B}$), and of course we also need an *Or* function.

Subtraction with an adder is an easy operation provided that the binary

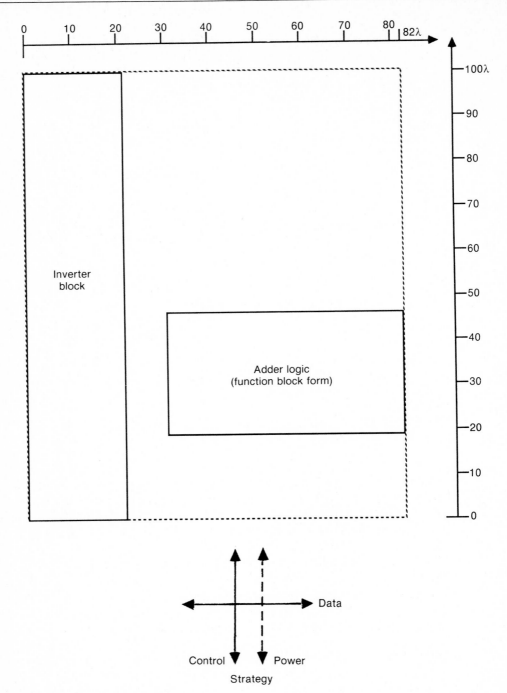

Figure 9–12   Approximate bounding box of adder element

(See Color Plates 10 and 11)

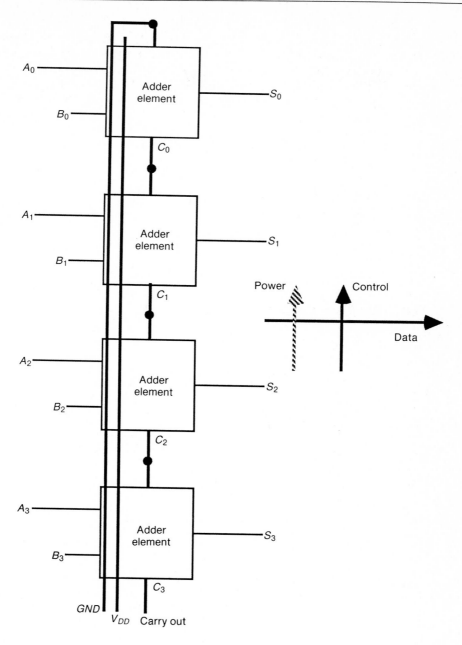

Figure 9–13   Four-bit adder (See Color Plate 11)

numbers A and B are presented in *twos complement* form. If this is the case, then to find the difference $A - B$ it is only necessary to complement B (exchange 1 for 0 and vice versa for all bits of B), add 1 to the number thus obtained, and then *add* this quantity to A using the standard addition process discussed earlier. The output of the adder will then be the required difference in twos complement form. Note that the complement facility necessary for subtraction can also serve to form the *logical complement* (which is indeed exchanging 0 for 1 and vice versa).

It is highly desirable that we keep the architecture of the ALU as simple as possible and it would be nice if the adder could be made to perform logical operations as readily as it performs subtraction. In order to examine this possibility, consider the standard adder equation set out in section 9.3.1 and reproduced here

$$\text{Sum} \quad S_k = H_k . \overline{C}_{k-1} + \overline{H}_k . C_{k-1}$$
$$\text{New carry} \quad C_k = A_k . B_k + H_k . C_{k-1}$$
$$\text{Half sum} \quad H_k = A_k . \overline{B}_k + \overline{A}_k . B_k$$

Consider, first, the sum output if C_{k-1} is held at logical 0. Then

$$S_k = H_k . 1 + \overline{H}_k . 0 = H_k$$

that is

$$S_k = H_k = A_k \overline{B}_k + \overline{A}_k B_k \quad - \text{ An } \textit{Exclusive-Or} \text{ operation}$$

Now, hold C_{k-1} at logical 1. Then

$$S_k = H_k . 0 + \overline{H}_k . 1 = \overline{H}_k$$

that is

$$S_k = \overline{H}_k = \overline{A}_k . \overline{B}_k + A_k B_k \quad - \textit{Exclusive-Nor}$$
$$\text{or } \textit{Equality} \text{ operation}$$

Next, consider the carry output of each element, first if C_{k-1} is held at logical 0. Then

$$C_k = A_k B_k + H_k . 0 = A_k B_k \quad - \textit{And} \text{ operation}$$

now, if C_{k-1} is held at logical 1. Then

$$C_k = A_k B_k + H_k . 1$$
$$= A_k B_k + A_k \overline{B}_k + \overline{A}_k B_k$$

Therefore

$$C_k = A_k + B_k \quad - \textit{Or} \text{ operation}$$

Thus, it may be seen that suitable switching of the carry line between adder elements will give the ALU logical functions. An arrangement of the adder elements for both arithmetic and logical functions is suggested in Figure 9–14.

9.4   Carry look-ahead adders

The adder design pursued in this text was not conceived with speed in mind but rather to provide a vehicle to demonstrate the design concepts and processes. In fact, when this design is simulated and later tested it will be found that the propagation time in forming the carry out of each bit is in the region of 40 nsec (for a 5 μm

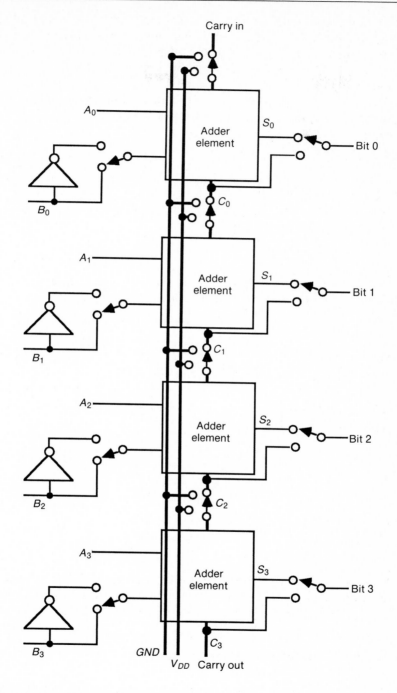

Figure 9-14   Four-bit ALU (See Color Plate 11)

nMOS realization). Furthermore, the design used for the overall four-bit adder is one in which the carry for each bit cannot be formed until the carry from the previous bit is available. Thus the forming of the carry for bit 3 must wait for C_0 then C_1 and then C_2 to be formed first; that is, a 'ripple through' effect is present in the carry chain.

A general solution to this problem is to be found in rearranging the expressions for the adder (given in section 9.3.1); in particular the expression for carry

$$C_k = A_k.B_k + H_k.C_{k-1}$$

(where $H_k = \bar{A}_k.B_k + A_k.\bar{B}_k$) can be rearranged into the form

$$C_k = A_k.B_k + (A_k + B_k).C_{k-1}$$

Thus for C_0 we may write

$$C_0 = A_0.B_0$$

since there is no previous carry; and, therefore, C_1 may then be written as

$$C_1 = A_1.B_1 + (A_1 + B_1).A_0.B_0$$

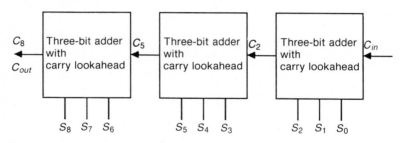

(a)   Partial carry look-ahead adder structure

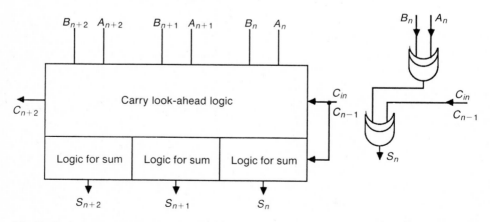

(b)   Basic three-bit adder cell with look-ahead

(c)   Logic for sum

Figure 9-15   Carry look-ahead and ripple through compromise

and, similarly

$$C_2 = A_2.B_2 + (A_2 + B_2).A_1.B_1 + (A_2 + B_2).(A_1 + B_1).A_0.B_0$$

The next stage would be

$$C_3 = A_3.B_3 + (A_3 + B_3).A_2.B_2 + (A_3 + B_3).(A_2 + B_2)A_1.B_1 +$$
$$(A_3 + B_3).(A_2 + B_2).(A_1 + B_1).A_0.B_0$$

and so on for further stages. Although these expressions become very lengthy as the bit significance increases, each expression is only three logic levels deep, so the delay in forming the carry is constant irrespective of bit position. However the logic does rapidly become over-cumbersome and also presents problems in 'fan-out' and 'fan-in' requirements on the gates used. A compromise, usually adopted, is a combination of 'carry look-ahead' and 'ripple through' as indicated in Figure 9–15. The three-bit groups shown were arbitrarily chosen to illustrate the approach.

9.5 Parallel multipliers

As ALUs sometimes include a multiplier it is convenient at this point to briefly mention a fast multiplier array. Multipliers are formed from adders and have carry propagation problems which are far worse than those of the adder. One approach to fast arithmetic, and to multipliers and dividers in particular, is to use a 'pipelined' architecture.

9.5.1 A pipelined multiplier array

Many parallel multipliers are iterative arrays. Some of these are carry-ripple structures with no storage elements, in which a given result must be output before new data words can be input. Such multipliers can be pipelined by introducing latches at appropriate positions in the array.

An example is a parallel multiplier based on *systolic array principles* as in Figure 9–16.* It comprises a diamond-shaped array of latched, gated full adder cells, connected only to immediately adjacent cells. This has practical advantages as no broadcasting of data right across the multiplier array occurs.

With multiplicand X, multiplier Y and product P, the kth bit of each partial product $x_{k-i}.y_i$ is formed in one of the cells in the kth vertical column of the array. The kth bit of the product

$$p_k = \sum_{i=0}^{k} x_{k-i}.y_i$$

is formed by letting these components accumulate as p_k passes down the column. Carries generated at each stage in the array are passed to the left (next most significant column).

---

* J. V. McCanny and J. G. McWhirter, 'Completely iterative, pipelined multiplier array suitable for VLSI', *IEE Proc.*, Vol. 129, Pt. G, No. 2, April 1982, pp. 40–6. This structure was designed by P. Evans as part of a VLSI course at the University of Adelaide, South Australia.

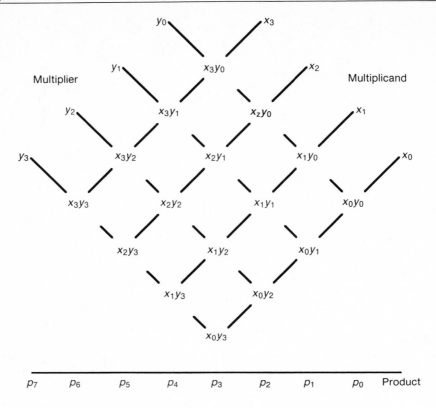

Figure 9-16 Systolic array multiplier

The residual carry bits passing across the lower left-hand boundary of the diamond must be added into the partial product sum to complete the multiplication. This is achieved with half of the above array placed at the lower left-hand boundary, retaining the iterative structure.

This gives the general structure shown in Figure 9–17. For an n-bit$\times n$-bit multiplier $\frac{1}{2}(3n+1)n$ cells are required. There is a further requirement of $3n^2$ latches to skew and deskew the input and output data. Note that each cell connects to six other cells provided it is not on the array boundary. All sum and carry inputs at the array boundary are set to zero.

The structure of the basic cell is shown in Figure 9–18. The gating function for unsigned numbers is

$$x.y$$

The delay of one operation through the pipeline is $3n$ clock cycles (i.e. it takes $3n$ clock cycles to obtain a product after X and Y are input). However, if the pipeline is kept full, a product will be output every clock cycle.

The clock period can be short as it must account for only the propagation time through one cell. The multiplier is thus a very high throughput structure (i.e. low average time per multiplication).

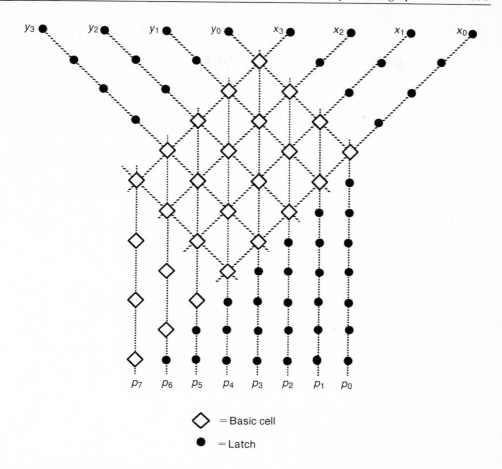

Figure 9-17 Multiplier structure

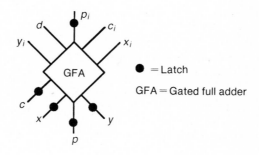

Note: Where p_i = partial product sum in
p = partial product sum out
c_i = carry in
c = carry out
d = line required for two's complement operation

Figure 9-18 Basic cell

If the product XY is rewritten

$$XY = x_{n-1}.2^{n-1}.\overline{Y} + x_{n-1}.2^{n-1} + \widetilde{x}.Y$$

where $\widetilde{x}$ is the $(n-1)$ least significant bits of X, then the structure can be used for multiplying twos complement numbers provided:

1. The gating function is replaced by

$$(y \oplus d).x$$

where $d=1$ for all cells on the upper left-hand boundary and $d=0$ elsewhere.

2. The value of x_{i-1} is fed to the carry input c_i as well as to the normal input x_i of the cell in the top row of the array.

3. Y is sign extended and suitably delayed sign extensions are input to left boundary y_i inputs.

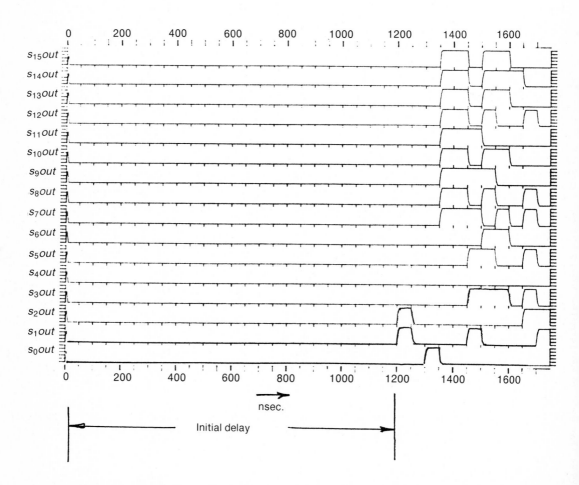

Figure 9-19   Performance of an eight-bit multiplier

The full adder chosen was a transmission gate adder because of its speed and because it generates the sum and the carry in equal time. The latches chosen were dynamic shift registers as the structure will be continuously clocked.

The following timing diagram (Figure 9–19) illustrates the performance of the eight-bit version. After the initial delay of about 1.2 µsec, the output is available after every 50 nsec.

9.6 Exercises

1. Referring to Figures 9–6 and 9–12, try to improve the layout and arrangement of the standard adder element to reduce the waste of space which is apparent in the floor plan of Figure 9–12. You must observe the overall strategy for data and control but have freedom to distribute the power in any suitable manner which will allow replication and butting together of elements.
2. Referring to Figure 9–14, design switches and other logic as necessary to implement the functions performed by the mechanical switches drawn in Figure 9–14. Work out the control lines needed to enable the ALU to perform add, subtract, logical *And*, logical *Or*, logical *Exclusive-Or*, and logical *Equality* operations.

9.7 Tutorial 4

1. Draw a bounding box representation with all inlet and output points shown (as in Figure 9–11) for the *logic circuitry* of an adder, using the multiplexer rather than the red–green function block representation used in Figure 9–11.

   Continue the design of the standard adder element (as represented in Figure 9–6) by working out a layout for the complete inverter block and then representing it as a bounding box with inlet and outlet points indicated by layer and position. *Hint*: represent each inverter circuit in bounding box form — with inlet and outlet points — so that inverters need not be drawn in detail in setting out your layout.

   Interconnect the inverter block bounding box with *either* the function block *or* the multiplexer-based adder logic (as in Figure 9–11, or as designed in this tutorial). Work out an accurate bounding box representation for the complete adder element showing inlet and outlet points, etc., by position and layer.
2. What are the overall dimensions of a four-bit adder?

   Using the bounding box representations draw an accurate floor plan of the whole four-bit adder showing position and layer of inlet and outlet points.
3. Carry out the design of a four-bit CMOS carry look-ahead adder up to stick diagram form. Then determine what standard cells are needed and design a mask layout for each.

10 Memory, registers, and aspects of system timing

'Everyone complains of his memory, but no one complains of his judgement.' Duc de la Rochefoucauld.

Having already designed two of the subsystems of the four-bit data path (Figures 8–3 and 9–1), it is now appropriate to consider the register arrangements in which the four-bit quantities to be presented to the adder and shifter will be stored. The question of data storage is an important one which has already been mentioned a number of times. It raises the question of the choice of storage elements or memory cells as well as the question of configuring arrays of such cells and the selection of a given cell or group of cells in an array.

Before looking at register arrangements, we should set out some ground rules for the design of the four-bit processor. It is essential that such rules should be established early in the piece so that a uniform approach to 'reading, writing, and refresh' is adhered to throughout. In practice, such rules should have been set out much earlier than this, but our progress through this text is such that in this case they are most effectively established here and would not have meant much earlier on.

10.1 System timing considerations

1. A two-phase nonoverlapping clock signal is assumed to be available and this clock alone will be used throughout the system.
2. Clock phases are to be identified as ϕ_1 and ϕ_2 where ϕ_1 is assumed to lead ϕ_2.
3. Bits (or data) to be stored are *written* to registers, storage elements, and subsystems on $\phi 1$ of the clock, that is, write signals *WR* are *Anded* with ϕ_1.
4. Bits or data written into storage elements may be assumed to have settled before the immediately following ϕ_2 signal, and ϕ_2 signals may be used to refresh stored data where appropriate.
5. In general, delays through data paths, combinational logic, etc. are assumed to be less than the interval between the leading edge of ϕ_1 of the clock and the leading edge of the following ϕ_2 signal.
6. Bits or data may be *read* from storage elements on the next ϕ_1 of the clock. That is, read signals *RD* are *Anded* with ϕ_1, but obviously *RD* and *WR* are generally mutually exclusive to any one storage element.
7. A general requirement for system stability is that there must be at least one clocked storage element in series with every closed loop signal path.

Strict adherence to a set of rules such as this will greatly simplify the task of system design and also help to avoid some of the disasters which will almost certainly occur if a haphazard approach is taken.

10.2 Some commonly used storage memory elements

In order to make a comparative assessment of some possible storage elements we will consider the following factors:

- area requirement;
- estimated dissipation per bit stored;
- volatility.

10.2.1 The dynamic shift register stage

One method of storing a single bit is to use the shift register approach previously introduced in section 5.5.4 (and also Figures 3–14, 5–36, 5–37, 5–38, 5–39 and 5–40).

10.2.1.1 Area

This calculation applies to an nMOS design (CMOS will be greater). Allowing for the sharing of V_{DD} and GND rails between adjacent rows of register cells, for Figure 5–40(a) with butting contacts, each bit stored will require

$$(20\lambda \times 20\lambda) \times 2 = 800\lambda^2$$

For example, for $\lambda = 2.5 \ \mu m$

$$\text{Area/Bit} = 5000 \ \mu m^2$$

To give an idea of what this implies, such area requirements would result in a maximum number of bits stored on a 4 mm × 4 mm chip area = 3.2 kbits.

10.2.1.2 Dissipation

Each inverter stage has a ratio of 8:1 and if the layout of Figure 5–40(a) (again, with butting contacts) is used, then

$$Z_{p.u.} = 2\tfrac{3}{4} R_S$$

and

$$Z_{p.d.} = \tfrac{1}{3} R_S$$

Therefore

$$\text{Current} = \frac{V_{DD}}{Z_{p.u.} + Z_{p.d.}} = \frac{5V \times 10^6}{3\tfrac{1}{12} \times 10^4} \ \mu A = \frac{500}{3\tfrac{1}{12}} \ \mu A \doteq 160 \ \mu A$$

Therefore

$$\frac{\text{Dissipation}}{\text{Bit stored}} = V_{DD} \times \text{current} = 5V \times 160 \ \mu A = 800 \ \mu W$$

Thus 3.2 kbits on a single chip would dissipate $3.2 \times 10^3 \times 800 \times 10^{-6} = 2.56$ watts.

Dissipation can be reduced to about one-third of this figure by using alternative geometry, but this is at the expense of increased area.

Clearly a CMOS design can have zero static power dissipation, but switching energy must be supplied.

10.2.1.3 Volatility

Data is stored by the charge on C_g, the gate capacitance of each inverter stage, so that data storage time (without refresh) is limited to 1 msec or less.

10.2.2 A modified nMOS lower power dynamic register element

A disadvantage of the nMOS dynamic shift register cell just discussed is the high dissipation per bit stored, due to the fact that one or other of the two inverters per bit is always on, that is, current always flows from V_{DD} to *GND*.

A modification to the pull-up transistor of each inverter can be made by replacing the conventional depletion mode with an enhancement mode transistor which is activated only during the Hi period of either the ϕ_1 or ϕ_2 clock signal. The arrangement used is indicated in Figure 10–1.

The action of the circuit may be considered by assuming, say, a logical 1 at port *A* waiting to be stored. This level will be read in on ϕ_1 of the clock and stored on C_g of the first inverter (while the current bit stored is read out of the second inverter to the next stage or output). When ϕ_1 drops Lo, the new bit level is stored on the gate to channel capacitance of the pull-down transistor of the first inverter. Subsequently, when ϕ_2 goes Hi, the state of the gate of the first inverter is sensed by virtue of the fact that the pull-up transistor of the first inverter will now conduct so that the output point is either pulled down to ground, if the stored value on C_g is a logic 1, or pulled up to $V_{DD} - V_t$ if C_g has a logic 0 stored (V_t is the necessary threshold voltage to enable the enhancement mode pull-up to conduct). The output of inverter 1 is the complement of the required bit to be stored, and this value is

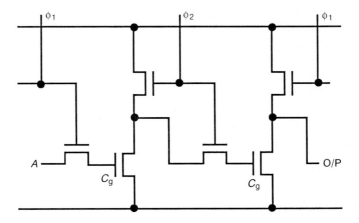

Figure 10–1 Low-power nMOS dynamic shift register

now coupled by the interstage pass transistor to be stored on the gate capacitance of the second inverter. The second inverter repeats the process outlined, but with ϕ_1 and ϕ_2 exchanged one for the other so that the true value of the stored bit is presented at the output of inverter 2; that is, one bit is stored.

10.2.2.1 Area

Slightly less than the standard nMOS shift register cell due to the lack of a butting or buried contact.

10.2.2.2 Dissipation

Will be less than that of the previous case by a factor equal to the duty ratio of the clock signals (assumed equal here). A typical factor would be in the region of 45 percent.

10.2.2.3 Volatility

As previously, data is only held while C_g holds its charge.

10.2.2.4 Other factors

Note that the logic level 1 generated at the output of each stage is degraded by V_t (due to the use of an enhancement mode pull-up transistor) and this must be allowed for.

10.2.3   A three-transistor dynamic RAM cell

An arrangement which has been used in RAM (random access memory) and other storage arrangements is set out in Figure 10–2.

With regard to Figure 10–2(a), the action is as follows:

1. With the *RD* control line in the Lo state, then a bit may be read from the bus through T_1 by taking *WR* to the Hi state so that the logic level on the bus is communicated to the gate capacitance of T_2. Then *WR* is taken Lo again.
2. The bit value is then stored for some time by C_g of T_2 while both *RD* and *WR* are Lo.
3. To read the stored bit it is only necessary to make *RD* Hi and the bus will be pulled down to ground through T_3 and T_2 if a 1 was stored. Otherwise, T_2 will be nonconducting and the bus will remain Hi due to its pull-up arrangements.

    Note that the complement of the stored bit is read onto the bus but this presents few problems and can be taken care of at some common point in the memory array.

A stick diagram for the cell identified in Figure 10–2(a) is presented as diagram (b) in the figure, and a possible layout of the superimposed masks follows in Figure 10–2(c). Note that this figure gives both nMOS and CMOS designs.

To return to our main theme, it is now appropriate to assess the three-transistor cells in the same manner as the previous ones.

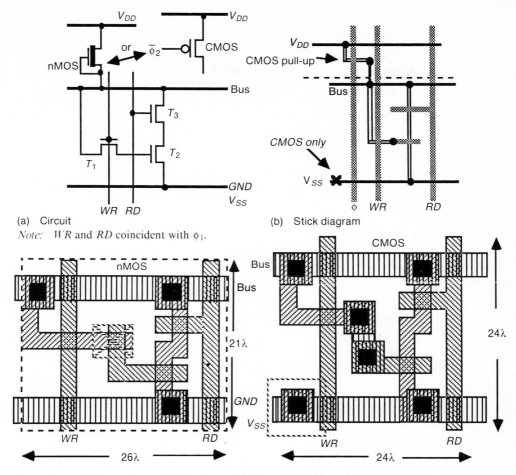

(a) Circuit

Note: *WR* and *RD* coincident with ϕ_1.

(b) Stick diagram

(c) Mask layout for part common to both nMOS and CMOS

Figure 10–2 Three-transistor memory cell

10.2.3.1 Area

From the layout it will be seen that an area of more than $500\lambda^2$ is required for each bit stored (less if *GND* (V_{SS}), and/or bus, and/or control lines are shared with other cells). Thus, for $\lambda = 2.5~\mu m$

$$\text{Area/Bit} \doteqdot 3000~\mu m^2$$

Thus, to use the previous example, the maximum number of bits which could be accommodated on a 4 mm $\times$ 4 mm silicon chip is > 4.8 kbits.

10.2.3.2 Dissipation

Static dissipation is nil since current only flows when *RD* is Hi and a 1 is stored. Thus, the actual dissipation associated with each bit stored will depend on the bus pull-up and on the duration of the *RD* signal.

10.2.3.3 Volatility

The cell is 'dynamic' and will hold data only for as long as sufficient charge remains on C_g (of T_2).

10.2.4 A one-transistor dynamic memory cell

The area occupied by each bit stored in each of the previous cases is quite considerable, which clearly limits, say, the number of bits which could be stored on a single chip of reasonable size.

Various approaches have been taken to reduce the area per bit requirements and one such approach is the one-transistor cell as shown in Figure 10–3.

The concept of the single transistor cell is quite simple, as may be seen from Figure 10–3(a). It basically consists of a capacitor C_m which can be charged during 'write' from the read/write line, provided that the row select line is Hi. The state of the charge C_m can be read subsequently by detecting the state of the charge via the same read/write line with the row select line Hi again, and a sense amplifier of a suitable nature can be designed to differentiate between a stored 0 and a stored 1.

However, in practice the cell is slightly more complex than first considerations might suggest since special steps must be taken to ensure that C_m has sufficient capacitance to allow ready detection of the stored content.

The most obvious and readily fabricated C_m in the structure under consideration would be to extend and enlarge the diffusion area comprising the source (S) of the pass transistor in Figure 10–3(b). We would then rely on the junction capacitance between the n-diffusion region and the p-substrate to form C_m. However, if we consult Table 4–2 (which gives capacitance values for a typical MOS process) we will see that the capacitance per unit area of diffusion path is much less than the capacitance per unit area between gate and channel (that is, between the channel under the thin gate oxide and the polysilicon gate area). If we use the diffusion to substrate capacitance alone, a comparatively large area will be required to give any significant value of capacitance; for example, at least $16\lambda^2$ will be needed to give a capacitance equal to $1\square C_g$ (i.e. 0.01 pF in the 5 µm MOS process being considered). A solution is to create a much more significant capacitor by using a polysilicon plate (which is connected to V_{DD}) over the diffusion area. Thus, C_m is formed as a three-plate structure as indicated in Figure 10–3(c). For example, for the area given in Figure 10–3(d), $C_{DIFF-POLY} = 10\square C_g$ ($= 0.1$ pF), while the contribution from the diffusion region to the substrate will be much smaller but will add some 25 percent to this figure, giving a total C_m of 0.125 pF for the layout considered. Even so, careful design is necessary to achieve consistent readability.

10.2.4.1 Area

The area enclosed to indicate the standard cell in Figure 10–3(d) is $200\lambda^2$. Thus for $\lambda = 2.5$ µm

$$\text{Area/bit stored} = 200\lambda^2 = 1250 \ \mu\text{m}^2$$

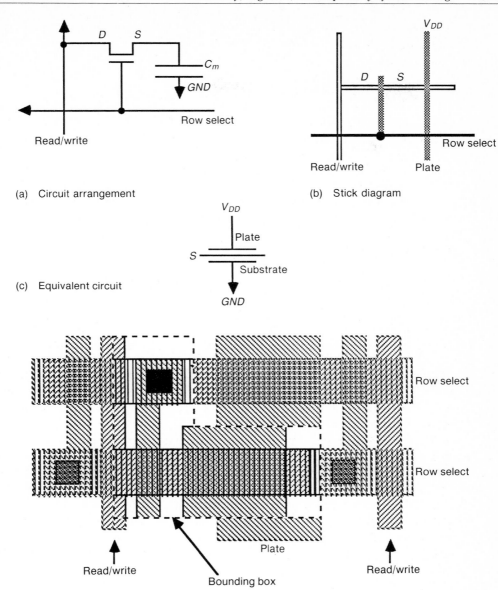

(a)   Circuit arrangement

(b)   Stick diagram

(c)   Equivalent circuit

(d)   Mask layout

Figure 10–3   One-transistor dynamic memory cell

Therefore, number of bits per 4 mm × 4 mm chip area is approximately 12 kbits (allowing some 'overheads' for sensing, etc.).

10.2.4.2 Dissipation

There is no static power associated with the cell itself, but there must be an allowance for switching energy while writing to and reading from the storage elements.

10.2.4.3 Volatility

Quite obviously, leakage current mechanisms will deplete the charge stored in C_m and thus the data will only be held for up to 1 msec or less. Therefore, there is a need to provide periodic refresh operations.

It will also be realized that reading the cell is a destructive operation and that the stored bit must be rewritten every time it is read.

10.2.5   A pseudo-static RAM/register cell

So far, all the storage elements considered have been volatile and, thus, have an implied need to be periodically refreshed. This is not always convenient and it is necessary to consider the design of a static storage cell which will hold data indefinitely. A common way of meeting this need is to store a bit in two inverter stages in series with feedback, say, on ϕ_2 to refresh the data every clock cycle. The circuit arrangement is shown in Figures 10–4(a) and 10–5(a) and it will be seen that a bit may be written to the cell from the bus by energizing the *WR* line. From our system timing consideration of section 10.1 we will assume *WR* to occur in coincidence with ϕ_1 of the clock. Thus, the bit is stored on C_g of inverter 1 and will be reproduced complemented at the output of inverter 1 and true at the output of inverter 2. It will be seen that during every ϕ_2 of the clock the stored bit is refreshed through the gated feedback path from the output of inverter 2 to the input of inverter 1. Thus the bit will be held as long as ϕ_2 of the clock recurs at intervals less

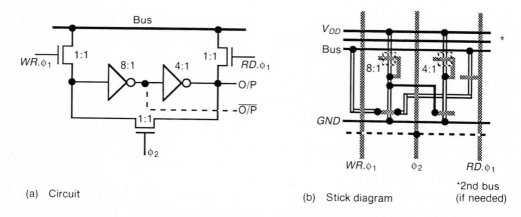

(a)   Circuit   (b)   Stick diagram

                                            *2nd bus
                                            (if needed)

Figure 10–4   nMOS pseudo-static memory cell

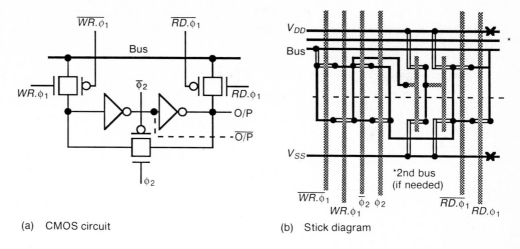

(a)   CMOS circuit

(b)   Stick diagram

Figure 10–5   CMOS pseudo-static memory cell (See Color Plate 12)

than the decay time of the stored bit. To read the state of the cell it is only necessary to energize the *RD* line, which is also assumed coincident with ϕ_1 of the clock, and the bit will be read onto the bus.

Note that:

1.   *WR* and *RD* must be mutually exclusive (but are both coincident with ϕ_1).
2.   If ϕ_2 is used for refresh, then the cell must not be read during ϕ_2 of the clock unless the feedback path is inhibited during *RD*. If an attempt is made to read the cell onto the bus during refresh, then charge sharing effects between the bus and input (C_g) capacitances may cause the destruction of the stored bit.
3.   Cells must be stackable, both side by side and top to bottom. This must be carefully considered *together* with the overall strategy to be observed when the layout is drawn.
4.   Allow for other bus lines to run through the cell so that register and memory arrays are readily configured.

With these factors in mind it is possible to draw up stick diagrams as in Figures 10–4(b) and 10–5(b), which show the basic cells.

Mask level layouts follow from this; a possible layout for an nMOS cell which can be written to from bus *A* and can be read onto bus *A* or bus *B* is given in Figure 10–6.

The mask layout shown occupies an area of $59\lambda \times 45\lambda = 2655\lambda^2$, but if we are considering a single bus and a more compact layout then the area requirement can be reduced to about $1750\lambda^2$ or less.

The CMOS version of this cell is *not* really a practical proposition other than for storing a few bits. Ten transistors are needed per bit stored, which makes the cell too demanding in area. However, it is mentioned here for completeness.

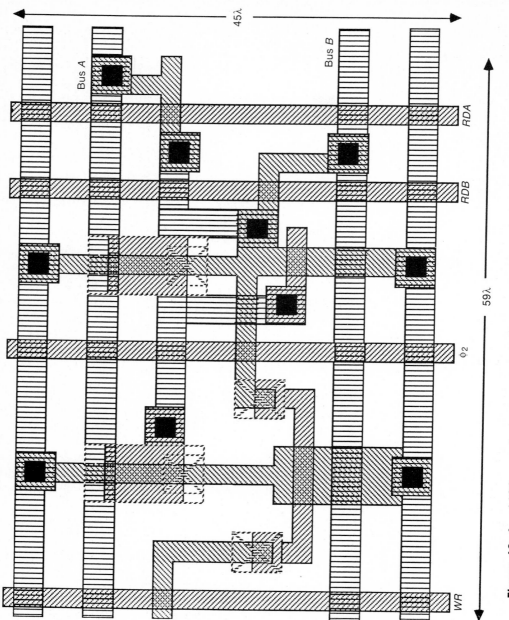

Figure 10-6 nMOS pseudo-static memory cell with read to either of two buses

A printer-produced plot of an alternative nMOS mask layout with read and write to a single bus, but with an additional bus line running through the cell, is given as Figure 10–7 and it will be seen that the area occupied is just over $2000\lambda^2$.

The way in which two such storage cells may be put together and the consequent need for selection circuitry to read or write to either cell is illustrated in

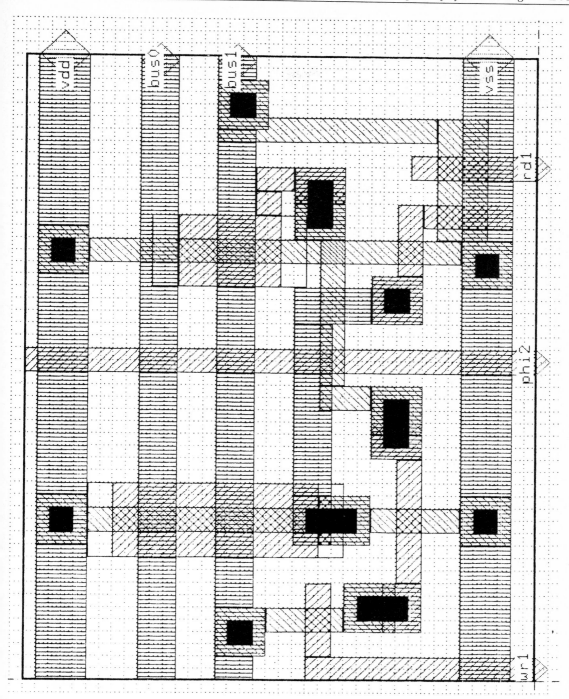

Figure 10–7 nMOS pseudo-static memory cell with two bus lines but read and write to one bus

Figure 10–8. This, again, is a printer-generated plot and you are asked to note that the extra heavily hatched areas are those where individual features of cell geometries overlap each other. It is not always the case that hatching is aligned globally and some plot routines used here will also display a small gap between areas butted together without overlap.

To complete the consideration of this geometry we have included Color Plate 13, which is a printer plot of 32 such cells forming a memory array. It will be seen that row and column decoders would be provided to enable addressing of the memory. The diagram serves to illustrate the way in which architecture evolves from relatively simple cells.

To return to the original purpose, we may now set out the relevant parameters for this popular and useful nMOS pseudo-static storage cell in the same terms as have been used previously.

10.2.5.1 Area

A typical area for a single cell with single bus is in the region of $1750\lambda^2$. Therefore, for $\lambda = 2.5~\mu$m

$$\text{Area/bit} \doteq 11000~\mu\text{m}^2$$

Thus, the maximum number of bits of storage per 4 mm × 4 mm chip is approximately 1.4 kbits.

10.2.5.2 Dissipation

The cell uses two inverters, one with an 8:1 and the other with a 4:1 ratio. Dissipation will depend on the current drawn and, thus, on the actual geometry of the inverters, but let us assume that inverters are based on minimum feature size gate areas so that the 8:1 stage will present a resistance of 90 kΩ and the 4:1 a resistance of 50 kΩ between the supply rails. Now when one stage is off, the other is on so that, say, each spends half-time in the conducting state.

Therefore

$$\text{Average current} = 0.5 \left(\frac{5\text{V}}{90~\text{k}\Omega} + \frac{5\text{V}}{50~\text{k}\Omega} \right) \doteq 80~\mu\text{A}$$

Therefore

$$\text{Dissipation per bit stored} = 80~\mu\text{A} \times 5\text{V} = 400~\mu\text{W}$$

Thus 1.4 kbits on a single chip would dissipate 560 mW.

10.2.5.3 Volatility

The cell is nonvolatile provided ϕ_2 signals are present.

10.2.6 Four-transistor dynamic and six-transistor static CMOS memory cells

Most of the preceding memory cells involved n-type transistors and can therefore be implemented in either nMOS or CMOS designs. The cells about to be described

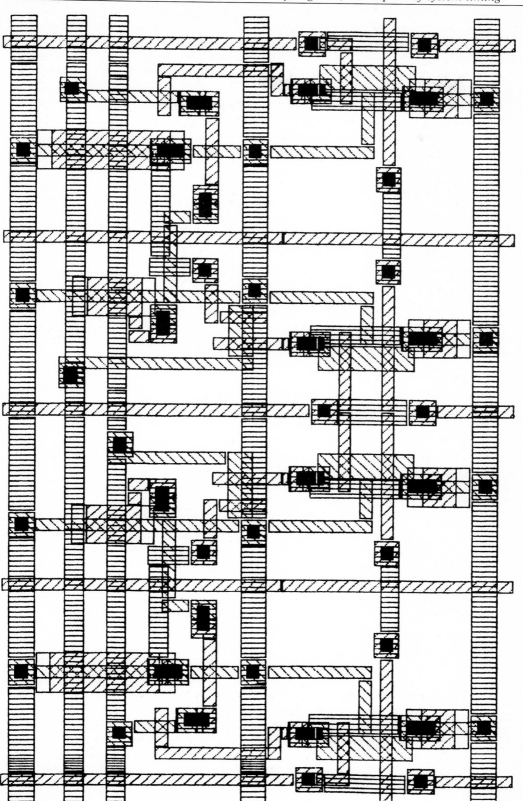

MEM2CELL.CIF

Figure 10–8 Two memory cells with select circuitry

(See also Figure 10–7 and Color Plate 13.)

utilise both n- and p-transistors and are therefore intended for CMOS systems only (although the dynamic element can be readily adapted to nMOS-only implementation).

Both the dynamic and static elements, set out in Figure 10–9, use a two bus per bit arrangement so that associated with every bit stored there will be a bit and a $\overline{\text{bit}}$ bus as shown. In both cases the buses are precharged to Logic 1 before read or write operations take place.

Figure 10–9(a) gives the arrangement for a four-transistor dynamic cell for storing one bit. Each bit is stored on the gate capacitance of two n-transistors T_1 and T_2 and a description of the write and read operation follows.

10.2.6.1   *Write operations*

Both bit and $\overline{\text{bit}}$ buses are precharged to V_{DD} (logic 1) in coincidence with ϕ_1 of an assumed two-phase clock. Precharging is effected via the p-transistors T_5 and T_6 in the diagram. Now (with reference to Figure 10–9(c)), the appropriate 'column select' line is activated in coincidence with the clock phase ϕ_2 and either the bit or $\overline{\text{bit}}$ line is discharged by the logic levels present on the I/O bus lines; the I/O lines acting in this case as a current sink when carrying a logic 0. The 'row select' signal is activated at the same time as 'column select' and the bit line states are 'written in' via T_3 and T_4 and stored by T_1 and T_2 as charges on gate capacitances C_{g2} and C_{g1} respectively. Note that the way in which T_1 and T_2 are interconnected will force them into complementary states whilst the row select line is high. Once the select lines are deactivated, the bit stored will be remembered until the gate capacitances lose enough charge to drop the 'on' gate voltage below the threshold level for T_1 or T_2.

10.2.6.2   *Read operations*

Once again both bit and $\overline{\text{bit}}$ lines are precharged to V_{DD} via T_5 and T_6 during ϕ_1 so that both lines will be at logic 1. Now if, say, a 1 has been stored, T_2 will be on and T_1 will be off and thus the $\overline{\text{bit}}$ line will be discharged to V_{SS} (logic 0) through T_2 and the stored bit thus reappears on the bit lines.

When such cells are used in RAM arrays, it is necessary to keep the area of each cell to a minimum and transistors will be of minimum size and therefore incapable of sinking large charges quickly. Thus it is important that the charges stored on the bit lines are modest and this may not be the case if they are directly paralleled by the I/O line and other associated capacitances through the column select circuitry. RAM arrays therefore generally employ some form of sense amplifier. A possible arrangement is shown in Figure 10–9(c) in which T_1, T_2, T_3, and T_4 form a *flip–flop circuit*. If we assume the sense line to be inactive, then the state of the bit lines is reflected in the charges present on the gate capacitances of T_1 and T_3 with respect to V_{DD} such that a 1 will turn off and a 0 turn on either transistor. Current flowing from V_{DD} through an on transistor helps to maintain the state of the bit lines and predetermines the state which will be taken up by the sense flip–flop when the sense line is then activated. The geometry of the single sense amplifier per column will be such as to amplify the current sinking capability of the selected memory cell.

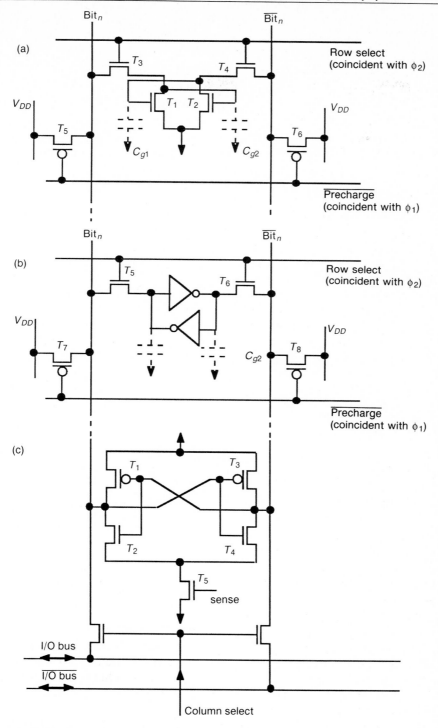

Figure 10-9 Dynamic and static memory cells

Figure 10–9(b) indicates an adaption of the basic dynamic cell, just considered, to form a static memory cell. At the expense of two additional transistors per bit stored, the transistors T_1 and T_2 of Figure 10–9(a) can each be replaced by an inverter as shown in Figure 10–9(b). This arrangement will clearly render the cell static in its data-storing capabilities.

The general arrangement of a RAM utilizing the circuits considered here appears later in this chapter (Figure 10–23).

10.2.7 A JK flip–flop circuit

No consideration of memory elements would be complete without the JK flip–flop. The JK flip–flop is a particularly widely used arrangement and is an example of static memory elements. It is also most useful in that other common arrangements such as the D flip–flop and the T flip–flop are readily formed from the JK arrangement.

Edge-triggered circuits are conveniently designed using an ASM (algorithmic state machine — see C. Clare, *Designing Logic Systems Using State Machines*, McGraw-Hill, 1983) approach and the design equations for a JK flip–flop, as in Figure 10–10, follow from an ASM chart setting out the requirements as in Figure 10–11. It should be noted that the flip–flop is assumed to have an asynchronous clear (*Clr*) input as well as the clocked *J* and *K* inputs, and that *J* and *K* are read in during the Hi level of ϕ of the clock, and the data thus read is transferred to the output on the falling edge of ϕ ($\nabla \phi$).

Design equations are readily derived from the ASM chart of Figure 10–11 and, using the secondary variable assignment (*AB* in the figure), we may express the requirements as follows

$$A = a.\overline{Clr}.(\overline{b} + \overline{\phi} + \overline{K}) + \overline{b}.\overline{Clr}.J.\phi$$

$$B = \overline{Clr}.(a.\overline{\phi} + b.\phi)$$

where output $Q = B$; and a and b are the fed back state of the secondary variables A and B respectively.

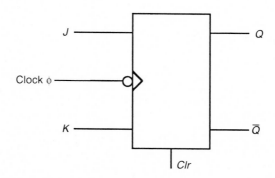

Figure 10–10   JK flip–flop

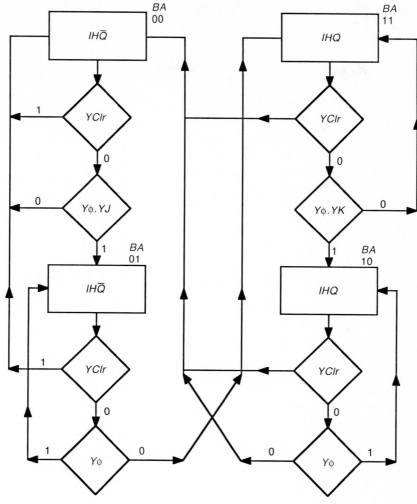

Note: $IHQ = Q$ output 'Hi' (Immediate)
$YClr$ = Yes clear
$Y\phi.YJ$ = Yes clock and J, etc.

Figure 10-11 ASM chart for JK flip-flop

It is convenient at this point to derive also the complementary expressions

$$\bar{A} = Clr + \bar{a}.\bar{J} + \bar{a}.\bar{\phi}.J + b.\phi.K + \bar{a}.b$$
$$= Clr + \bar{a}.(\bar{J} + b + \bar{\phi}) + b.\phi.K$$
$$\bar{B} = Clr + \bar{a}.\bar{b} + \bar{b}.\phi + \bar{a}.\bar{\phi}$$

and output $\bar{Q} = \bar{B}$.

10.2.7.1 *Logic gate implementations*

We are now faced with a choice of implementations based on *Nand* or *Nor*, on switch logic; or, of course, on a combination.

The expressions for *A* and *B* are readily realized in *Nand* or *Nor* logic, as shown in Figure 10–12, and it will be seen that the master/slave arrangement is fairly obvious in each case.

However, an initial inspection of each arrangement will reveal that, for nMOS, the *Nand* arrangement is impractical, due to the relatively large number of gates requiring three or more inputs which are inherently large in area and slow in performance. The obvious nMOS alternative is a *Nor* gate arrangement which is a practical proposition and can be readily implemented.

For CMOS, both *Nand* and *Nor* gates are suitable although the *Nor* gate is generally slower.

10.2.7.2 *Switch logic and inverter implementation*

In setting out an arrangement of *n* pass transistors to realize the logical requirements, we must bear in mind earlier considerations on the nature of switch logic networks (i.e. no more than four pass transistors in series (section 4.10); pass tran-

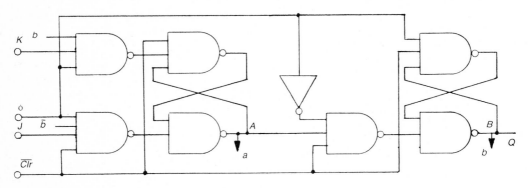

(a) *Nand* gate version

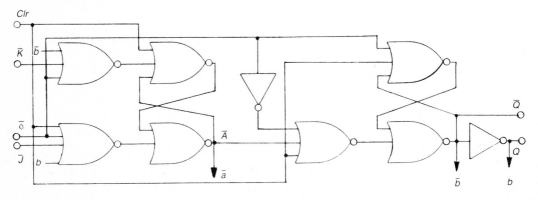

(b) *Nor* gate version

Figure 10–12 Logic arrangement for JK flip-flop

sistors not to be used to drive the gates of other pass transistors (Figure 5–2); the logic 0 as well as the logic 1 transmission conditions to be deliberately satisfied (section 5.4.2)). Thus, we need to implement the expressions for A and B *and* the expressions for $\bar{A}$ and $\bar{B}$ given earlier in this section. The resulting arrangement is given as Figure 10–13 and is a realization of the JK flip–flop based on n-pass transistor logic and inverters only.

10.2.7.3   *Comparison of the nMOS Nor gate and switch logic implementation*

Turning first to Figure 10–12(b), it will be seen that the *Nor* gate realization requires:

- 1×4 I/P *Nor* gate;
- 4×3 I/P *Nor* gate;
- 2×2 I/P *Nor* gate;
- $4 \times$ Inverters (two of which invert J and K at the input).

So that we can compare complexity we may 'convert' each *Nor* gate into an inverter plus pass transistors (e.g. 1×2 I/P *Nor* gate is equivalent to one inverter plus one pass transistor, etc.)

Thus, allowing for inverters for ϕ and K inputs, the *Nor gate realization* is equivalent to 11 *inverters* + 13 *pass transistors*. This may be directly compared with the circuit of Figure 10–13. It will be seen that the *switch logic realization* comprises 8 *inverters* + 25 *pass transistors*. Thus, the switch logic realization is the more complex and will require much more area because of the greater number of interconnections present on the diagram. However, the current drawn by the *Nor* gate version will be higher than the switch logic circuit by almost 50 percent. Thus, the *power dissipation* of the circuit of Figure 10–12(b) will be something like 50 percent greater than the circuit of Figure 10–13.

As far as switching speed is concerned, the relative response times can be assessed from following the sequences required to form A and B in the two circuits.

To form A
    Nor gate form: Input inverters + 3 *Nor* gates (max.) in series
    Switch logic form: Input inverters + 4 pass transistors in series (max.) + 2
                        inverters for output

To form B (assuming A is stable at end of $\phi = $ Hi)
    Nor gate form: 2 *Nor* gates (max.) in series + 1 inverter
    Switch logic form: 3 pass transistors (max.) in series + 2 inverters

The time needed to form A determines the minimum period for which ϕ must be Hi, and the time needed to form B will be the delay between the falling edge of the clock signal ($\nabla\phi$) and the response at output Q.

It is thus likely that the *Nor* gate version will be faster, but at the expense of increased power consumption, and quite obviously the static memory cell constituted by the JK flip–flop will occupy considerably more (>4 times) the area and

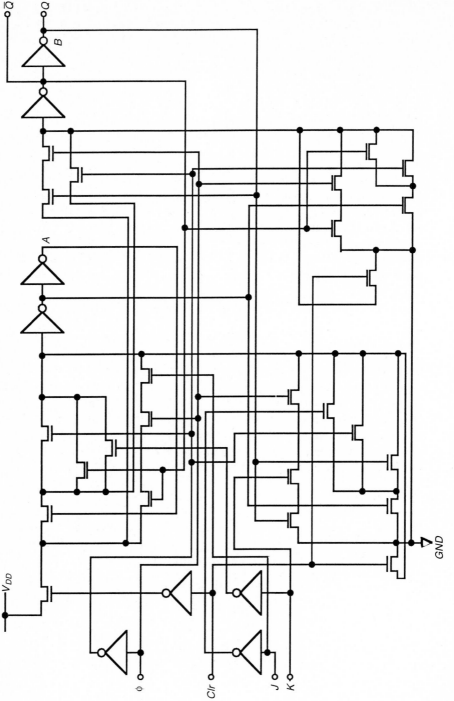

Figure 10–13 Switch logic implementation of JK flip–flop

dissipate much more power (>4 times) compared to the pseudo-static cell of section 10.2.5 of this text. Similar comparisons can be made for the equivalent CMOS arrangements.

10.2.8   D flip–flop circuit

A D flip–flop is readily formed from a JK flip–flop by renaming the J input D and then replacing connections to K by $\overline{D}$ (Figure 10–12). Similarly, a T (Toggle) flip–flop is formed from the JK by making $J = K = 1$ (Hi).

It should also be noted that the arrangements given may be simplified by the omission of the *Clr* input, or that a *Preset* input can be substituted for or added to the *Clr* input if required. Furthermore, the way in which clock activation takes place may be modified by a reshaping of requirements in the ASM chart of Figure 10–11 and a consequent reformulation of the JK flip–flop design equations given at the beginning of section 10.2.6 of this text.

However a much simpler version of the D flip–flop is obtained from a pseudo-static approach, as in Figure 10–14 for CMOS. Clearly, an nMOS version is also readily configured.

10.3 Forming arrays of memory cells

The memory cells discussed in section 10.2 and others will most often be used in arrays of some form or other. Typical arrays are registers and random access memories (RAM) and these arrays will be used as examples in this section. We must not forget, however, that another common application is to use memory elements individually as 'flags' or 'status bits' in system design. In any event, there must be some means of *selecting* a particular cell or group of cells and some means of effecting *read* or *write* operations.

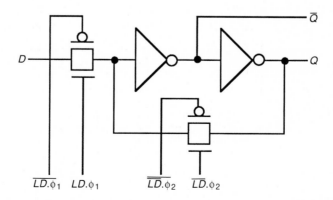

Figure 10–14   A CMOS pseudo-static D flip–flop

10.3.1 Selection of cells or groups of cells

An example would be to consider an eight-bit register, say one of the working registers in a system, in which data is presented and stored in parallel. For purposes of *selection*, all eight cells comprising the eight-bit word of the desired register must be selected simultaneously and the appropriate read (*RD*) or write (*WR*) signals applied at the same time, so that data may be written to or read from the register from or to an eight-bit data bus (presumably). Again, in a RAM arrangement, an individual word of *n* bits must be selected from a large number of similar *n*-bit words and written to or read from.

It is appropriate, then, to consider ways of selecting a register from a group of registers. To give some meaning to these considerations, it is most appropriate now to take the design of the four-bit data path one step further and consider the array of 4 × 4-bit registers which form the next subsystem of the overall design (Figures 8–3 and 9–1). Note that all 'write to register' operations will come from, say, bus *A*, while any register can be read to bus *A* and/or bus *B* so that two four-bit quantities are connected simultaneously to the adder (ALU).

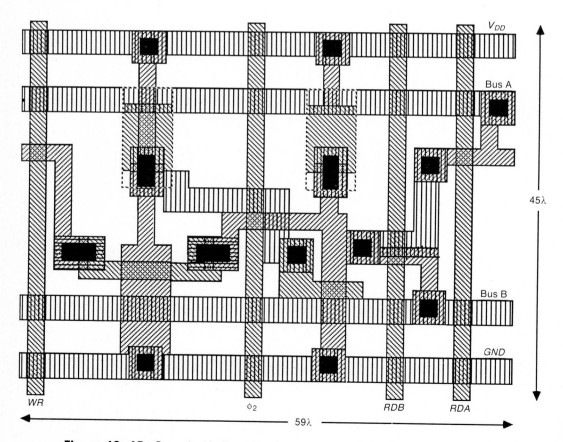

Figure 10–15 Pseudo-static memory cell with read/write to bus A and read only to bus B

10.3.2 Building up the floor plan for a 4×4-bit register array

This will be the final subsystem to be designed for the four-bit data path; the I/O port facilities will be left to the reader as an exercise in completing the system design (prior to adding inlet and outlet pads through which the chip will be bonded to the outside world).

Starting with a bounding box representation of the chosen memory cell — in this case the pseudo-static cell with two bus lines — we can arrive at a bounding box for a single four-bit register and hence the floor plan for a 4×4-bit register array. Allowing for two connections to bus *A* and one to bus *B*, a layout for the cell, using butting contacts, can be set out as indicated in Figure 10–15, and the corresponding bounding box representation of the cell then follows at Figure 10–16. For the cell layout, it may readily be seen that the $59\lambda \times 45\lambda$ boundary is arrived at by combining the contact and associated diffusion path from the output of one cell with that to the input of the next cell, both being connections to bus *A*.

The bounding box representation of the cell may then be 'stacked' to form a four-bit register floor plan as in Figure 10–17. Note the way in which the cells stack

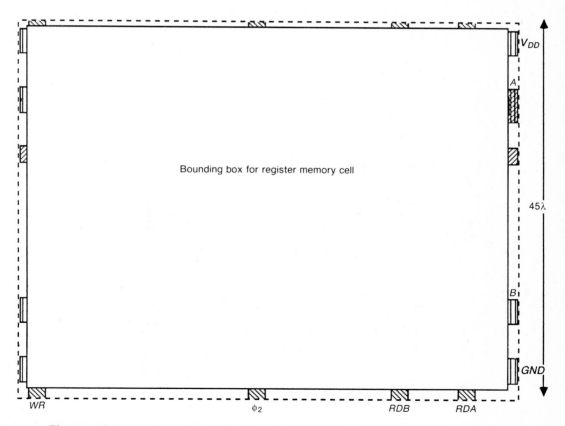

Figure 10–16   Bounding box for cell of figure 10–15

'vertically' to form a four-bit word and it will also be seen that a 'vertical' distribution of power has been assumed from other areas of the chip. Note also that short, wide diffusion 'duck unders' have been used to allow the ground rail to cross the V_{DD} rail, but it must be stressed that V_{DD} and GND (V_{SS}) connections must

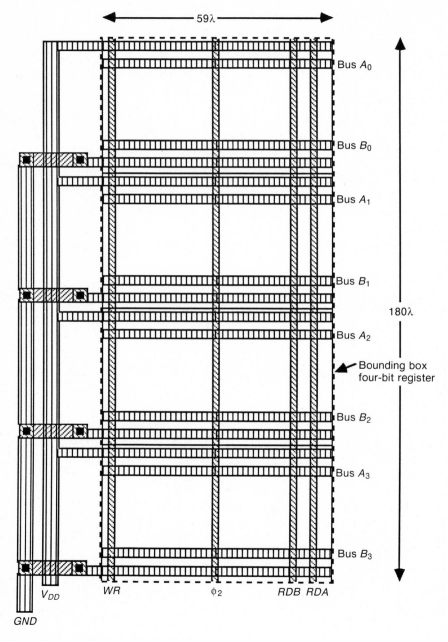

Figure 10–17 Four-bit register outline

always be made through metal rails except where crossovers are unavoidable; such crossovers should then normally be by means of short diffusion duck unders.

The required architecture may then be built up by stacking complete registers, side by side in this case, to form the desired four-register array. The floor plan is given as Figure 10–18 and the diagram clearly shows the direction of data flow and control signal distribution. It must be noted that this floor plan does *not* include the selection and control circuitry as yet.

10.3.3 Selection and control of the 4×4-bit register array

With reference to Figure 10–18, it will be seen that the register array must be provided with the control signals *WR*, *RDB*, and *RDA*, combined with register select so that each register may be selected for read or write. We must also note that we need the capability to select two registers simultaneously for connection to the adder and that, in some cases, we may wish to read the contents of a single register to both *A* and *B* buses. One approach is to make use of decoder (or demultiplexer) circuits to route the control signals, as suggested in Figure 10–19. (For the reader unfamiliar with demultiplexer circuits, the select lines allow routing of a single input to any one of the output lines, that is, like a multiposition switch, and is the converse of the multiplexer which selects any one of a number of input lines to be routed to a single output.)

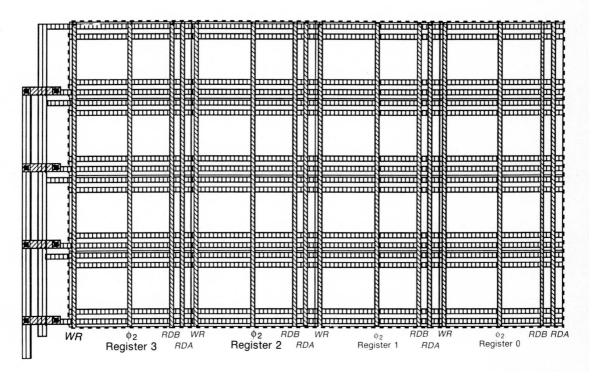

WR ϕ_2 RDB WR ϕ_2 RDB   WR ϕ_2 RDB WR ϕ_2 RDB RDA
Register 3   RDA   Register 2   RDA   Register 1   RDA   Register 0

Figure 10–18 4×4-bit register floor plan

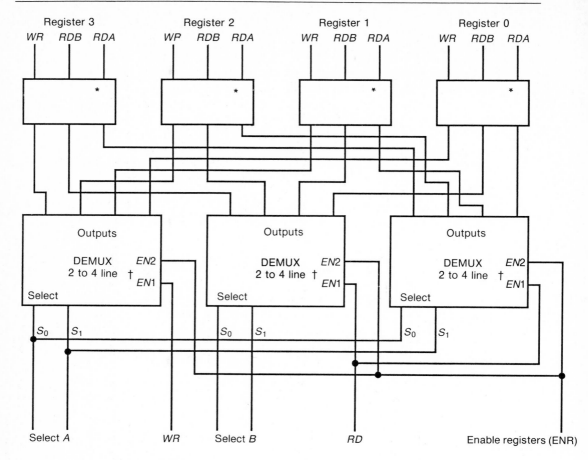

Note: †In this case, the effective input to each decoder is *EN*1.*EN*2.
*Indicates buffers/drivers if required.

Figure 10–19 Decoder-based selection and control

An alternative, and in this case the chosen approach, is to make use of a demultiplexer, buffers, and logic circuitry to combine and route control signals, and provide the necessary drive to each read and write line. Design equations may be written as follows (remembering that 'writes' take place from bus *A* while 'reads' are to both buses).

$$(WR.REGX) = (WR).(BUSA.REGX.ENR)$$

which may be put into *Nor* form

$$(\overline{WR.REGX}) = \overline{WR} + (\overline{BUSA.REGX.ENR})$$

where

$$ENR = \text{Enable Registers}$$

$$BUSA.REGX = \text{Select Register } X \text{ for Bus } A$$

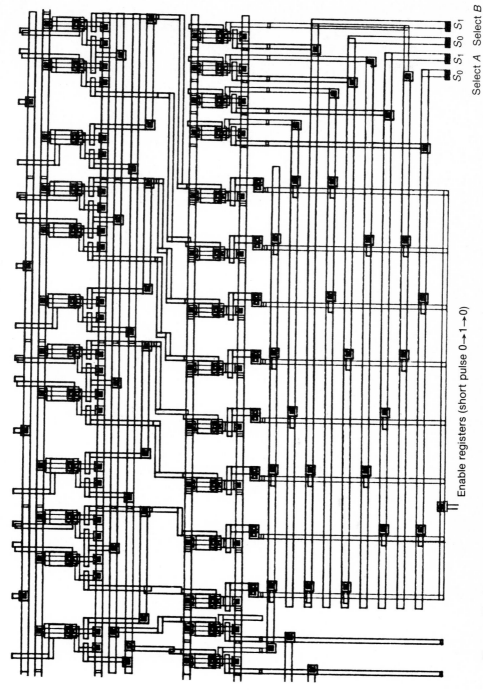

Enable registers (short pulse $0 \rightarrow 1 \rightarrow 0$)

S_0 S_1 S_0 S_1
S_1 S_0 S_1

Select A Select B

Figure 10–20 Mask level layout for 4×4-bit register selection and control

Similarly for

$$RDA.REGX = (RD).(BUSA.REGX.ENR)$$

the *Nor* form is

$$(\overline{RDA.REGX}) = \overline{RD} + (\overline{BUSA.REGX.ENR})$$

and

$$RDB.REGX = (RD).(BUSB.REGX.ENR)$$

has *Nor* form

$$(\overline{RDB.REGX}) = \overline{RD} + (\overline{BUSB.REGX.ENR})$$

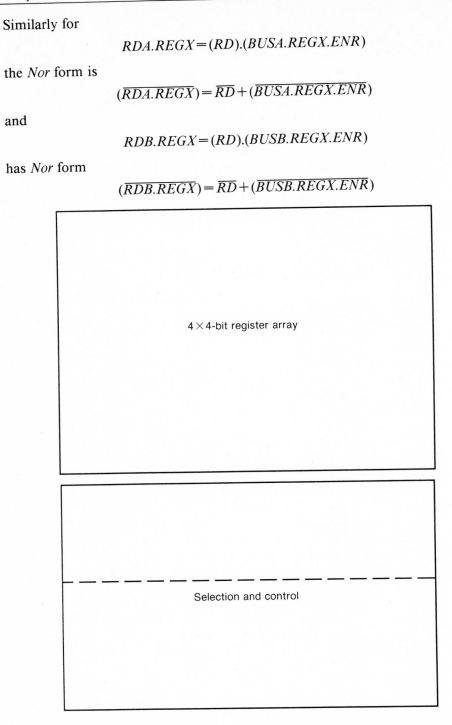

Figure 10–21 Floor plan of 4×4-bit register with selection and control

The composite *And* forms (*BUSB.REGX.ENR*, etc.) are conveniently formed by a multiplexer followed by an inverter to form the complementary signals needed by a *Nor* gate-based circuit for driving the register control lines.

A possible arrangement is given as Figure 10–20. In creating the stick diagram and layout it will be seen that control signals must flow through the network and emerge in positions *compatible* with the disposition of control inputs to the register array. This again demonstrates the importance of carefully considering communication paths in designing the subsystems of any architecture, and in having set out a strategy for control and data flow at an early stage.

The whole register array and selection and control circuitry may then be represented in floor plan form, as in Figure 10–21. The architecture of the whole array with select and control is included in Figure 11–19 and Color Plate 14, which is a mask level layout of the four-bit data path chip which was manufactured and tested.

10.3.4   Random access memory (RAM) arrays

Having considered individual memory cells, some of which are quite small in area and low in dissipation, and having considered the use of memory cells in an array of registers, it is not a large step to consider much larger arrays of which the RAM is the most commonplace.

It is relatively easy to form 'words' of memory cells, and Figure 10–22 indicates a possible layout for four-bit word storage locations derived from the nMOS pseudo-static memory cell of Figure 10–4 (etc.). The CMOS memory cell of Figure 10–9(b) and associated circuits will form a RAM array as shown in Figure 10–23.

Finally, the architecture of a typical RAM array is illustrated by the floor plan and some of the interconnections for a 16-location×4-bit word array in Figure 10–24. It will be seen that, in this case, the incoming address lines are decoded into row and column (with *RD* or *WR*) select lines, which are then used to select individual words in the memory. It will be noted that V_{DD} and *GND* (V_{SS}) rails are not shown, but it is clear that they may be interleaved with the data bus lines. Note that in large arrays in particular, the data bus lines will become relatively long and must, therefore, be run on the metal layer to avoid excessive capacitance or series resistance. As discussed earlier, the bus capacitance *and* the control line capacitances *must* be allowed for in the design.

To complete this section, Figure 10–25 is a plot of the *metal layer* only for a 16-location×4-bit memory. The regularity of the memory array, the way in which the buses are run, and the various subsections of the floor plan are clearly evident.

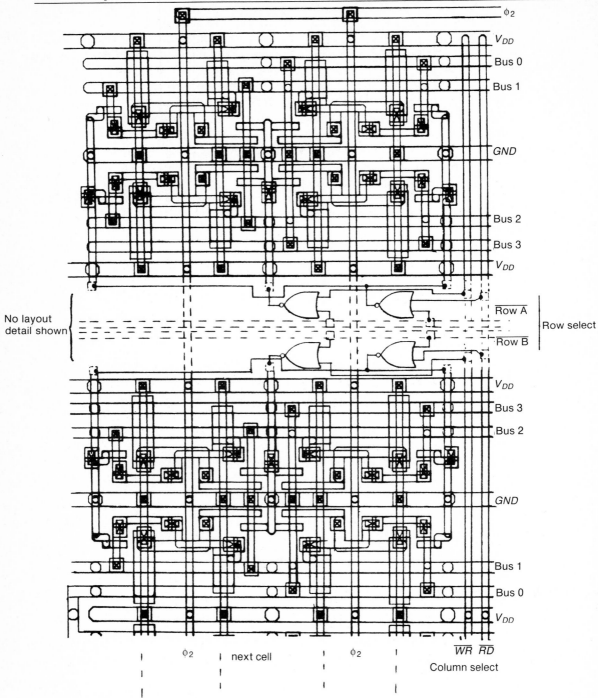

Figure 10-22 Two four-bit words of nMOS RAM array

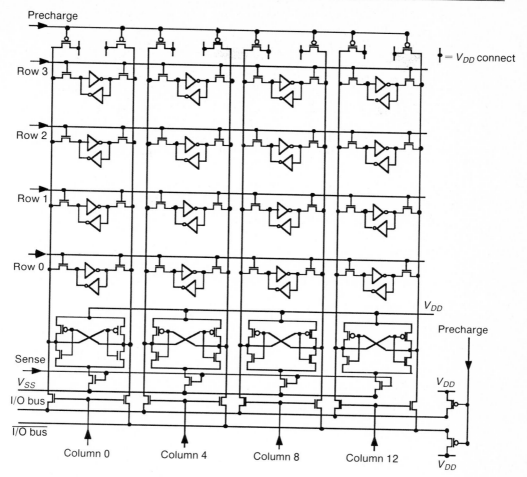

Figure 10-23 16-bit CMOS static memory array

10.4 Exercises

1. Design a two-line to four-line decoder (demultiplexer) circuit to the mask layout level and determine its bounding box. Then work out the arrangement of and area occupied by the 4×4-bit register select and control circuit of Figure 10–19.

2. Taking a 16-location×2-bit RAM arrangement as an example, suggest (with sketches only) the way in which such an arrangement could be configured for a two-port operation (that is, data can be read or written to any location from either of *two* two-bit data buses).

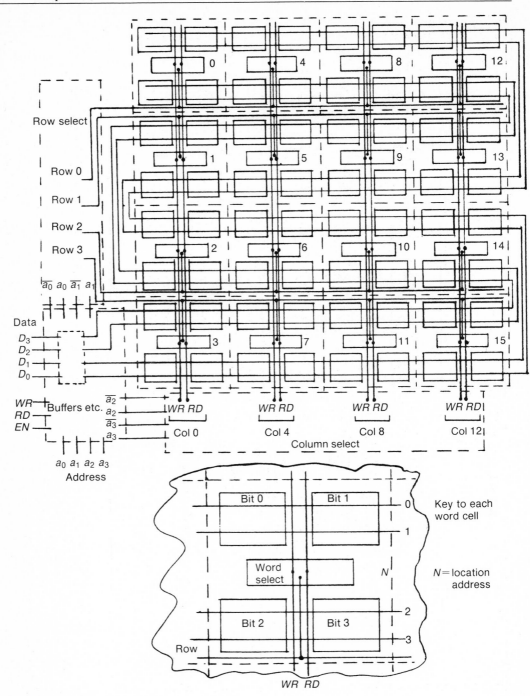

Figure 10-24 Floor plan of 16×4-bit RAM

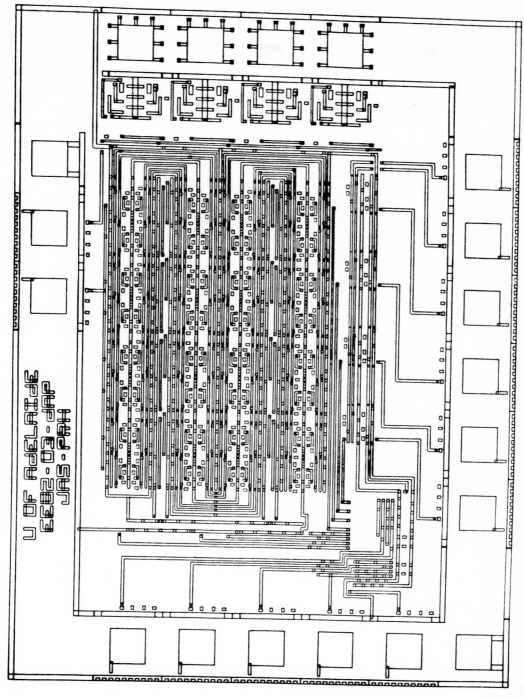

Figure 10–25 Metal layer only for 16×4-bit RAM

10.5 Tutorial 5

1. Using the 4×4-bit register and select and control circuit developed in Chapter 10 (or use the select and control circuit designed in Exercise 1 above), work out all communication paths and interconnections between the three subsystems of the four-bit data path which we have so far designed. Use a bounding box representation for each subsystem and clearly indicate the layers on which interconnections are made. What is a suitable overall area for the processor as so far designed?

2. nMOS: Using a four-bit word arrangement of Figure 10–22 and having regard to the RAM arrangement of Figure 10–24, draw a mask level layout for the word select circuit associated with each four-bit word and, thus, determine the overall area needed for each word stored. Next, design stick diagram level arrangements for the remaining blocks on the floor plan — that is, the row and column selection circuits and the input buffers and drivers, etc. Hence, *estimate* the area needed for the 16×4-bit RAM as a whole (without I/O pads).

3. CMOS: Starting with the 16-bit RAM array of Figure 10–23, design suitable decoding and control circuitry to allow row and column selection and read and write operation of the array. (You will find it useful to refer back to section 10.2.6.)

    Design *one* memory cell as far as the mask layout and determine a suitable area per bit stored.

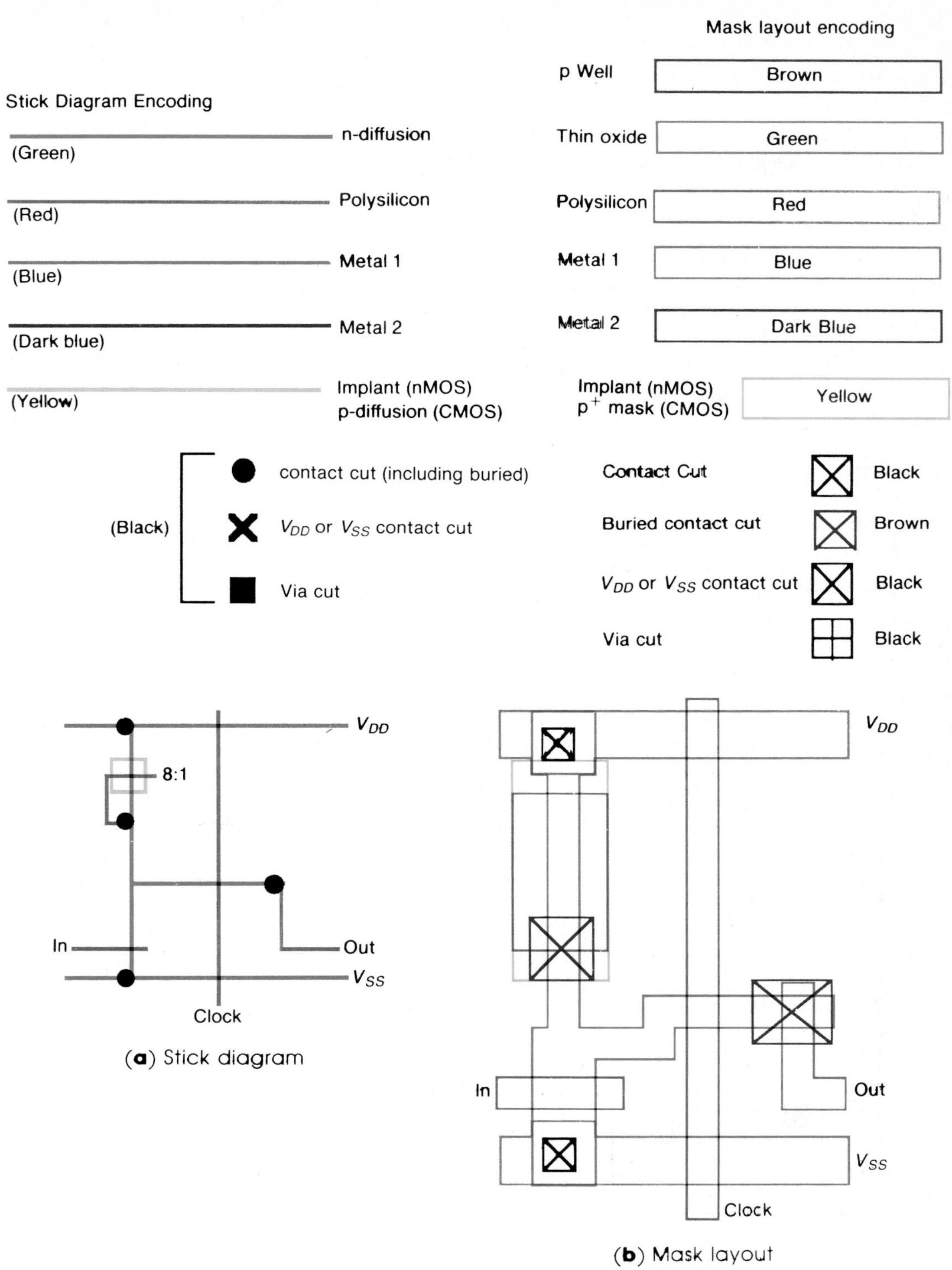

Mask layout encoding
p Well
Brown
Thin oxide
Green
Polysilicon
Red
Metal 1
Blue
Metal 2
Dark Blue
Implant (nMOS)
p$^+$ mask (CMOS)
Yellow
Contact Cut
Black
Buried contact cut
Brown
V_{DD} or V_{SS} contact cut
Black
Via cut
Black
Stick Diagram Encoding
n-diffusion
(Green)
Polysilicon
(Red)
Metal 1
(Blue)
Metal 2
(Dark blue)
Implant (nMOS)
p-diffusion (CMOS)
(Yellow)
(Black)
contact cut (including buried)
V_{DD} or V_{SS} contact cut
Via cut
V_{DD}
8:1
In
Out
V_{SS}
Clock
(a) Stick diagram
V_{DD}
In
Out
V_{SS}
Clock
(b) Mask layout

Color Plate 1 nMOS and CMOS stick and layout encoding (see Figure 3–1)
nMOS shift register cell (with buried contacts) (see Figure 5–40(a))

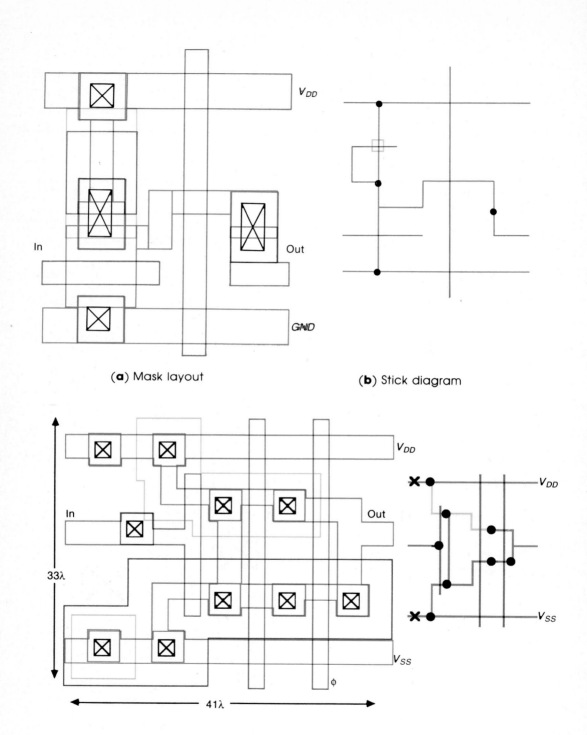

(a) Mask layout   **(b)** Stick diagram

Color Plate 2 *Top:* nMOS shift register cell (with butting contact) (see Figure 5–40(a))
Bottom: CMOS shift register cell (see Figure 5–40(b))

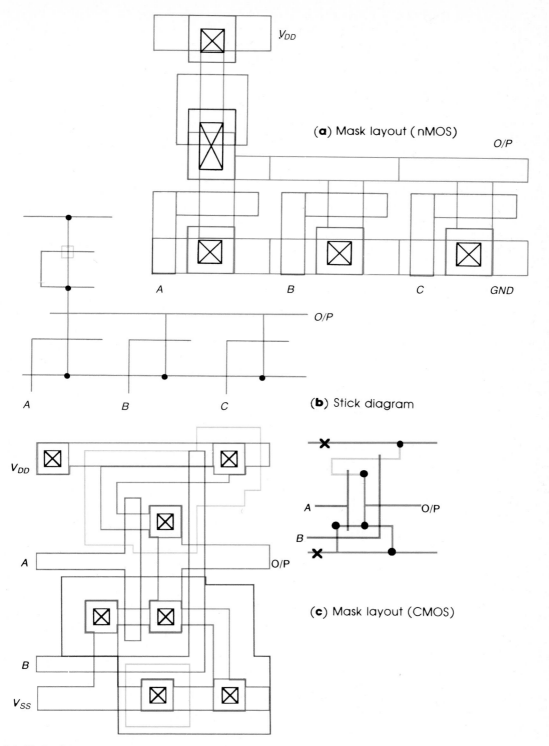

(a) Mask layout (nMOS)

(b) Stick diagram

(c) Mask layout (CMOS)

Color Plate 3 *Top:* nMOS 3 I/P *Nor* gate
Bottom: CMOS 2 I/P *Nor* gate

(**a**) (i) and (ii) Mask layout for standard cells

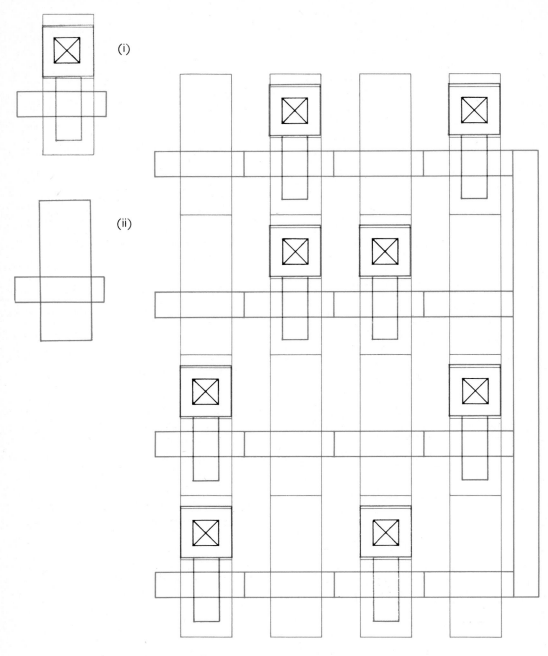

(i)

(ii)

(**b**) Mask layout of four-way multiplexer

Color Plate 4　nMOS four-way multiplexer (see Figure 5–25)

(a) Mask layout

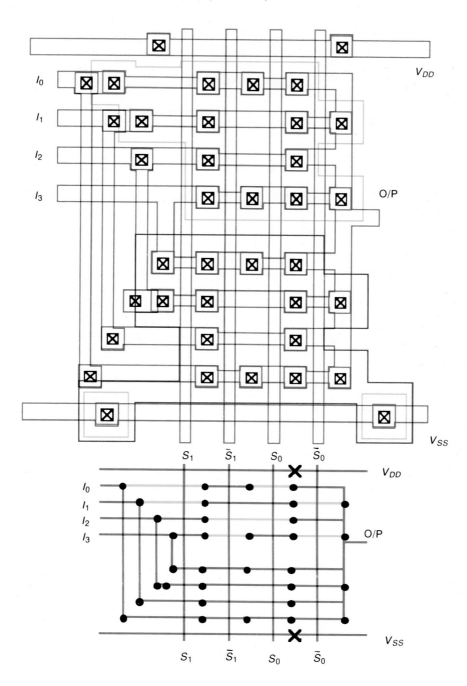

(b) Stick diagram

Color Plate 5 CMOS four-way multiplexer (see Figure 5–24(b))

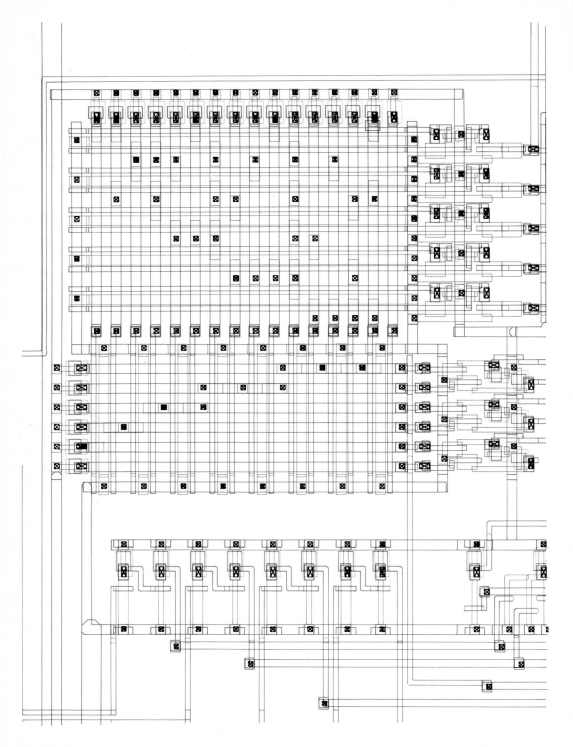

Color Plate 6 nMOS PLA design example (using contact cuts) (c.f. Figures 7–12 and 7–13)

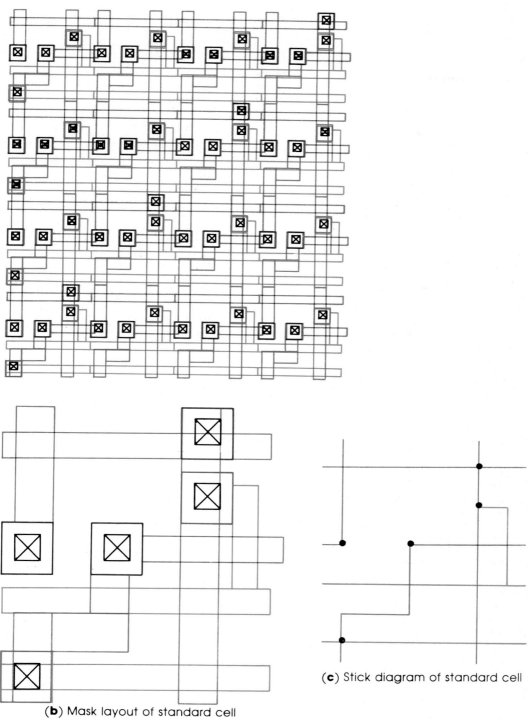

(a) Mask layout

(b) Mask layout of standard cell

(c) Stick diagram of standard cell

Color Plate 7 4×4 barrel shifter (see Figures 8-8 and 8-9)

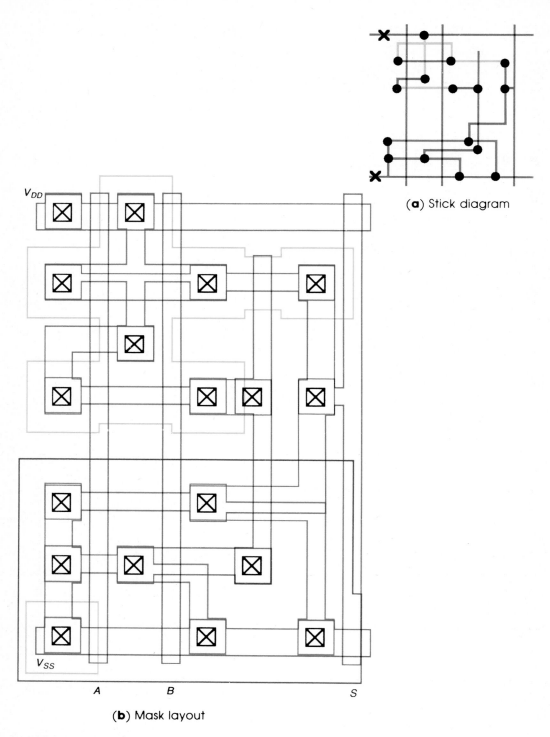

(a) Stick diagram

(b) Mask layout

Color Plate 8 CMOS *Exclusive-Or* (see Figure 5–31)

(a) Inverter stick diagram (see Figure 5–3)

(b) 8:1 ratio inverter mask layout (see Figure 9–8)

(c) 4:1 ratio inverter mask
layout (see Figure 9–9)

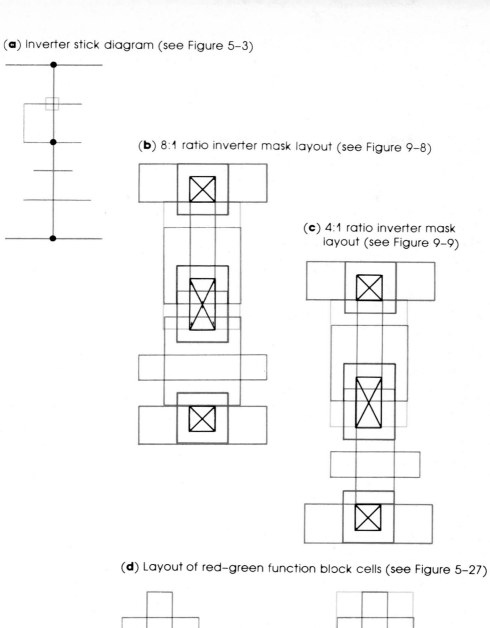

(d) Layout of red–green function block cells (see Figure 5–27)

(i) without implant　　　　　　(ii) with implant

Color Plate 9　nMOS Inverters and n-type function block cells

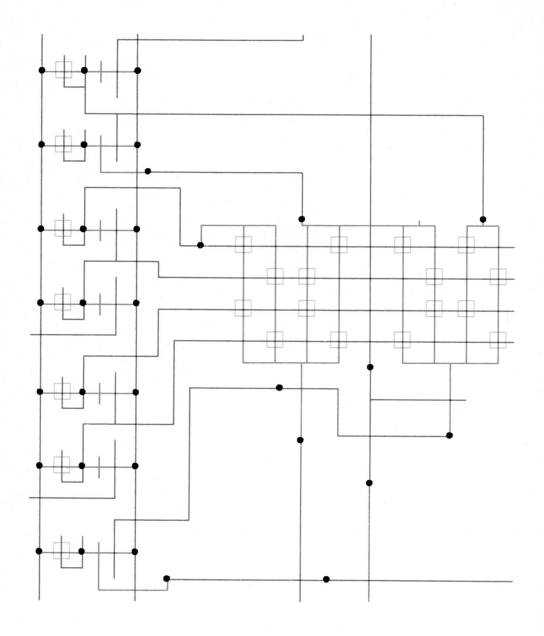

Color Plate 10   Adder element stick diagram — created from cells of Color Plate 9
(see Figure 9–6)

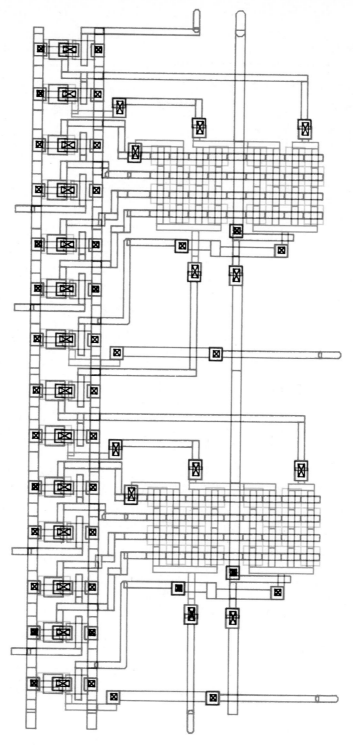

Color Plate 11 Two-bit adder mask layout—formed from elements of Color Plates 9 and 10 (see Figure 9–13)

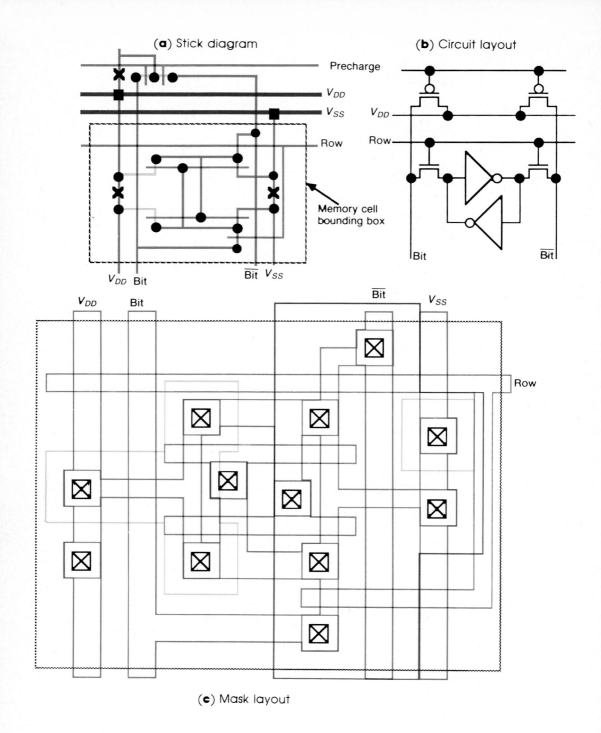

(a) Stick diagram

(b) Circuit layout

(c) Mask layout

Color Plate 12 CMOS static memory cell (see Figures 10–9(b) and 10–23)

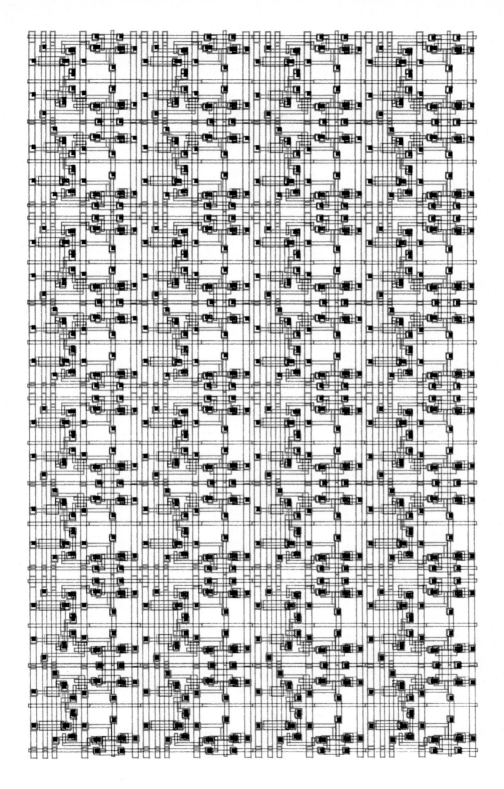

Color Plate 13 32-bit nMOS memory array (16×2-bit) with select circuits (see Figure 10–8)

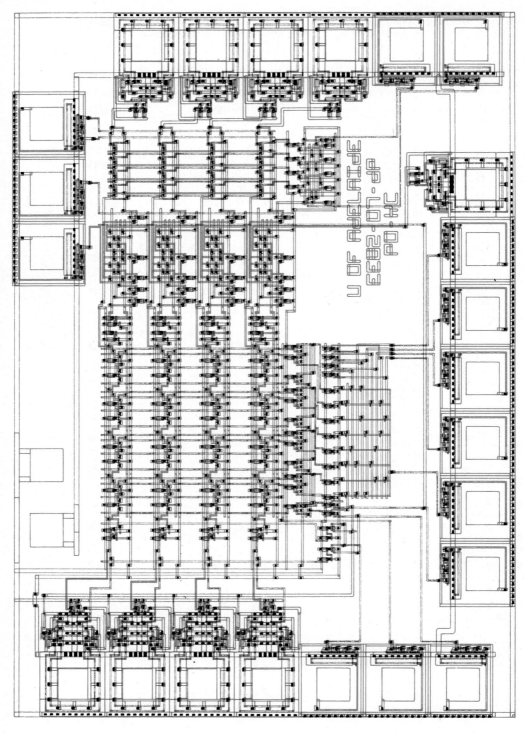

Color Plate 14 Complete four-bit data path chip mask layout (see Figure 11–9)

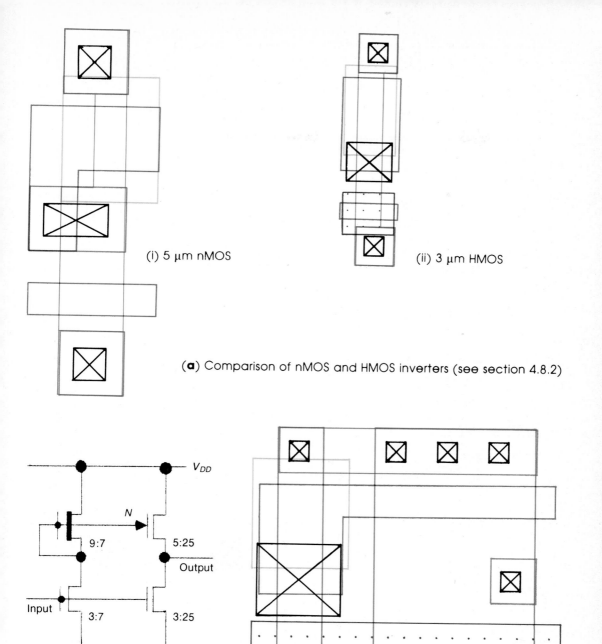

(i) 5 μm nMOS   (ii) 3 μm HMOS

(**a**) Comparison of nMOS and HMOS inverters (see section 4.8.2)

(**b**) Native super buffer for 2 pF load (inverting type) (see section 4.8.4)

Color Plate 15

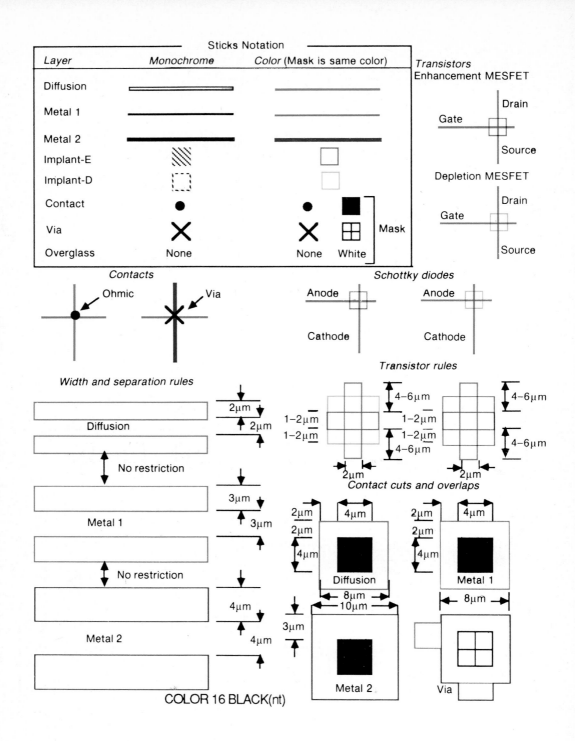

Color Plate 16 Gallium arsenide stick and layout encoding and rules (see sections 14.3 and 14.4)

11 Practical realities and ground rules

'Is it not strange that desire should so many years outlive performance?'
Shakespeare: King Henry IV.

11.1 Some thoughts on performance

Two important parameters (other than 'does it work at all?'), are speed and power dissipation. It is generally the case that these factors are interrelated. It is also the case that power dissipation and area are interrelated in MOS technology.

Take, for example, the simple case of an nMOS 8:1 inverter which may be set out with a minimum feature size pull-down transistor (i.e. $2\lambda \times 2\lambda$ pull-down gate area and the consequent 16λ long $\times$ 2λ wide pull-up channel) giving a total resistance from V_{DD} to GND of 90 kΩ. The power dissipation of this particular design will thus be

$$\frac{(5 \text{ V})^2}{90 \text{ k}\Omega} = 0.278 \text{ mW}$$

An alternative form of 8:1 inverter is to use a pull-down geometry 2λ long and 6λ wide with a 6λ long, 2λ wide pull-up channel giving a V_{DD} to GND resistance of $33\frac{1}{3}$ kΩ and a consequent power dissipation of

$$\frac{(5 \text{ V})^2}{33\frac{1}{3} \text{ k}\Omega} = 0.744 \text{ mW}$$

that is, about three times the dissipation. However, comparing the total transistor areas for each case we have, in the first case, $2\lambda \times 2\lambda + 16\lambda \times 2\lambda = 36\lambda^2$ area and, in the second case, $2\lambda \times 6\lambda + 6\lambda \times 2\lambda = 24\lambda^2$.

In other words, the 3:1 (approximate) reduction in power dissipation is at the expense of a 50 percent increase in area.

Now consider the aspect of speed (or circuit delays) and take the simple case of one 8:1 inverter driving another similar inverter. The longest delays will occur when the output of the first stage is changing from logic 0 (Lo) to logic 1 (Hi), that is,

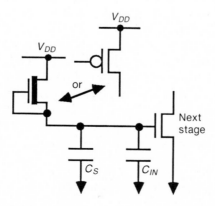

Figure 11-1 Circuit model for inverter driving an inverter on a △O/P transition

the $\triangle$ transition of the output, and the capacitances associated with the output and the input of the next stage must be charged through the pull-up resistance of the first stage as in Figure 11–1. Asymmetry is also present in CMOS devices. It is obvious also that during the complementary $\triangledown$ transition the same capacitances must be discharged through the pull-down transistor of the first stage.

For the minimum pull-down feature size nMOS 8:1 inverter, for example

$$R_{p.u.} = 8\,R_S$$
$$R_{p.d.} = 1\,R_S$$
$$C_{IN} = 1\square C_g$$

Allow stray and wiring capacitances

$$C_S = 4\square C_g \text{ (say)}$$

Then

$$\triangle \text{ transition delay} = 8R_S \times 5\square C_g = 40\tau$$

and

$$\triangledown \text{ transition delay} = 1R_S \times 5\square C_g = 5\tau$$

For the alternative 8:1 inverter design discussed earlier

$$R_{p.u.} = 3R_S$$
$$R_{p.d.} = \tfrac{1}{3}R_S$$
$$C_{IN} = 3\square C_g$$

and allowing the same stray and wiring capacitances ($C_S = 4\square C_g$)

$$\triangle \text{ transition delay} = 3R_S \times 7\square C_g = 21\tau$$

and

$$\triangledown \text{ transition delay} = \tfrac{1}{3}R_S \times 7\square C_g = 2\tfrac{1}{3}\tau$$

Thus, it may be seen that a speed-up factor of about 2:1 in this case is bought at the expense of a 3:1 increase in power consumption but has the bonus of reducing area by a factor of 2:3. Similar considerations apply to the switching energy of CMOS circuits.

Therefore, as in most engineering situations, there are trade offs to be made, and it is essential that the would-be designer has a good fundamental understanding of the discipline to be able to make sound decisions.

But remember, in the end there will always be limits imposed by the technology and some specifications will be impossible to meet.

11.1.1 Optimization of nMOS and CMOS inverters*

The approximate calculations presented here should be useful from a qualitative point of view and are intended to give the reader some appreciation of basic CMOS

* The authors are indebted to Professor K. S. Trivedi of Duke University for providing this material on inverter optimization.

and nMOS circuit optimization problems. For a more rigorous treatment of circuit optimization methods, the reader should refer to the articles cited at the end of the chapter.

11.1.1.1   CMOS inverter

The *area* of a basic CMOS inverter is proportional to the total area occupied by the p- and n-devices.

$$A \propto (W_p L_p + W_n L_n)$$

where

$$W_p = \text{width of the p-device}$$
$$L_p = \text{length of the p-device}$$
$$W_n = \text{width of the n-device}$$
$$L_n = \text{length of the n-device}$$

Minimum area can be achieved by choosing minimum dimensions for

$$W_p, \ L_p, \ W_n \text{ and } L_n, \text{ that is}$$

$$W_p = L_p = W_n = L_n = 2\lambda \text{ (minimum)}$$

Hence

$$\frac{W_p}{W_n} = 1$$

Switching power dissipation, P_{sd}, can be aproximated by $C_L V_{DD}^2 f$ where

$$C_L = \text{load capacitance of the inverter}$$
$$V_{DD} = \text{power supply voltage}$$
$$f = \text{frequency of switching}$$

For fixed V_{DD} and f, minimizing P_{sd} requires minimizing C_L which can be achieved by minimizing the area A since C_L is proportional to the gate areas in A.

Asymmetry in rise and fall times, t_r and t_f (transition times between 10 percent and 90 percent logic levels), can be equalized by using $\beta_n = \beta_p$. (Notice that t_r and t_f are proportional to the average resistance of the device which is approximately given by $\dfrac{2}{\beta V_{DD}}$, *where* $\beta = \beta_n$ *or* β_p.) This requires

$$\frac{W_p}{L_p} = \left(\frac{\mu_n}{\mu_p}\right) \frac{W_n}{L_n}$$

to compensate for the lower hole mobility μ_p, compared to electron mobility μ_n. Assuming $L_p = L_n = 2\lambda$, $\dfrac{\mu_n}{\mu_p} \doteq 2$, we require $\dfrac{W_p}{W_n} \doteq 2$. This yields $t_r = t_f$.

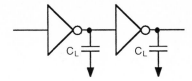

Figure 11–2 Inverter pair

Note that equalizing rise and fall times is not possible in static or pseudo nMOS inverters because of the ratio requirement.

Asymmetry in Noise Margins, NM_H and NM_L, can be equalized by choosing $\beta_n = \beta_p$ and hence $\dfrac{W_p}{W_n} \doteq 2$ for $L_p = L_n = 2\lambda$. This yields $NM_H = NM_L$. (See Figure 11–4(b).)

Basic inverter pair delay — Consider a basic inverter pair shown in Figure 11-2 where C_L is the capacitive load driven by the two identical inverters, inverter pair delay $D (= t_r + t_f)$ is proportional to $(R_p + R_n)C_L$ where $R_p = 2/(\beta_p V_{DD})$ and $R_n = 2/(\beta_n V_{DD})$ are the average resistances of the p- and n-transistors respectively.

Also

$$C_L = C_E + (W_p L_p + W_n L_n)C_g$$

where

C_E = lumped parasitic capacitance
C_g = gate capacitance per unit area

Hence

$$D = D_0 \left[\left(\frac{2}{\beta_p V_{DD}} + \frac{2}{\beta_n V_{DD}} \right) (C_E + (W_p L_p + W_n L_n)C_g) \right]$$

where D_0 is a constant of proportionality. Assuming $\dfrac{\mu_n}{\mu_p} \doteq 2$

$$D = D_0 \left[C_E \left(\frac{2L_p}{W_p} + \frac{L_n}{W_n} \right) + C_g \left(2L_p{}^2 + 2L_p L_n \frac{W_n}{W_p} + L_p L_n \frac{W_p}{W_n} + L_n{}^2 \right) \right]$$

Since D increases with L_n and L_p, for minimum D, choose $L_n = L_p = 2\lambda$ (minimum). Minimizing D with respect to W_p yields a solution

$$W_p / W_n = \sqrt{2} \left[1 + \frac{C_E}{C_g L_n W_n} \right]^{1/2}$$

$W_p / W_n \doteq \sqrt{2}$ for $C_E \ll C_g L_n W_n$ (normal case)

However D does not vary significantly with W_p / W_n in the range $1 \leqslant \dfrac{W_p}{W_n} \leqslant 2$ (see

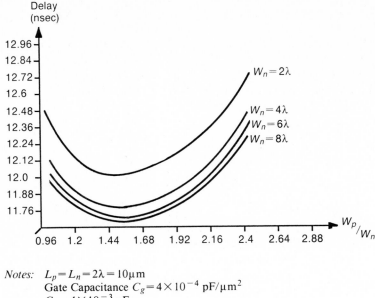

Notes: $L_p = L_n = 2\lambda = 10\mu m$
Gate Capacitance $C_g = 4 \times 10^{-4}$ pF/μm^2
$C_E = 4 \times 10^{-3}$ pF

Figure 11-3 Delay (nsec) vs. W_p/W_n for CMOS inverter

Figure 11–3). Hence simultaneous optimization of various parameters mentioned above seems to be easily achievable in the CMOS inverter, without greatly increasing the delay D.

11.1.1.2 nMOS inverter

Let $Z_{p.u.}/Z_{p.d.} = \dfrac{L_{p.u.} W_{p.d.}}{W_{p.u.} L_{p.d.}} = k$ where the subscripts *p.u.* and *p.d.* refer to the pull-up and pull-down transistors respectively. Then area

$$A = A_0 (L_{p.d.} W_{p.d.} + L_{p.u.} W_{p.u.})$$
$$= A_0 \left(L_{p.d.} W_{p.d.} + k W_{p.u.}^2 \frac{L_{p.d.}}{W_{p.d.}} \right)$$

where A_0 is a constant of proportionality. For a fixed k, to achieve minimum A, we need $L_{p.d.} = W_{p.u.} = 2\lambda$. Minimizing A with respect to $W_{p.d.}$ yields a solution $W_{p.d.} = \sqrt{k} W_{p.u.} = \sqrt{k} 2\lambda$.

Hence, using $Z_{p.u.}/Z_{p.d.} = k$, we obtain

$$L_{p.u.} = \sqrt{k} L_{p.d.} = \sqrt{k}\ 2\lambda$$

This implies $Z_{p.u.} = \sqrt{k}$ and $Z_{p.d.} = 1/\sqrt{k}$. Giving

$$\text{Minimum area} = 8 A_0 \lambda^2 \sqrt{k}$$

Static power dissipation, $P_d = P_0 \dfrac{V_{DD}^2}{(k+1)Z_{p.d.}}$, where P_0 is a constant of proportionality — for fixed k and V_{DD}, P_d is minimized by choosing as large a $Z_{p.d.}$ as possible. However, a large $Z_{p.d.}$ requires a large a $Z_{p.u.}$ ($Z_{p.u.} = kZ_{p.d.}$), and hence the delay D of the inverter pair increases. One has to choose the maximum $Z_{p.d.}$ possible for a given maximum allowed delay D.

If we use $Z_{p.d.} = 1$ with $L_{p.d.} = W_{p.d.} = 2\lambda$, and $Z_{p.u.} = k$ with $L_{p.u.} = 2k\lambda$ and $W_{p.u.} = 2\lambda$ we obtain

$$P_d = \frac{P_0 V_{DD}^2}{(k+1)}$$
$$A = 4A_0(k+1)\lambda^2$$

Inverter pair delay — Proceeding in a similar manner to the CMOS case

$$C_L = C_E + C_g W_{p.d.} L_{p.d.}$$
$$D = t_r + t_f = D_0(Z_{p.d.} + Z_{p.u.})C_L$$
$$= D_0[Z_{p.d.} C_E(1+k) + C_g(1+k)L_{p.d.}^2]$$

To minimize D:

1.   Choose minimum $L_{p.d.} = 2\lambda$.

2.   For maximum $W_{p.d.}$, choose $L_{p.u.} = 2\lambda$ as $W_{p.d.} = 2k\lambda\dfrac{W_{p.u.}}{L_{p.u.}}$ which yields $W_{p.d.} = kW_{p.u.}$

Choosing large $W_{p.d.}$ to minimize D, increases A. Hence for a given area A ($= W_{p.d.}L_{p.d.} + W_{p.u.}L_{p.u.}$) with $L_{p.d.} = L_{p.u.} = 2\lambda$, we must have

$$W_{p.u.} = \frac{A}{2\lambda(k+1)} \qquad W_{p.d.} = \frac{kA}{2\lambda(k+1)}$$

With $W_{p.u.} = 2\lambda$, we have $W_{p.d.} = k2\lambda$. Hence $Z_{p.u.} = 1$ and $Z_{p.d.} = 1/k$ for minimum D.

$$\text{Minimum } D = D_0(1+k)(C_E/k + 4\lambda^2 C_g)$$

Table 11–1 shows the summary of optimization of the three parameters, D, A and P_d. Notice that the solution for minimum power dissipation also gives the lowest power delay product among the three designs.

Table 11–1 Optimum parameters for nMOS inverters

	$L_{p.d.}$	$W_{p.d.}$	$Z_{p.d.}$	$L_{p.u.}$	$W_{p.u.}$	$Z_{p.u.}$
Minimum D	2λ	$2k\lambda$	$1/k$	2λ	2λ	1
Minimum A	2λ	$2\lambda\sqrt{k}$	$1/\sqrt{k}$	$2\lambda\sqrt{k}$	2λ	$\sqrt{k}$
Minimum P_d	2λ	2λ	1	$2\lambda k$	2λ	k

Table 11–1 continued

	A/A_0	D/D_0	$P_d/(P_0 V_{DD}{}^2)$
Minimum D	$4\lambda^2(k+1)$	$(1+k)(C_E/k+4\lambda^2 C_g)$	$\dfrac{k}{k+1}$
Minimum A	$8\lambda^2\sqrt{k}$	$(1+k)\left(\dfrac{C_E}{\sqrt{k}}+4\lambda^2 C_g\right)$	$\dfrac{\sqrt{k}}{(k+1)}$
Minimum P_d	$4\lambda^2(k+1)$	$(1+k)(C_E+4\lambda^2 C_g)$	$\dfrac{1}{(k+1)}$

11.1.2 Noise margins

Noise margins have been mentioned in the preceding section and it is appropriate to now consider this factor in more detail.

Noise margins are a measure of a logic circuit's tolerance to noise voltages in either of the two logic states; in other words, by how much the input voltage can change without disturbing the present logic output state. In order to examine this, it is convenient to consider a pair of inverters (nMOS or CMOS) and derive the noise margins for signals applied to the input of the second inverter, inverter 2, which is driven from the output of a similar inverter, inverter 1, as in Figure 11–4(a).

Referring now to Figure 11–4(b) we see the transfer characteristics (V_{out} vs. V_{in}) for a pair of CMOS inverters set out in such a way that the output voltage of inverter 1 is applied as the input voltage to inverter 2. By first considering the point at which output 1 starts to enter the transition region (the Unity gain point A) and calling this voltage V_{OHmin} and then considering the input voltage level V_{IHmin} (point B) at which the transition of the output of inverter 2 commences, we are able to define the high level noise margin of inverter 2 as NM_H where

$$NM_H = V_{OHmin} - V_{IHmin} \text{ (a positive voltage)}$$

Similarly, a consideration of the low logic level conditions gives

$$NM_L = V_{OLmax} - V_{ILmax} \text{ (a negative voltage)}$$

A similar approach will yield noise margins for the nMOS inverter as shown in Figure 11–4(c). It may be seen that generally the CMOS inverter will have better noise margins than the nMOS inverter particularly for the low condition.

In both cases, symmetry about V_{inv} is assumed (where V_{inv} is the point at which $V_{out} = V_{in} = V_{DD}/2$). This assumes that $\beta_p = \beta_n$ for CMOS and that the correct ratio of $Z_{p.u.}$ to $Z_{p.d.}$ has been observed for nMOS.

Changes in the β_n/β_p ratio for CMOS or to the $Z_{p.u.}/Z_{p.d.}$ ratio for nMOS will result in a shift in the V_{out} vs. V_{in} characteristics (see Figure 2–7 for nMOS and 2–15 for CMOS) and consequent degradation of one or the other noise margin in each case.

Thus the effect of ratios on noise margins performance must be taken into account in design.

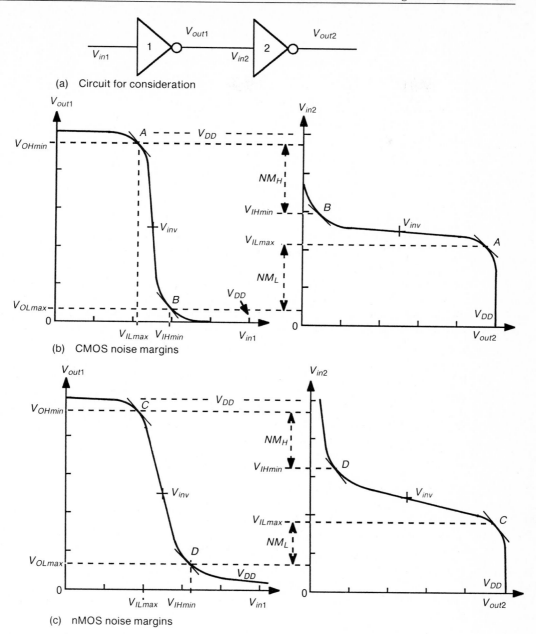

(a) Circuit for consideration

(b) CMOS noise margins

(c) nMOS noise margins

Note: *A* and *B*, *C* and *D* are unity gain points.

Figure 11–4 Inverter noise margins

11.2 Further thoughts on floor plans/layout

In considering the layout of the four-bit data path used as a design exercise, we could have waited until we knew the minimum size and disposition of connections to each functional block in order to finalize the floor plan. Indeed, this is a possible approach if communications will allow. Quite accurate floor plans can be set out at an early stage if a library of properly dimensioned and characterized elements/cells is available to the designer.

However, an alternative approach is to draw up quite specific floor plans at the outset and then design/configure the subsystems to conform to the required floor plan. This approach is more general than that we have used to date.

The same four-bit processor will be used to illustrate the method and considerations involved.

First (as before) determine an *overall strategy* (perhaps as suggested in Figure 11–5) and then use this to determine the best relative disposition of subsystems in the light of data flow and control paths through the system. For the four-bit data path, a suitable layout is shown in Figure 11–6.

When approached this way, a reasonably well thought out floor plan can be developed in advance of knowing any real detail of the subsystem/block areas. In the event, features of individual subsystems will, in general, dominate the overall layout and other blocks may then be stretched and/or reconfigured as necessary to conform with the dominant features.

Taking the four-bit data path for example, one of the main features is the bus spacing, that is, the spacing between buses A_n and B_n and between A_n and A_{n+1}, etc., and in this respect it will be seen that for the designs pursued in this text, the spacings for the adder subsystem dominate those of the other subsystems. It is also essential to set out unambiguously and clearly the way in which data will flow on the buses. In this case:

1. Floating bus lines are envisaged.
2. All read and write operations are coincident with ϕ_1.
3. Bus A connects the I/O port to the register array and carries one operand from the registers to the adder. It will also be used to carry the output of the shifter back to the register array (and I/O port). Bus A is therefore *bidirectional*.

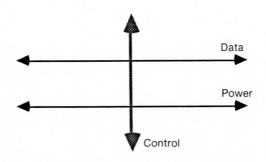

Figure 11–5 A communications strategy

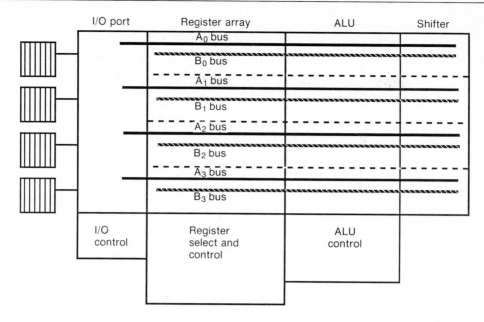

Figure 11-6 Possible floor plan for four-bit processor

4. Bus *B* connects the register array with the other input of the adder and could also be used to carry the sum output from the adder to the input of the shifter. Bus *B* is *unidirectional*.

Rearrangements consequent on these definitions affect the barrel shifter in particular. It is necessary to interchange the relative position of the in and out bus lines and also make the cell stretchable to match the height of the dominant (adder) block and its bus spacing. Also, to mate with the bus structures of the other blocks, the in and out bus lines should be in metal rather than polysilicon and diffusion, as used in our original design of Figures 8–8 and 8–9.

The way in which this may be done is indicated in the revised standard cell layout (Figure 11–7); when using a layout language, it will be advantageous to parameterize the layout to allow for stretching, *and* to cope with optional features which result from the various versions of the standard cell which are needed, thus ensuring generality.

Since there are four versions of the standard cell needed (due to optional contacts) the need for parameterization of the layout becomes quite apparent. The concept of the use of a Y RIFT which is extendable from 0λ minimum upwards and X EXTN and Y EXTN which are extensions of the cell from 0λ upwards make the barrel shifter configurable to match any bus disposition.

The reader should note that rifts and extensions should be placed where they cut a minimum amount of simple geometry; for example, Y RIFT involves the stretching of two wires — one in polysilicon and the other in diffusion. Once such a degree of freedom is available, then subsystems may be mated with a smooth flow through of buses as suggested in Figure 11–8 where the shifter is on the right.

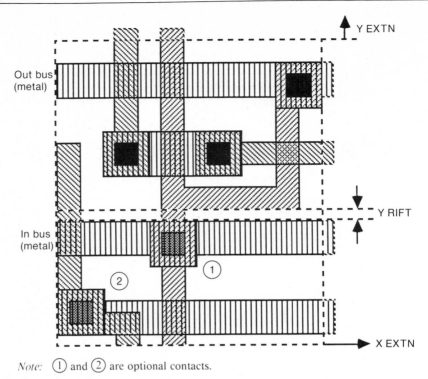

Note: ① and ② are optional contacts.

Figure 11-7 Standard cell for modified barrel shifter

11.3 Floor plan layout of the four-bit processor

Having designed the three main subsystems and determined their bounding boxes and interconnection dispositions, we can now envisage a complete system in which they are disposed relative to each other as set out in Figure 11-6.

Having already determined the dominant feature of the layout (the interbus spacing of the adder circuit) and having already redesigned the shifter to allow stretching to match the adder, a consideration of the bounding box and of connections to the register array will reveal a need for some stretching of this cell also so that an easy interconnection of the subsystem can take place.

A possible arrangement, and in fact one actually fabricated as a student project, is now included as Figure 11-9. Although layer encoding is lost in this particular black and white reproduction of a color-pen plotter representation of the superimposed mask layouts for the chip design, the architecture and placement of the subsystems is quite readily apparent. The detail of the subsystems has been set out in previous sections of the text and the system as a whole is best appreciated from an inspection of the color plot of the layout included as Color Plate 14.

Connections to and from the outside world are made through input and output pads which allow for bonding.

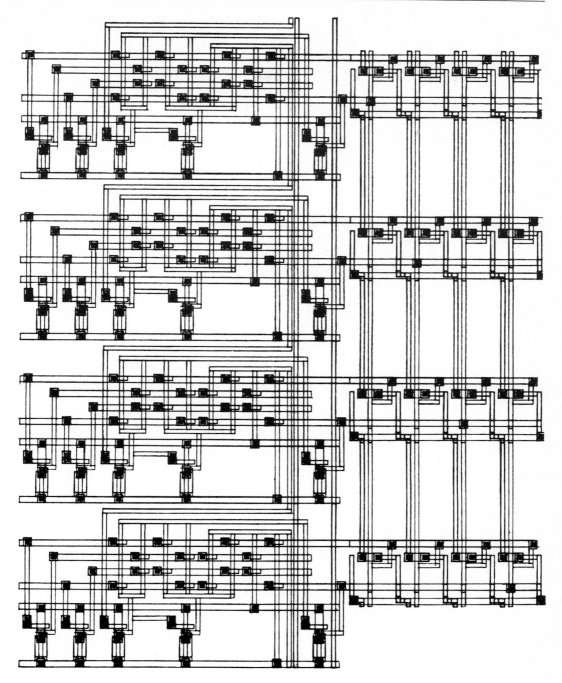

Figure 11-8 A possible interconnection of the adder and shifter subsystems

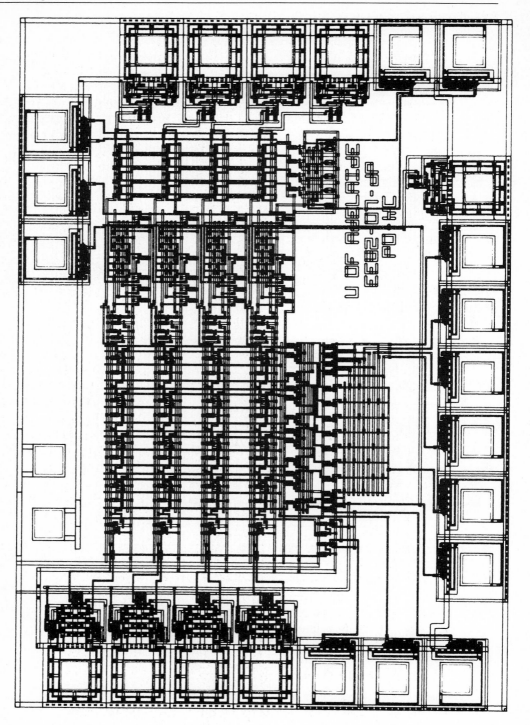

Figure 11–9 Complete layout of four-bit data path multi-project chip

11.4 Input/output (I/O) pads

As well as allowing bonding of leads from the chip to the pins on the package, the I/O pads also cover a number of other requirements for which there are usually several alternative designs of pad. It is not within the scope of this text to present designs for a family of pads and, in most cases, pad designs are readily obtainable as basic library cells. However, some general observations are in order on the purposes served by the circuitry associated with pads. The following needs must be met:

1. Protection of circuitry on chip from damage from static electricity and capacitive discharge effects: this can be a serious problem and care must be exercised in handling all MOS (and other integrated) circuits (the reader is referred to Hewlett Packard, *Bench Briefs: Static Zap makes Scrap*, March–May 1983). The problem of 'static zap' may be put in perspective by considering the breakdown voltage of the thin oxide between gate and channel in a 2.5 μm $= \lambda$ MOS circuit. For a breakdown voltage in the region of 10^9 volts/meter in silicon dioxide and for a gate oxide thickness of 0.1 μm, the maximum allowable voltage gate/channel is

$$V_{gcMAX} < \frac{10^9 \text{ volts}}{\text{meter}} \times \frac{0.1}{10^6} \text{ meter} = 100 \text{ volts}$$

This may sound generous in the light of rail voltages of the order of 5 to 10 volts, but relatively high voltages are readily generated on one's person. Quite innocent pastimes, such as walking across a vinyl floor or a synthetic carpet, can generate voltages of several hundred volts under conditions of high relative humidity (RH) and more than 10 kV if the RH is low. In either case, the voltages are well in excess of 100 volts and, although in some cases immediate failure may not occur, there may be significant degradation of reliability and/or life.
2. Provide the necessary buffering between the environments on and off chip. For example, buffers are needed to drive the relatively large capacitances associated with circuits off the chip.
3. Provide for the connection of power supply rails.

A minimum set of pads should include:

1. V_{DD} connection pad;
2. *GND* (V_{SS}) connection pad;
3. Input pad;
4. Output pad;
5. Bidirectional I/O pad (usually tristate logic).

In all cases when input and output (or bidirectional) pad designs from a library are used, the designer *must* be aware of the nature of the circuitry embodied in the pad design, that is:

1. be aware of the ratios/size of inverters/buffers onto which output lines are connected;
2. be aware of the way in which input lines pass through the pad circuit (e.g. are the input signals fed in through pass transistors or do they come from inverter-like stages?)

Unless there are exceptional circumstances pads must *always* be placed around the *periphery* of the chip area, otherwise bonding difficulties may be encountered.

A sample set of nMOS 5 µm pad designs may be consulted in Hon and Sequin, *A guide to LSI implementation*, 2nd edn, Xerox, 1980, and in Newkirk and Mathews, *The VLSI Designer's Library*, Addison-Wesley, 1984. CMOS pad designs are often available from fabricators or, for example, from Integrated Silicon Design Pty. Ltd.

A factor which the designer must allow for is the way in which input and output pads tend to proliferate and the very significant area which they occupy. Take, for example, a simple processor of the type discussed in this text together

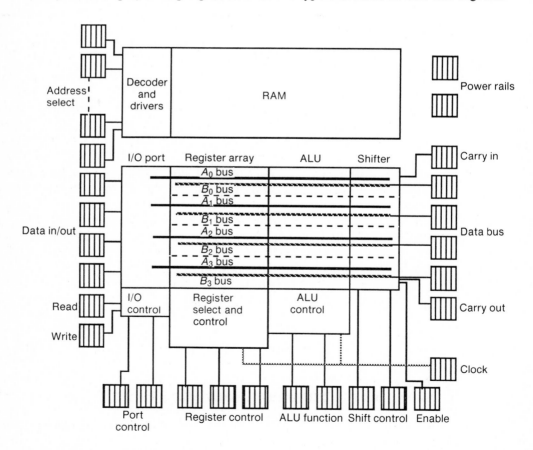

Figure 11–10 Four-bit processor

with some RAM memory to form a basic microprocessor circuit. A typical arrangement could be that shown as Figure 11–10. Allowing for eight memory address lines (i.e. 256 locations of RAM), the complete chip as shown will need more than 30 pads which must, therefore, be accommodated in the layout. Such a number is readily bonded to, say, a 40-pin header but the designer must also bear in mind that the package to be used will impose an ultimate limitation on the allowable number of pads.

11.5 'Real estate'

'Give me land, lots of land ...'
(words of a popular song of yesteryear).

One of the most common mistakes among beginners is to assume that phenomenal amounts of circuitry occupy very little area on the chip (VLSI = very little silicon indeed?). In order to correct such over-optimism it is necessary to consider only one or two of the practical factors which arise in system design.

For example, consider the area required by the I/O pads for the floor plan of Figure 11–10. The connections shown require 33 pads and typical standard 5 μm pad layouts require an area of 105λ by 100λ to 200λ (depending on the nature of the pad). An average pad then occupies some 105λ by 150λ, say, that is, an area of $15750\lambda^2$. Thus the area required for 33 pads is over $500,000\lambda^2$. To put this into perspective, the average area allowance for each student project for a multiproject chip (MPC) design was typically somewhere in the region of $1000\lambda \times 1000\lambda$, that is, $10^6\lambda^2$. For the floor plan given in Figure 11–10, the pads would occupy one-half of this total area. Certainly, the design given here is somewhat pad-intensive but, as a rule of thumb, the small system designer should allow *one-third* of the chip area for pads.

Having come to terms with this reality, the budding designer may then consider what to do with the layout of the remaining two-thirds of the chip area (i.e. about $700,000\lambda^2$ for an example MPC design). What is the prognosis?

An assessment of what could be fitted into such an area could be approached by considering the basic enhancement mode pass transistor of *minimum size* occupying an area of $4\lambda^2$. If 2λ clearance is allowed all around then *on chip area* will not exceed $36\lambda^2$. Thus, one might conclude that almost 20,000 such devices could be fitted into the area under discussion. However, MOS circuitry necessitates the use of inverters or inverter-like circuits. When two transistors are put together and contacts, etc. are added, then, typically, a single inverter occupies at least $200\lambda^2$. Viewed from this point, the same area could accommodate about 3500 inverters. Both these figures give an over-optimistic assessment of the possible circuit density, since one has to consider the effect of interconnections even within a leaf cell. Consider the simple memory cell of Figure 11–11 (also discussed in section 10.2.5), which we might use to implement the RAM of Figure 11–10.

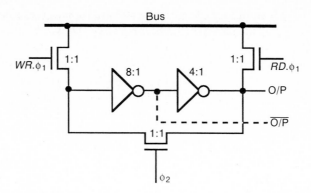

Figure 11-11 Pseudo-static memory cell

The temptation is to assess area requirements by reasoning thus

$$\text{two inverters} + \text{three pass transistors} = 2 \times 200\lambda^2 + 3 \times 36\lambda^2 = 508\lambda^2$$

However, when design rule clearances, buses, power, and control are allowed for, this cell can occupy $1500\lambda^2$ or more (i.e. a factor of 3:1 over the 'coarse' estimates).

Now, consider the available area on the floor plan and further assume that about half this area (ie. approximately $350{,}000\lambda^2$) is to be devoted to the RAM. This area will allow no more than 256 bits of storage and if each RAM location must hold a four-bit word, then the designer can be no more ambitious than a 64-word RAM. The running of extra bus lines, as in the register array, will further substantially increase the area occupied by each memory cell.

11.6 Further thoughts on system delays

11.6.1 Buses

> *'He thought he saw (an operand),*
> *descending from a bus,*
> *he looked again and saw it was*
> *a hippopotamus.'*
> (With apologies to Lewis Carroll.)

The use of bus lines is a convenient concept in distributing data and control through a system. However, it is easy to lose sight of what is *really* happening and for bus-derived signals not to be what was expected.

Bidirectional buses are convenient but conflicts must be avoided since data cannot flow in both directions at once. Clearly, in our data path design, the sum S_k must be stored and then subsequently read onto the bus, since it becomes obvious that two buses cannot carry two input operands and the sum simultaneously.

A significant problem which is often underestimated is that of speed restrictions imposed by the capacitive load presented by long bus lines.

The largest capacitance (for a typical bus system) is contributed by C_{BUS} (the bus wiring capacitance), and for small chips with, say, a 1000λ long bus this can be as high as .75 pF for a metal layer bus in 5 μm technology. In total, the bus and associated circuitry for the system being considered could contribute a capacitive load of about 1 pF, which must be *driven* through pull-up (typically 20 to 40 kΩ 'on' resistance) and pull-down (typically 10 kΩ 'on' resistance) transistors and through at least one pass transistor or transmission gate in the series in each case.

Therefore, sufficient time must be allowed to charge the total bus capacitance during say, ϕ_1 of the clock. In the data path system considered here, the time required for the total bus capacitance to charge to an appropriate level (to, say, >90 percent of V_{DD}) is in the region of 120 nsec. Thus, it may be seen that equal ϕ_1 and ϕ_2 clock periods would result in an upper clock frequency limitation for the processor due to bus loading alone of $\doteq 4$ MHz, but this can be increased by using asymmetric ϕ_1 and ϕ_2 periods.

11.6.2 Control paths, selectors, and decoders

A basic operation of the data path is to add together the numbers stored in any two registers to produce a sum and a carry at the 'carry out' pad (for cascading, etc.).

In terms of *delays* involved and in the context of the system considered here, the following delay mechanisms are encountered during this process:

1. *Select register* and open pass transistors (or transmission gates) to connect cells to bus. For our particular design the select logic and associated drivers have the equivalent circuit as shown in Figure 11–12.

    The overall *delay* of this arrangement may be assessed in terms of τ (where τ is the time constant of $1\square C_g$ charging through a minimum-size n-type pass transistor).

Element(s) Contributing	*Delay*
Inlet pad	30τ (typical)
Three pass transistors $= n^2\tau = 9\tau$	9τ
Driver pair turning on $(\triangle A \rightarrow \triangledown B \rightarrow \triangle C)$	
Assume gate and wiring $= 2\square C_g$	
Delay A to $B = 2\square C_g R_S = 2\tau$	

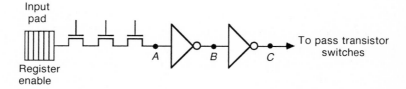

Figure 11–12   Register select circuit

Then, for a fan out of 4 . . .

Delay B to $C = 4 \times 2 \square C_g (4 R_S) = 32 \tau$

Pair delay $= (2 + 32) \tau =$ \hfill 34τ

Sum of delays (select register) $=$ \hfill 73τ

(where R_S = sheet resistance = on resistance of minimum-size n-type pass transistor).

2. *Data propagation along bus* — This has already been calculated as 120 nsec.

3. *Carry chain delay* — The longest delay in the particular design of adder used is that of forming the 'carry out' which, in effect, propagates through all four bits of the adder and then through the outlet pad as shown in Figure 11–13. Note that both the multiplexer (upper) and R/G function block (lower) arrangements are indicated in Figure 11–13. Timing simulator results for both arrangements are given as Figures 11–14 and 11–15.

A similar calculation for the multiplexer version and allowing for peripheral capacitances will yield a total carry chain delay $= 268 \tau$ which is more optimistic than the simulation of Figure 11–15.

Thus, the overall delay = select registers + bus delays + carry chain delays = $(73 \tau) + (120 \text{ nsec}) + (268 \tau)$.

Now, for $\tau = 0.2$ nsec

$$\text{Delay} = 14.6 + 120 + 54 \doteq 190 \text{ nsec}$$

Thus, ϕ_1 of the clock must have a duration > 190 nsec, say 200 nsec.

11.6.3 Use of an asymmetric two-phase clock

11.6.3.1 Clock period ϕ_2

In the system considered here, ϕ_2 of the clock is used only to refresh memory/register cells and, from Figure 11–16, it can be seen that ϕ_2 has to be long enough in duration to allow C_{in} to charge through $4 R_S + R_S = 5 R_S$. If time is

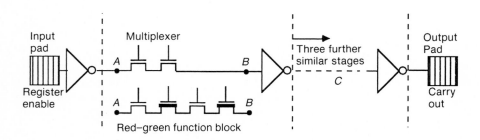

Figure 11–13 Carry chain

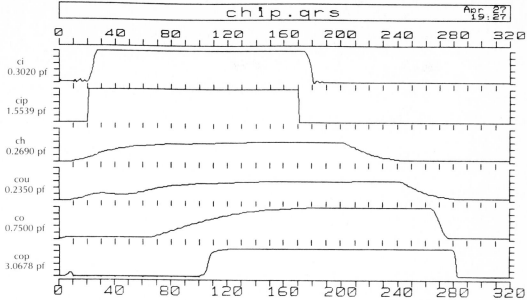

Figure 11–14 Timing simulator results for a two-bit version of the R/G function block adder

Key: from top to bottom

ci	carry input after input pad.		cou	carry out unbuffered.
cip	input to "carry in" pad.		co	carry out to pad.
ch	carry signal (unbuffered) after 1 bit.		cop	"carry out" pad output.

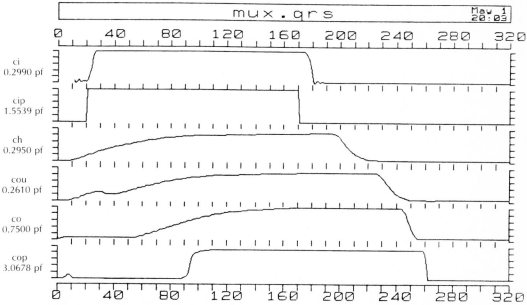

Figure 11–15 Timing simulator results for a two-bit version of the multiplexer-based adder

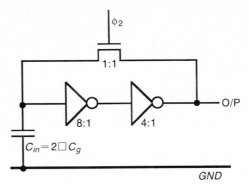

Note: C_{in} = Gate and wiring C

Figure 11-16 Memory cell refresh

allowed for C_{in} to charge to within <10 percent of its final value, then refresh time $\geqslant 2.5 \times 2 \square C_g \times 5R_S \geqslant 25\tau$.

ϕ_2 signals must also propagate through wiring etc., so some extra time should be allowed for the ϕ_2 period. For safety allow, say, 100τ (i.e. 20 nsec), for ϕ_2 period and also allow 15 nsec underlap between each of the phases. Thus

$$\text{total clock period} = 200 + 15 + 15 + 20 = 250 \text{ nsec}$$

Therefore, *in theory*, our simple modelling suggests that the data path chip design should operate on add instructions with a 4-MHz clock.

11.6.4 More nasty realities

'Life wasn't meant to be easy' ... Malcolm Fraser.

The simple calculations made on the particular processor design would appear to indicate that a clock frequency in the region of 4 MHz would be possible. In practice, this may not happen and, in fact, the particular design in question, when realized as a 5 μm multiproject chip (MPC) design, operated at an upper frequency of around 1 MHz.

Why was this so? To answer this it is necessary to consider practical as well as theoretical realities.

From the theoretical aspect, our predictions have mostly ignored the quite significant effects of peripheral capacitance in diffusion regions.

Although τ was assumed to be in the range 0.1 to 0.3 nsec for $\lambda = 2.5$ μm, the value of τ measured for the fabricated chip may not be within this range. In fact, the value of τ measured on the MPC circuits fabricated and tested for this project was in the region of 0.6 nsec.

Compared with the 0.2 nsec assumed in these notes the actual value of τ is up by a factor of $3:1$. Thus, we may see that measured operating frequency is not far from the predicted value, provided that all significant nasty realities are taken into account.

The designer, therefore, must be aware of and allow for all the significantly nasty realities which affect the performance of the design, *including* a good knowledge of the parameters of the processing plant or fabrication line where that design is to be implemented in silicon. Even so, there are two main points of difference between expectations and realization which characterize many of the designs of beginners. They are:

1. The system being designed occupies far more area than was anticipated.
2. The system when manufactured is slower than the designer had estimated.

However, if the first few designs are carefully carried out and are *not* over-ambitious, so that they can be readily checked for logical and design rule errors, then the beginner is usually pleasantly surprised by the fact that the system does in fact function as intended.

11.7 Ground rules for successful design

This section is intended to provide a convenient focus for design information. From our considerations of system design up to this point a number of ground rules, aspects of philosophy, and some basic data have emerged which help to ease the design process and ensure success. These and one or two other considerations which are important (but which have not as yet been formally set out in the text) are presented or referenced here under twenty subheadings.

1. *The ratio rules* (Chapter 2)
    (a) for nMOS inverters and inverter-like stages

    $$\text{Ratio } \frac{Z_{p.u.}}{Z_{p.d.}} = \frac{4}{1} \text{ when driven from another inverter}$$

    $$= \frac{8}{1} \text{ when driven through pass transistor(s)}$$

    where
    $$Z = L/W \text{ for channel in question}$$

    (b) for CMOS, a 1:1 ratio is normally used to minimize area but for pseudo-nMOS inverters (etc.) a ratio $Z_{p.u.}/Z_{p.d.} = 3$ is required.

2. *Design rules* (Chapter 3). Never bend the rules.
3. *Typical parameters for* 5 μm ($\lambda = 2.5$ μm) *feature size MOS* (from Chapter 4, grouped here as Tables 11–2, 11–3, 11–4, and 11–5) and 'ground rules' for signal interconnections.

Table 11-2 Typical Resistance Values

Layer	R_S ohm per square
Metal	0.03
Diffusion	$10 \rightarrow 50$
Silicide	$2 \rightarrow 4$
Polysilicon	$15 \rightarrow 100$
n-transistor channel	10^4†
p-transistor channel	2.5×10^4†

† *Note*: Approximate values only. Resistance can be calculated from V_{ds} and the expressions for I_{ds}.

Table 11-3 Typical area capacitance values

Capacitance		Value in pF/μm^2	Relative value
Gate to channel		4×10^{-4}	1
Diffusion		1×10^{-4}	0.25
Polysilicon		0.4×10^{-4}	0.1
Metal 1	To substrate	0.3×10^{-4}	0.075
Metal 2		0.2×10^{-4}	0.05
Metal 2 to metal 1		0.4×10^{-4}	0.1
Metal 2 to polysilicon		0.3×10^{-4}	0.075

Table 11-4 Typical values for diffusion capacitances

Diffusion capacitance	Typical values	
	Minimum	*Maximum*
Area (C_{area}) (as in Table 4-2)	0.8×10^{-4} pF/μm^2	1.2×10^{-4} pF/μm^2
Periphery (C_{periph})	6.0×10^{-4} pF/μm	10×10^{-4} pF/μm

C_{periph} values are for relatively deep diffusion and do not apply to shallow implants.

Standard unit of capacitance $\square C_g = .01$ pF
Standard unit of delay $\tau = 0.2$ to 0.3 nsec

Taking account of resistances and total capacitances we may set out practical guidelines on signal path lengths as in the following table noting that the figures given are conservative but safe.

Table 11–5 Electrical rules (guide lines)

Layer	Maximum length of communication 'wire'
Metal	20,000λ
Silicide	2,000λ
Polysilicon	200λ
Diffusion	20λ*

* Taking account of peripheral and area
capacitances

Calculated wiring capacitance should be increased to allow for fringing fields.

4. *Inverter pair delay* (Chapter 4)

$$\text{Delay nMOS } \tau_d = \left(1 + \frac{Z_{p.u.}}{Z_{p.d.}}\right)\tau$$

For minimum size CMOS $\tau_d = 7\tau$

5. *Cascaded inverters driving a large capacitive load* (C_L) (Chapter 4)
    For optimum performance each stage should be larger than the preceding stage by factor f where

$$f = e \doteq 2.7 \; (f = 3 \text{ is commonly used}).$$

Then,

$$\text{number of stages } N = \ln(y)$$

where

$$y = \frac{C_L}{\Box C_g}$$

Then, for nMOS

delay $t_d = 2.5fN\tau$ (for N even)

or

delay $t_d = (2.5(N-1)+1)f\tau$ for $\triangle V_{in}$

or

$\left.\vphantom{\begin{array}{c}a\\b\\c\end{array}}\right\}$ (for N odd)

delay $t_d = (2.5(N-1)+4)f\tau$ for $\triangledown V_{in}$

And, for CMOS, assuming minimum size transistors

delay $t_d \doteq 2fN\tau$ (for N even)

or

$$\text{delay } t_d \doteq (2(N-1)+1)f\tau \text{ for } \triangle \dot{V}_{in}$$

or

$$\text{delay } t_d \doteq (2(N-1)+3)f\tau \text{ for } \triangledown V_{in}$$

(for N odd)

6. *Propagation delay through cascaded pass transistors or transmission gates* (Chapter 4)

$$\tau_d = n^2 rc\tau$$

where

$n =$ number in series

$r =$ relative series resistance per transistor or per transmission gate in terms of R_S

$c =$ relative capacitance gate to channel per transistor or per transmission gate in terms of $\square C_g$.

Normally no more than four pass transistors should be connected in series without buffering.

7. *Factors influencing choice of layer for wiring* (Chapter 4, Table 11–6)

Table 11-6 Choice of layer

| Layer | Relative | | Comments |
	R	C	
Metal	Low	Low	Good current carrying without large voltage drop. Best for buses. Essential for V_{DD} and GND (V_{SS}) lines and for global signals.
Diffusion	Moderate	High	Moderate IR drop but high C, therefore hard to drive
Polysilicon*	High	Moderate	Moderate RC product. High IR drop.
Silicide*	Low	Moderate	Modest RC product and low IR drop. Reasonably long wires are possible.

* Alternatives, depending on process line.

Note: V_{DD} and V_{SS} (or GND) rails must always be run in metal, except for very short 'duck unders' where crossovers are unavoidable.

8. *Subsystem/leaf cell design guidelines* (Chapter 5)
   (a) Define the requirements properly and carefully.
   (b) Consider communication paths most carefully in order to develop sensible placing of subsystems and leaf cells.
   (c) Draw a floor plan (alternating with (b) as necessary).
   (d) Aim for regular structures so that design is largely a matter of replication.

   (e)   Draw stick diagrams for basic cells, leaf cells, and/or subsystems

   (f)   Convert each cell to a mask level layout.

   (g)   Carefully and thoroughly check each mask layout for design rule errors and simulate circuit or logical operation. Correct as necessary, *rechecking* as corrections are made.

9.   *Restrictions associated with MOS pass transistors* (Chapter 5)

   (a)   No more than four in series without buffering (see 6 above).

   (b)   No pass transistor gate must be driven from the output of one or more pass transistors, since logic 1 levels are degraded by V_{tp} (where V_{tp} can be as high as 0.3 V_{DD}).

   (c)   When designing switch logic networks of pass transistors or transmission gates care must be taken to deliberately implement *both* the logic 1 *and* logic 0 output conditions.

Note: An *if, then, else* approach to specifying requirements will help to make sure that this is done.

10.   *Special conditions associated with nMOS Nand gates* (Chapter 5)

   (a)   *Nand* ratio for *n* input gate

$$\frac{Z_{p.u.}}{nZ_{p.d.}} = \frac{4}{1} \left(\text{or } \frac{8}{1} \text{ if appropriate}\right)$$

   (b)   *Nand* delay for *n* inputs

$$\tau_{Nand} = n\tau_{inv}$$

where τ_{inv} is the delay associated with similar inverter.

   (c)   Storage of bits — see 11(c) below.

11.   *Storage of logic levels on gate capacitance of transistors*:

   (a)   Gate/channel capacitance is suitable for storing a bit, but care must be taken to allow for the finite decay time (about 0.25 msec at room temperature) (Chapter 5).

   (b)   It is quite allowable to construct pass transistors, etc. *under* metal layers to save space. This is often convenient and is used, for example, in some multiplexer layouts, but care must be taken with *overlying* metal wires where gate/channel capacitance is used for bit storage.

Consider Figure 11–17(a). Three such instances are illustrated here, all of which lie under metal wires. Two of these cases, T_1 and T_3, will operate satisfactorily, since for T_1 the metal wire is actually connected to the gate and for T_3 the metal wire is at a fixed, unvarying potential (i.e. V_{DD} in this case). However, T_2 gate region lies under a metal bus which has no connection with the gate of T_2. If a bit is stored on T_2 gate by momentarily connecting Control A to the required level, then the bit will be stored but can be disturbed or destroyed by variation of the voltage on the overlying bus, as a consideration of Figure 11–17(b) will reveal.

   (c)   Similar considerations apply to logic level storage on the input capacitance of a *Nand* gate except for the input *nearest* the *GND* or V_{SS} rail. Conditions are indicated in Figure 11–18.

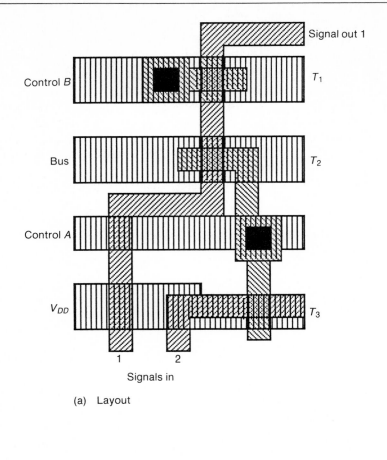

(a)   Layout

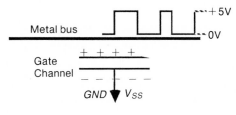

(b)   Circuit model

Figure 11–17   Pass transistors under metal wires

12.   *Enhanced clocking* — One of the basic limitations on the use of simple MOS pass transistors (see 9 above) is the degradation of logic 1 levels by V_{tp} and the consequent inability of one pass transistor to drive the gate of a second (or more) pass transistor. This is particularly bothersome in clocking networks and a solution to this problem is to run all clock lines at a voltage level above V_{DD}, as shown in Figure 11–19.

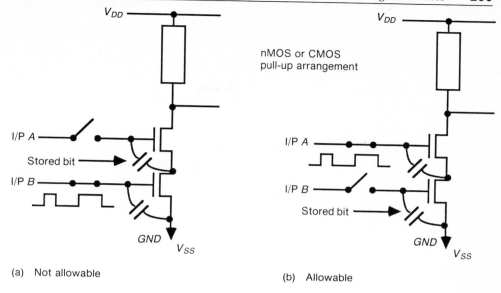

(a) Not allowable   (b) Allowable

Figure 11–18 Storage nodes in gate arrangements

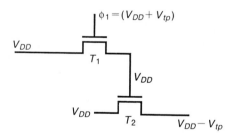

Figure 11–19 Enhanced clocking

It will be seen that the signal propagated through T_1 is V_{DD} while that propagated through T_2 is $V_{DD} - V_{tp}$.

13. *Further thoughts on the red–green function block.* (Chapter 5, section 5.4.4)

The problem of ensuring that such arrangements function correctly was foreshadowed in section 5.4.4. Consider any one path through the arrangement of Figure 5–26, as set out in Figure 11–20.

The main problem with such structures is that processing variations can result in a large spread of V_{td} (depletion mode threshold voltage). This variation is primarily caused by the changes in the implant level that may occur in various processing runs.

It is instructive to examine the effect that such changes have on the performance of the network, and this has been done both for the inverter

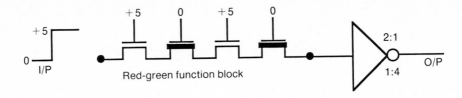

Figure 11-20   One path through a red-green function block

output versus input voltage in Figure 11-21 and for the output response time in Figure 11-22 for the path of Figure 11-20.

From Figure 11-21 we may deduce that the logic threshold voltage V_{inv} (i.e. the point at which input and output voltages are equal) changes from 1.1 to 1.7 volts as V_{td} changes from -1.5 to -4.0 volts.

Thus the inverter will continue to operate over a wide range of V_{td}. However, note the reduced noise margins at low negative values V_{td}.

With regard to Figure 11-22, the response is plotted for an input voltage step from 0 to V_{DD} with a delay time $t_d = 10$ nsec and a rise time $t_r = 1$ nsec.

The response time assumes no load on the output of the inverter so that we see the response of the function block path and inverter only.

The time responses illustrate that the structure always works but that *considerable delays* can be expected when V_{td} is less negative than -2.5 volts.

14. *The maximum allowable current density* in aluminum wires is 1 mA/μm^2. Otherwise, metal migration may occur (Chapter 5). Current density must be carefully considered if the circuit is to be scaled down.

15. *Scaling effects*:
     (a) on transistors — see Chapter 6, Table 6-1.
     (b) on interconnections — see Chapter 6, Table 6-3.

16. *System design process* (Chapter 8) — refer also to 8 in this section:
     (a) Set out a specification together with an architectural block diagram.
     (b) Suitably partition the architecture into subsystems which are, as far as possible, self-contained and give interconnections which are as simple as possible.
     (c) Set out a tentative floor plan showing the proposed relative physical disposition of subsystems on the chip.
     (d) Determine interconnection strategy.
     (e) Revise (b), (c), and (d) interactively as necessary.
     (f) Choose layers on which to run buses and main control signals.
     (g) Take each subsystem in turn and conceive a *regular* architecture to *conform* to the strategy set out in (d). Set out circuit and/or logic diagrams as appropriate. *Remember* that switch-based logic is such that both logic 1 and logic 0 output conditions must be deliberately satisfied (see 9).

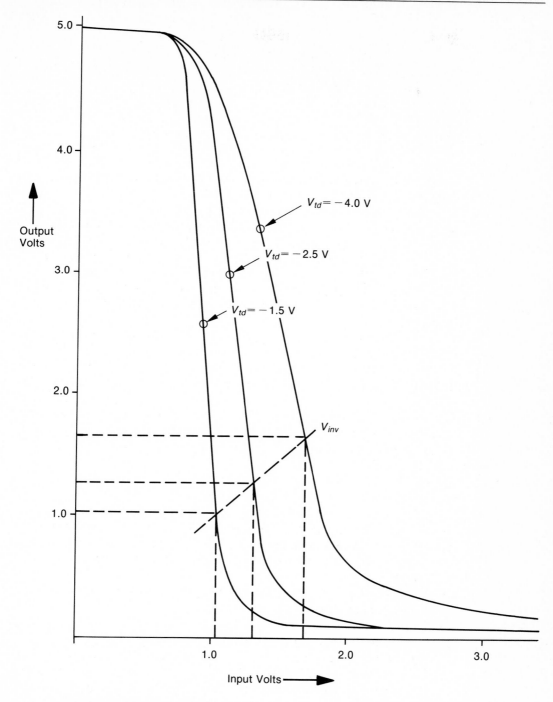

Figure 11–21 Transfer characteristics of inverter with function block path for figure 11–20 as a function of variation in depletion threshold

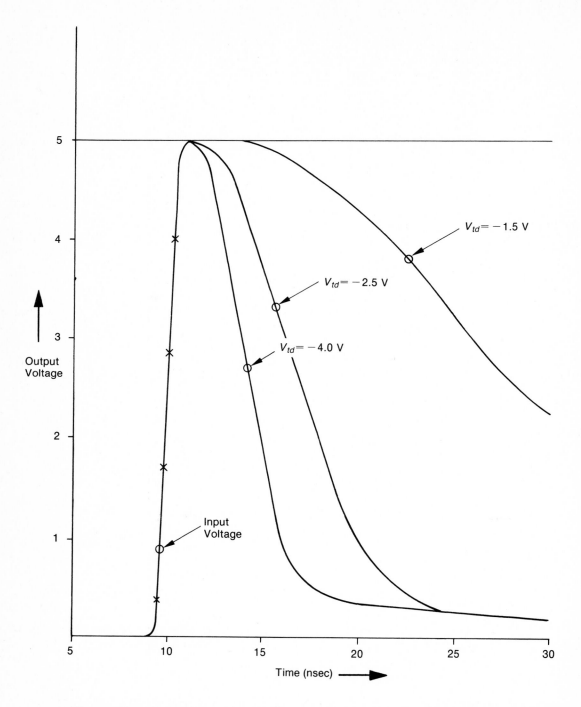

Figure 11-22 Output response time for arrangement of figure 11-20 with step input $t_r = 1$ nsec, $t_d = 10$ nsec

(h)   Develop stick diagrams adopting suitable tactics to meet the overall strategy (d) and choice of layers (f). Determine suitable *standard cell(s)* from which the subsystem may be formed.

(i)   Produce mask layouts for the standard cells *making sure* that cells can be butted together, side by side and/or top to bottom, without design rule violation or waste of space. Carefully check for any design rule errors in each standard cell itself. Determine overall dimensions of each cell and characterize in bounding box form if convenient.

(j)   Cascade the replicate standard cells as necessary to complete the desired subsystem. This may now be characterized in bounding box form with positions and layers of inlets and outlets. External links, etc. *must* be allowed for. Check for design rule errors.

17.   *Further observations on the design process* (based on Chapter 9):

(a)   First and foremost, try to put requirements into words (often an *if, then, else* approach helps to do this) so that the most appropriate architecture or logic can be evolved.

(b)   If a standard cell (or cells) can be arrived at, then the actual detailed design work, including simulation, is confined initially to small areas of simple circuitry.

(c)   Aim for generality as well as regularity, that is, standard cells, etc. should not be highly specialized unless it is absolutely necessary.

(d)   Communications dominate any system design.

(e)   A good library of basic standard cells and subsystems will allow accurate floor planning at an early stage.

(f)   A structured and orderly 'top down' approach to system design is highly beneficial and becomes essential for large systems.

18.   *Set out rules of system timing* at an early stage in design. A sample set of such rules is set out in Chapter 10 (section 10.1).

19.   *Avoid bus contentions* by setting out bus utilization diagrams or tables, particularly in complex systems and/or where bidirectional buses are used.

20.   *Do not take liberties with the design rules* but *do* take account of the ground rules and guidelines (set out in this section).

11.8 A final footnote on design processes

Remember, IC designers should expect their systems to function first time around* and this will happen if the design concepts are correct and if the rules are obeyed. (We do *not* subscribe to the view 'If it works, it's out of date' (Stafford Beer, 1972) but we do contend that poorly conceived and badly designed systems may well be out of date before they work!)

---

* Not necessarily at optimum speed ... this may take longer and depends on the designer's understanding of the properties of circuits produced in silicon.

11.9 Special reference material for Chapter 11

For a detailed discussion of circuit optimization methods with yield maximization and optimal design of CMOS polycells refer to

1. M. R. Lightner and S. W. Director, 'Multiple criterion optimization with yield Maximization', *IEEE Transactions on Circuits and Systems*, Vol. CAS–28, No. 8, pp. 781–91, 1981.
2. R. K. Brayton et al., 'A Survey of Optimization Techniques for Integrated Circuit Design', *Proc. IEEE*, Vol. 69, pp. 1334–62, 1981.
3. K. J. Antreich and S. A Huss, 'An Interactive Optimization Technique for the Nominal Design of Integrated Circuits', *IEEE Transactions on Circuits and Systems*, Vol. CAS–31, No. 2, pp. 203–12, 1984.
4. Sung Mo Kang, 'A Design of CMOS Polycells for LSI Circuits', *IEEE Transactions on Circuits and Systems*, Vol. CAS–28, No. 8, pp. 838–43, 1981.

12 The real world of VLSI design

'Knowledge comes, but wisdom lingers.' Alfred Lord Tennyson

The preceding chapters of this book have attempted to give the reader an understanding of the way in which system, circuit, and logic requirements may be turned into silicon and a feeling for the nature of silicon circuits. The authors believe that a sound understanding of cause and effect is essential if the maximum benefits are to be obtained from VLSI and the fullest range of applications opened up to VLSI realizations. Thus it is without apology that we have dwelt on the fundamental aspects of design in silicon for the past 11 chapters.

From a sound foundation, a VLSI designer can operate with confidence, but must face up to the following requirements when contemplating large system designs in silicon.

1. *CAD.* The designer will need computer-aided design assistance, not only to assist in the design but also to handle the sheer complexity of the information needed to express the physical aspects of the design in a form suitable for translation into silicon.
2. *Verification.* Tools to verify that the design is physically and logically correct and will perform correctly at the desired speed.
3. *Testability.* The designer must, from the outset, face up to the requirements of being able to test a system once it is realized in silicon.
4. *Test Facilities.* Not only must testability be designed in but complex systems need sophisticated equipment to actually test for correct operation.

Thus, it is the purpose of this chapter to present an overview of these important topics in order to put them in perspective for the budding VLSI designer. However, it is not our intention to provide a complete or comprehensive coverage of any of these topics in this chapter.

Although the topics are listed separately it will be readily apparent that they are closely interrelated and can be significantly interdependent.

12.1 Design styles and philosophy

'Style, like sheer silk, too often hides eczema.' Albert Camus.

When wishing to implement a system design in silicon, a variety of approaches are possible and, of course, a wide range of technologies is available to choose from. The designer must choose an appropriate design style, but at this point it must be stressed that in no case will the choice of style hide the lack of a competent and systemic approach by the designer. However, we may summarize the possibilities into three broad categories:

1. Full custom design of the complete system for implementation in the chosen technology. In this case, the designer designs all the circuitry and all interconnection/communication paths.

2. Semi-custom design using a library of standard cells together with specially designed circuits and subsystems which are placed as appropriate in the floor plan and interconnected to achieve the desired functional performance. In this case, the designer designs a limited amount of circuitry and the majority of interconnections/communications.

3. Gate array (uncommitted logic array)-based design in which standard logic elements are presented for the designer to interconnect to achieve the desired functional performance. In this case, the design is that of the interconnections and communications only.

Once again the boundaries between these categories may be blurred. For example, full custom design will seldom involve the complete design of the entire chip. Input/output pad circuits are more or less accepted as standard components and would be available to the custom designer.

In all cases it is desirable to take a hierarchical approach to the system design in which the principles of iteration (regularity) can be used to reduce the complexity of the design task.

The designer is usually concerned with a number of key design parameters. These will include:

1. performance, in terms of the function to be performed, the required speed of operation and the power dissipation of the system;
2. time taken for the design/development cycle;
3. testability;
4. the size of the die, which is determined by the area occupied by the circuitry and in turn has a marked impact on the likely yield in production and on the cost of bonding and packaging and testing. Large die sizes are generally associated with poor yields.

Full custom design tends to achieve the best results, but *only* if the designer is fully conversant with the fundamental aspects of design in silicon so that the parameters can be optimized. However, full custom design parameter optimization is usually at the expense of parameter 2, the time taken to design.

Semi-custom and gate array designs both have penalties in area and often in speed and this is contributed to by the fact that not all the available logic will be used, due to the need for generality in gate array and standard cell geometries. However, it may often be the case that gate arrays will be faster than a prototype full custom design in, say, MPC form and the final design must be carefully optimized.

Once the approach is chosen, there remains the design philosophy which ranges through the following general possibilities.

1. *Hand-crafted design* in which, for example, the mask layouts are drawn on squared paper with layer encoding and are then digitized to give a machine readable form of the mask detail. Digitization can be 'by hand' with entry of coordinates through, say, a keyboard or by more direct digitization of the drawn layout using a digitizer pad and cursor.

2. *Computer-assisted textual entry* of mask detail through a keyboard using some specially developed language employing a text-editing program. Such programs may have relatively low-level capabilities, allowing the entry of rectangular boxes, and 'wires', etc. only, or may be at a higher level and allow symbolic entry of circuit elements such as transistors and contact structures.

3. *Computer-assisted graphical entry* of mask geometry through either a monochrome or color graphics terminal, again with the aid of the appropriate entry, display, and editing software.

In cases 2 and 3 the software usually aids the processes of hierarchical system design in that leaf cells (symbols) can be instanced many times, each instance being placed as appropriate in the floor plan. Subsystems thus created may themselves be repeatedly instanced and placed as required to build up the system hierarchy.

Such tools obviously encourage *regularity* and are generally used with a *generate* then *verify* design philosophy.

Silicon compiler-based design in which a high level approach is taken to design, and special languages, analogous to high level programming language compilers, are developed to allow the designer to specify the system requirements in a manner which is convenient and compact. The silicon compiler program then translates this input code into a mask design which will generate a circuit in silicon to meet the specified system requirements. Such programs are the subject of much research and development work at this particular time. Indeed, the work has reached a stage at which silicon compilers have been in use for some time and text books on the subject are beginning to appear (e.g. R. F. Ayres, *VLSI silicon compilation and the art of automatic microchip design*, Prentice-Hall, 1983).

12.2 The interface with the fabrication house

'Knowledge without practice makes but half an artist.' Proverb.

Obviously, real world designs in silicon are intended to be fabricated and there is no doubt that the learning processes associated with VLSI design depend heavily on actually designing systems in silicon, on having them *fabricated* and then on *testing* the fabricated chips.

In all cases, then, good *two-way* communications between the fabrication house or silicon broker and the designer must be established.

Communication from the former to the latter usually takes the form of a set of design rules which specify clearances, widths, spacing, etc. for the process to be used. The design rules used in this test, based on the work of Mead and Conway, are an example of such rules which will work for a large selection of MOS process lines. The fabrication house will also supply design parameters relevant to its process. These include layer resistance values, layer to layer capacitance values, etc. and figures for a typical 5 µm MOS process have been given and used in this text.

In return, the designer must communicate his mask layout designs to the fabricator in a form which is convenient and clearly understandable. Methods of expressing mask geometry are not entirely standardized, but a *de facto* standard appears to be CIF code.

12.2.1 CIF (Caltech. Intermediate Form) code

CIF is a low level graphics language for specifying the geometry of integrated circuits (Hon and Sequin, *A Guide to LSI Implementation*, Xerox). The purpose of CIF code is to communicate chip geometry in a standard machine-readable form for mask making. CIF code is reasonably compact and can cope with small and large system geometry. Its format is straightforward and it has the added advantage of being easily read. It has been widely used for the electronic transport of designs between universities and industrial laboratories, using such facilities as ARPANET in the United States and CSIRONET within Australia. Thus, it is appropriate to briefly examine some of the features of CIF so that the reader may appreciate general attributes of the code.

12.2.1.1 Geometric primitives

Various geometric structures such as boxes, polygons, and wires are readily defined. In general, the position, dimensions, and orientation must be specified and, also of course, the layer on which the box exists in the silicon. When examining the attributes of CIF code, the reader should be aware that CIF dimensions and positions are given in X, Y coordinate form but are in absolute dimension units, *not* in lambda form.

A few examples (Figure 12–1) serve to illustrate the features of the representation.

Boxes (B) are specified as

Box   Length (L)   Width (W)   Center (C)   Direction (D)

Note that direction is given as a vector assumed parallel to the length. If not given, then a vector 1,0 (*x,y*) is assumed (i.e. length will be parallel to the *x*-axis).

Boxes I and II in the diagram would, therefore, appear in code as

B25   60   50 80   − 10   10;   (box I)
.   .
.   .
.   .
(L)   (W)   (C)   (D)   (L, W, C, D would not appear
.   .   .   in the actual code.)
.   .   .
.   .   .
B40   20   40   35;   (box II)

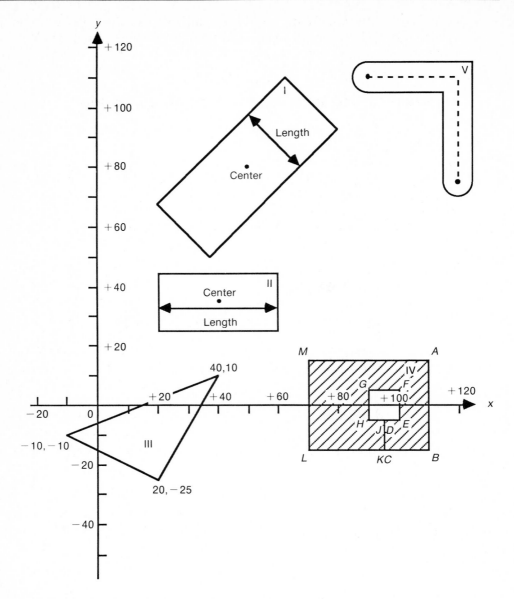

Figure 12–1 CIF primitives — examples

Polygons (P) are specified in terms of the vertices in order. An *n*-sided polygon requires *n* vertices and a connection between first and last is assumed to complete the boundary.

Polygon III in Figure 12–1 would therefore appear in code as

P−10   −10   40   10   20   −25   (box III)

In order to represent areas with holes in them, as in polygon (IV), the vertices A, B, C, D, E, F, G, H, J, K, L, M would be used to specify the area.

Wires (W) are specified in terms of their width followed by the center lines coordinates of the wire's path. Figure 12–1, wire (V) would be specified as follows:

W10   90   110   120   110   120   75

Note that each segment of wire ends in a semicircular 'flash' which will overlap any connecting area.

12.2.1.2 Layers

Layer selection and subsequent changes are treated by mode setting prior to or during the entry of geometric primitives. Layer setting must precede the entry of the first piece of geometry and must then precede the geometric inputs on any change of layer.

For the MOS processes dealt with in this text the layers are named as follows:

ND	(nMOS diffusion/thinox)	CD	(CMOS diffusion/thinox)
NP	(nMOS polysilicon)	CP	(CMOS polysilicon)
NC	(nMOS contact cut)	CC	(CMOS contact cut)
NM	(nMOS metal 1)	CM	(CMOS metal 1)
NN	(nMOS metal 2)	CN	(CMOS metal 2)
NI	(nMOS implant)	CS or CPP	(CMOS p^+ mask)
NB	(nMOS buried contact)	CW or CPW	(CMOS p-well)
NG	(nMOS overglass cuts)	CG	(CMOS overglass cuts)

Layer changes are indicated by the letter L followed by the layer name.

CIF also accommodates Calls (C) and rotations and translations, etc., but the elementary review given here should serve to convey the essential features to the reader. CIF code will be given later for design examples pursued in a following section of this chapter.

12.3 CAD tools for design and simulation

'*Efficiency is intelligent laziness.*' Arnold Glasgow, *Reader's Digest*, 1974.

The design of a chip of reasonable complexity can in time be completed 'by hand' but it is both a hard and inefficient way of doing things. As far as the design of very large systems is concerned, it is *essential* to have computer aids to design so that the design can be completed in a reasonable time and, indeed, so that it can be completed at all. Whatever the size or nature of the design task, there is no doubt that well-conveived tools can make it much easier *and* do it better. Tools are, therefore, essential to ensure first time (and every time) success in silicon. At the very least, the designer's tool box should include:

1. *physical design layout and editing* capabilities, either through textual or graphical entry of information;

2. *structure generation/system composition* capabilities, which may well be part of the design layout software implementing 1;
3. *physical verification.* The tools here should include design rule checking (DRC), circuit extractors, ratio rule and other static checks, and a capability to plot out and/or display for visual checking.
4. *behavioral verification.* Simulation at various levels will be required to check out the design before one embarks on the expense of turning out the design in silicon.

Simulators are available for logic (switch level) simulation and timing simulation. Circuit simulation via such programs as SPICE is also possible, but may be expensive in terms of computing time and therefore impractical for other than small subsystems. Recent advances in simulators have made it possible to use the software as a probe on various parts of the circuit to examine the simulated responses to input stimuli provided via the simulator. Such a facility, known as a software probe (and analogous to a CRO and associated hardware probe), is available, for example, in the Integrated Silicon Design suite of programs.

The authors can only stress that the joy of discovering that it does what it's supposed to is only exceeded by the dismay of discovering that it doesn't work once a chip is fabricated (the designer having failed to carry out proper simulation testing).

Because CAD tools are so important and because the first link in the CAD VLSI chain is the physical layout and editing aspects, a brief overview of some typical tools will be taken at this point in the text.

12.3.1   A basic textual entry layout language

It is not uncommon to approach the generation of such a language by embedding it in a suitable high level language which then conveys much of the power of the high level language to the embedded layout language. Such a language is BELLE (Basic Embedded Layout Language) which is embedded in PASCAL. BELLE was developed by the CSIRO (Commonwealth Scientific and Industrial Research Organisation) VSLI Program in Adelaide, Australia, and is similar to the SIMULA package LAP developed at the Californian Institute of Technology (Caltech.) in the United States. Because of the different base language, the syntax of user statement is rather different.

BELLE was originally distributed throughout Australia to support the VLSI educational and associated AUSMPC (Australian Multiproject Chip) program. However, an example of the use of BELLE serves to illustrate the general characteristics of this class of programs. BELLE is basically a leaf cell tool, that is, it is intended to describe the geometrics of relatively small circuit cells or groups of cells but it may also be used to compose complete layout. BELLE is composed of a set of PASCAL procedures and generates its output in CIF code. The use of PASCAL as the base language allows parameterization of circuit cells and circuits so that, say, one cell design can be used in many applications by simply changing the parameters for, for example, size, number of inputs, etc.

12.3.1.1 Design process using BELLE

Typically, designs are performed using BELLE in the following manner:

1. Beginning with an initial sketch or stick diagram of the circuit being designed, the circuit must then be laid out on graph paper to aid digitization. This process usually takes more than one attempt to generate an acceptable layout.
    Hints for layout:
    (a) Use colored pens to help distinguish between masks.
    (b) Graph paper with 2 mm or 5 mm grid spacing are good sizes. (2 mm representing 1 lambda produces quite legible layouts.)
    (c) Liquid Paper or equivalent is almost a necessity to remove those occasional mistakes.
    (d) Don't worry too much about achieving very dense layout packing in early attempts at design. Densely packed layouts are more likely to contain design rule violations than are sparse layouts.
    (e) Always check and recheck your layout for design rule violations, circuit correctness, etc. Some violations are often very difficult to detect (e.g. metal to metal violations involving butting contacts). It is wise to have at least one other person check your layout since a fresh outlook may spot elusive errors.
    (f) Some layouts, such as address decoders, are highly repetitive with only slight variations from section to section of the layout. In these cases, it is not necessary to draw the entire layout on paper, but to design the basic cell common to all sections and determine how to program the cells to achieve the desired function.

2. Once the layout has been completed on paper, programmability and parameterization must be determined. For example:
    (a) Is there a need to program a cell by conditional placement of transistors or contact cuts?
    (b) Should a variable number of inputs or outputs be provided to enable the same BELLE routine to be used for several different sections of the layout?
    (c) Should a cell be stretchable and, if so, where and by how much?
    (d) Should the width of power supply buses be variable?
    (e) Should the transistor ratios be adjustable?

    Strategy for implementing these parameters should be decided upon.

3. At this stage, coding the circuit in BELLE can commence. Coordinates which are to be parameterized should be expressed in terms of variables during digitization. By expressing coordinate positions relative to reference lines (e.g. the lower left corner of the cell, a vertical line, etc.), stretching the cell is made easy. Coding the circuit in BELLE is effectively the same as writing a PASCAL procedure, with the added benefit that many of the required procedures and functions have been prewritten.

12.3.1.2 *Design examples using BELLE*

Two examples are considered here. First, the design of a leaf cell for an nMOS dynamic shift register which is constructed from a chain of inverters separated by clocked pass transistors. This is followed by a design of an *n*-bit dynamic shift register to illustrate the composition aspects.

Routine to generate a dynamic shift register cell

```
procedure design proc;
var  srcellwidth, srcellheight:sizeunit: {Variables:srcellwidth,srcellheight}
{sizeunit is a BELLE defined type: all lambda-based variables can be of this
type}
Begin {design proc}
define ('srcell'); {define the basic S/R cell}
    layer (metal);
    wire (4, 0,2); dx (19);       {gnd bus}
    wire (4, 0,25); dx (19);      {Vdd bus}
{define the inverter part}
diffcut (4,2);                    {connect to gnd}
diffcut (4,25);                   {connect to Vdd}
buttcontact (4,14, 90);           {connect source and gate of pull-up}
layer (diffusion);
wire (4, 4,3); y (12);            {source and drain of pull-down}
wire (2, 4,24); y (14);           {source and drain of pull-up}
layer (poly);
box (0,7,8,9);                    {gate of inverter}
box (1,14, 7,22);                 {gate of pull-up}
layer (implant);
box (1,12, 7,24);                 {make pull-up depletion mode}
{now define the part with the clock gating the output}
buttcontact (16,10, −90);         {connect to poly, for next stage}
layer (diffusion);
wire (2, 5,12); x (15);           {output connection}

layer (poly);
wire (2, 17,8); x (19);           {output connection}
wire (2, 11,0); y (27);           {clock forming gate of pass transistor}
srcellwidth: = 19;
srcellheight: = 27;
enddef;
draw ('srcell', 0,0);
End; {design proc}
```

The layout to which this code corresponds has been plotted out in Figure 12–2 and the corresponding CIF code printed out in Table 12–1.

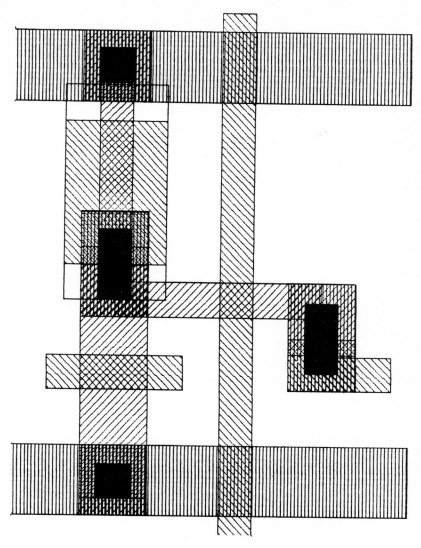

Figure 12-2   Layout of 'srcell' (Plotted from the CIF code of Table 12-1)

Routine to generate an n-bit dynamic shift register

In the previous routine only half a bit of a shift register was designed. In this part our intention is to extend the program to form an *n*-bit shift register using the basic cell.

To proceed we need to declare *n*-bits to be a constant at the top of the program. It is important to structure the program so that it can handle a different number of bits simply by changing this constant.

After the definition of the basic cell, we need to start with a new definition for the register. This should include a 'for' loop somewhere to repetitively draw the cell.

Table 12-1 CIF code for SRCELL

```
25 Lambda = 250;
DS 1001;
9 SRCELL;
42  − 500, − 250 5250,7000;
        L  NM  :
                    W 1000 0,500 4750,500;
                    W 1000 0,6250 4750,6250;
        L  ND  :
                    B 1000 1000 1000,500;
        L  NC  :
                    B 500 500 1000,500;
        L  NM  :
                    B 1000 1000 1000,500;
        L  ND  :
                    B 1000 1000 1000,6250;
        L  NC  :
                    B 500 500 1000,6250;
        L  NM  :
                    B 1000 1000 1000,6250;
        L  ND  :
                    B 1000 1000 1000,3250;
        L  NP  :
                    B 1000 750 1000,3875;
        L  NC  :
                    B 500 1000 1000,3500;
        L  NM  :
                    B 1000 1500 1000,3500;
        L  ND  :
                    W 1000 1000,750 1000,3000;
                    W 500 1000,6000 1000,3500;
        L  NP  :
                    B 2000 500 1000,2000;
                    B 1500 2000 1000,4500;
        L  NI  :
                    B 1500 3000 1000,4500;
        L  ND  :
                    B 1000 1000 4000,2750;
        L  NP  :
                    B 1000 750 4000,2125;
        L  NC  :
                    B 500 1000 4000,2500;
        L  NM  :
                    B 1000 1500 4000,2500;
        L  ND  :
                    W 500 1250,3000 3750,3000;
        L  NP  :
                    W 500 4250,2000 4750,2000;
                    W 500 2750,0 2750,6750;
    DF;
        C 1001 T 0,0;
    End
```

A loop should also be used to connect the clock bus to the appropriate cells. The modified program is:

```
procedure design proc;
const nbits = 4;

var srcellwidth, srcellheight: sizeunit;
regwidth, regheight: sizeunit;
i: integer;
rx: cornerunit;

Begin {design proc}
define ('srcell');

         .
         .
         .                    (previous SRCELL)
         .
         .

enddef;
{draw 2n of the cells side by side to form an n-bit shift register}
define ('shiftreg');
     for i: = 1 to 2*nbits do
          draw ('srcell', (i − 1)*srcellwidth,5);
{place the clock lines: phi 1 top, phi 2 bottom}
     layer (poly);
     wire (2, 0, srcellheight + 9); dx(nbits*2*srcellwidth);
     {phi 1 along top}
     wire (2, 0,1); dx(nbits*2*srcellwidth); {phi 2 along bottom}
     for i: = 1 to nbits do
          begin
          rx: = (i − 1)*2*srcellwidth + 11;
          wire (2, rx,srcellheight + 9); dy(− 4); {connect to phi 1}
          rx: = rx + srcellwidth;
          wire (2, rx,1); dy(4); {connect to phi 2}
          end;
regwidth: = 2*nbits*srcellwidth;
regheight: = srcellheight + 10;
enddef;
draw ('shiftreg', 0,0);
End;
```

A printout of the CIF code for a four-bit register is set out as Table 12–2, and the layout as Figure 12–3.

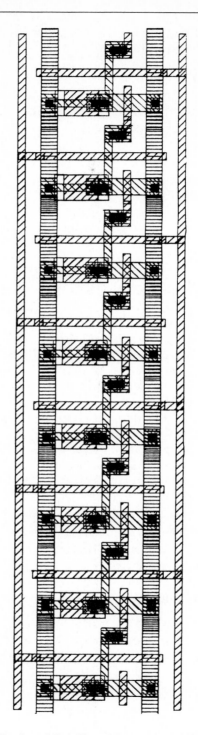

Figure 12–3 Layout of the four-bit shift register 'shiftreg' (Plotted from the CIF code of Table 12–2)

Table 12–2 CIF code for four-bit shift register

```
25 Lambda = 250;
DS 1001;
9 SRCELL;
42 −500, −250 5250,7000;
        L  NM  ;
                     W 1000 0,500 4750,500;
                     W 1000 0,6250 4750,6250;
        L  ND  ;
                     B 1000 1000 1000,500;
        L  NC  ;
                     B 500 500 1000,500;
        L  NM  ;
                     B 1000 1000 1000,500;
        L  ND  ;
                     B 1000 1000 1000,6250;
        L  NC  ;
                     B 500 500 1000,6250;
        L  NM  ;
                     B 1000 1000 1000,6250;
        L  ND  ;
                     B 1000 1000 1000,3250;
        L  NP  ;
                     B 1000 750 1000,3875;
        L  NC  ;
                     B 500 1000 1000,3500;
        L  NM  ;
                     B 1000 1500 1000,3500;
        L  ND  ;
                     W 1000 1000,750 1000,3000;
                     W 500 1000,6000 1000,3500;
        L  NP  ;
                     B 2000 500 1000,2000;
                     B 1500 2000 1000,4500;
        L  NI  ;
                     B 1500 3000 1000,4500;
        L  ND  ;
                     B 1000 1000 4000,2750;
        L  NP  ;
                     B 1000 750 4000,2125;
        L  NC  ;
                     B 500 1000 4000,2500;
        L  NM  ;
                     B 1000 1500 4000,2500;
        L  ND  ;
                     W 500 1250,3000 3750,3000;
        L  NP  ;
                     W 500 4250,2000 4750,2000;
                     W 500 2750,0 2750,6750;
```

Table 12-2 continued

```
                    DF;

                    DS 1002;
                    9 shiftreg;
                    42 − 500,0 38500, 9250;
                              C 1001 T 0,1250;
                              C 1001 T 4750,1250;
                              C 1001 T 9500,1250;
                              C 1001 T 14250,1250;
                              C 1001 T 19000,1250;
                              C 1001 T 23750,1250;
                              C 1001 T 28500,1250;
                              C 1001 T 33250,1250;
                    L NP     ;
                              W 500 0,9000 38000,9000;
                              W 500 0,250 38000,250;
                              W 500 2750,9000 2750,8000;
                              W 500 7500,250 7500,1250;
                              W 500 12250,9000 12250,8000;
                              W 500 17000,250 17000,1250;
                              W 500 21750,9000 21750,8000;
                              W 500 26500,250 26500,1250;
                              W 500 31250,9000 31250,8000;
                              W 500 36000,250 36000,1250;
              DF;
                    C 1002 T 0,0;
              End
```

12.3.2 A symbolic textual entry layout language and virtual grid-based design

The main disadvantages of a textual entry layout language such as BELLE may be summarized as follows:

1. Layouts are on a fixed grid where each grid line represents a particular distance in numbers of λ from a given datum. Thus, all circuit elements must be drawn in positions such that no design rule violations are present in any direction or between any layers. The designer must therefore be fully conversant with the layout rules applicable to the process to be used for fabrication and must observe those rules at all stages of the layout work.

2. As a consequence of this, the layouts must be subjected to checking by a design rule checker (DRC) program which takes as input, say, the complete CIF code and checks for design rule violations which must then be corrected by the designer.

3. As a further consequence, the designed layout is both technology and fabrication house dependent (except where a set of rules such as those published by Mead and Conway are applicable for a number of fabrication houses).

4.   The geometric primitives are such that all layouts must be built up from boxes, wires, and contact cuts, etc.

12.3.2.1   The ABCD (A Better Circuit Description) language

ABCD is a symbolic layout language for CMOS and nMOS system designs which supports the *virtual grid* style of layout. It was developed at the Microelectronics Center of North Carolina (MCNC) and is based on the ICDL language developed at Bell Laboratories. In a virtual grid system, the grid lines on which layout takes place serve to indicate *relative* geometric topology but *not* any absolute physical spacings. Thus, the virtual grid lines are used for capturing the designer's intent and the designer does *not* have to be aware of any design rules while carrying through the layout work.

The virtual grid, of course, also captures the desired connectivity requirements, and symbols are placed on the grid to build a circuit with the desired general topology.

A function of the symbolic language is that the user can create and define symbols that describe the layout of system cells. Symbols may then be 'instanced' any number of times in forming the system layout. In this respect, it may be likened to a macro assembler where the macro instructions correspond to the symbols in ABCD.

The designer is, therefore, decoupled from design rules and fabrication house constraints. Such factors are taken into account by subsequent processing through which the required design rules are implemented. Such processing is known as compaction and serves to convert the virtual grid layout into a real mask layout which has the same general topology but obeys the required design rules. A feature of compaction software is that any reasonable set of design rules can be built in and thus implemented.

A simple example of compaction from a virtual grid layout is included in Figure 12–4. Brief notes on ABCD now follow, noting that the examples are for

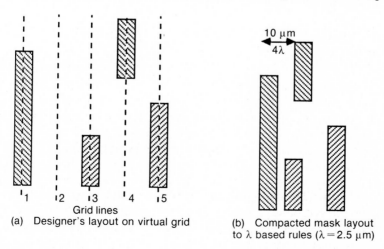

(a)   Designer's layout on virtual grid

(b)   Compacted mask layout
to λ based rules (λ = 2.5 μm)

Figure 12–4   Example of virtual grid layout and subsequent compaction

nMOS circuits, although both CMOS and nMOS environments are provided by the software.

12.3.2.2 *Brief notes on ABCD: ABCD symbolic primitives*

An ABCD file contains the following primitives:

- devices;
- loads;
- wires;
- contacts;
- pins;
- marks or points;
- instances.

Typical statements might be as follows (for an nMOS inverter):

```
# pull-up with length to width ratio of 2:1; (Figure 12-5(a))
        pull-up: load ntype (3,5) l=2 or=north
# pull-down with length to width ratio of 1:2; (Figure 12-5(b))
        pull-down: device ntype (3,2) w=2 or =north
```

\# V_{DD} and V_{SS} rails; (Figure 12-5(c))

```
                wire alum (0,7) (7,7)
                wire alum (0,0) (0,7)
# Connect devices together and to supply rails; (Figure 12-5(d))
                wire ndiff (3,3) (3,4)
                wire ndiff (3,6) (3,7)
                wire ndiff (3,0) (3,1)
                contact md (3,7)
                contact md (3,0)
# Connect the gate of pull-up to the source; (Figure 12-5(e))
                wire poly (3,5) (2,5) (2,4) (3,4)
                contact pd (3,4)
# Connect input and output connections; (Figure 12-5(f))
                wire poly (0,2) (3,2)
                wire ndiff (3,3) (5,3)
```

Figure 12-5 illustrates the one-to-one correspondence between the ABCD text and the symbolic layout that is generated. In order to differentiate between the depletion transistor (load) and the enhancement transistor (device), the encoding used in this text for layout layers is extended as in Table 12-3.

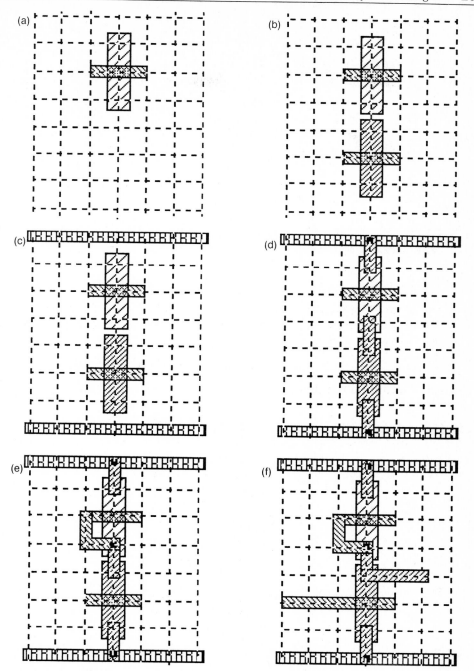

Figure 12–5 Symbolic layout of nMOS inverter

Transistor type	Description	Symbol
n-enhancement	Green transistor	
n-depletion	Yellow transistor	

This symbolic approach relieves the designer of any necessity to consider the implant layer.

Table 12-3 ABCD symbols

12.3.2.2 Instances

Instances of previously defined cells are used to establish hierarchy. For example, we may have used ABCD to create a cell $C1$ that has corners (0,0) and (4,4). Then the following statement:

$$C1: \text{instance cell } 1 \ ll=(0,0) \ n=4 \ dir=\text{vertical}$$

places four copies (that is, $n=4$) of $C1$ onto the virtual grid of the calling cell

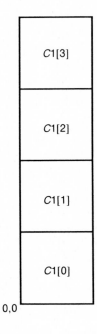

Figure 12-6 Cell composition

vertically, and associates the names $C1[0]$, $C1[1]$, $C1[2]$, and $C1[3]$ with each of the four copies.

It should be noted that the four corners of a cell are referred to as follows:

lower-left $= ll$	upper-left $= ul$
lower-right $= lr$	upper-right $= ur$

The hierarchical composition of the four instances is shown in Figure 12–6.

Details of the ABCD language were contributed by Professor J. Rosenberg of MCNC, North Carolina.

12.3.3 Graphical entry layout

A convenient and highly interactive method of producing layouts is to make use of monochrome or color graphics terminals on which the layout is built up and displayed during the design process. Such systems are mostly 'menu driven', in that menus of possible actions at various stages of the design are displayed on the screen beside the display of the current layout detail. Some form of cursor allows selection and/or placement of geometric features, etc., and the cursor may also allow selection of menu items or, alternatively, these may often be selected from a keyboard. Positioning of the cursor may be effected from the keyboard in simple systems and/or position may be controlled from a bitpad digitizer or from a 'mouse', etc.

Two available graphical entry layout packages are KIC, developed at the University of California, Berkeley, USA, and PLAN, originally developed at the University of Adelaide. PLAN makes use of low-cost monochrome, as well as color, graphics terminals and is marketed by Integrated Silicon Design Pty Ltd, Adelaide. The use of an early version of PLAN to generate layouts is illustrated in Figures 12–7 to 12–11.

It is hoped that the inclusion of these figures which show various stages of design is sufficient to convey an idea of the nature of this class of software tools.

12.4 Design verification prior to fabrication

'Try your skill in gilt first, and then in gold.' Proverb.

It is not enough to have good design tools for producing mask and system layout detail. It is essential that such tools should be complemented by equally effective verification software capable of handling large systems and with reasonable computing power requirements.

The nature of the tools required will depend on the way in which an integrated circuit design is represented in the computer. Two basic approaches are:

1. Mask level layout languages, such as CIF, which are well-suited to physical layout description but serve poorly for capturing the design intent.

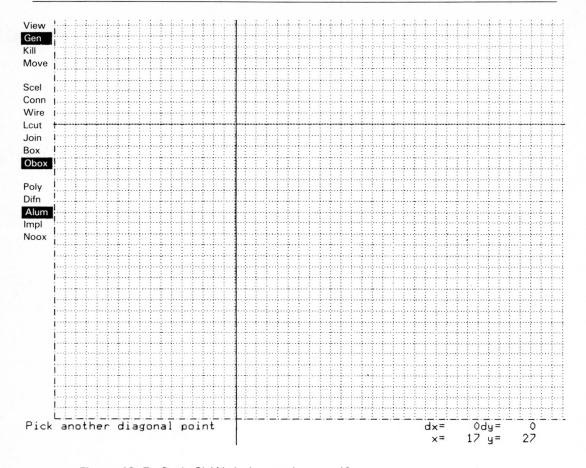

Figure 12-7   Basic PLAN design environment*

*Figure shows λ grid, cross hair cursor, and menu (selected items in inverse video). *x* and *y* values of current or previous cursor position may also be displayed as shown. OBOX is selected to establish an outline (bounding) box. Then a name (SRCL) is allocated to the enclosed cell.

2. Circuit description languages such as are used by ABCD where the primitives are circuit elements such as transistors, wires, and nodes. In general, such languages capture the design intent but do not directly describe the physical layout associated with the design.

The need for physical layout verification 'design rule checking (DRC)' will also depend on whether or not layout is on a fixed or virtual grid.

By and large therefore, the designer's needs may include:

12.4.1   Design rule checkers (DRC)

The cost in time and facilities in mask making and in fabricating a chip from those masks is such that all possible errors must be eliminated before mask making pro-

View
Gen
Kill
Move

Scel
Conn
Wire
Lcut
Join
Box
Obox

Poly
Difn
Alum
Impl
Noox

```
Pick a diagonal point of the box          dx=    17dy=    -4
                                          x=     17 y=    23
```

Figure 12-8 Layout of metal geometry using the BOX generate feature*

*V_{DD} and *GND* rails have been drawn by specifying diagonally opposite corners of each box (the Alum or metal layer is selected). *x* and *y* values shown are for the last corner specified and *dx* and *dy* give the relative movement of the cursor between corners of the last box drawn.

ceeds. Once a design has been turned into silicon there is little that can be done if it doesn't work.

The wise designer will check for errors at all stages of the design, namely:

1. at the pencil and paper stage of the design of leaf cells;
2. at the leaf cell level once the layout is complete (say, when the CIF code for that leaf cell has been generated);
3. at the subsystem level to check that butting together and wiring up of leaf cells is correctly done;
4. once the entire system layout has been completed.

A number of DRC programs, based on various algorithms, are available to the designer, for example, CHECK from Integrated Silicon Design Pty Ltd.

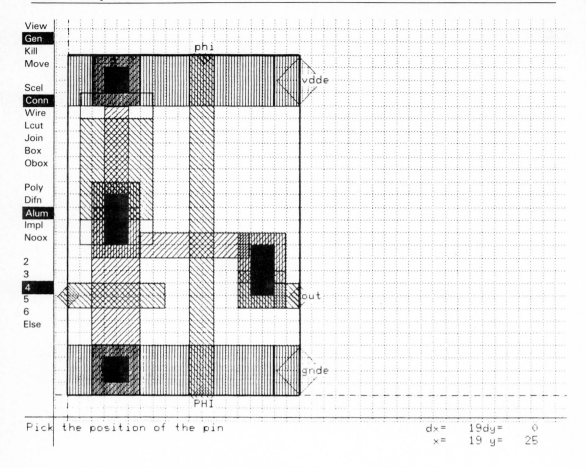

Figure 12-9 Completed layout of shift register cell (SRCL)*

*Identical to that of Figure 12–2. Note the labelled nodes or pins.

12.4.2 Circuit extractors

If design information exists in the form of physical layout data (as in CIF code form), then a circuit extractor program which will interpret the physical layout in circuit terms is required. Although the designer could use the extracted data to check against his design intent, it is normally fed directly into a simulator so that the computer may be used to interpret the findings of the extractor. An example of a circuit extractor program is NET from Integrated Silicon Design Pty Ltd.

12.4.3 Simulators

In this section we briefly consider the very important topic of simulation prior to the VLSI design being committed to silicon.

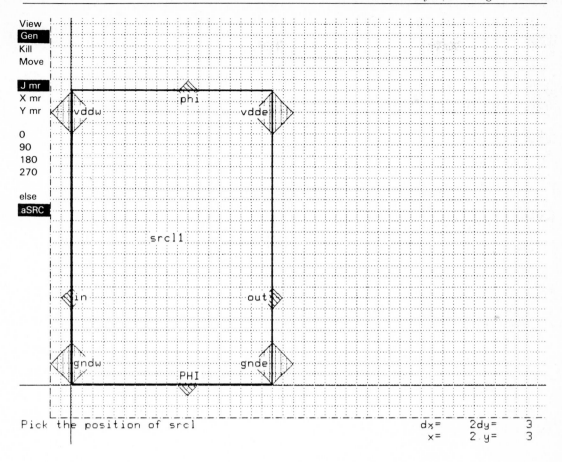

Figure 12-10 Bounding (outline) box representation of SRCL*

*From now on, SRCL may be instanced from the SCEL item on the previous menu and placed as required as shown. Note that the cell is shown now as a bounding box with pins.

From mask layout detail it is possible to extract a circuit description in a form suitable for input to a simulator. Programs which do this are referred to as circuit extractors. The circuit description contains information about circuit components and their interconnections. This information is subsequently transformed by the simulator into a set of equations from which the predictions of behavior are made.

The topology of the circuit determines two sets of equations:

- Kirchoff's Current Law — determining the branch currents; and
- Kirchoff's Voltage Law — determining node voltages.

The electrical behavior is defined by mathematical modeling, the accuracy of which determines two key factors:

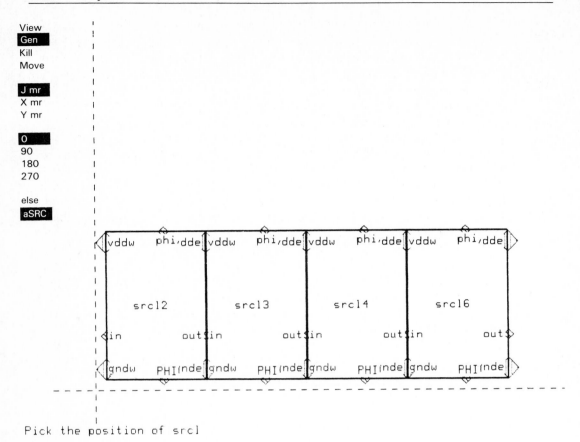

Figure 12–11   Instancing SRCL to form a register*

*Several instances of SRCL may be set out as shown to form a complete register (two-bits only shown) and a bounding box and a name can be given to the whole structure.

- the accuracy of the simulation; and
- the computing power and time needed for the simulation.

We are often interested in relatively simple models to enable the high-lighting of the salient features of performance in the design stage and to be able to observe trends as aspects of a design are changed by means of on-line simulation.

Various types of simulators are available but generally they may be grouped into:

- circuit simulators;
- timing simulators;
- logic level (switch level) simulators;
- system level simulators.

Circuit simulators are concerned with the electrical behavior of the various parts of the circuit to be implemented in silicon. Such simulation programs as SPICE can do this quite well, but take a lot of computing time to simulate even relatively small sections of a system and are completely impractical for circuits of any real magnitude.

Timing simulators such as PROBE from Integrated Silicon Design Pty Ltd and QRS (developed at MCNC) have attempted to improve matters in these respects by concentrating on active nodes and ignoring quiescent nodes in simulation. Work is proceeding in many establishments on improving the nature and performance of simulators; in particular, the way in which devices/circuits are modeled is vital. In all cases, the accuracy of simulation depends on the accuracy of the fabrication house parameters which must be fed into the simulator. In most cases, simulators attempt to predict the electrical performance with an accuracy of 20 percent or better. Examples of the output form of typical timing simulators may be examined in Figures 11–14, 11–15, 13–6, 13–13, 13–21, and 13–22.

Simulators such as PROBE are becoming increasingly important during the design phase. The structure of these tools ensures that run times are strictly linearly-related to the number of devices and nodes being simulated. Speed-up is usually achieved through the use of a simple simulation cycle, a somewhat restricted network model and reasonably simple transistor models.

The simulation cycle is organized around the concept of a timestep. Each node voltage V is updated within each timestep by applying the following relation

$$V_{new} = V_{old} + \frac{I_{ds}}{C} \Delta t$$

where

$$I_{ds} = \text{drain to source current}$$

$$C = \text{node capacitance}$$

$$\Delta t = \text{timestep}$$

In order to improve transistor modeling it is possible to include:

- body effect;
- channel length modulation;
- carrier velocity saturation.

The last two effects are particularly important for short channel transistors, that is, channel lengths $\leqslant 3 \ \mu m$, and their effects should be taken into account.

Channel length modulation — for voltages exceeding the onset of saturation there is an effective decrease in the channel length of a short channel transistor. For example, the change in channel length ΔL for an n-transistor is approximated by

$$\Delta L = \sqrt{\frac{2\varepsilon_0 \varepsilon_{Si}}{qN_A} (V_{ds} - V_t)}$$

The resultant drain to source current $I^1{}_{ds}$ is approximated by

$$I^1{}_{ds} = I_{ds} \frac{L}{L - \Delta L}$$

where I_{ds} is given by the simple expressions developed in Chapter 2.

Velocity saturation — when the drain to source voltage of a short channel transistor exceeds a critical value, the charge carriers reach their maximum scattering limited velocity before pinch off. Thus, less current is available from a short channel transistor than from a long channel transistor with similar width to length ratio and processing.

Logic level simulators can cope with large sections of the layout at one time but, of course, the performance now is measured in terms of logic levels only. However, there may be large sections of a system which can be satisfactorily dealt with and verified this way, provided that leaf cell elements have been subjected to a more rigorous treatment.

When considering complete systems, logic simulators may be replaced by simulators which operate at the register transfer level.

In all cases, the designer should carefully consider the availability of all such tools when choosing VLSI design software.

12.5 Test and testability

'The proof of the pudding is in the eating.' Proverb.

Although this topic has been left to last it is by no means least in significance.

Three factors conspire to create considerable difficulties for the test engineer and, indeed, for the designer testing his own prototypes:

1. the sheer complexity of VLSI systems;
2. the fact that the entire surface of the chip, other than over the pads, is sealed by an overglass layer and, thus, circuit nodes cannot be probed for monitoring or excitation.
3. With minor exceptions, there is no way that the circuit can be modified during tests to make it work.

Thus, not only will mistakes be very costly, both in terms of time and money but, for a complex system, lack of thought may mean that it cannot be properly tested.

It is, therefore, *essential* that the requirements of testing be considered and that a satisfactory and sufficient measure of *testability* be built into the architecture from the outset. So important is testability that many designers are prepared to dedicate 30 percent or more of chip area for this purpose alone.

12.5.1   System partitioning

The problems of testing, particularly at the prototype stage, are greatly eased if the system is sensibly partitioned into subsystems, each of which is as self-contained and independent as possible. To take the example of the four-bit data path chip used earlier in the text, the partitions used — namely the register array, the adder, the shifter — are functionally independent to a large extent and have relatively simple interconnections.

At the prototyping stage it is possible to provide special test points (by providing extra pads for probing) at the interface between the subsystems. It is also possible, in a prototype, to provide double pad and fusible link connections in key paths between subsystems. This allows these connections to be open circuited if necessary so that one system can be divorced from another as a last resort in prototype testing.

For production items, also, it helps greatly if subsystems can be checked out individually by providing the appropriate additional inlet/outlet pads for test purposes. The test requirements for exhaustive testing of large digital systems are quite prohibitive if the system is tested as a whole. Take, for example, a finite state machine realized as a mixture of combinational logic and memory elements. Let us assume n possible inputs to the combinational logic and m memory elements, and that m outputs of the memory elements are fed back as inputs to the combinational logic.

In this case, to fully exercise the system for every possible combination of inputs and internal states would involve the generation of 2^{m+n} test vectors.

If, say, $n = 24$ and $m = 20$, the resultant number of test vectors for exhaustive testing is 2^{44} and, even if these are generated at a rate of 10^6 vectors/sec, then testing will take six months at 24 hours per day.

On the other hand, if the system is partitioned for testing, exhaustive testing can be reduced to $2^n + 2^m$ vectors, a much more reasonable proposition (and for the figures given above would result in a test time of less than 20 seconds).

12.5.2   Layout and testability

Although it is impossible to generalize on this topic, common sense and a thoughtful approach to system layout may well considerably ease the problems associated with testing. For example, the inclusion of key point test pads or pads to energize special test modes are possible when the design is evolving.

The designer should also be aware of practical factors which will reduce the likelihood of short and open circuits. In particular, for nMOS circuits, it has been shown that short circuits and open circuits in the metal layer and short circuits in the diffusion layer, were the dominant faults experienced. Careful observance of design rules and ground rules should help to reduce the incidence of such faults.

12.5.3 Reset/initialization

One simple but very effective aid to testing and testability is to design a reset facility into all digital systems of any complexity. This has the considerable advantage of setting all internal states to known values, and testing may then at least proceed from known conditions.

The simple expedient is quite often overlooked or omitted.

12.5.4 Design for testability

There are two key concepts underlying all considerations for testability. They are:

1. controllability;
2. observability.

Quite simply, these concepts ensure that the designer considers the provision of means of setting or resetting key nodes in the system and of observing the response at key points.

The effects of testability or lack of it are such that it has been predicted that testability will soon become the main design criterion for VLSI circuits. The alternative is to save area by ignoring testability, but the penalties are such that even for modest complexity (e.g. 10,000 gates per chip) the test costs could rise by a factor of 5 to 10, compared with the same system designed for testability. Given that test is already a significant component of LSI chip costs, then the effects will be quite dramatic and could well cause the test costs to exceed all other production costs by a significant factor. (See G. Grassl, *Design for Testability*, NATO Advanced Study Course on VLSI Design, 1980.)

12.5.5 Notes on test and testability

Particular approaches to design, known as *design for testability*, have gained momentum in recent years.

In general, the approaches fall into two categories — either design for testability with hard and fast rules or with sets of guidelines. Within these categories, various techniques are possible, such as:

1. *ad hoc* testability features;
2. structured testability approaches;
3. self-test circuitry.

12.5.5.1 Ad hoc testability

An *ad hoc* approach is often quite effective, since the nature of the architecture can be taken into account and the most appropriate testability arrangements configured without changing the architecture dramatically.

For example, for long sequential sections, subdivisions into smaller subsections is readily effected. Consider the simple example of a 20-bit counter which would need 2^{20} steps for an exhaustive test. If the counter is split into four five-bit sections, only four sets of 2^5 steps are needed.

Again, bus-oriented structures can exploit the buses in any testing strategy.

Thus, *ad hoc* testing can be a very effective method if the designer approaches the task in an intelligent manner. However, being essentially unstructured, it is not readily compatible with automatic test generators.

12.5.5.2 Structured testability

In this approach the concepts of controllability and observability are implemented and structural test pattern generation is characterized by:

1. Controllability — being able to set known internal states.
2. Combinatorial testability — being able to generate all states to fully exercise all combinations of circuit states.
3. Observability — being able to read out the result of the state changes as they occur.

One popular structured testing technique is to form storage elements into large shift register chains for testing. This approach is known as level sensitive scan design (LSSD) and a number of parallel paths rather than a simple scan path can be used to reduce testing time.

The design rules for LSSD combine two concepts:

1. Correct operation of a design must *not* be dependent on risetimes or falltimes, or on minimum delays in signals propagating through the architecture.
2. All internal storage elements other than memory arrays have to be capable of configuration as shift register stages.

The essence of the LSSD approach is to design all circuitry in a register-to-register format. This implies compact blocks of combinational logic with registers on input and output sides and all feed-back lines being register-to-register as shown in Figure 12–12.

In the operational mode the registers merely latch the signal lines between blocks of logic. In test mode the registers become shift registers.

The scan design concept attempts to solve the general problem of test generation for sequential circuits. It takes advantage of the fact that if all flip–flops can be set to any specific value, and if their state can be observed in a straightforward manner, then the test generation task can be reduced to the complexity of testing combinational logic.

Scan design allows the designers to control and observe the state, or value, of all the internal flip–flops by connecting each flip–flop into one or more shift registers when the circuit is in the test (scan) mode.

In order to reconfigure flip–flops appropriately, it is necessary to be able to include a double throw switch in the data path. One possible arrangement is suggested in Figure 12–13.

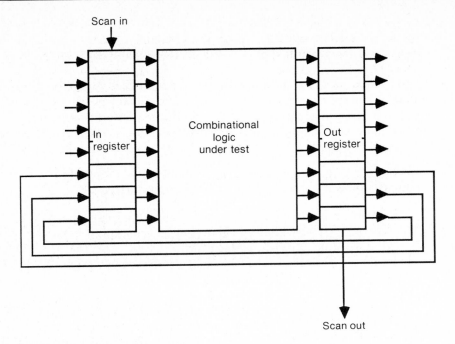

Figure 12-12 LSSD approach

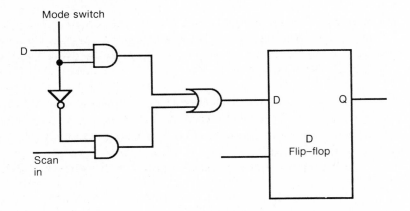

Figure 12-13 D flip-flop with double throw switch

A typical sequence of events in structured testing would be:

1. scan in an appropriate pattern;
2. apply primary inputs;
3. assert the system clock;
4. observe primary outputs;
5. scan out the results.

12.5.5.3 Self-test circuitry

Another effective way of implementing design for testability is to deliberately design self-test circuitry for the architecture on the chip. In this way, testing is completed by initiating a self-test mode by the chip itself and the results are reported through the output facilities to the outside world. Some of the approaches include:

1. Functional testing — for example, a microprocessor testing itself. This approach does not result in a high coverage of possible faults, because the approach is dependent on all essential features of the architecture being functional for the testing process to work at all.
2. The inclusion of replicated sections of the architecture (i.e. parallel redundancy) and the implementation of majority voting circuitry.
3. Signature analysis techniques — such techniques have been extensively pioneered by Hewlett–Packard and the effectiveness depends on the planning done at the design stage. In other words, signature analysis cannot effectively be tacked on as an afterthought.

The approach is based on linear feedback shift register principles, as shown in Figure 12–14, and *Exclusive/Or* gates are used to connect outputs from appropriate points back to the input of the register. A clocked system is generally implied, as shown.

Generally, there must be a test sequence which requires that the circuit is initialized to a known state and then a sequence of known length and characteristics is generated. If the circuit is functioning correctly then the signatures (i.e. state of the shift register outputs) at the end of the sequence may be checked against those predicted by the designer. Incorrect signatures indicate faults in the circuitry and the nature of the errors can give rise to a fault identification process.

12.5.5.4 Built-in logic block observation (BILBO)

A natural extension to the techniques considered is to merge an LSSD scan path with a linear feedback shift register to form a BILBO facility.

This also provides a pseudo-random number generator and, thus, a source

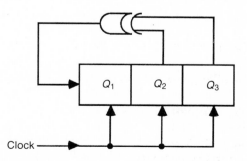

Figure 12–14 General arrangement for signature analysis

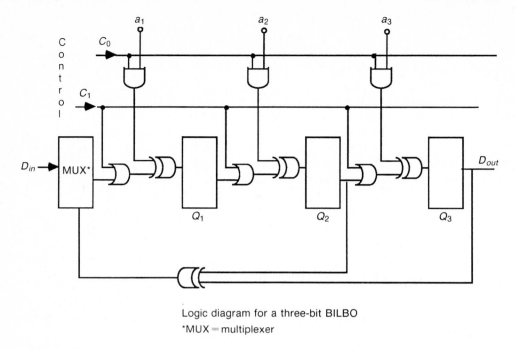

Logic diagram for a three-bit BILBO
*MUX = multiplexer

Figure 12–15 Basic BILBO arrangement and modes

of random test patterns. It is generally found that random pattern testing is very effective for testing combinational logic.

The BILBO facility has the general arrangement of Figure 12–15.

1. *Linear Shift Mode.* $C_0 = C_1 = 0$: data are serially clocked into *S/R* through D_{in} and can be either read out at the Q outputs, or alternatively may be clocked out through the output D_{out}.
2. *Signature Analysis Mode.* $C_0 = 1$: $C_1 = 0$: can perform either signature analysis or alternatively generate pseudo-random sequences.
3. *Data Latch.* $C_0 = C_1 = 1$: the inputs a_1, a_2, a_3 are clocked into the flip–flops and can be read out on the Q outputs.
4. *Reset Mode.* $C_0 = 0$: $C_1 = 1$: all registers are reset.

The operation of the BILBO facility is such that the monitoring of patterns in the BILBO is by means of *Exclusive-Oring* into the linear feedback shift register at multiple points, which corresponds to a signature analyzer with multiple inputs.

The results stored in the signature analyzer are scanned out after a number of random test patterns have been applied. This is achieved by changing the modes of operation from the linear feedback to the simple shift register mode. The various modes are selected by the control lines C_0 and C_1 of Figure 12–15.

One possible approach for using the BILBO facility in a bus-oriented architecture is to include BILBO facilities in each subsection (see Figure 12–16).

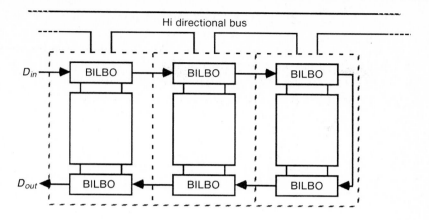

Figure 12–16   One approach to using BILBOs

In such a system, the scan path mode may be used for initialization followed by the self-test (signature analysis) mode for a specified length of sequence. The signature which may contain fault messages is then clocked out in the scan path mode.

It should be noted that the function of the BILBO arrangements is not necessarily confined to testing alone, and in the normal (non-testing) mode they may be used as shift registers, latches, or storage elements of the architecture.

12.6 Some observations

Having worked through this text, the budding VLSI designer should have come to terms with the essential techniques and rules for designing nMOS and CMOS circuits. It is possible to design small simple ICs, or even larger (but regular) digital circuits using a pencil and paper to generate mask layouts and hand digitization of layouts into CIF code. However, although that would provide a thorough grounding in the fundamentals and the design rules, it is an inefficient and tedious process to say the least and does not readily provide for checking the correctness or the likely performance of the design. Thus any serious entry into VLSI design requires access to suitable CAD tools. This does not necessarily imply a need for large sophisticated computer systems, although, of course, VLSI design tools will run very well in such environments. Suites of software are readily available to run in a personal computer/workstation environment. Thus the investment needed to be able to tackle custom VLSI chip design is not excessive and the time saved by acquiring and using proper facilities will repay the capital outlay over a very short period of chip design activity.

This text has, so far, exercised the reader in the use of lambda-based Mead and Conway style design rules with which we have designed a number of nMOS and CMOS leaf-cells and subsystems, and a small nMOS system — the four-bit data path. However, micron-based rules generally allow for more aggressive designs in terms of speed and area.

The next chapter presents three CMOS project designs which utilized the micron-based rules set out in Appendix A for mask layout and fabrication.

Faster and smaller area designs may utilize double metal two-micron technology for which a rule set is presented in Appendix B. In practice (and after practice) the designer may well wish to use this state-of-the-art approach.

13 | Some CMOS design projects

'You cannot create experience — you must undergo it.' Albert Camus

13.1 Introduction to project work

The main design exercise tackled earlier in this text was chosen to illustrate the design processes and to introduce the reader to the type of project suitable as a first design in silicon. The design has been proven as a student design exercise and through fabrication. The technology, nMOS, was chosen for a number of reasons including the relatively simple design rules and access to fabrication at the time.

Although the design processes are similar it is nevertheless instructive to formally tackle CMOS design work and to this end three projects are set out in this chapter.

The following projects, which have also been fabricated and tested, are part of the material used by Integrated Silicon Design Pty Ltd of Adelaide in the conduct of training courses and we are indebted to that company for their permission to reproduce this work in this text.

Up to this point in the text we have made exclusive use of lambda-based design rules and all the layout examples given, conform to the rules set out in Chapter 3. However sooner or later the designer will want to pursue a more aggressive design layout than the lambda rules allow. Earlier in the text we introduced micron-based rules and, by way of example, the rules utilized by AWA Ltd and Orbit Semiconductor Inc. Complete sets of these rules are contained in Appendix A (AWA) and Appendix B (Orbit). The design examples in this chapter employ AWA design rules.

13.2 CMOS project 1 — an incrementer/decrementer

The design to be pursued is that of a four-bit incrementer/decrementer, but the design is general in that the standard cell envisaged can be cascaded at will to n bits.

13.2.1 Behavioral description

The truth table for a binary one-bit incrementer is shown in Figure 13–1, where C_i is the carry bit from the previous stage, Cl is the clock input, C_{i+1} is the carry bit output, and Q_n is the stage output.

The logic expressions for the incrementer are as follows

$$Q_n = C_i \oplus Q_{n-1} \tag{13.1}$$
$$C_{i+1} = C_i \cdot Q_{n-1} \tag{13.2}$$

The n stages are isolated by the clock signal Cl, and it will be seen that the truth table

Truth table

Inputs			Outputs	
CI	C_i	Q_{n-1}	Q_n	C_{i+1}
0	0	0	0	0
1	0	0	0	0
0	1	0	0	0
1	1	0	1	0
0	0	1	0	0
1	0	1	1	0
0	1	1	0	0
1	1	1	0	1

Note: Where Q_{n-1} is state of output prior to clocking.

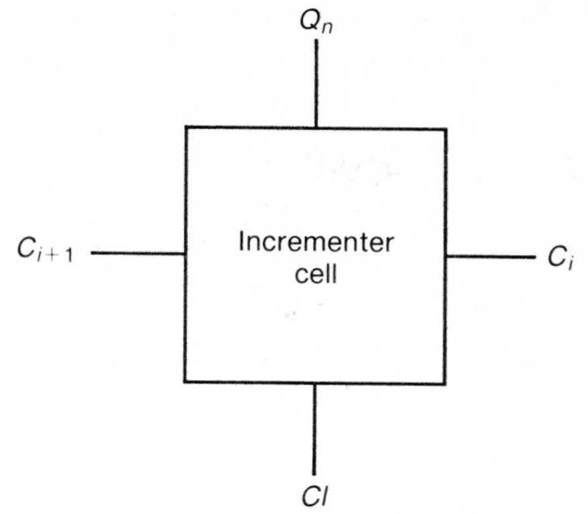

Figure 13–1 One-bit incrementer cell

assumes positive-edge clocking. A reset signal *Rs* should also be provided, for the incrementer to be able to start from zero at any instant in time.

For the incrementer to function as a decrementer the additional equation that needs to be implemented is as follows:

$$C_{i+1} = C_i \cdot \overline{Q_{n-1}} \tag{13.3}$$

A particular, but not the only possible, approach to designing this subsystem follows. For those readers who wish to 'fly solo' in tackling this design, the next project is introduced in section 13.3.

13.2.2 Structural description

13.2.2.1 *Logic representation*
An incrementer/decrementer cell is realized by direct implementation of expressions (13.1), (13.2), and (13.3) as in Figure 13–2, for example. A reset control line may be provided to the flip-flop to enable the circuit to start from zero at any time. The control line which is required to set the circuit operation to that of an incrementer or a decrementer is shown in the figure.

13.2.2.2 *Operation of the circuit*
The circuit functions like an adder or a subtractor with one of its three inputs set to zero. The cell uses its current state as one input and the carry in from the previous stage as the other input. The current state and the carry out are modified according to the two inputs.

13.2.2.3 *Critical paths*
The critical delay in this circuit is the propagation delay of the carry bit — analogous to the adder situation. Since the circuit is clocked, the minimum allowable clock period is set by the maximum circuit delay; in this case the time that the carry bit needs to propagate from the first to the last stage. The carry bit passes through only one *And* gate per stage.

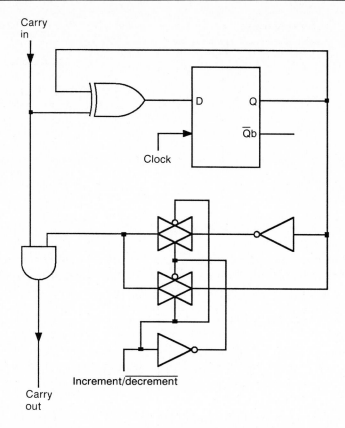

Figure 13–2   Logic diagram for incrementer/decrementer cell

13.2.3   Physical description

13.2.3.1   System floor plan of a four-bit incrementer

For simplicity, we will pursue the floor plan design of an incrementer which readily extends to a decrementer. The four-bit incrementer is realized by abutting four identical cells. The height of the incrementer remains constant while the width grows linearly with n—the number of bits. Therefore the width of each cell should be made as small as possible. The control lines run right across the whole structure and adequate driving capability should be supplied. The resulting floor plan is shown in Figure 13–3.

If the width of the leaf cell is w then the width of an n-bit incrementer/decrementer is nw. This dimension must be pitch matched to the rest of the data path (e.g. a VLSI processor etc.) of width W. Therefore

$$w = W/n$$

provided that

$$w_{min} \leqslant W/n$$

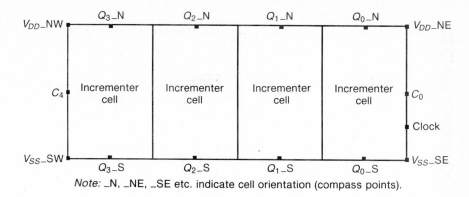

Note: _N, _NE, _SE etc. indicate cell orientation (compass points).

Figure 13–3 Proposed floor plan — four-bit incrementer

where w_{min} is the minimum width of a cell. In the event that $w_{min} > W/n$ then the design must be adjusted to be thinner and taller.

13.2.3.2 Leaf cell floor plan

The floor plan of the four-bit incrementer basically determines the floor plan of the leaf cell which is given as Figure 13–4. The width w of each cell is set by the total allowable maximum incrementer/decrementer width W which cannot be exceeded if the circuit is to be properly pitch matched to the data path for which it is being designed. The minimum height h of the leaf cell is set by its complexity once the width has been fixed. The decision about the output connection and the power rail placements is made at the system's level (the system here being the four-bit incrementer/decrementer).

In a complex design the number of leaf cells should be kept to the absolute minimum which implies that the complexity of the leaf cells should be as high as possible. This greatly simplifies the global floor plan. A 50 to 100 transistor leaf cell can usually be readily realized with available design tools. The incrementer/decrementer leaf cell is of a medium complexity and should not be further subdivided into subleaf cells.

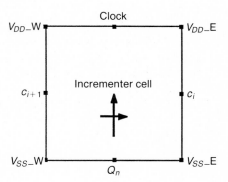

Figure 13–4 Leaf cell — floor plan for an incrementer

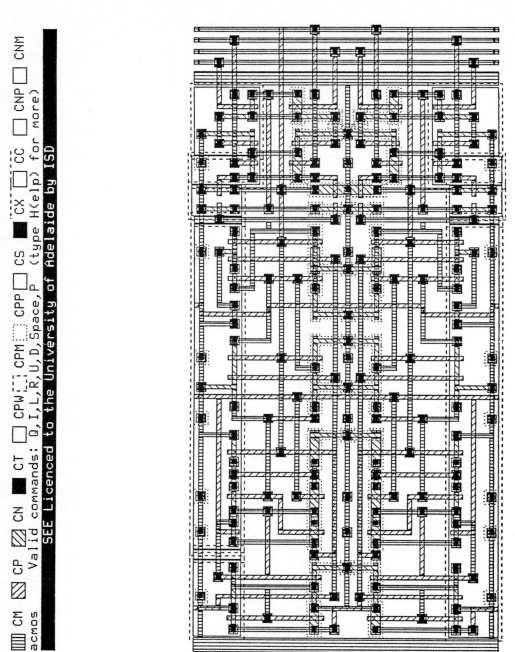

Figure 13-5 Mask layout for two bits of an incrementer/decrementer

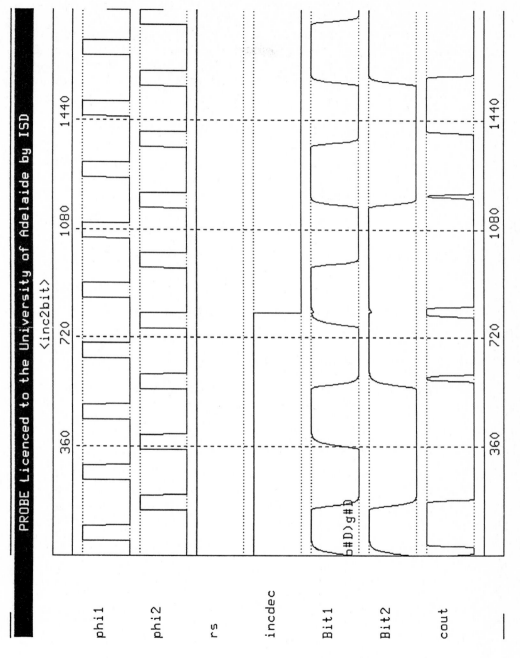

Figure 13–6 Simulation results for the two-bit system

The leaf cell floor plan for a general purpose incrementer/decrementer is similar to Figure 13–4 with the addition of an increment/decrement control line and an overall reset function control line ($\overline{Rs}$).

The design may be pursued to mask layout level using available design tools. The mask layout for two bits of an incrementer/decrementer system is given as Figure 13–5 (details plotted from the CIF code description of the mask layout). Note that the two bits are in vertically reflected form from the layout point of view and share a common V_{DD} rail.

13.2.4 Design verification

The circuit detail present in the CIF code specification was extracted with a circuit extractor (*NET*) and then simulated with a circuit simulator (PROBE). The simulation results are given as Figure 13–6.

13.3 CMOS project 2 — left/right serial/parallel shift register

This project is concerned with the design of a shift register cell capable of expansion to form an *n*-bit register.

13.3.1 Behavioral description

Table 13–1 defines the shift register connections that apply to the Figures 13–7 and 13–8. A single shift register cell is shown in Figure 13–9.

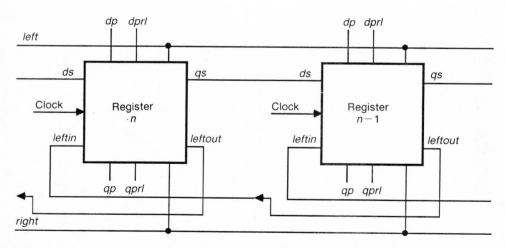

Figure 13–7 Two-bit shift register block diagram

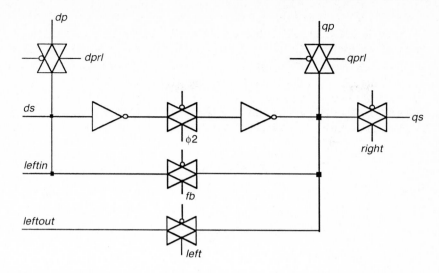

Figure 13-8   Shift register logic diagram

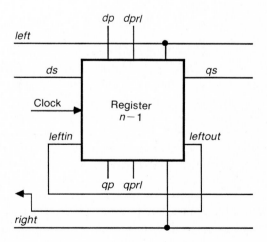

Figure 13-9   Shift register cell

Table 13-1 Shift register control functions

Controls	Function	Conditions Required
dp	parallel data input	latched when *dprl* is asserted
dprl	parallel input data control	$\overline{left} \cdot \overline{right} . \phi1$
qp	parallel data output	valid when *qprl* is asserted
qprl	parallel output data control	data valid on $\phi2$ of clock
ds	serial right data input	valid when *right* is asserted
qs	serial right data output	valid when *right* is asserted
right	shift right control	$\overline{dprl} \cdot \overline{left} \cdot \phi1$
leftin	serial left data input	valid when *left* is asserted
leftout	serial left data output	valid when *left* is asserted
left	shift left control	$\overline{dprl} \cdot \overline{right} \cdot \phi1$
fb	internal refresh control	$\overline{dprl} \cdot \overline{right} \cdot \overline{left} \cdot \phi1$
$\phi2$	second clock phase	data latch to output node

13.3.2 Structural description

13.3.2.1 *Logic representation*
The complete four-bit shift register is made up of single shift register cells abutted as shown in part in Figure 13–7.

13.3.2.2 *Operation of the circuit*
The operation of the complete shift register may be understood by considering the single shift register cell of Figures 13–8 and 13–9. The advantage of this cell is that it may be loaded or unloaded in parallel and the bits may be shifted either left or right within the shift register. The register also uses a two phase nonoverlapping clock of which $\phi1$ allows loading, shifting, and refreshing to occur while $\phi2$ isolates the two inverters so that the cells may be loaded.

The operations of the shift register (Figure 13–8) in detail are as follows:

1. *The refresh loop.* Refreshing *fb* (or feedback) occurs in coincidence with $\phi1$ and when no other control is asserted (namely *dprl*, *right*, and *left*). The transmission gate takes the output of the second inverter and uses it to refresh the logic level stored on the two gates of the first inverter.
2. *In parallel load mode.* The inputs *dp* and control *dprl* are used to load the registers in parallel. Asserting *dprl* when $\phi1$ is at logic level 1 will cause the input of the first inverter to assume the state of *dp*. At this time $\phi2 = 0$ and the inverters are isolated. Subsequently $\phi2 = 1$ and the second inverter output assumes the state of *dp* which is stored dynamically at the first inverter input.
3. *In shift right mode.* The signals associated with the shift right operation are *right*, *qs*, and *ds*. Asserting *right* when $\phi1$ is at logic level 1 effectively loads the subsequent register with *qs*, while the output *qs* of the register cell to the left of the current one is connected through a transmission gate to *ds* of the present

cell. Hence the cell is loaded in the same manner as with a parallel load but the data input comes from the adjoining cell to the left (i.e. a shift right operation).

4. *In shift left mode.* The signals associated with the shift left operation are *left*, *leftout*, and *leftin*. Asserting *left* when $\phi 1$ is a logic level 1 effectively loads the previous register with *qs* via the feedback line *leftout*. The register cell to the right of the current one has its *leftout* connected through a transmission gate to *leftin* of the present cell. Hence the cell is loaded in the same manner as with a parallel load but the data input comes from the adjoining cell to the right (i.e. a shift left operation).

5. *For parallel output.* The output data is correctly read at the end of $\phi 2$ when there can be no change to the input. This is achieved by asserting *qprl* in which case *qp* assumes the state of the cell and all outputs are read in parallel.

6. *Isolation of the inverters by $\phi 2$.* The second phase of the clock ($\phi 2$) is used to isolate the inverters during a write operation so that the register array does not become transparent. Consider a shift right operation but allow $\phi 2 = 1$. Here the first inverter output would become $\overline{ds}_{i-1}$ (from the next left cell) while the second inverter would become ds_{i-1} also. However ds_{i-1} can now be passed on to cell $i + 1$ since *right* is asserted and $qs = ds_{i-1}$. Hence ds_{i-1} would ripple throughout the entire array. This undesirable effect is eliminated by loading on a separate clock phase.

13.3.2.3   Critical paths

The system is restricted to shifts of one bit only in either direction and hence any shifts of more bits will take proportionally more time. In this case there is a minimum time t_1 for which $\phi 1$ must be asserted, since the data must be stored at the first inverters input gate. After this delay the data is passed to the output on $\phi 2$ which must have time duration t_2 for the carry bit to change its state if required. The total delay (T) is governed by the sum of t_1 and t_2 and the number of shifts n required (i.e. $T = n \times (t_1 + t_2)$). To reduce this delay a fast shifting cell is required.

The most critical path at the leaf cell level is associated with the output of the second inverter which must drive four transmission gate input capacitances. For this reason the second inverter is not made minimum size. Note however that the second inverter cannot be made too large since the first inverter (which is minimum sized) must drive its input when $\phi 2 = 1$. The final sizing of the transistors may be determined after a series of simulations after extracting the circuit from the mask description.

13.3.3   Physical description

13.3.3.1   System floor plan

The four-bit shift register may be formed by abutting four identical one-bit register cells. The most convenient arrangement for an n-bit shift register is to have the parallel data inputs and outputs running perpendicular to the direction of the register array. The control lines are also conveniently run perpendicular to the

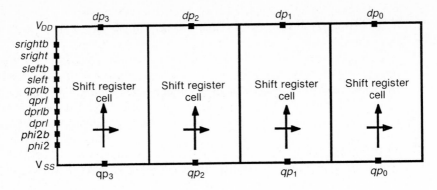

Figure 13–10 Proposed floor plan — four-bit shifter

register array but, on exiting a register cell, may be run along the array with appropriate connections made to adjoining cell control signals. The power rails must be implemented in metal and also run perpendicular to the parallel input/output data. The resulting floor plan is shown in Figure 13–10.

If the width of the leaf cell is w then the width of an n-bit register is nw. This dimension must be pitch matched to the rest of the data path (e.g. a VLSI processor etc.) of width W. Therefore

$$w = W/n$$

13.3.3.2 Leaf cell floor plan

The floor plan of the four-bit shifter basically specifies the floor plan of the leaf cell. The width w is set by the total maximum register width and this cannot be exceeded if the register is to be properly pitch matched, for example, to a processor. The

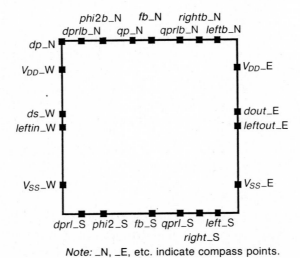

Note: _N, _E, etc. indicate compass points.

Figure 13–11 Shift register cell floor plan

minimum height *h* of the leaf cell is set by its complexity once the width has been fixed. The decision about the input/output connection and the power rail placements is made at the system's level.

In a complex design the number of leaf cells should be kept to the absolute minimum which implies that the complexity of the leaf cells should be as high as possible. This greatly simplifies the global floor plan. A 50 to 100 transistor leaf cell

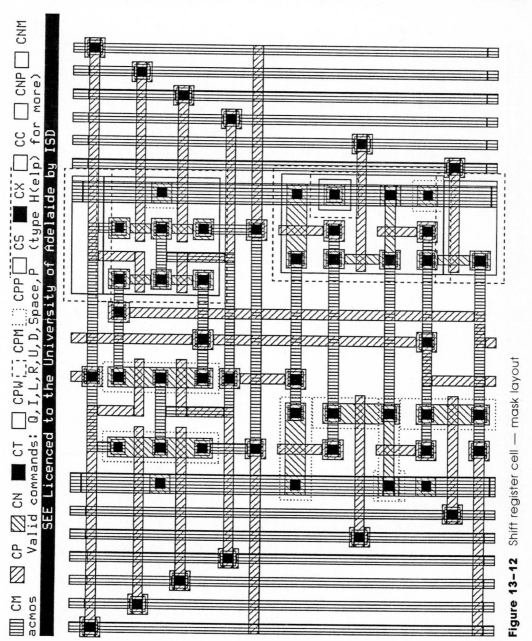

Figure 13–12 Shift register cell — mask layout

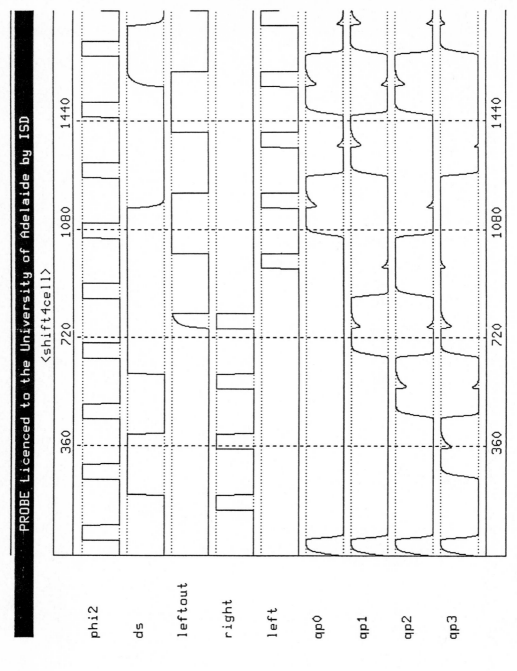

PROBE Licenced to the University of Adelaide by ISD

<shift4cell>

Figure 13–13 Simulation over four shift register cells

can usually be readily realized with available design tools. The register leaf cell described here is of small/medium complexity and should not be further subdivided into subleaf cells. The shift register cell floor plan is shown in Figure 13–11 and a mask layout follows as Figure 13–12.

13.3.4 Design verification

Results of simulation using *PROBE* for a four-bit register are presented as Figure 13–13.

13.4 CMOS project 3 — a comparator for two *n*-bit numbers

This section describes the design methodology, layout strategy, and simulation results for comparator cells. A four-bit comparator was designed using these cells, the general arrangement being as suggested in Figure 13–14.

13.4.1 Behavioral description

The truth table and general arrangement for a binary one-bit comparator is shown in Figure 13–15 where A_i and B_i are the two numbers to be compared, C_{i+1} and D_{i+1} are the inputs from outputs of the previous stage and C_i and D_i are the outputs of the current stage. $C_i = 1$ if $A_i > B_i$; $D_i = 1$ if $A_i < B_i$; and $C_i = D_i = 0$ if $A_i = B_i$.

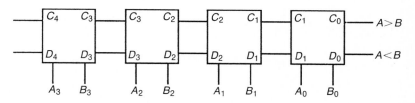

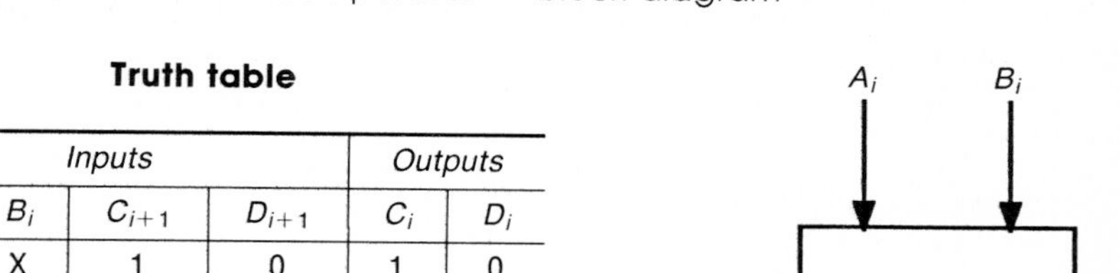

Figure 13–14 Four-bit comparator — block diagram

Truth table

Inputs				Outputs	
A_i	B_i	C_{i+1}	D_{i+1}	C_i	D_i
X	X	1	0	1	0
X	X	0	1	0	1
0	0	0	0	0	0
0	1	0	0	0	1
1	0	0	0	1	0
1	1	0	0	0	0

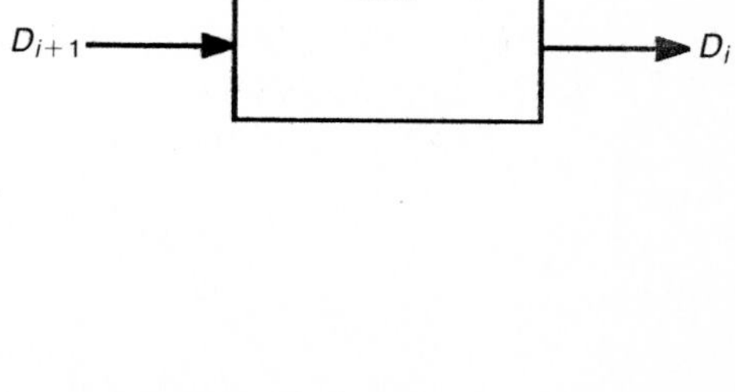

Figure 13–15 Comparator cell behaviour

The logic expressions for the two output signals in terms of the four input signals are as follows

$$C_i = C_{i+1} + \overline{C}_{i+1} \cdot A_i \cdot \overline{B}_i \cdot \overline{D}_{i+1} \tag{13.4}$$

$$D_i = D_{i+1} + \overline{D}_{i+1} \cdot \overline{A}_i \cdot B_i \cdot \overline{C}_{i+1} \tag{13.5}$$

The two logic expressions may be rearranged into the form

$$C_i = \overline{\overline{C}_{i+1} \cdot \overline{(\overline{C}_{i+1} \cdot \overline{D}_{i+1} \cdot A_i \cdot \overline{B}_i)}}$$

$$= \overline{\overline{C}_{i+1} \cdot \overline{(C_{i+1} + \overline{A}_i + B_i) \cdot \overline{D}_{i+1}}} \tag{13.4a}$$

$$D_i = \overline{\overline{D}_{i+1} \cdot \overline{(\overline{D}_{i+1} \cdot \overline{C}_{i+1} \cdot \overline{A}_i \cdot B_i)}}$$

$$= \overline{\overline{D}_{i+1} \cdot \overline{(D_{i+1} + \overline{B}_i + A_i) \cdot \overline{C}_{i+1}}} \tag{13.5a}$$

A further simplification may be achieved if alternate logic is used between subsequent cells. Stage i implements

$$\overline{C}_i = \overline{\overline{C_{i+1} + D_{i+1} + \overline{A}_i + B_i}} \tag{13.4b}$$

$$\overline{D}_i = \overline{\overline{D_{i+1} + C_{i+1} + A_i + \overline{B}_i}} \tag{13.5b}$$

and stage $i-1$ implements

$$C_{i-1} = \overline{\overline{\overline{C}_i \cdot \overline{D}_i \cdot A_{i-1} \cdot \overline{B}_{i-1}}} \tag{13.4c}$$

$$D_{i-1} = \overline{\overline{\overline{D}_i \cdot \overline{C}_i \cdot \overline{A}_{i-1} \cdot B_{i-1}}} \tag{13.5c}$$

13.4.2   Structural description

13.4.2.1   *Logic representation*

The comparator is implemented with complementary cells, that is, the ith stage has true inputs and inverted outputs while the $i+1$ stage has inverted inputs and true outputs. The two cells are realized by direct implementation of expressions (13.4c) and (13.5c) (COMPCELLA) and expressions (13.4b) and (13.5b) (COMPCELLB) as shown in Figure 13–16.

13.4.2.2   *Operation of the circuit*

The operation of the complete circuit is as follows:

- The two numbers are compared starting with the most significant bits. The outputs from this comparison are connected to the next most-significant-bit-stage inputs etc. The two output signals C_i and D_i remain at zero as long as the two bits being compared are the same.
- As soon as a difference is detected the two outputs are set to one of two possible states: if $A > B$ then $C_i = 1$ and $D_i = 0$; if $A < B$ then $C_i = 0$ and $D_i = 1$.

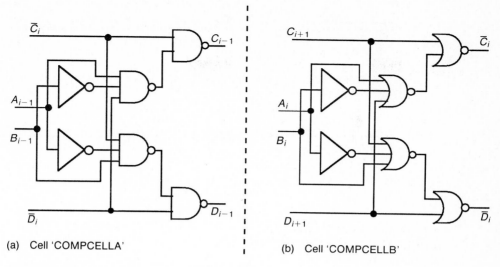

Figure 13-16 Comparator — logic diagram

- All the remaining pairs of less significant bits then have no further effect on the state of subsequent outputs C_i and D_i.
- If all pairs of bits of the two numbers being compared are equal, then the outputs stay at zero signifying equality.

13.4.2.3 Critical paths

The critical delay in this circuit is the propagation delay of the two outputs through all the stages. The gates passing both outputs should be sized appropriately. The delay is only one gate per stage and should not be the limiting factor on a system's scale. The final sizing of the transistors is usually determined after a series of simulations.

13.4.3 Physical description

13.4.3.1 System floor plan

The four-bit comparator is realized by abutting cells of each type on an alternate basis. One possibility would be to have both bit inputs on the same side of a cell with the two outputs propagating at right angles to the input data path. Another possible layout would be to have the two bit inputs on opposite sides of a cell. The second approach was adopted here. The height of the comparator remains constant while the width grows linearly with n — the number of bits. Therefore the width of each cell should be made as small as possible. A possible floor plan is shown in Figure 13-17: the inputs A_i and B_i come in at the top and bottom of each cell respectively, and C_i and D_i propagate horizontally. V_{DD} and V_{SS} rails may also propagate horizontally in global terms but may be distributed at right angles within a cell if convenient.

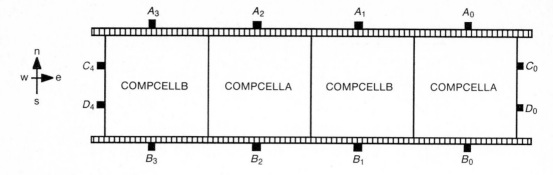

Figure 13-17 Proposed floor plan — four-bit comparator

If the width of the leaf cell is w then the width of an n-bit comparator is nw. This dimension must be pitch matched to the rest of the system (e.g. a VLSI processor etc.) of width W. Therefore $w = W/n$.

13.4.3.2 Leaf cell floor plan

The floor plan of the four-bit comparator basically specifies the floor plan of the leaf cells as shown in Figure 13–18. The width w is set by the total maximum comparator width and this cannot be exceeded if the comparator is to be properly pitch matched to the data path for which it is being designed. The minimum height h of the leaf cell is set by its complexity once the width has been fixed. The decision about the input/output connection and the power rail placements is made at the system's level (the system here being the four-bit comparator).

In a complex design the number of leaf cells should be kept to the absolute minimum which implies that the complexity of the leaf cells should be as high as possible. This greatly simplifies the global floor plan. A 50 to 100 transistor leaf cell can usually be readily realized with available design tools. The comparator leaf cell

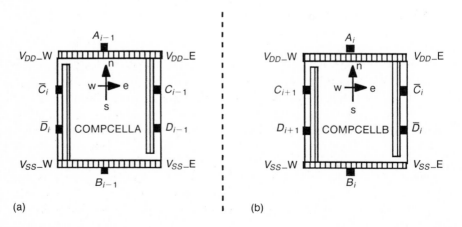

Figure 13-18 Leaf cells — floor plan

is of medium complexity and should not be further subdivided into subleaf cells.

13.4.4 Symbolic or stick representation to mask transformation

A mask representation may be obtained from a symbolic cell specification by the process of compaction. A compactor is a tool that takes a symbolic representation of the given cell and produces a mask description of the cell according to some predefined process design rules. A mask description of the cell may also be obtained by direct mapping from a stick diagram using PLAN or a similar graphics editor.

A few basic rules need to be observed when designing a circuit:

1. Start the design by placing an imaginary demarkation line. This line separates the *p*-type devices, which are placed above it, from the *n*-type devices, which are placed below it; that is, the two types of transistors should not be inter-mixed. This style of design allows easy placements of the p-well and the p$^+$ masks (Figure 13–19).
2. Keep the V_{DD} and V_{SS} supply rails well separated. This allows all the devices to be placed close to the required rail and be completely within the V_{DD} to V_{SS} boundaries, greatly simplifying the intercell connections.

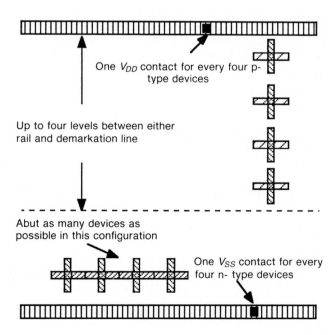

One V_{DD} contact for every four p-type devices

Up to four levels between either rail and demarkation line

Abut as many devices as possible in this configuration

One V_{SS} contact for every four n- type devices

Figure 13–19 Layout design style

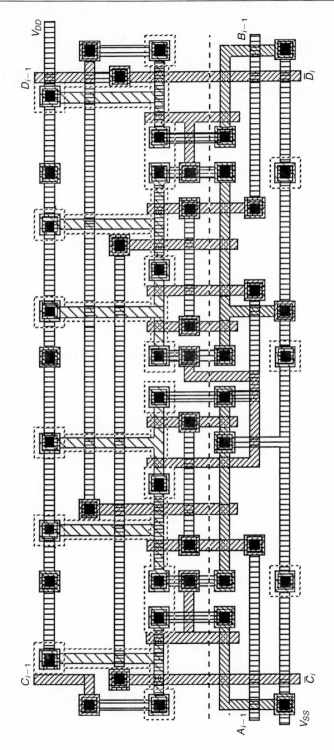

Figure 13–20 COMPCELLA mask layout

3. Place the devices in horizontal (diffusion) orientation (watch out for sensitive nodes) and abut as many devices as possible to minimize the interconnect resistance and capacitance between them.
4. Do not use more than four levels of devices between a rail and the demarkation line (as shown).
5. Place one V_{SS} contact for every four n-type devices and one V_{DD} contact for every four p-type devices.

A possible mask layout for COMPCELLA (*Nand* gate based) is given as Figure 13–20. This layout is readily adapted to form cell COMPCELLB by exchanging *Nand* for *Nor* gates. Note that input A_i defines the top of the cell and B_i the bottom.

13.4.5 Design verification

Before the actual layout can be submitted for fabrication, the whole design must be carefully checked and verified. A simulator (e.g. PROBE) is used during the design process to verify and improve the timing behavior of each leaf cell. When the layout is completed, it must be passed through a design rule checker to verify its compliance with the design rules of the fabrication process to be used and an electrical rules checker to test for the number of V_{DD} and V_{SS} contacts etc. The necessary steps are:

- Pass the design through a design rule checker (e.g. CHECK) and correct any errors.
- Extract the circuit from the mask layout (e.g. using NET). This produces a file which is a circuit description containing connectivity information obtained from the CIF description.
- Simulate the cell (e.g. using PROBE) and make any necessary changes to the transistor dimensions etc. to improve the performance. Remember to apply correct capacitance loadings to the output terminals when simulating. The results obtained in this case are presented in Figures 13–21 and 13–22.

- Recheck for design rule errors.
- Check the circuit for any electrical rule errors using an electrical rules checker (e.g. ELEC).
- Carry out the final simulation at cell level.
- Assemble the complete four-bit comparator (using an editor, for example, PLAN). Simulate and design rule check the complete circuit.
- Place the input and output pads around the circuit as suggested in the floor plan in Figure 13–23. Note that the overall system, including the pads, should now have its operation checked by simulation.

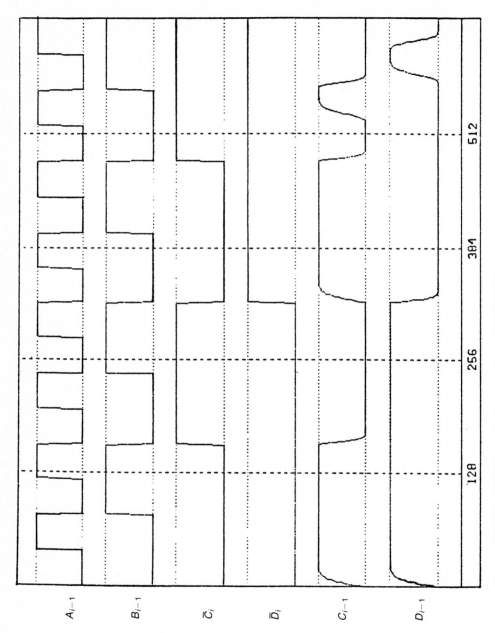

Figure 13–21 PROBE simulation results — COMPCELLA

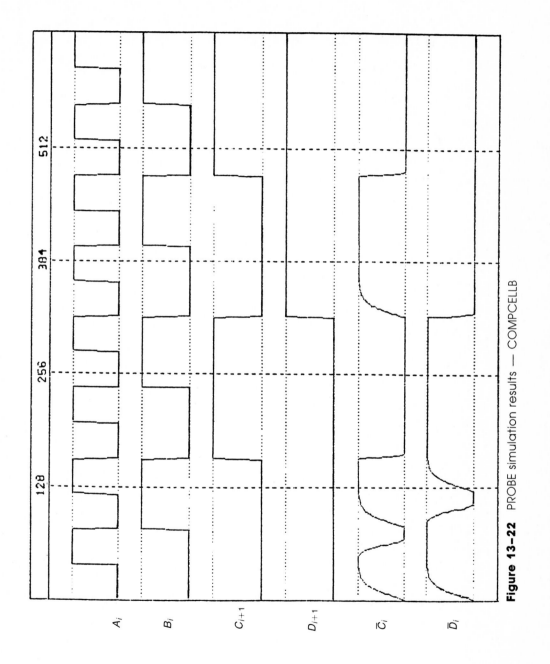

Figure 13-22 PROBE simulation results — COMPCELLB

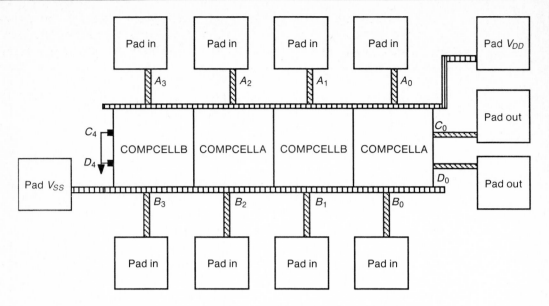

Figure 13–23 Four-bit comparator with pad placement indicated

13.5 Summing up

We have seen that the design process for nMOS and CMOS circuits are of a similar nature and that the design of digital systems in silicon is a reasonably straightforward proposition, provided that an orderly and structured approach is taken. The tutorials, exercises, and project work in the text have illustrated design in both technologies, and readers should, by now, begin to feel comfortable in their ability to tackle the design of systems of modest size and complexity. An ability to understand the technologies and design processes should enable the system designers to specify and, where necessary, design 'custom' digital chips which in the future may be present in up to 10 percent of all new electronic systems. In view of the large volume of current and predicted business in electronic systems this represents a large volume of chips to be custom designed.

This text has not attempted to seriously address the problems of complexity management, testability, and the design time associated with the design of large digital systems. We have also largely ignored the ever-growing need for custom designed analog circuits in MOS technologies, both for pure analog applications and for 'on-chip' interfaces between the analog world and digital systems. These topics are most important and are the subject of texts in their own right.

We have seen that there are factors which limit the ultimate scaling of silicon circuits and thus there are ultimate limitations on the speed of silicon circuitry. This will not be a problem in any but the fastest areas of application, but emerging needs in real-time control and in signal processing applications, to name just two, will impose needs beyond the capability of MOS silicon systems alone.

It is in such applications that other technologies, such as gallium arsenide, will find application for 'front-end' processors to silicon systems. To introduce the reader to this important area, the next, and final, chapter introduces gallium arsenide technology.

14 The future — fast VLSI circuits and systems

> '*He that will not apply new remedies must expect new evils:*
> *for time is the greatest innovator.*' Francis Bacon

In this final chapter we will briefly consider some of the limitations of silicon devices and then look at one of the emerging alternatives — gallium arsenide.

14.1 Submicron CMOS technology

Speed and smaller device dimensions are closely interrelated and we have already touched on the fact that the foreseeable limits on channel length for MOS transistors is in the region of 0.25 µm, after which further scaling down results in unworkable transistor geometry due to the encroachment of depletion regions from the source and drain areas into the entire channel.

In CMOS devices we have also seen that the p-transistors have inherently slower performance than similar n-transistors. This is primarily due to the lower mobility µ of holes compared to electrons. Typically

$$\mu_p \doteqdot 240 \ \text{cm}^2/\text{V.sec}$$
$$\mu_n \doteqdot 650 \ \text{cm}^2/\text{V.sec}$$

In long-channel devices this means a difference in current drive transition times of about 2.5:1.

However, as the channel lengths are scaled down, the influence of mobility µ starts to diminish as the effects of velocity saturation begin to be felt.

For long-channel MOS transistors, the current/voltage relationship below saturation can be approximated by

$$I_{ds} = \frac{W \mu C_{OX}}{L} [(V_{gs} - V_t) V_{ds} - 0.5 V_{ds}^2]$$

where

$$C_{OX} = \text{gate/channel capacitance per unit area}$$
$$= \frac{\varepsilon_{ins} \varepsilon_0}{D}$$

This implies that current drive is proportional to mobility and inversely proportional to channel length.

Transconductance g_m is similarly influenced.

When velocity saturation occurs along the entire channel length, then the current/voltage relationship is given by

$$I_{dsat} = W C_{OX} v_{sat} (V_{gs} - V_t)$$

where v_{sat} is the saturation *velocity*. Current is now independent of both mobility and channel length but dependent on the saturation velocity. Transconductance is constant and thus independent of channel length.

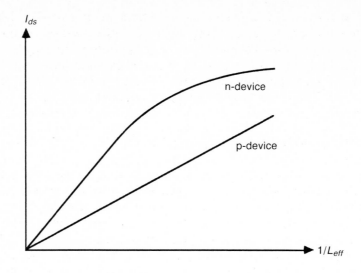

Note: L_{eff} = effective channel length.

Figure 14–1 Velocity saturation effect

It should be noted that velocity saturation occurs at lower electric field strengths in n-devices due to their higher mobility compared to p-devices. Thus, as dimensions are scaled down, the current drive from n-transistors tends to a constant value independent of channel length while the current drive from p-transistors does not tend to a constant value until, at a shorter channel length, the holes start to run into velocity saturation. The trends are indicated in Figure 14–1.

We must therefore look to other than silicon-based MOS technology to provide for the faster devices which will undoubtedly be required as the sophistication of our system design capabilities increases.

An alternative technology is based on gallium arsenide.

14.2 Gallium arsenide VLSI technology

> '*There was a young lady named Bright,*
> *Whose speed was far faster than light,*
> *She set out one day*
> *In a relative way,*
> *And returned home the previous night.*'
>
> Arthur Henry Buller

Silicon MOS technology has been the main medium for computer and system applications for a number of years and will continue to fill this role. However, there are speed limitations that are already becoming apparent in state-of-the-art fast digital system design. Paralleling developments in silicon technology, some very interesting results are beginning to be seen with gallium arsenide (GaAs). This new technology promises to satisfy the speed requirements of present-day computers and, indeed, the super computers of the 1990s, which are conjectured to operate at 10 BFLOPS (1 BFLOPS is 1 billion floating-point operations per second).

Gallium arsenide will not displace silicon but may be used in conjunction with silicon to satisfy the need for very high speed integrated (VHSI) technology in the many new and innovative systems that are beginning to emerge. This means that GaAs technology may be utilized for fast front-end processor sections of high-speed single stream processors for digital data (e.g. 1–5 Gigasamples/second). Fast data stream operations can subsequently be subdivided into lower rate parallel streams suitable for processing in silicon subsystems at lower frequencies. By mixing GaAs and Si technologies it is possible to exploit high system clock rates in high bandwidth signal processing environments.

Although the technology is confronted with the same kind of constraint as was silicon in the mid 1970s, advances in GaAs-integrated circuitry have progressed to the point where it is now feasible to introduce a design methodology. Foundries providing GaAs fabrication are now in operation and typically have the following characteristics.

- one-micron gate geometry;
- three to four-micron metal pitch;
- two-layer metal;
- three to four-inch diameter wafers;
- suitability for clock rates in the range 500MHz–10GHz.

Gallium arsenide technology is therefore attractive for high-speed digital systems. This is mainly due to the higher mobility of electrons, and this and other attractions follow.

- Electron mobility is six to seven times that in silicon, resulting in very fast electron transit times.
- Saturated drift velocity is twice that of silicon at lower electric field strengths (less than 10^4V/cm). (At higher field strengths the saturated velocities in GaAs and Si are approximately equal, but what is significant is the fact that GaAs devices require less voltage to enter saturation.)
- Intrinsic bulk resistivity is higher, which minimizes parasitic capacitances and allows easy isolation of multiple devices in a single substrate.
- Radiation resistance is stronger.
- A wider operating temperature range is possible due to the larger bandgap. GaAs devices are tolerant of wide temperature variations over the range -200 to $+200°$C.
- Efficient integration of electronics and optics is provided.

Table 14–1 provides some comparisons between silicon and gallium arsenide.

Table 14–1 Comparison between Si and GaAs

Properties (*typical values*)	*Si*	*GaAs*
Intrinsic mobility		
Electrons	1300 cm^2/V.sec	7000 cm^2/V.sec
Holes	500 cm^2/V.sec	400 cm^2/V.sec
Saturation velocity of electrons	0.5×10^7 cm/sec	1×10^7 cm/sec
Intrinsic resistivity	2.2×10^5 Ω.cm	1×10^8 Ω.cm
Dielectric constant	11.9	13.1
Density	2.33 gm/cm^3	5.32 gm/cm^3
Energy gap	1.12 eV	1.4 eV
Thermal conductivity	1.4 W/cm.°C	0.5 W/cm.°C

Since the introduction of the first very high speed GaAs MESFET in 1974 a considerable amount of research has been directed toward improvement of the fabrication process as well as the development of various device and circuit structures using this technology. Progress can be assessed from the trends indicated in Figure 14–2.

In pursuing this technology, important objectives have been to develop very high speed, low power devices that can be laid out in a small area.

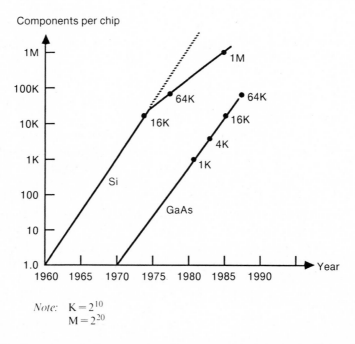

Figure 14–2 Progress of silicon and gallium arsenide-integrated circuits

14.2.1 A compound semiconductor

Gallium arsenide is a compound semiconductor which may be defined as a semi-conductor made of a compound of two or more elements (as opposed to silicon, which is a single-element semiconductor).

From Table 14–2, which shows the materials in the periodic table, it is possible to deduce the manner in which III–V semiconductors can be produced. For example, gallium having three valence electrons can be combined with arsenic which has five valence electrons.

It should be noted that group IV elements such as silicon can act as either donors (i.e. on Ga sites) or acceptors (i.e. on As sites). Since arsenic is smaller than gallium and silicon, group IV impurities tend to occupy gallium sites. Thus, silicon is usually used as the dopant for the formation of n-type material.

Table 14–2 Periodic table

GROUP II	GROUP III	GROUP IV	GROUP V	GROUP VI
$Be_{9.01}^{4}$	$B_{10.82}^{5}$	$C_{12.01}^{6}$	$N_{14.008}^{7}$	$O_{16.0}^{8}$
$Mg_{24.32}^{12}$	$Al_{26.97}^{13}$	$Si_{28.09}^{14}$	$P_{31.02}^{15}$	$S_{32.07}^{16}$
$Zn_{65.38}^{30}$	$Ga_{69.72}^{31}$	$Ge_{72.60}^{32}$	$As_{74.91}^{33}$	$Se_{79.0}^{34}$
$Cd_{112.4}^{48}$	$In_{114.8}^{49}$	$Sn_{118.7}^{50}$	$Sb_{121.8}^{51}$	$Te_{127.6}^{52}$

Note: Numbers in the table refer to the atomic number and the atomic weight.

Figure 14-3 shows the arrangement of atoms in a gallium arsenide substrate material. Note the alternate positioning of gallium and arsenic atoms in their exact crystallographic locations.

Since gallium arsenide is a binary semiconductor, special care is required during the processing to avoid high temperatures that could result in dissociation of the surface.

14.2.2 GaAs devices

During the last few years a number of different devices have been developed. The so-called 'first generation' of GaAs devices includes:

- depletion-mode metal semiconductor field-effect transistor: D–MESFET;

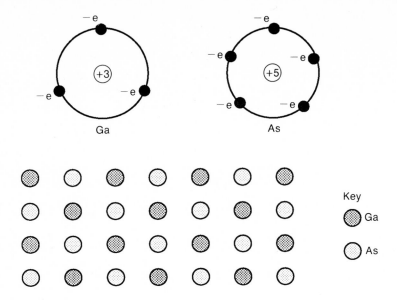

Figure 14-3 Arrangement of atoms in GaAs

- enhancement-mode metal-semiconductor field-effect transistor: E–MESFET;
- enhancement-mode junction field-effect transistor: E–JFET;
- complementary enhancement-mode junction field-effect transistor: CE–JFET.

First-generation GaAs gates have exhibited switching delays as low as 80 psec for 1 to 2.5 mW power dissipation.

There are other more sophisticated 'second generation' devices such as:

- high-electron mobility transistor: HEMT;
- heterojunction bipolar transistor: HJBT.

Electron mobility in second-generation transistors can be up to five times greater than in the first generation. In consequence, very fast devices should be possible.

In the following section we will concentrate on establishing some of the fundamental principles of GaAs design methodology for the first generation devices, particularly the predominant MESFETs, which are now at a stage of development to be incorporated in fast system designs.

14.2.2.1 Metal semiconductor FET (MESFET)

The metal-gallium arsenide field-effect transistor, a bulk-current-conduction majority-carrier device, is fabricated from bulk gallium arsenide by ion implantation and high-resolution photolithography. Processing is relatively simple, requiring no more than seven or eight masking stages.

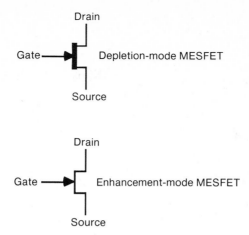

Figure 14–4   MESFET circuit symbols

GaAs MESFETs are somewhat similar to Si MOSFETs. The major difference is the presence of a Schottky diode at the gate region which separates two thin n-type active regions (source and drain) connected by ohmic contacts. The D-MESFET is normally 'on' and its pinch-off voltage V_{pdep} is negative.

The E-MESFET is normally 'off'. Its pinch-off voltage V_{penh} is positive and is determined by the channel thickness and doping. A highly doped, thick channel exhibits a larger negative pinch-off voltage but, by reducing the channel thickness, a normally 'off' enhancement mode MESFET with a positive pinch-off voltage can be fabricated.

The MESFET has a maximum gate to source voltage V_{gs} of about 0.8 volt due to the diode action of the Schottky diode gate. Circuit symbols for the depletion and enhancement MESFETs are set out in Figure 14–4.

14.2.2.2   Depletion-mode MESFET

The depletion-mode MESFET (D-MESFET), the most mature of the current GaAs technologies, is illustrated in Figure 14–5.

The basic structure, in which a thin n-type region joins two ohmic contacts with a narrow metal Schottky barrier gate, is very simple. The depletion-mode devices are fabricated using the planar process where n-type dopants are directly implanted into the semi-insulating GaAs substrate to form the channel as well as the heavier doped source and drain regions. The semi-insulating substrate is ideal for 'all ion implantation' planar technology. The gate and first level interconnect metalizations are deposited by E-beam evaporation techniques. The operation is similar to that of silicon JFET, in which the conducting n-channel is confined between the gate depletion region and the semi-insulating GaAs substrate. By varying the thickness and doping level of the active region, it is possible to vary the pinch-off voltage V_p to the desired negative value and the saturated channel current I_{ds}.

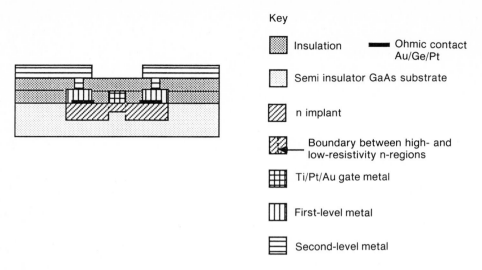

Key

▨ Insulation ▬ Ohmic contact
Au/Ge/Pt

☐ Semi insulator GaAs substrate

▨ n implant

▨ Boundary between high- and
low-resistivity n-regions

⊞ Ti/Pt/Au gate metal

Ⅲ First-level metal

☰ Second-level metal

Figure 14-5 Depletion-mode MESFET

Circuits utilizing D-MESFETs pose the least problems during the fabrication process. This is primarily because:

● Schottky barrier diodes on GaAs are easier to fabricate than pn junctions; and

● logic swings typically in the order of one volt can be obtained. This reduces to some extent the stringent requirements for the uniformity of the pinch-off voltage.

14.2.2.3 *Planar GaAs fabrication*

Due to the absence of a stable native oxide, GaAs technologies rely on deposited dielectric films for passivation and/or encapsulation. The fabrication process entails the utilization of three to four inch liquid-encapsulated Czochralski (LEC) wafers. The starting material is a semi-insulating GaAs substrate, coated with a thin layer of Si_3N_4 insulation, in which the active device regions are formed by ion implantation of Si^+ through the insulating layer. Photoresist is the usual mask for this step. Normally there are two implantation steps:

● a high-resistivity n^- channel layer with donor concentration $N_D \doteq 10^{17}/cm^3$;

● a low-resistivity n^+ layer for the formation of source and drain with high donor concentration $N_D \doteq 10^{18}/cm^3$ allowing for low contact resistance.

The ohmic contacts between the metal and the source and drain are created by deposition through E-beam evaporation of a thin layer of gold-germanium-nickel (or platinum) alloy. The metals must be carefully alloyed to ensure reliable low resistance contacts.

The multilayer insulation that provides encapsulation of the substrate is plasma-deposited silicon nitride and silicon dioxide. Encapsulation is particularly important in preventing the diffusing out of arsenic due to the high vapor pressure occurring when GaAs is subjected to temperatures in excess of 600°C during annealing. The metalization for gates and first and second level interconnects is titanium-platinum-gold (Ti/Pt/Au) alloy. The gate metalization is the most critical step in the process and is often recessed to achieve the desired pinch-off voltage.

The planar process entails a number of localized ion implantations directly into the semi-insulating GaAs substrate. The unimplanted areas provide electrical isolation between circuit elements.

It is interesting to note the close similarity between the planar implanted D-MESFET GaAs fabrication process and the Si planar process. This can readily be observed by noting that the GaAs substrate is totally protected by dielectric layers throughout the fabrication process. Cuts are made in the dielectric only where ohmic contacts, Schottky barriers, or interconnect metalizations are required.

Probably the most difficult layer to control is the shallow, lightly doped high-resistance n^- MESFET channel layer. This implant layer determines the pinch-off voltage V_p of the MESFETs. The n^+ implant, in contrast, has more relaxed specification since it is used mainly for the high-speed switching diodes, the main concern being that the diode must be fabricated on a relatively high conductance layer.

In more advanced processes the second level metalization uses what is known as the 'airbridge' technique to minimize the intermetal line capacitances.

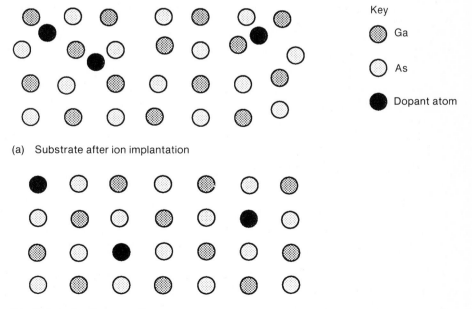

(a)　Substrate after ion implantation

(b)　Substrate after annealing

Figure 14–6　Ion implantation

This approach provides a good yield at the crossover points. Furthermore this approach significantly reduces the interconnect capacitances.

The ion implantation and subsequent annealing are very significant in this technology. The original arrangement of atoms on the crystal lattice was indicated in Figure 14–3. After ion implantation, the dopant atoms come to rest in the crystal and, as a result of interactions and collisions, the crystal lattice is disrupted as indicated in Figure 14–6(a). Ions now occupying interstitial positions are electrically inactive. The annealing process now moves the interstitial dopant ions into lattice positions where they become electrically active and furthermore moves the displaced substrate atoms back to their crystallographic lattice locations (Figure 14–6(b)), which then gives high electron mobility.

The fabrication process is relatively straightforward and is outlined in Figure 14–7.

14.2.2.4 GaAs process steps details

First level metalization is accomplished by:

1. delineating photoresist patterns;
2. plasma etching the underlying insulator;
3. evaporating the appropriate metal;
4. photoresist lift-off.

The metal contacts and interconnects are precisely registered with the plasma-etched insulator windows.

By fabricating the first-level metal within windows in the first-level insulator, and by ensuring that the first-level metalization thickness is close to the insulator thickness as in Figure 14–5, it is feasible to fabricate a more complex multilevel interconnect due to the planar nature of the surface.

Since any regions of the source or drain channel that are not under the gate are automatically strongly conducting in D-MESFETs, one does not require the precise alignments of the gate. However, logic gates that employ D-MESFETs require a voltage shifter to ensure that next stage turnoff requirements are met. This usually necessitates two supply lines. Thus there is a penalty for simplicity in the utilization of the wafer area.

14.2.2.5 Schottky barrier diode

The steps involved to fabricate the Schottky barrier diode are similar to those already described. However in this structure either the source or drain is missing as may be seen in Figure 14–8.

14.2.2.6 Enhancement-mode MESFET

The E-MESFET structure is similar to that of the D-MESFET, except for a shallower and more lightly doped channel. This means the channel is in 'pinch-off' at zero gate voltage, due to the built-in potential of the metal Schottky barrier gate. A positive gate voltage (i.e. threshold voltage) is required for the channel to begin conduction. The advantages of a self-aligned Si gate process have already been

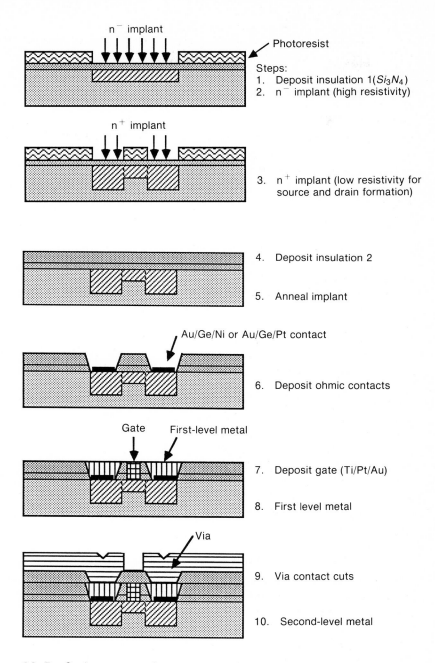

Figure 14–7 GaAs process steps

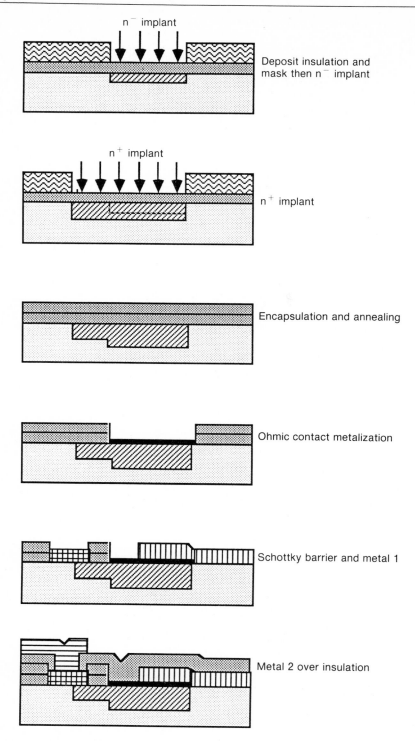

Figure 14-8 Process steps for a Schottky barrier diode

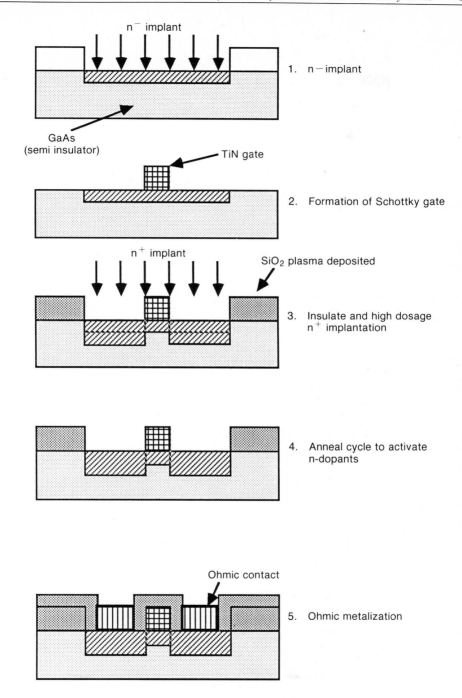

Figure 14-9 Self-aligned processing for GaAs E-MESFET

discussed. Similarly, here we will outline the process steps for a GaAs self-aligned gate.

Process steps for a GaAs self-aligned gate are as follows (see Figure 14–9):

1. formation of a Schottky gate on an n-type GaAs layer;
2. a high-dosage n^+ implantation;
3. an anneal cycle at 800°C to activate dopants and the formation of the self-aligned regions;
4. ohmic metalization of the source and drain regions.

Due to the anneal cycle that requires a temperature up to 800°C to activate the dopants, it is necessary to choose a high-temperature-stable gate. Tungsten nitride has been found to be satisfactory. It has film resistivity $\rho \doteq 70 \ \mu\Omega$ cm and Schottky barrier height $\phi_R \doteq 0.8$ volt to n-type GaAs.

As can be seen, the self-aligned GaAs fabrication process is similar to that of the Si gate nMOS process, except for the omission of the oxide layer under the metal gate.

It should be noted that a Schottky barrier diode can be created through this same process. However the source, or alternatively the drain, is left out in this case.

Due to the positive pinch-off voltage, E-MESFETs require only one power source and therefore provide for circuit simplicity.

Since Schottky barrier gates on GaAs cannot be forward biased above 0.7 to 0.8 volt without drawing excessive currents, the permissible voltage swing is somewhat low. This limits the noise immunity of the gate and places stringent fabrication requirements on pinch-off voltage control and uniformity. A further point to be noted is that E-MESFETs require more complex device processing than D-MESFETs due to the channel structure.

14.2.2.7   *Enhancement-mode junction FET (E-JFET)*

An E-JFET's operation is very similar to that of an E-MESFET. Its source and drain regions are formed by n^+ ion implantation, and channel is formed by n-type implantation but, in contrast with an E-MESFET where the metal gate rests above the channel, in an E-JFET, the gate is buried below the channel surface by p-type implantation. Through this process a pn junction is formed between the gate and the channel. This structure is illustrated in Figure 14–10.

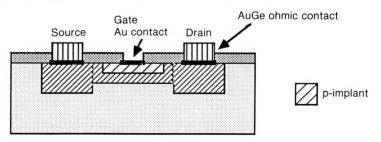

Figure 14–10   E-JFET structure

The permissible voltage swing for E-MESFETs is somewhat low, since Schottky barrier gates on GaAs cannot be forward biased above 0.6 to 0.8 volt without drawing excessive current. However, with E-JFETs, because of the larger built-in voltage of the pn junction, the device can be biased to about $V_{gs} \doteqdot 1$ volt without incurring excessive conduction. Thus, the control on the threshold voltage deviation can be relaxed.

14.2.2.8 Complementary enhancement-mode junction FET (CE-JFET)

A CE-JFET device is similar to the silicon complementary MOSFET (CMOS) and the basic structure is illustrated in Figure 14–11.

Here the depletion-mode transistor or, alternatively, the resistive load is replaced by a p-channel E-JFET. The n-channel and p-channel JFET is fabricated by a sequence of ion implantations into the semi-insulating GaAs substrate. The sequence entails:

1. n^+ implantation
2. n-channel implantation
3. p-channel implantation
4. p^+ implantation.

In a CE-JFET, the ratio of the effective channel electron mobility μ_n of the n-channel device to that of the hole mobility μ_p of the p-channel device is given by

$$\frac{\mu_n}{\mu_p} \doteqdot 10$$

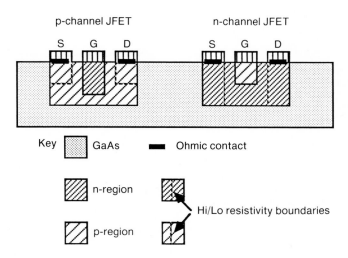

Figure 14–11 Complementary enhancement mode JFET structure

Thus, for a p-channel E-JFET requiring the same drain current I_{ds} as that of the n-channel E-JFET, it is necessary to have

$$W_p = 10W_n$$

where

$$W_p = \text{channel width for p-channel device}$$

$$W_n = \text{channel width for n-channel device.}$$

This means that circuits requiring the same number of p- and n-devices will consume large areas. Therefore one must resort to precharge techniques in which a single pull-up p-transistor serves a number of n-transistors performing the logical operation.

Of particular importance is the improved tolerance of GaAs J-FETs to doses of ionizing radiations and cosmic rays, when compared with Si MOSFETs.

14.3 GaAs design methodology

14.3.1 Sticks notation for GaAs MESFETs

Stick diagrams are once again used to convey layer information through the extension of the color code already developed for nMOS and CMOS. The overall scheme is illustrated in Table 14–3.

Table 14–3 Sticks notation for GaAs

Layer	Color	Monochrome sticks notation	CIF
Diffusion†	Green		GD
Metal 1	Blue		GM
Metal 2	Deep Blue		GN
Implant – E*	Red		GP
Implant – D*	Yellow		GI
Contact	Black		GC
Via	Black		GV
Overglass	White	None	GG

Note: Implant – E: channel implant for enhancement device. Implant – D: channel for depletion device. Regions inside Red or Yellow are n^- implants with n^+ outside.

† This layer is actually an n^- implant region but the term diffusion has been used to be consistent with nMOS and CMOS notation.

14.3.2　Transistor formation and layer connections

A transistor is formed wherever blue crosses green surrounded by implant E or D and a cut is present at the gate region. Stick representations for the two transistors are given in Figure 14–12.

It should be noted at the sticks level that the cut is transparent to the designer. However, at a later stage the cut is usually generated to allow for the removal of gate oxide prior to gate-metal deposition.

The approach used for transistor representation may also be extended to the Schottky barrier diode as in Figure 14–13.

Apart from a missing source or drain, the Schottky barrier diode is similar to the MESFET.

As for nMOS and CMOS, intersections on the same layer form connections, as in Figure 14–14(a).

Intersections on different layers do not form connections or transistors as shown in Figure 14–14(b).

Different layers may also be connected by a contact or a via as in Figure 14–14(c).

Once again, as for silicon gate technology, the interaction with the foundry is through a CIF (Caltech Intermediate Form) design file. The CIF layer description code is shown in Table 14–3. Here the first letter is used to identify the technology (i.e. G for GaAs). This free format approach to layout allows the designer to concentrate on the design instead of the details of the technology.

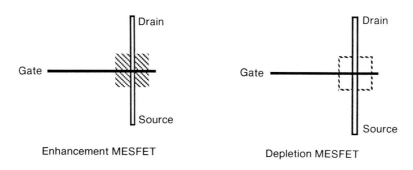

Enhancement MESFET　　　　　Depletion MESFET

Figure 14–12　Stick representations

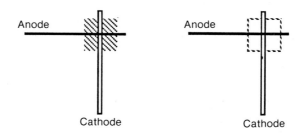

Figure 14–13　Schottky diode stick diagrams

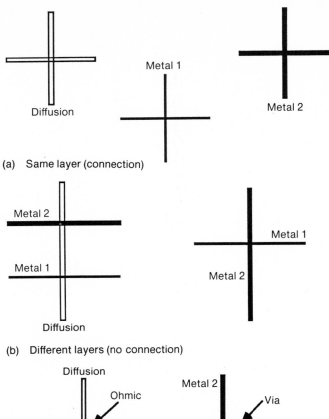

(a) Same layer (connection)

(b) Different layers (no connection)

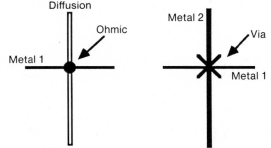

(c) Connection by contact or via

Figure 14-14 Layer connectivity

The step from sticks to mask may be carried out by hand by using mask level CAD software, or, alternatively, through a software-based approach of compaction. This process entails compacting or stretching a circuit layout to conform to some design rule specification.)

14.3.3 Symbolic approach to layout for GaAs

The application of some restrictions to the free-format stick layout results in a symbolic approach to design. The basic primitives are given in Figure 14–15 and an inverter in Figure 14–16.

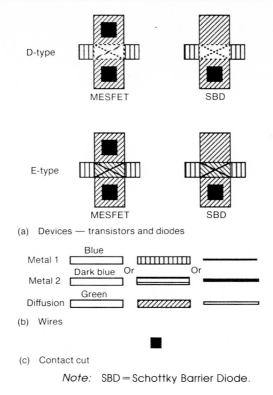

(a)   Devices — transistors and diodes

(b)   Wires

(c)   Contact cut

Note: SBD = Schottky Barrier Diode.

Figure 14–15   Symbolic representation for transistors and Schottky diodes

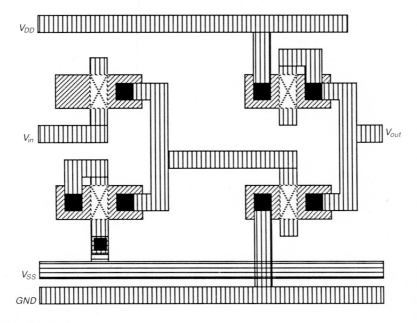

Figure 14–16   Symbolic layout for an inverter

14.4 Micron design rules for GaAs MESFET

14.4.1 Width and spacing rules (See Color Plate 16 and Figure 14–17)

The simplified rules are as follows:

1. Diffusion, Metal 1, and Metal 2 can cross each other without interaction.
2. All width and separation rules given in Figure 14–17 are dependent upon the width of the photoresist.
3. Diffusion width is a function of:
   (a) field-oxide encroachment;
   (b) width of the photoresist;
   (c) diffusion width giving an acceptable voltage drop across an interconnect.
4. As for nMOS and CMOS, we need to ensure that the depletion regions of two unrelated diffusions do not contact. The separation between diffusion is determined from:

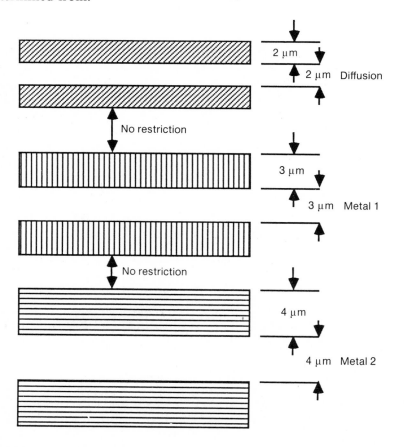

Figure 14–17 GaAs width and separation rules

(a)   width of depletion region;
(b)   width of the photoresist;
(c)   field-oxide encroachment.

14.4.2   Transistor rules (See Figure 14–18)

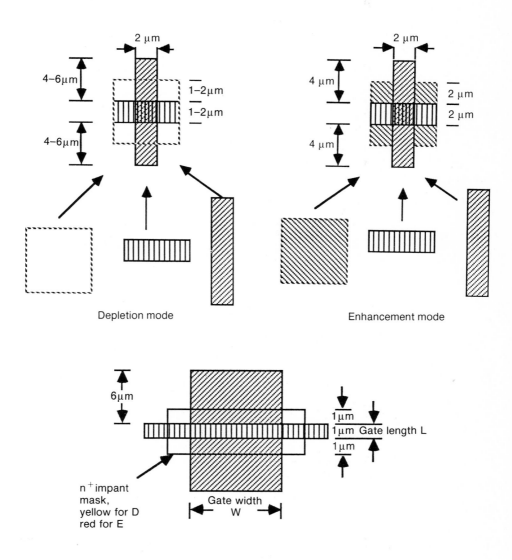

Figure 14–18   Transistor rules

By logical operation of the appropriate layer masks, it is possible to generate a contact cut at the MESFET gate area before metal deposition for the formation of the gate.

14.4.3 Contact cut rules (See Figure 14–19)

Generally the size of a cut is established from the knowledge of the minimum dimensions necessary to give an acceptable resistance. The rules that one may follow are:

1. Dimensions of a cut are 4 μm × 4 μm.
2. Dimension of diffusion overlap with cut is 2 μm.
3. Dimension of metal 1 overlap with cut is 2 μm.
4. Dimension of metal 2 overlap with cut is 3 μm. This rule may be relaxed to an overlap of 2 μm for some processes.

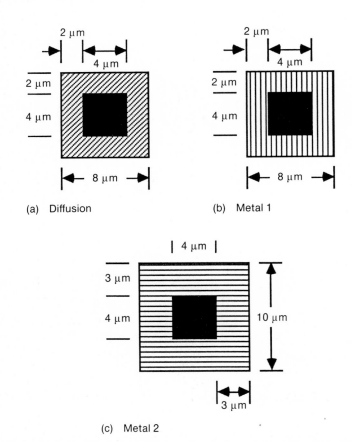

(a) Diffusion

(b) Metal 1

(c) Metal 2

Note: Contact resistances in range of 0.5 to $1m\Omega/cm^2$ can be expected. This leads to a contact resistance of about 500Ω to 1000Ω for a 4 μm × 4 μm contact.

Figure 14–19 Contact cuts and overlap

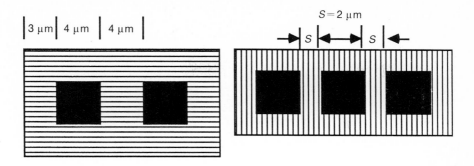

Figure 14-20 Multiple contacts

5. Multiple contact separation (Figure 14–20):

   (a) first-layer metal 2 μm;
   (b) second-layer metal 4 μm.

6. Via size is 4 μm×4 μm (see Figure 14–21):

   (a) metal 1 overlap of via 2 μm;
   (b) metal 2 overlap of via 2 μm.

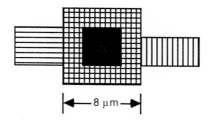

Figure 14-21 Via

In this section we have concentrated on one technology, namely D-MESFET, but the approach is readily extended to include other forms of GaAs technology as set out in the preceding sections of this chapter.

14.5 Device modeling and performance estimation

14.5.1 V–I characteristics

As for nMOS and pMOS transistors, the saturation drain current I_{ds} for GaAs transistors with $V_{gs} > V_{ds} - V_p$ is given by

$$I_{ds} = \frac{\mu_n \varepsilon}{d} \left[\frac{W}{L} \right] [V_{gs} - V_p]^2$$

where

μ_n = electron mobility
V_p = pinch-off voltage
L = gate length
W = gate width
d = depletion layer thickness
V_{gs} = gate-to-source voltage
ε = permittivity in gate/channel region

It should be noted that here the pinch-off voltage is the value of gate-to-source voltage at which the depletion layer thickness equals the thickness of the channel region.

The characteristics for a typical D-MESFET are illustrated in Figure 14–22.

As can be seen, the characteristic is similar to that of silicon gate technology, with the exception of the magnitude of the gate-to-source voltage V_{gs}, which is limited to about 0.8 volt. This limit is brought about by the presence of the Schottky diode at the gate region.

A more accurate representation of the MESFET requires an extension to our simple model. A more accurate representation is

$$I_{ds} = \frac{\mu_n \varepsilon}{d} \left[\frac{W}{L} \right] [V_{gs} - V_p]^2 [1 + \lambda V_{ds}] [\mathrm{Tanh}(k V_{ds})]$$

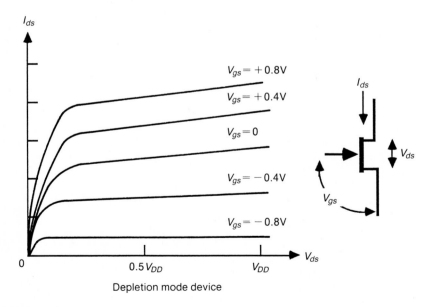

Figure 14–2 V–I characteristics for D-MESFET

where

$$V_{ds} = \text{drain to source voltage}$$
$$k = \text{an empirically derived constant}$$
$$\lambda = \text{constant}$$

For large electric fields E, the drain current I_{ds} may be modeled by

$$I_{ds} = \frac{\varepsilon \, v_{sat} \, W}{d} [V_{gs} - V_p]$$

This relation shows that, as the magnitude of the electric field is increased, the drain current I_{ds} is governed by the saturation velocity v_{sat} of the electrons. Comparing

$$v_{sat} \text{ for Si} \doteqdot 0.5 \times 10^7 \text{ cm/sec}$$

with

$$v_{sat} \text{ for GaAs} \doteqdot 1.0 \times 10^7 \text{ cm/sec}$$

indicates that degradation of GaAs devices occurs at finer geometries than their Si counterpart.

It is the drift velocity that determines the switching speed of a device. Here it should be noted that the drift velocity v_s is given by

$$v_s = \mu_n E$$

where

$$E = \text{electric field}$$

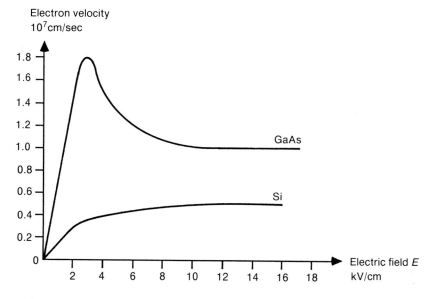

Figure 14-23 Electron velocity versus electric field

In high electric fields, due to an increased scattering, the electron mobility μ_n decreases. A particularly important feature of GaAs in relation to electron velocity versus electric field is shown in Figure 14–23.

As a result of the velocity overshoot, GaAs devices generally switch faster than if the velocity rose monotonically to the saturation value (as with Si).

14.5.2 Transconductance

The transconductance in the saturation region for a long-channel device can be modeled by

$$g_m = \frac{dI_{ds}}{dV_{gs}}\bigg|_{V_{ds}} = \text{constant}$$

$$= \frac{\mu_n \varepsilon}{d}\left[\frac{W}{L}\right][V_{gs} - V_p]$$

Similarly, for large electric fields, the transconductance may be expressed as

$$g_m = \frac{\varepsilon \, v_{sat} \, W}{d}$$

where

$$v_{sat} = \text{saturation velocity}$$

It may be seen that transconductance g_m is directly proportional to v_{sat} and is independent of gate length L.

14.5.3 Simplified model for MESFET device

A simplified circuit model for MESFET can be constructed as in Figure 14–24 where

$C_{gs} = $ gate-to-source capacitance
$C_{ds} = $ drain-to-source capacitance
$C_{gd} = $ gate-to-drain capacitance
$R_{ds} = $ drain-to-source resistance

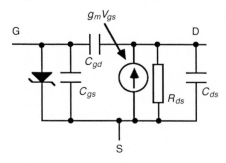

Figure 14–24 MESFET model

Using this model, one is able to calculate the instrinsic speed of a GaAs device from a knowledge of the gain-bandwidth product f_τ given by

$$f_\tau = \frac{g_m}{2\pi\, C_{gs}}$$

$$= \frac{\mu_n}{2\pi\, L^2}\,(V_{gs} - V_p)$$

The current gain-bandwidth product f_τ illustrates that switching speed depends upon:

- gate length L;
- carrier mobility μ_n in the channel;
- gate voltage.

Thus, to improve switching speed, the options are:

- increase logic voltage swing (logic voltage swing is comparable with the gate voltage above threshold);
- reduce gate length.

Although the former option is possible, the switching energy in this case is increased, resulting in an increase in dissipation. That is

$$P_d = C_L\, V^2 f$$

where

$$P_d = \text{dynamic dissipation}$$
$$C_L = \text{load capacitance}$$
$$V = \text{logic voltage swing}$$
$$f = \text{frequency of switching}$$

14.5.4 Device parameters

Typical parameters for a MESFET with $L = 1.2\ \mu\text{m}$ and $W = 12\ \mu\text{m}$ are illustrated in Table 14–4.

Table 14–4 Typical device parameters

(a) Capacitances

Device parameter	Value
C_{gs}	0.015 pF
C_{ds}	0.003 pF
C_{gd}	0.005 pF

Table 14-4 continued

(b)   Resistance

Device parameter	Value
R_{ds} (saturated)	15,000 ohm

(c)   MESFET

MESFET	Value	
Device parameter	Min	Max
V_p	$-0.8V - 1.0V$	
g_m	110	150

(d)   Schottky barrier diode

SBD	Value
Device parameter	(Typical)
V_F	0.8V
η	1

Note: where V_F is the SBD forward voltage and η is the ideality factor

With typical value for transconductance g_m being in the order of 1 mmho the intrinsic speed of a GaAs MESFET can be determined. Thus

$$f_\tau = \frac{g_m}{2\pi \, C_{gs}}$$

$$\doteq 11\text{GHz}$$

(For Si gate technology with $L = 1.2 \ \mu$m: $f_\tau \doteq 3\text{GHz}$)

14.6 GaAs logic families

There are a number of approaches one may take in developing the basic logic gates. The approaches include:

- unbuffered FET logic (UFL);
- direct-coupled FET logic (DCFL);
- capacitor-coupled FET logic (CCFL);
- D-MESFET Schottky diode FET logic (SDFL).

14.6.1   Unbuffered FET logic (UFL)

The basic structure of a gate is shown as Figure 4–25. Here the Schottky diode that is connected at the gate output provides the mechanism for level shifting.

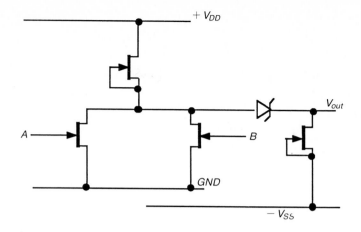

Figure 14-25   Basic structure for unbuffered FET logic (UFL)

14.6.2   Direct-coupled FET logic (DCFL)

In this class of logic, the enhancement mode FETs are utilized as illustrated in Figure 14–26. From the figure it is evident that, firstly, there is no need for level shifting, and, secondly, that the design of the logic gate closely resembles that of nMOS circuitry. However, it should be noted that the problems encountered with enhancement mode FETs somewhat detract from the attractiveness of this type of logic.

14.6.3   Capacitor-coupled FET logic (CCFL)

Capacitor-coupled FET logic needs only one supply. However the necessity to clock above a minimum clock frequency can cause some problem with testing.

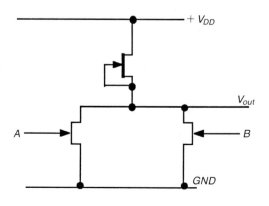

Figure 14-26   Basic structure for direct-coupled FET logic (DCFL)

14.6.4 D-MESFET Schottky diode — FET logic (SDFL)

In this class of logic, a cluster of Schottky diodes is used to perform the logical *Or* function. This is followed by a level shifter and a buffer.

The basic circuits are built up around the SDFL inverter, the circuit and sticks diagrams for which are given in Figures 14–27 and 14–28.

Since some form of voltage level shifting is necessary to ensure that the buffer stage can be turned off, an additional negative supply line is necessary. Thus some penalty in terms of area is paid for routing this additional bus.

The SDFL structure permits a large fan-in at the first logic level without influencing the dynamic response. However, a limitation of 2 (and sometimes 3) is imposed at the second logic level (i.e. the *Nand* operation).

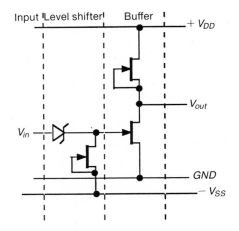

Figure 14–27 SDFL inverter circuit

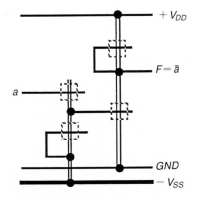

Figure 14–28 SDFL inverter stick diagram

It should be noted that the independence of switching behavior of the buffer from the number of inputs is brought about by the gate turn-off current for the buffer-switching transistor being provided by the pull-down transistor and not by the preceding switch (c.f. nMOS and CMOS), due to the presence of an isolating diode.

To complete this section, typical *Nor* gate and *Nand* gate arrangements, with corresponding stick diagrams are given in Figures 14–29 to 14–32.

14.7 Design of very high speed logic (VHSL)

A basic consequence of increased clock frequency is that the time-alignment of signals travelling different paths within the microsystem becomes critical and somewhat difficult to achieve. This means that propagation delays are required to be carefully balanced in order to obtain optimum performance.

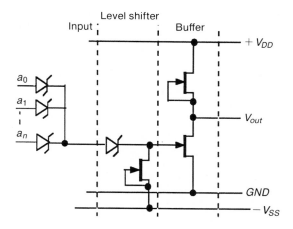

Figure 14–29   SDFL *Nor* gate circuit

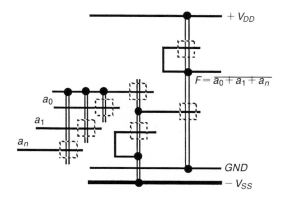

Figure 14–30   SDFL *Nor* stick diagram

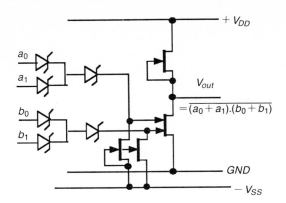

Figure 14-31 *Or/Nand* gate circuit

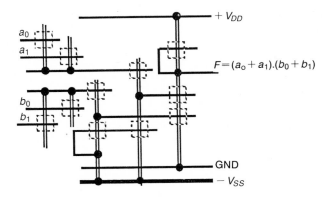

Figure 14-32 *Or/Nand* gate stick diagram

Another issue that needs consideration is that logic signals in the Gigahertz range require low-impedance transmission lines to ensure that the levels and pattern are reproduced. Power dissipation well beyond that of circuits operated in the MHz range can be expected. Thus the conflicting constraints that we are faced with in the design of very high speed logic are:

- signal and clock skews;
- cross talk;
- low-impedance signal lines;
- power dissipation.

It should be noted that high system clock rates produce a very high degree of cross talk and a consequent need for low-impedance signal lines. The need for low-impedance signal lines results in somewhat high system power dissipation.

14.8 VLSI design — the final ingredients

We are living in an age of unprecedented revolutionary change in engineering, particularly electronic engineering. The digital computer and associated processing revolution of the past two or more decades has been complemented and augmented by the even more dramatic advances in microcircuitry in silicon. We have come to accept world-shattering advances as a matter of course, and predictions such as the computing power of a CRAY1 computer in one's pocket hardly raise an eyebrow. Further, the potential of newer technologies, such as GaAs has yet to be explored.

However, it is a fact that unlike the situations faced by engineers of the past, we are no longer technology-bound or limited. Indeed we have solutions to problems that don't even exist yet! This is a situation in which the potential applications of VLSI technology are limited only by the creativity and imagination of those working in engineering or computer science.

VLSI design is also an enjoyable area in which to work. The designer has a great deal of freedom as there are few constraints associated with VLSI system designs. It is also an area which captures the imagination and it is hard not to become highly motivated.

The authors, therefore, recognize *enthusiasm founded on a knowledgeable base* as the final ingredient. We feel it appropriate to end with two quotations from R. W. Emerson:

'*Nothing great was ever achieved without enthusiasm.*'

'*The reward of a thing well done is to have done it.*'

14.9 References for GaAs

Curtice, W. R., 'A MESFET model for use in the design of GaAs integrated circuits,' *IEEE Trans. Microwave Theory and Techniques*, Vol. JMTT–28, No. 5, 1980, pp. 448–56.

Deming, et al. 'A Gallium Arsenide Configurable Cell Array Using Buffered FET Logic', *IEEE Journal of Solid State Circuits*, Vol. SC–19, No. 5, Oct. 1984, pp. 728–38.

Eden, R. C. (Ed.), 'Very Fast Solid-State Technology', *Proc. IEEE* 70 (1), 1982.

Einspruch, N. G. (Ed.), *VSLI Handbook*, Academic Press, 1985.

Elmasay, M. I., 'Stick-Layout Notation for Bipolar VLSI', *VLSI Design*, March/April 1983.

Ishii, Y., et al. 'Processing Technologies for GaAs Memory LSIs', *Proc. GaAs IC Symposium*, Oct. 1984, pp. 121–4.

Kazuyoshi, A., et al. 'GaAs 1Kbit Static RAM with Self Aligned FET Technology', *IEEE Journal of Solid State Circuits*, Vol. SC–19, No. 2, April 1984, pp. 260–2.

Milutnovic, Fura and Helbig, 'An introduction to GaAs Microprocessor Architecture for VLSI', *Computer*, Vol. 19, No. 3, March 1986, pp. 30–42.

Welch, B. M., et al., 'LSI Processing Technology for Planar GaAs Integrated Circuits', *IEEE Trans. Electron Devices* ED–27 (6), 1980.

Appendix A —
AWA design rules

The micron-based design rules for the AWA process are specified in terms of delta (δ), where delta $= 1.25$ μm.

Design rules cover the minimum spacings, notches, and widths allowed. The relevant layers are listed in Table A–1. The design rules are specified below and in Figures A–1 to A–7.

Table A–1 AWA CMOS layer encoding

Name	CIF layer
Metal	'CM'
Polysilicon	'CP'
Nitride (diffusion)	'CN'
p-Well	'CPW'
Contact	'CT'
p-Plus	'CPP'
n-Plus	'CPN' Process mask: photoreversal of CPP
p-Minus	'CPM' Derived by oversizing CPW by 3δ
n-Minus	'CNM' Process mask: photoreversal of CPW
Silox	'CS'
V_{tp} adjust	'CTA' Process mask: generated from CPP

1. *Layer: metal 'CM'*
   - (a) minimum metal width 4
   - (b) minimum spacing 4
   - (c) minimum notch 4
   - (d) minimum contact overlap (all sides) 1
   - (e) minimum clearance to bond pad metal 28
   - (f) minimum separation between metal and scribe area edge 32
   - (g) minimum overlap of bond pad over silox opening 4
   - (h) minimum bond pad dimension 100
   - (i) minimum pad-to-pad spacing 60
   - (j) minimum metal-to-pad metal 30
   - (k) An arrow should indicate the bond pad for pin 1 and point in the increasing pin number direction.
   - (l) Bond pads must not be placed over active circuit components.
   - (m) A 45 degree fillet should be provided where tracks join a pad.
2. *Layer: polysilicon 'CP'*
   - (a) minimum width 4
   - (b) minimum polysilicon to polysilicon spacing 4
   - (c) polysilicon to gate overlap beyond nitride 3
   - (d) minimum spacing between polysilicon and nitride wires 2
   - (e) minimum self-aligned diffusion width 4
   - (f) minimum spacing between polysilicon and bond pad metal 28

    (g)   minimum spacing between polysilicon and edge of scribe area   28
    (h)   polysilicon to be placed under bond pads and extend around
            bond pad metal by   4

3. *Layer: nitride 'CN'*
    (a)   minimum width   4
    (b)   minimum spacing (for 6 volts or greater)   6
                           (for < 6 volts)   4
    (c)   minimum notch   4
    (d)   minimum clearance to scribe channel   32

4. *Layer: p-well 'CPW'*
    (a)   minimum width   4
    (b)   minimum spacing   16
    (c)   minimum notch   16
    (d)   minimum p-well overlap of nitride   2
    (e)   external nitride clearance   7
    (f)   scribe minimum clearance   32
    (g)   p-well to be placed under all bond pads and extending around bond pad
            metal.
    (h)   *Important*: No part of the p-well shall be more than 60 delta (75 μm)
            from an ohmic contact (V_{SS} contact). Similarly, no part of a p-channel
            nitride (or p$^+$ wires) shall be more than 120 delta (150 μm) from an
            ohmic contact (V_{DD} contact).
    (i)   'CPM' is defined as a 3 delta overlap of 'CPW'.

5. *Layer: contact 'CT'*
    (a)   minimum contact size   4
    (b)   maximum contact size   20
    (c)   minimum contact to contact spacing   4
    (d)   minimum contact to nitride (inside)   2
            and to guardband nitride   1
    (e)   minimum separation from contact within nitride to polysilicon   3
    (f)   minimum polysilicon overlap of contact (all sides)   2
    (g)   minimum metal overlap of contact (all sides)   1
    (h)   Contact to polysilicon over active area is not allowed.

6. *Layer: p-plus 'CPP'*
    (a)   minimum width (diffusion/nitride intersects)   4
    (b)   minimum spacing or notch   4
    (c)   minimum overlap of nitride   2
    (d)   minimum clearance from n$^+$ nitride   2

7. *Layer: n-plus 'CNP'*
  Process mask generated by photoreversal of p-plus mask 'CPP'.

8. *Layer: silox 'CS'*
    (a)   minimum opening   4
    (b)   minimum clearance inside metal   4

9. *Layer: p-minus 'CPM'*
  Process mask generated by 3 delta oversizing of p-well ('CPW').

10. *Layer: n-minus 'CNM'*
    Process mask generated by photoreversal of p^- mask ('CPM').

11. *Layer: VTP adjust 'CTA'*
    Process mask generated from p-plus ('CPP') and used for threshold voltage adjustment (process step is optional and generally not used).

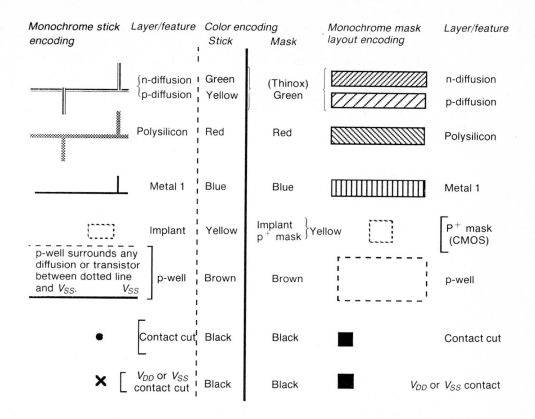

Monochrome stick encoding	Layer/feature	Color encoding Stick	Mask	Monochrome mask layout encoding	Layer/feature
	{n-diffusion	Green	(Thinox)		n-diffusion
	{p-diffusion	Yellow	Green		p-diffusion
	Polysilicon	Red	Red		Polysilicon
	Metal 1	Blue	Blue		Metal 1
	Implant	Yellow	Implant p⁺ mask }Yellow		P⁺ mask (CMOS)
p-well surrounds any diffusion or transistor between dotted line and V_{SS}. V_{SS}	p-well	Brown	Brown		p-well
•	Contact cut	Black	Black	■	Contact cut
✕	V_{DD} or V_{SS} contact cut	Black	Black	■	V_{DD} or V_{SS} contact

Monochrome stick diagram examples

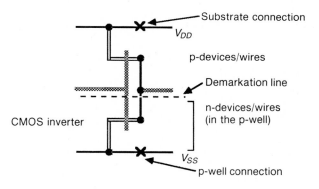

- Substrate connection
V_{DD}
p-devices/wires
Demarkation line
n-devices/wires (in the p-well)
CMOS inverter
V_{SS}
p-well connection

Note: Layers are insulated from each other unless deliberately joined by a contact. However, wherever polysilicon crosses diffusion, a transistor is formed.

Figure A–1 Layer/feature encoding scheme

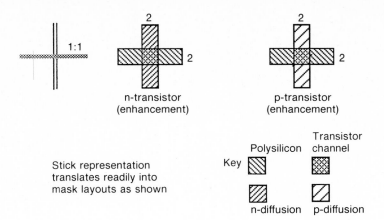

Figure A-2   A stick diagram and corresponding mask layouts

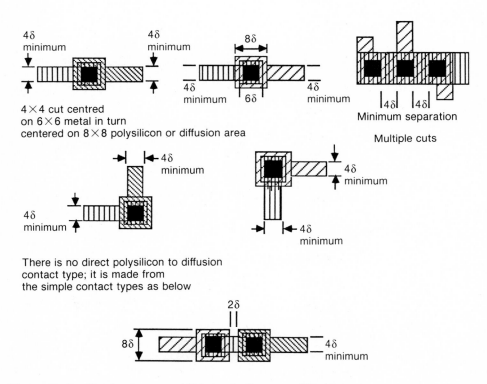

Figure A-3   Contacts — metal to polysilicon or diffusion

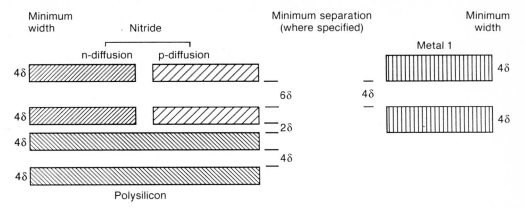

Figure A–4   Design rules for wires (AWA CMOS)

Note: Where no separation is specified, wires may overlap or cross (e.g. metal is not constrained by any other layer). Note that n-diffusion wires can only exist inside and p-diffusion wires outside the p-well.

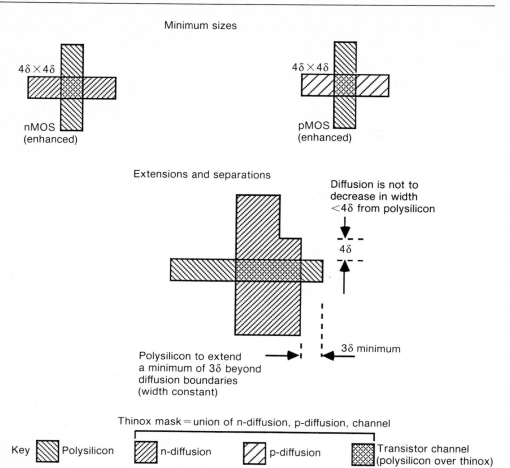

Figure A–5   Transister design rules (AWA CMOS)

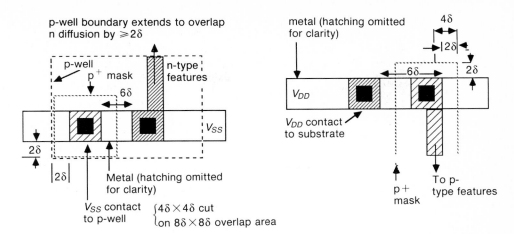

Figure A-6 V_{SS} and V_{DD} contacts

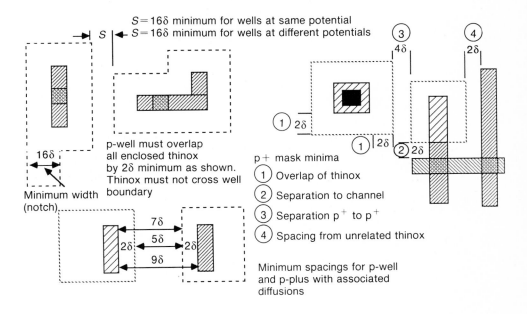

Figure A-7 p-well and p$^+$ mask

Appendix B — Orbit Semiconductor Inc. design rules

These design rules are for a 2 µm single polysilicon, double metal CMOS process and apply to both p-well or n-well CMOS. The p-well CMOS is illustrated here. For n-well design, transform all p to n and n to p.

The n^+ and p^+ mask fields listed in Table B–1 are purely incidental. This is the case if one digitizes only the n^+ mask, then p^+ is obtained by mask field reversal. Other design houses might choose to digitize the p^+ instead of n^+, and that results in p^+ being the dark field and n^+ the clear field. Another possible convention would be digitizing n^+ and p^+ separately, then both layers would be a dark field.

Table B–1   'Orbit'® double metal ISO-CMOS mask designation and encoding

Mask	Description	Field	Scribe	Align to	Mask layout encoding
1	p-well	Dark	No	Flat	
2	Source/drain diffusion	Clear	Yes	1	 n-type 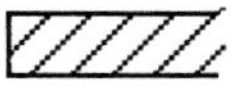 / p-type
3	Field implant	Clear	No	2	Not drawn, oversize p-well by 2.5 µm
4	Polysilicon, gate	Clear	No	2	 Polysilicon
5	n^+ mask	Dark	Yes	2	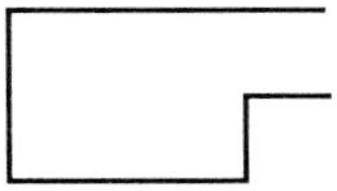
6	p^+ mask	Clear	No	2	Not drawn, field reverse of 5
7	Contact mask	Clear	Yes	2&4	Cut
8	Metal 1	Clear	No	7	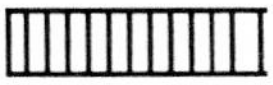 Metal 1
9	Via	Dark	Yes	8	Via
10	Metal 2	Clear	No	9	 Metal 2
11	Pad mask	Dark	Yes	10	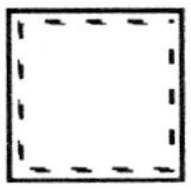
12	Depletion (ROM)	Dark	No	2	See Figure B–15
13	Buried contact	Dark	Yes	2	

Table B–2 lists the design as drawn, the mask, and the resultant 'on-wafer' dimensions. It is important to note the shrink in source/drain dimension, that is, the width of the active device, after processing.

The photolithography is PE300 projection aligner, with positive resist and plasma etching of polysilicon, contact, via, and metal. The design rules are based on a worst case layer-to-layer registration of 1 μm.

The following design rules should be read in conjunction with Figures B–1 to B–15. The process and device parameters for the p-well and n-well technologies are given in Tables B–3 and B–4 respectively. Note that V_{CC} is used in place of V_{DD}.

Table B–2 Drawn/mask/wafer dimensions for positive resist

Design		Mask dimensions (μm) ±0.2 μm on critical layers	Skew factor (μm) Delta per side	Wafer (μm)
	Microns			
p-well	3	2.8	−0.1	3.0 ± 0.25
Source/drain (5.5 μm pitch)	3	3.5	+0.25	2.0 ± 0.25
Field implant	8	8.0	0	8.0 ± 0.5
Polysilicon gate (4.5 μm pitch)	2	2.3	+0.15	2.0 ± 0.2
n^+ mask	3	3.0	0	3.25 ± 0.25
p^+ mask	3	3.5	+0.25	3.25 ± 0.25
Contact (dry etch)	2	2.2	+0.1	2.5 ± 0.25
Metal 1 (6 μm pitch)	3	3.5	+0.25	3.0 ± 0.25
Via	2	2.2	+0.1	2.75 ± 0.25
Metal 2 (7 μm pitch)	4	4.5	+0.25	3.5 ± 0.25
Pad	5	5.0	0	3.0 ± 0.5
Depletion, ROM, capacitor	5	4.8	−0.1	5.0 ± 0.25
Buried contact	3	2.7	−0.15	3.0 ± 0.25

Design rule detail:

1. *p-well mask* (Layer 1) *Refer to Figure B–1*
   - (a) minimum p-well width $d_1 = 3\ \mu m$
   - (b) p-well to p-well spacing $d_2 = 8.5\ \mu m$
2. *Source/drain* (n^+, p^+ diffusion) (Layer 2) *Refer to Figure B–2*
   - (a) minimum width (n^+, p^+)
     - (i) Interconnect $d_1 = 3\ \mu m$
     - (ii) Active device $d_1{}^* = 3.5\ \mu m$
   - (b) minimum spacing
     - (i) n^+ to n^+ $d_2 = 2.5\ \mu m$
     - (ii) p^+ to p^+ $d_3 = 2.5\ \mu m$
     - (iii) n^+ to p^+ in the same substrate $d_4 = 2.5\ \mu m$
   - (c) p^+ to p-well (electrical isolated) $d_5 = 6.5\ \mu m$
     p^+ inside p-well to p-well edge $d_6 = 0\ \mu m$

    (d) n^+ (substrate contact) to p-well $d_7 = 4\,\mu m$

    (e) n^+ (inside p-well) to p-well edge $d_8 = 2.5\,\mu m$

3. *Field implant* (Layer 3)

    (a) oversize of p-well mask by $2.5\,\mu m$

4. *Polysilicon gate* (Layer 4)   *Refer to Figure B–3*

    (a) minimum polysilicon width $d_1 = 2\,\mu m$

    (b) minimum polysilicon to polysilicon spacing $d_2 = 2.5\,\mu m$

    (c) minimum gate overlap field $d_3 = 2\,\mu m$

    (d) minimum gate to diffusion edge $d_4 = 2.5\,\mu m$

    (e) minimum polysilicon in field to edge of

          diffusion $d_5 = 1\,\mu m$

5. n^+ *diffusion mask* (Layer 5)   *Refer to Figure B–4*

    This mask defines area to be n^+ doped

    (a) overlap all n^+ source/drain (except butted

          contacts) $d_1 = 1\,\mu m$

    (b) n^+ diffusion mask to p^+ $d_2 = 1.5\,\mu m$

    (c) minimum n^+ diffusion mask width/spacing $d_3 = 3\,\mu m$

6. p^+ *diffusion mask*

    (a) reverse field of n^+ mask

7. *Contact mask*   *Refer to Figure B–5*

    (a) minimum contact size and spacing (except

          butted contacts) $d_1 = 2\,\mu m$

    (b) maximum contact size (except protection

          devices and butted contacts) $d_2 = 5\,\mu m$

    (c) spacing between large contacts $d_3 = 3\,\mu m$

    (d) n^+, p^+ diffusion overlap contacts $d_4 = 1.5\,\mu m$

    (e) n^+, p^+ diffusion contacts to polysilicon gate $d_5 = 2.5\,\mu m$

    (f) polysilicon overlap contacts $d_6 = 1.5\,\mu m$

    (g) polysilicon contacts to diffusion edge $d_7 = 2.5\,\mu m$

    (h) maximum distance between V_{CC} contacts $d_8 = 200\,\mu m$ }Not

    (i) maximum distance between V_{SS} contacts $d_9 = 100\,\mu m$ }shown

    (j) p-well substrate contacts:

        (i) p^+ guard ring extends $3\,\mu m$ around

             p-well

      (ii) p^+ (V_{SS}) to n^+ butted contacts

            — minimum butted contact

                $2.0 \times 6\,\mu m$, extends $3.0\,\mu m$

                each side of n^+, p^+ diffusion

                mask $d_{10} = 2.0 \times 3.0\,\mu m$

            — p^+ mask can be coincident with

                p^+ source/drain $d_{11} = 0\,\mu m$

            — p^+ mask to adjacent n-channel

                gate $d_{12} = 2\,\mu m$

      (iii) n^+ to p^+ to n^+ butted contacts

            — minimum contact size

                 $2.0 \times 8.0\,\mu m$, extends $2.5\,\mu m$

                for n^+ and $3.0\,\mu m$ for p^+

            — p^+ mask overlap contact $d_{13} = 2\,\mu m$

            — p^+ mask to gate $d_{14} = 3\,\mu m$

(k)   n-well substrate contacts:
  (i) n^+ guard ring for input and output devices
  (ii) n^+ (V_{CC}) to p^+ butted contacts   *Features not illustrated*
    — minimum butted contact
      2×6 µm, extends 3.0 µm each
      side of n^+, p^+ diffusion mask $d_{15} = 2.0 \times 3.0$ µm
    — n^+ mask can be coincident with
      n^+ source/drain $d_{16} = 0$ µm
    — n^+ mask to adjacent p-channel $d_{17} = 2$ µm
      gate
  (iii) $p^+/n^+/p^+$ butted contacts
    — minimum contact size
      2.0×8.0 µm, extends 2.5 µm
      for p^+ and 3.0 µm for n^+
    — n^+ mask overlap contact $d_{18} = 2$ µm
    — n^+ mask to p-channel gate $d_{19} = 3$ µm

8.   *Metal mask* (Layer 8)   *Refer to Figure B–6*
  (a)   metal width $d_1 = 3$ µm
  (b)   metal spacing $d_2 = 3$ µm
  (c)   metal overlap contacts
    (i)   in direction of diffusion, polysilicon
          and metal $d_3 = 1.5$ µm
    (ii)   other directions $d_4 = 1$ µm
  (d)   metal pad size $d_5 = 110 \times 110$ µm
  (e)   pad to pad (not shown) $d_6 = 75$ µm
  (f)   pad to active circuitry $d_7 = 30$ µm
  (g)   pad to inner edge of scribe ring $d_8 = 30$ µm

9.   *Via mask*   *Refer to Figure B–7*
  (a)   via's not allowed over 1st contact
  (b)   minimum via opening $d_1 = 2.0$ µm
  (c)   minimum via spacing $d_2 = 2.5$ µm
  (d)   via to diffusion $d_3 = 2.5$ µm
  (e)   via to polysilicon $d_4 = 2.5$ µm
  (f)   via to contact $d_5 = 2.5$ µm
  (g)   metal 1 overlap via $d_6 = 1.5$ µm
  (h)   metal 1 overlap via in bonding pad (not
        shown) $d_7 = 5$ µm

10.   *Metal 2 mask*   *Refer to Figure B–8*
  (a)   metal 2 minimum width $d_1 = 4$ µm
  (b)   metal 2 minimum spacing $d_2 = 3$ µm
  (c)   metal 2 overlap via $d_3 = 1.5$ µm
  (d)   metal 2 overlap via in bonding pad (not
        shown) $d_4 = 5$ µm

11.   *Step coverage rule*   *Refer to Figure B–9*
  (a)   metal 2 to metal 1
    (i)   avoid metal 2 coincident with metal 1
    (ii)   metal 2 overlap metal 1 $d_1 = 1.5$ µm
    (iii)   metal 2 edge to metal 1 edge spacing $d_2 = 3$ µm

12. *Pad mask*   *Not illustrated*
    (a) pad opening $d_1 = 100 \times 100 \ \mu m$
    (b) metal overlap pad $d_2 = \ 5 \ \mu m$
13. *Scribe ring*   *Refer to Figure B–10*
    (a) scribe ring consists of source/drain, n^+
         diffusion mask (not shown), contact, metal
         and pad layers.
14. *Input protection devices*   *Refer to Figure B–11*
    (a) static discharge protection:
         (i)   double diode and polysilicon resistor
         (ii)   minimum contacts area 100 μm^2
         (iii) minimum diode area 400 μm^2
         (iv)   minimum polysilicon resistor width
                8 μm
         (v)   typical polysilicon resistor value 500 Ω
         (vi)   guard rings are required for latch up
                prevention
         (vii) use ample overlap of diffusion to
                contact and metal to contact
                typically 5 μm.
    (b) Other types of input protection devices use
         p-well resistor instead of polysilicon. P-well
         resistor is typically 2 kilo-ohms per square
         and can be placed under the pad. It also
         acts as a p to n diode.
15. *Output protection*   *Refer to Figures B–12 and B–13*
    (a) Output pads connected to drivers with large
         transistor width do not need additional
         protection.
    (b) Other output pads can use the same structure
         as 14(a) for static protection.
    (c) Output devices are heavily guard ringed for
         SCR protection.
16. *Latch up*
    (a) Parasitic bipolar transistors
         (i)   Vertical NPN's base width is fixed by
                the p-well and n^+ diffusion
                junctions.
         (ii)   Lateral PNP's Beta is determined by
                the p^+ (outside p-well) to p-well
                spacing. This Beta can be reduced by
                increasing internal p^+ diffusion to
                p-well spacing of output devices.
    (b) Guard ring:
         Guard rings are collectors for injected
             currents at input and output devices. This
             prevents current paths from establishing
             forward biased PN and NP junctions
             concurrently which initiates SCR action.

(c) N-channel impact ionisation current:
For scale down processes, impact ionisation current can be substantial especially at high V_{ds}. This impact current or I_b can cause a forward bias potential of p-well to n^+ diffusion junction. This is minimised by adhering to the maximum distance between p-well substrate contacts.

17. V_{CC} bus around the die periphery for substrate bias can be used. This replaces the scribe ring structure in Figure B–10.   *Refer to Figure B–14*

18. *Process options*   *Refer to Figure B–15*

   (a) Depletion devices (n-channel) and ROM code implant
      (i) Implant mask overlap polysilicon gate in direction of diffusion $d_1 = 2\ \mu m$
      (ii) Implant mask overlap field $d_2 = 1\ \mu m$
      (iii) Implant mask to adjacent gate in the same diffusion $d_3 = 2\ \mu m$
      (iv) Implant mask to unrelated diffusion $d_4 = 1.5\ \mu m$

   (b) Capacitor implant
      (i) To form the bottom plate of capacitor in p-well. The dielectric is the gate oxide thickness sandwiched between polysilicon (n^+) and the implant layer. Implant dose is heavier than typical depletion to improve the voltage coefficient parameter.
      (ii) Capacitor implant mask overlap S/D $d_1 = 1\ \mu m$
      (iii) Diffusion overlap polysilicon capacitor $d_2 = 2.5\ \mu m$

   (c) Buried contact, n-channel side only
      (i) Polysilicon to diffusion contact minimum dimension $d_1 = 3 \times 3\ \mu m$
      (ii) B.C. mask extends in direction of field $d_2 = 1\ \mu m$
      (iii) B.C. mask extends in direction of diffusion $d_3 = 2\ \mu m$
      (iv) B.C. mask to adjacent gate $d_4 = 2\ \mu m$
      (v) B.C. to unrelated diffusion and polysilicon $d_5 = 1.5\ \mu m$

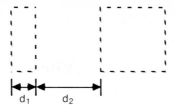

Figure B-1   p-well width and spacing

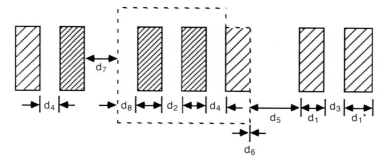

Figure B-2   Widths and spacings for source/drain regions

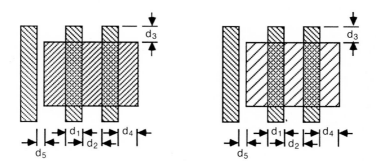

Figure B-3   Width and spacings for polysilicon gate regions

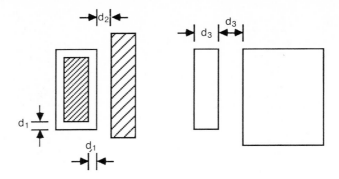

Figure B–4 n^+ mask overlap, width, and spacing

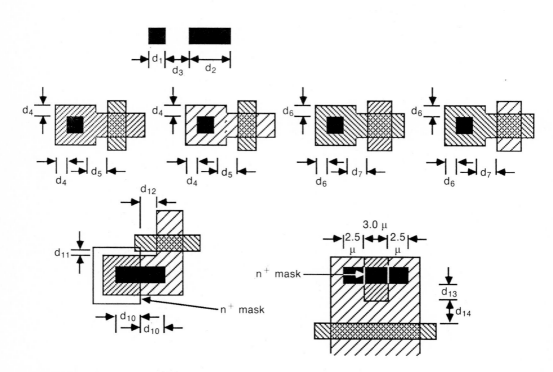

Figure B–5   Contacts — dimensions, separation, and overlaps

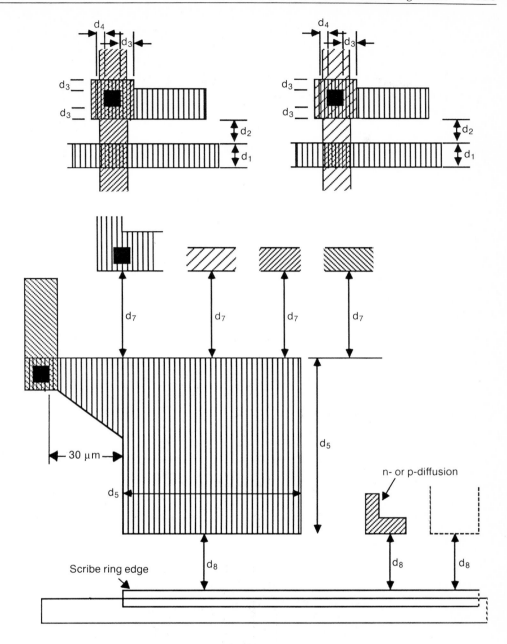

Figure B–6   Metal mask (not to scale)

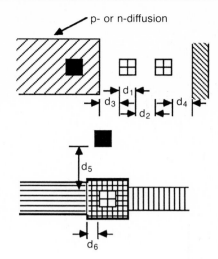

Figure B-7   Via mask separations and overlaps

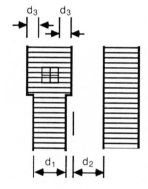

Figure B-8   Metal 2 mask width, separation, and overlaps

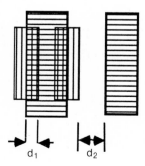

Figure B-9   Metal 2/metal 1 step coverage and separation

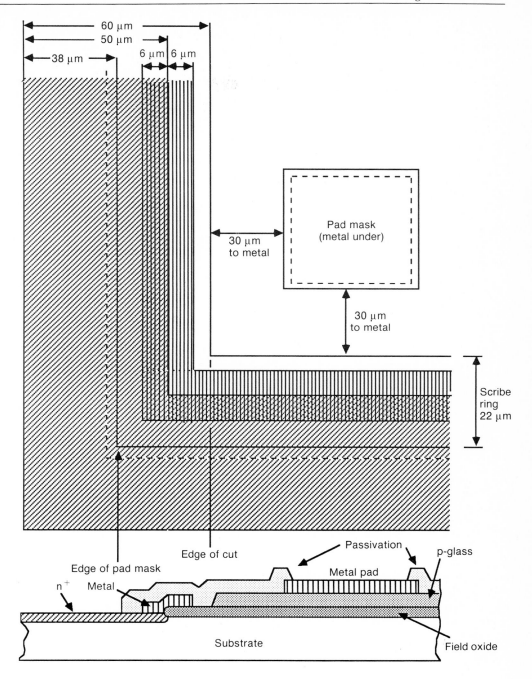

Figure B–10 Scribe ring detail (not to scale)

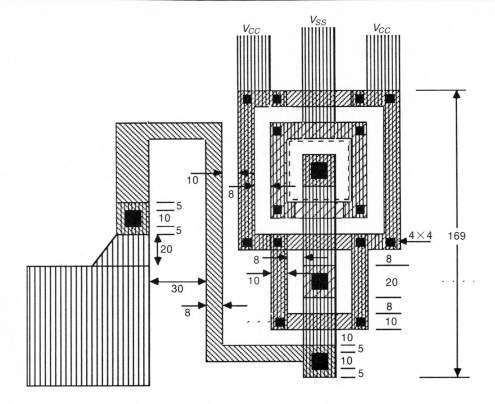

All dimensions in μm (drawing is not to exact scale)

Figure B-11 Input protection

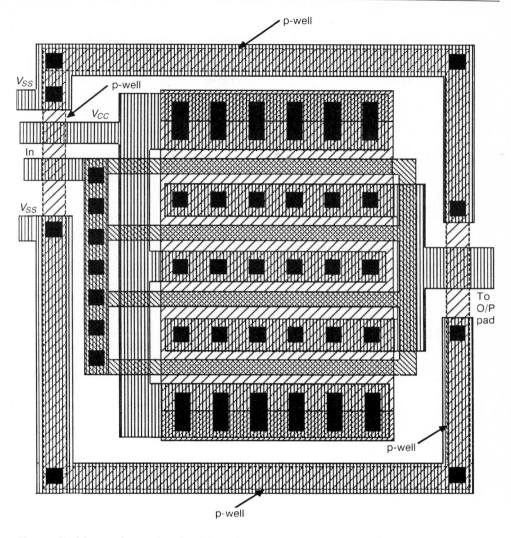

Figure B–12 p-channel output transistor and protection (not to scale)

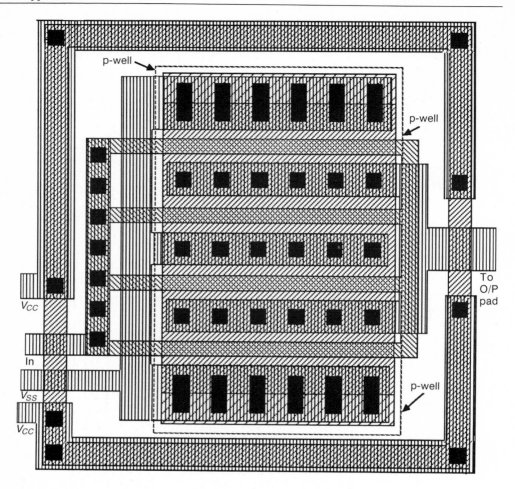

Figure B–13 n-channel output transistor and protection (not to scale)

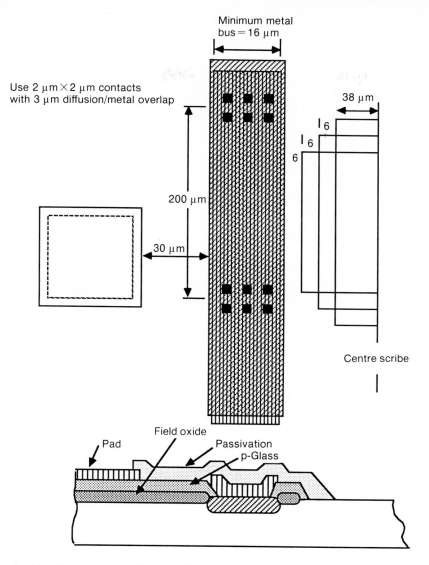

Figure B-14 V_{CC} peripheral bus (not to scale)

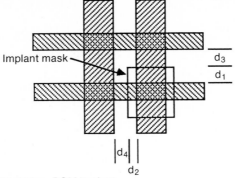

Implant mask

d_3
d_1

d_4
d_2

(a) Depletion, ROM implant

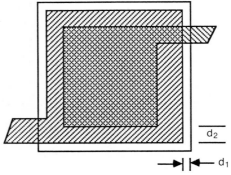

d_2

d_1

(b) Capacitor implant

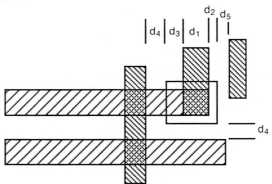

d_2 d_5

d_4 d_3 d_1

d_4

(c) Buried contact

Figure B–15 Process options

Table B–3 2 µm single polysilicon, double metal p-well CMOS device parameters

	n-channel	*p-channel*	*Condition*
V_{TEO} (extrapolated)	0.5–1.0 V	0.5–1.0 V	30 µm × 2 µm device saturation
BV_{DSS}	$\geqslant 10$ V	$\geqslant 10$ V	30 µm × 2 µm device $V_{GS}=0$, $I_{DS}=1$ µA
$K'\left(\dfrac{\mu C}{2}\right)$	22–25 $\dfrac{\mu A}{V^2}$	6.5–8.5 $\dfrac{\mu A}{V^2}$	30 µm × 30 µm device $V_{DS}=0.1$ V, $V_{GS}=2, 3$ V
B_E (long channel body effect)	0.8–1.2 $V^{1/2}$	0.4–0.6 $V^{1/2}$	30 µm × 30 µm $B_E = \Delta V_{TE} \rbrack {\,V_{BS}=2\text{ V} \atop \,V_{BS}=0\text{ V}}$
B_E (short channel body effect)	0.6–0.9 $V^{1/2}$	0.25–0.45 $V^{1/2}$	30 µm × 2 µm $B_E = \Delta V_{TE} \rbrack {\,V_{BS}=2\text{ V} \atop \,V_{BS}=0\text{ V}}$
Gate oxide capacitance (10^{-4} pF/µm^2)	8.0–10.0	8.0–10.0	Based on 400 ± 30Å
Polysilicon to substrate capacitance (10^{-4} pF/µm^2)	0.55–0.65	0.55–0.65	Based on 5500–6000Å
Metal to diffusion capacitance (10^{-4} pF/µm^2)	0.55–0.65	0.55–0.65	Based on 5500–6500Å
Metal to substrate capacitance (10^{-4} pF/µm^2)	0.27–0.32	0.27–0.32	Based on 1.1–1.25µm
Metal to polysilicon capacitance (10^{-4} pF/µm^2)	0.55–0.65	0.55–0.65	Based on 5500–6500Å
Diffusion JCN capacitance (10^{-4} pF/µm^2)	1.8	1.68	Zero bias
Diffusion capacitance periphery (10^{-4} pF/µm)		Negligible	"Diffusion" is a shallow implant
Diffusion JCN depth	0.5 ± 0.1 µm	0.3 ± 0.1 µm	
Diffusion ρ_s	20–40Ω/□	60–100Ω/□	
Diffusion surface concentration (ion/cm^3)	5×10^{19}	1.0×10^{19}	
Polysilicon ρ_s	15–30Ω/□	15–30Ω/□	
Diffusion contact resistance (2.5 µm × 2.5 µm)	20Ω	35Ω	
Polysilicon contact resistance (2.5 µm × 2.5 µm)	15Ω	15Ω	
p-well JCN	2.5–3.5 µm		
p-well ρ_s	2–3kΩ/□	1.0–1.5Ω–cm	
ΔW (Weff= Wdrawn + ΔW)	−1.0 ± 0.2 µm	−1.2 ± 0.2 µm	
Leff	1.20 ± 0.2 µm	1.55 ± 0.2 µm	

Gate delay: 19 stage ring oscillator 1.0–1.4 nsec.

Table B-4 2 μm single polysilicon, double metal n-well CMOS device parameters

	n-channel	p-channel	Condition
V_{TEO} (extrapolated)	0.5–1.0 V	0.5–1.0 V	30 μm × 2 μm device saturation
BV_{DSS}	⩾ 10 V	⩾ 10 V	30 μm × 2 μm device $V_{GS} = 0$, $I_{DS} = 1$ μA
$K' \left(\dfrac{\mu C}{2} \right)$	21–25 $\dfrac{\mu A}{V^2}$	6.5–8.5 $\dfrac{\mu A}{V^2}$	30 μm × 30 μm device $V_{DS} = 0.1$ V, $V_{GS} = 2, 3$ V
B_E (short channel body effect)	0.15–0.35 V$^{1/2}$	0.45–0.65 V$^{1/2}$	30 μm × 2 μm $B_E = \Delta V_{TE} \rbrack \begin{array}{l} V_{BS} = 2 \text{ V} \\ V_{BS} = 0 \text{ V} \end{array}$
Gate oxide capacitance (10^{-4} pF/μm^2)	8.0–10.0	8.0–10.0	Based on 400 ± 30Å
Polysilicon to substrate capacitance (10^{-4} pF/μm^2)	0.55–0.65	0.55–0.65	Based on 5500–6000Å
Metal to diffusion capacitance (10^{-4} pF/μm^2)	0.55–0.65	0.55–0.65	Based on 5500–6500Å
Metal to substrate capacitance (10^{-4} pF/μm^2)	0.27–0.32	0.27–0.32	Based on 1.1–1.25μm
Metal to polysilicon capacitance (10^{-4} pF/μm^2)	0.55–0.65	0.55–0.65	Based on 5500–6500Å
Diffusion JCN capacitance (10^{-4} pF/μm^2)	0.9–1.1	2.5–3.0	Zero bias
Diffusion capacitance periphery (10^{-4} pF/μm)		Negligible	"Diffusion" is a shallow implant
Diffusion JCN depth	0.2 ± 0.25 μm	0.28 ± 0.38 μm	
Diffusion ρ_s	25–45Ω/□	50–80Ω/□	
Diffusion surface concentration (ion/cm^3)	1×10^{20}	7×10^{19}	
Polysilicon ρ_s	15–35Ω/□	15–35Ω/□	
Diffusion contact resistance (2.5 μm × 2.5 μm)	20Ω	35Ω	
Polysilicon contact resistance (2.5 μm × 2.5 μm)	15Ω	15Ω	
n-well JCN		3 ± 0.3 μm	
Substrate	38–60Ω–cm	2–3 kΩ/□	
ΔW (Weff = Wdrawn + ΔW)	− 1.0 ± 0.2 μm	− 1.2 ± 0.2 μm	
Leff	1.7 ± 0.2 μm	1.6 ± 0.2 μm	

Gate delay: 19 stage ring oscillator 1.0 nsec.

Bibliography for general reading

Allison, J. *Electronic Integrated Circuits — Their Technology and Design*, McGraw-Hill, 1975.

Ayers, R. F. *VLSI — Silicon Compilation and the Art of Automatic Microchip Design*, Prentice-Hall, USA, 1983.

Barbe, D. F. (ed.). *Very Large Scale Integration — VLSI — Fundamentals and Applications*, Springer-Verlag, West Germany/USA, 1982.

Barna, A. *VHSIC (Very High Speed Integrated Circuits) — Technologies and Trade Offs*, Wiley, USA and Canada, 1981.

Camenzind, H. R. *Circuit Design for Integrated Electronics*, Addison-Wesley, USA, 1968.

Cobbold, R. S. *Theory and Application of Field-Effect Transistors*, Wiley, USA, 1970.

Colclaser, R. A. *Microelectronics: Processing and Device Design*, Wiley, USA, 1981.

Eichelberger, E. B. and Williams, T. W. *A Logic Design Structure for LSI Testability*, Journal of Design Automation and Fault-Tolerant Computing, Vol. 2, No. 2, May 1978, pp. 165–78.

Einspruch, N. G. and Wisseman, W. R. (ed.) *VLSI Electronics, Microstructure Science, Vol. II, Ga As Microelectronics*, Academy Press, 1985.

Fortino, A. *Fundamentals of Computer Aided Analysis and Design of Integrated Circuits*, Reston, USA, 1983.

Glasser, L. A. and Dobberpuhl, D. W. *The Design and Analysis of VLSI Circuits*, Addison-Wesley, 1985.

Gray, J. P. *VLSI 81 — Very Large Scale Integration*, Academic Press (London), UK, 1981.

Grove, A. S. *Physics and Technology of Semiconductor Devices*, Wiley, 1981.

Haskard, M. and May, I. *Analog VLSI Design, nMOS and CMOS*, Prentice-Hall, 1987.

Hicks, P. J. *Semi-Custom IC Design and VLSI*, Peter Peregrinus Ltd, UK, 1983.

Hon, R. W. and Sequin, C. M. *A Guide to LSI Implementation*, 2nd edn, Xerox, USA, 1980.

Lindmayer, J. and Wrigley, C. Y. *Fundamentals of Semiconductor Devices*, Van Nostrand, USA, 1965.

McCarthy, O. J. *MOS Device and Circuit Design*, Wiley, USA, 1982.

Maly W. *Atlas of I. C. Technologies: An Introduction to VLSI Processes*, Benjamin/Cummings Publishing, 1987.

Marcus M. *Switching Circuits for Engineers*, 2nd edn, Prentice-Hall, USA, 1967.

Mavor, J., Jack, M. A., and Denyer, P.B. *Introduction to MOS LSI Design*, Addison-Wesley, UK, 1983.

Mead, C. A. and Conway, L. A. *Introduction to VLSI Systems*, Addison-Wesley, USA, 1980.

Mukherjee, A. *Introduction to nMOS and CMOS Systems Design*, Prentice-Hall, 1986.

Muroga, S. *VLSI System Design*, Wiley, USA, 1982.

Nadig, H. J. *Signature Analysis-Concepts, Examples, and Guidelines*, Hewlett Packard Journal, USA, May 1977, pp. 15–21.

Newkirk, J. A. and Mathews, R. G. *The VLSI Designer's Library*, Addison-Wesley, USA and Canada, 1984.

Rene Segers, M. T. M. *The Impact of Testing on VLSI Design Methods*, IEEE Journal of Solid-State Circuits, USA, Vol. SC-17, No. 3, June 1982, pp. 481–6.

Richman, P. *Characteristics and Operation of MOS Field-Effect Devices*, McGraw-Hill, USA, 1967.

Rubin, S. M., *Computer Aids for VLSI Design*, Addison-Wesley, 1987.

Streetman, B. G. *Solid State Electronic Devices*, Prentice-Hall, USA, 1980.

Sze, S. M. (ed.) *VLSI Technology*, McGraw-Hill, USA, 1983.

Till, C. W. and Luxon, J. T. *Integrated Circuits: Materials, Devices, and Fabrications*, Prentice-Hall, USA, 1982.

Weste, N. H. E. *Mulga — An Interactive Symbolic System for the Design of Integrated Circuits*, Bell System Technical Journal 60, USA, pp. 823–57, July–August 1982.

Weste, N. H. E. and Eshraghian, K. *Principles of CMOS VLSI Design — A Systems Perspective*, Addison-Wesley, USA, 1984.

Westinghouse Defense and Space Center. *Integrated Electronic Systems*, Prentice-Hall, USA, 1970.

Index